Alexander Hieke, Hannes Leitgeb (Eds.)

Reduction – Abstraction – Analysis

Publications of the
Austrian Ludwig Wittgenstein Society.
New Series

Volume 11

Alexander Hieke, Hannes Leitgeb

Reduction – Abstraction – Analysis

ontos
verlag

Frankfurt I Paris I Lancaster I New Brunswick

Bibliographic information published by Deutsche Nationalbibliothek
The Deutsche Nationalbibliothek lists this publication in the Deutsche Nationalbibliographie;
detailed bibliographic data is available in the Internet at http://dnb.ddb.de

Gedruckt mit Förderung des
Bundesministeriums für Wissenschaft und Forschung in Wien
und der Kulturabteilung der NÖ Landesregierung

North and South America by
Transaction Books
Rutgers University
Piscataway, NJ 08854-8042
trans@transactionpub.com

United Kingdom, Ire, Iceland, Turkey, Malta, Portugal by
Gazelle Books Services Limited
White Cross Mills
Hightown
LANCASTER, LA1 4XS
sales@gazellebooks.co.uk

Livraison pour la France et la Belgique:
Librairie Philosophique J.Vrin
6, place de la Sorbonne ; F-75005 PARIS
Tel. +33 (0)1 43 54 03 47 ; Fax +33 (0)1 43 54 48 18
www.vrin.fr

©2009 ontos verlag
P.O. Box 15 41, D-63133 Heusenstamm
www.ontosverlag.com

ISBN 13: 978-3-86838-047-7

2009

Printed on acid-free paper
ISO-Norm 970-6
FSC-certified (Forest Stewardship Council)
This hardcover binding meets the International Library standard

Printed in Germany
by buch bücher **dd ag**

Introduction

Philosophers often have tried to either reduce "disagreeable" entities or concepts to (more) acceptable entities or concepts, or to eliminate the former altogether. Reducing a class of entities to another one is regarded attractive by those who subscribe to an ideal of ontological parsimony. For instance, nominalism is concerned with denying the existence of universals; modern versions of nominalism object to abstract entities altogether; as a consequence, nominalists have to show how reference to abstract entities in mathematics, in the sciences and in philosophy can be eliminated or is merely apparent. *Reduction* and elimination very often have to do with the question of "What is really there?", and thus these notions belong to the most fundamental ones in philosophy. But the topic is not just restricted to traditional metaphysics or ontology. In the philosophy of mathematics, logicism aimed at deriving every true mathematical statement from purely logical truths by reducing all mathematical concepts to logical ones. In the last twenty years, (neo-)logicism has experienced an amazing revival. *Abstraction* principles, such as Hume's principle, have been suggested to support a "quasi-logicist" reconstruction of mathematics in view of their quasi-analytical status. In the philosophy of language and the philosophy of science, the logical *analysis* of language has long been regarded to be the dominating paradigm. Although the importance of projects such as Russell's paraphrasis of definite descriptions and Carnap's logical reconstruction and explicatory definition of empirical concepts is still acknowledged, many philosophers now doubt the viability of the programme of logical analysis as it was originally conceived. At the same time, liberalized projects of logical analysis remain to be driving forces of modern philosophy.

The articles in this volume originate from the 31st International Wittgenstein Symposium, August 2008, Kirchberg am Wechsel, which was devoted to *Reduction and Elimination in Philosophy and the Sciences*. We want to thank the authors for their great support, and we are confident that their work will stimulate further philosophical progress.

Alexander Hieke & Hannes Leitgeb
Spring 2009

Table of Contents

I. REDUCTION

II. ABSTRACTION

III. ANALYSIS

CONTEXTUALISM, RELATIVISM, AND FACTIVITY. ANALYZING 'KNOWLEDGE' AFTER THE NEW LINGUISTIC TURN IN EPISTEMOLOGY

ELKE BRENDEL

I.
Reduction

A PROOF OF NOMINALISM:
AN EXERCISE IN
SUCCESSFUL REDUCTION IN LOGIC

JAAKKO HINTIKKA
Boston University

Symbolic logic is a marvelous thing. It allows for an explicit expression of existence, viz. by means of the existential quantifier, and by it only. This is the true gist in Quine's slogan "to be is to be a value of a bound variable." Accordingly, one can also formulate explicitly the thesis of nominalism in terms of such logic. What this thesis says is that all the values of existential quantifiers we need in our language are particular objects, not higher-order objects such as properties, relations, functions and sets.

This requirement is satisfied by the first-order languages using the received first-order logic. The commonly used basic logic is therefore nominalistic. But this result does not tell anything, for the received first-order logic is far too weak to capture all we need in mathematics or science. According to conventional wisdom, we need for this purpose either higher-order logic or set theory. Now both of them deal with higher-order entities and hence violate the canons of nominalism. This does not refute nominalism, however. For I will show that both set theory and higher-order logic can be made dispensable by developing a more powerful first-order logic that can do the same job as they do.

Moreover, there are very serious problems connected with both of them. This constitutes an additional reason for dispensing with them in the foundations of mathematics. I will show how we can do just that. But we obviously need a better first-order logic for the purpose. Hence my first task is to develop one.

But is this a viable construal of the problem of nominalism? The very distinction between particular and higher-order entities might perhaps seem to be hard to capture in logical terms – harder than has been indicated so far. Logicians like Jouko Väänänen (2001) have emphasized the complexities involved in trying to distinguish first-order logic from higher-order logic. The first step of an answer is that the distinction cannot be made purely formally but has to depend on the interpretation of one's logic, in particular on the specification of the values of bound variables.

But how does such an interpretation come about? This question should be generalized. How does a mathematical or scientific theory formulated in a logically explicit language work? The answer is obvious: By specifying a class of models. These models are the structures that the theory studies. In those models, the values of first-order quantifiers are particular objects (individuals) while the values of higher-order quantifiers are higher-order entities, such as sets, functions, predicates, relations etc.

But now the usual axiomatizations of set theory seem to belie the distinction. Such axiomatizations use the nominalistic first-order logic even though they are supposed to deal with sets, which are higher-order entities, albeit seemingly more concrete than properties and relations. The answer, which will be expounded more fully elsewhere, is that this is precisely what is wrong with first-order axiomatizations of set theory. (See here Hintikka, forthcoming (a) and (b).) They simply represent a wrong approach to set theory. They are based on a serious misunderstanding as to how an axiomatic theory works. Their models are structures of particulars, not structures of sets. Hence it is extremely difficult to try to extract information about structures of sets from a first-order axiomatization of set theory. Indeed, it can be explicitly proved that there cannot exist a set theory using the received first-order logic whose variables range over all sets.

Moreover, it is an important strategic defect of the usual axiomatic set theories that their logic is the usual first-order logic. For because of their reliance on conventional first-order logic it is impossible to define the concept of truth for such a set theory by means of its own resources. As a consequence one cannot discuss the model theory of set theory in set theory itself. This is a tremendous limitation foreshadowed in the so-called semantical paradoxes of set theory of yore. In this light, it is only to be expected that important questions concerning set-theoretical structures cannot be answered in the usual set theories. For instance the results by Cohen and Gödel concerning the unsolvability of the continuum problem on the basis of Zermelo-Fraenkel set theory thus only serve to confirm the reality of the predicted limitations.

Another mixed case seems to be obtainable by considering the higher-order logic known as type theory as a many-sorted first-order theory, each different type serving as one of the "sorts". One can try to interpret the logics of Frege and of Russell and Whitehead in this way. The attempt fails (systematically if not historically) because there are higher-order logical principles that cannot be captured in terms of the usual formulations of many-sorted first-order logic. An important case is the so-called axiom of choice. (But see below how the axiom of choice can become a truth of a reformulated first-order logic). This example from set theory in fact reveals the crucial watershed between first-order logic and higher-order logic. It is not the style of variables, which only means pretending that one is dealing with this or that kind of entity, that is, first-order (particular) objects or higher-order ones. The crucial question is whether principles of inference are involved that go (or do not go) beyond the logical principles of first-order (nominalistic) logic.

These are vital problems to any serious thinker who tries to understand all mathematical reasoning nominalistically. A case in point is Hilbert. (See Hilbert (1918) and (1922).) Indeed, it is his nominalism that is largely responsible for Hilbert's having been labelled a "formalist". He wanted to interpret all mathematical thinking as dealing with structures of particular concrete objects. Now for mathematicians' deductions of theorems from axioms the interpretation of nonlogical primitives does not matter. In other words it does not matter what these objects are as long as they are particulars forming the right kind of structure. In this sense Hilbert could say that for the logical structure of his axiomatization of geometry he could have named his primitives "table", "chair" and "beer mug" instead of "line", "point" and "circle". One could not carry out such a reformulation of axioms and deductions from them if the values of a geometer's variables were entities which already have a structure like e.g. sets. A deduction is invariant with respect to a permutation of individuals but not of structures of individuals. One cannot hope to exchange the terms "triangle" and "quadrangle" in a geometrical proof and expect it to remain valid. Because of this invariance, Hilbert could say that the concrete particular objects in one of the models of his theory could be thought of as symbols and formulas. To use his own vivid language, Hilbert could have said that he could have named his geometrical primitives "letter", "word" and "formula", quite with the same justification as the envisaged terms "chair", "table" and "beer mug". This gambit was in fact put to use later as a technical resource by logicians, among them Henkin (1949) and Hintikka (1955) in building up the models they used to prove the completeness of the received first-order logic. It is thus a radical misunderstanding to label Hilbert a formalist

Hilbert blamed all the problems in the foundations of mathematics on the use of higher-order concepts. And he tried to practice nominalism and not only profess it. He tried to show the dispensability of higher-order assumptions in mathematics. His test case was the controversial axiom of choice. Hilbert (1922) expressed the belief that in a proper perspective this "axiom" could turn out to be as obvious as 2+2=4. Hilbert tried to accomplish this reduction to first-order level by replacing quantifiers by certain choice terms, so-called epsilon terms. These epsilon-terms are expressions of certain choice functions. Hilbert's mistake was not to spell out what the choices in question depend on and thereby in effect ruling out some relevant kinds of dependence.

Hilbert did not succeed even though he was on the right track. There is in fact a far simpler way of showing that the axiom of choice can be understood as a first-order logical principle. All we need for the purpose is a slightly more flexible formulation of the usual first-order logic. One of its usual rules is existential instantiation that allow us to replace a variable x bound to a sentence-initial existential quantifier in a sentence $(\exists x)F[x]$ by a new individual constant, say β, at the same time as we omit the quantifier itself. This β can be thought of as a sample (some writers say "arbitrarily chosen") representative of the truth making values of x. Hence such a β is like the legalese pseudo-names "John Doe" and "Jane Roe" representing existing but unknown individuals.

This rule cannot be applied to an existential quantifier $(\exists y)$ inside a formula, because the choice (sic) depends on the values of the universal quantifiers $(\forall z_1),(\forall z_2),\ldots$ within the scope $(\exists y)$ occurs (assuming that the formula is in the negation normal form). But the rule of existential instantiation becomes applicable when we allow the substituting term to be a function term $\beta(z_1, z_2,\ldots)$ which takes into account the dependencies in question. However, what is now introduced is not an individual constant, but a new function constant.

This reformulation of first-order logic is totally natural, and can be seen as following directly from certain eminently obvious truth-conditions of first-order (quantificational) sentences. The most obvious truth-condition for a first-order sentence S is the existence of suitable "witness individuals" that together show the truth of S. Thus for instance $(\exists x)F[x]$ is true iff there is an individual a that satisfies $F[a]$ and $(\forall x)(\exists y)G[x,y]$ is true iff for any given a there exists an individual b that satisfies $G[a,b]$. As this example shows, witness individuals may depend on other individuals. Hence their existence amounts to the existence of the functions (including constant functions) that yield as their values suitable witness individuals.

These functions are known as the Skolem functions of S. The functions β mentioned earlier are merely examples of "John Doe" Skolem functions.

This rule is a first-order one, for no higher-order quantifiers are involved. It seems to effect merely an eminently natural and eminently obvious reformulation of the rules of first-order logic. But when this reformulated first-order logic is used as the basis of second-order logic or set theory, the axiom of choice becomes a truth of logic without any further assumptions.

This result may at first seem too elementary to be of much interest. In reality, it puts the very idea of axiomatic set theory into jeopardy. In a historical perspective, Zermelo axiomatized set theory in the first place in order to defend his use of the axiom of choice in his proof of the well-ordering theorem. (See Zermelo 1908 (a) and (b), Ebbinghaus 2007.) We can now see that his axiomatizing efforts were redundant. Zermelo could have vindicated the axiom of choice by showing that it is a purely logical principle. First-order axiomatic set theory was right from the outset but logicians' labor lost.

I am intrigued by the question why this exceedingly simply way of vindicating the status of the axiom of choice as a logical principle has not been used before. I suspect that the answer is even more intriguing. The new rule of functional instantiation is context sensitive, and hence makes first-order logic noncompositional. Now compositionality seems to have been an unspoken and sometimes even overt article of faith among logicians. It was what prevented Tarski from formulating a truth definition for a first-order language in the same language, as is shown in Hintikka and Sandu (1999). It might also be at the bottom of Zermelo's unfortunate construal of the axiom of choice as a non-logical, mathematical assumption.

Systematically speaking, and even more importantly, the version of the axiom of choice that results from our reformulation is extremely strong. It is so strong that it is inconsistent with all the usual first-order axiom system of set theory. For instance, in a von Neumann-Bernays type set theory (Bernays 1968) it applies also to all classes and not only to sets. Accordingly, first-order set theories turn out to be inconsistent with (suitably formulated) first-order logic. This already shows that something is rotten in the state of first-order set theories.

But the axiom of choice is only the tip of the iceberg of problems (and opportunities) here. Earlier, I promised to develop a better first-order logic in order to defend nominalism. It turns out that we have to develop one in any case. The most fundamental insight here is that the received first-order logic (logic of quantifiers) does not completely fulfill its job description. The semantical job of quantifiers is not exhausted by their expressing the nonemptyness and the exceptionlessness of (usually complex) predicates. But in the reconstructed axiom of choice another aspect of the meaning of quantifiers comes to play. By their formal dependence on each other, quantifiers also express the real-life dependence of the variables on each other that are bound to them. Such dependence is precisely what Skolem functions codify.

The formal dependence of a quantifier (Q_2y) on another quantifier (Q_1x) is in the received logic expressed by the fact that (Q_2y) occurs in the syntactical scope of (Q_1x). But this scope (nesting) relation is of a special sort, being among other features transitive and antisymmetric. Hence the received first-order logic cannot express all patterns of dependence and independence between variables. Since such dependence relations are the bread and butter of all science, this is a severe limitation of the received logic.

This defect is corrected in the independence-friendly (IF) logic that I have developed together with associates. (For it, see Hintikka 1996.) Its semantics is completely classical and can be obtained from the usual game-theoretical semantics simply by allowing our semantical games to be games with incomplete information.

The resulting logic is deductively weaker than the received first-order logic but richer in important ways in its expressive capacities. For instance, the equicardinality of two sets can be expressed by its means. Incidentally, this would have made it possible for Frege to define number on the first-order level, thus depriving him of one reason to use higher-order logic (as he does).

Because IF logic merely corrects a defect in the received "classical" first-order logic and because its semantics does not involve any new ideas (except independence, of course), it is not an alternative to the received first-order logic. It is not a special "nonclassical" logic or "alternative" logic. It is an improved version of the basic first-order logic. It replaces our usual logic.

In IF logic, the law of excluded middle does not hold, in spite of the classical character of its semantics. In other words, the negation ~ in it is not the contradictory negation but a strong (dual) negation.

An interesting feature of IF first-order logic is that its implications differ from those of the received first-order logic also when it comes to finite models. Since we have to replace the latter by the former, we must also reconsider all finitary metamathematics and its prospects, including Hilbert's. This means that Hilbert's project has to be re-evaluated. It is no longer clear that Gödel's second incompleteness implies the impossibility of Hilbert's program. Indeed, there already exists an elementary proof of the consistency of an IF logic based elementary arithmetic in the same arithmetic. (See Hintikka and Karakadilar 2006.)

I will later show that IF first-order logic is as strong as the Σ^1_1 fragment of second-order logic (to be defined below). In simpler terms, second-order existential quantifiers are expressible in IF first-order logic.

This has major implications for the theme of this meeting which includes reduction. Reductions between theories are often implemented by mappings of the models of the reduced theory into the reduct theory. The existence of such a mapping is an existential second-order statement. If the theories in question are formulated by means of IF first-order logic, such reductions can be discussed in the same terms as theories themselves, which is impossible to do if the conventional first-order logic is used instead. What this means is that IF logic typically enables us to turn what used to be thought of as a metatheoretical examination of reductions into (object-language) scientific questions. Such algebras were studied already in Jónsson and Tarski (1951) and (1952).

IF logic can be extended unproblematically by introducing a sentence-initial contradictory negation $\neg$. The result can be called extended IF logic or EIF logic. This logic is the true new basic logic. Algebraically it is a Boolean algebra with an additional operator $\neg\sim$.

The contradictory negation $\neg S$ of S says that such winning strategies do not exist. Since semantical games are not all determinate, S may fail to be true and yet not necessarily be false. Thus $\neg S$ means game theoretically that for any strategy of the verifier there exists a strategy for the falsifier that defeats it if known to the falsifier. This can be expressed by a Π^1_2 second-order sentence.

One of the main advantages of IF logic is that it makes it possible to define truth for a sufficiently rich IF first-order theory in the same theory, thus overcoming the main handicap of conventional set theories. In terms of game-theoretical semantics, the truth-condition for a sentence S will say that there exists a winning strategy for the verifier in the semantical "verification" game $G(S)$ connected with S. This is a second-order condition, but it will be shown to reduce back to IF first-order logic. Technically, such winning strategies are codified in the Skolem functions explained earlier. Hence S is true if and only if its Skolem functions all exist. This can be expressed by a second-order sentence with a string of second-order existential quantifiers followed by a first-order formula, i.e. by what is known as a Σ_1^1 sentence. They turn out to have IF first-order equivalents, as will be seen later in this paper.

Our new basic logic, the EIF first-order logic, is in many ways a highly interesting structure. It does not rely on the law of excluded middle and hence can be considered a realization of intuitionists' intuitions. Indeed, its systematic motivation makes it a more natural "intuitionistic logic" than the formal systems so-called. In spite of this essential kinship, it allows for much of the usual mathematics, including analysis. For instance, the unrestricted axiom of choice is valid in it. Precisely how much analysis can be handled by its means, is an important largely open problem to be investigated. This question means asking how much of analysis can be done by unproblematic elementary means.

EIF logic can be extended further by allowing $\neg$ to occur also within the scope of quantifiers. The result can be called a fully extended IF logic (FEIF logic). This does not mean leaving the first-order level but requires further explanations (to be supplied later) for its semantics. It incorporates both the received first-order logic and IF logic as subsystems.

A clarifying comment is in order here. What precisely is the relation of the received first-order (RFO) logic to IF first-order logic, EIFFO logic and FEIFFO logic? The answer is that as long as tertium non datur holds, RFO logic and IFFO logic are analogous. RFO logic is the logic of those formulas for which the law of excluded middle holds. It is in this sense a part of IFFO logic. It is also that part of EIF logic whose formulas do not contain independence indicators (slashes) and for whose atomic sentences obey the law of excluded middle.

This FEIF logic can now serve the purpose of the reduction foreshadowed in my title. FEIF logic can be shown to be as strong as the entire second-order logic. And even though I have been speaking of higher-order logic, the fact is that second-order logic is strong enough to capture all the modes of reasoning used in mathematics and in science. In this sense, second-order logic is the true *Begriffsschrift* in Frege's ambitious terminology.

Second-order logic formulas are divided into fragments according to the number of changes of sign in their prenex form. Thus the $\Sigma_0^0 = \Pi_0^0$ fragment consists of first-order formulas, Σ_1^1 of formulas with a string of existential second-order quantifiers followed by a Σ_0^0 formula, and the Π_1^1 fragment consists of contradictory negations of Σ_1^1 formulas. In general, the Σ_{n+1}^1 fragment consists of a string of existential quantifiers of the order

8

$n+1$ followed by a formula in the Π_n^1 fragment. The Π_n^1 fragment consists of the contradictory negations of Σ_n^1 formulas.

The second-order logic that I propose to reduce to the first-order level is to be understood as the received "classical" second order logic. (It is this logic that is generally recognized as a sufficient medium of all normal mathematical reasoning.) That means that no independence indicator slashes occur in them. Consequently, the law of excluded middle holds. All sentences can be assumed in the negation normal form.

The reduction can be introduced by means of an example. Consider a Σ_1^1 sentence of the simple form $(\exists f)G[f]$ where $G[f]$ is a first order formula in its prenex form. Since $G[f]$ can be assumed to be an IF first-order formula, its prenex form can be assumed to begin with a string of universal quantifiers. In the simplest case, there is only one of them, say $(\forall x)$.

Let us assume also that f does not appear nested in (1). That means that it occurs in F only in contexts like $A(f(x))$ or $f(x) = a$. Hence (1) is of the form

(1) $(\exists f)(\forall x)F[x, f(x)]$

Now (1) is easily seen to be equivalent with the following formula

(2) $(\forall x_1)(\forall x_2)(\exists y_1/\forall x_2)(\exists y_2/\forall x_1)$ & $((x_1 = x_2) \supset (y_1 = y_2)$ & $F^*)$

Here F^* is like F except that $A(f(x))$ has been replaced by $(\forall w)(w = y_1 \supset A(w))$ and $f(x) = a$ by $(\forall w)(w \supset y_1 \supset w = a)$.

This equivalence can be shown to hold as follows: The Skolem function translation into second-order form is

(3) $(\exists f_1)(\exists f_2)(\forall x_1)(\forall x_2)((x_1 = x_2) \supset (f_1(x_1) = f_2(x_2))$ & F^{**}

where F^{**} is like F^* except that $f_2(x_2)$ replaces y_2. Now the first conjunct in (3) says that f_1 and f_2 are the same function. Hence (3) and (2) are equivalent to (1).

This elimination is obviously repeatable so as to be extendable to any number of initial universal quantifiers in the prenex form of F and to any number of initial existential quantifiers $(\exists f_1)(\exists f_2),\ldots$ instead of the single one $(\exists f)$.

If there is nesting of the functions $f_1, f_2,\ldots$ in F, it can be eliminated by introducing new functions f_i and new universal quantifiers $(\forall x_i)$. For

9

instance, if in F there occurs a term $f_i(f_2(x))$, we can add a new initial existential quantifier $(\exists g)$ and add after the prenex of F the conjunct

$$(4)\ (\forall z)(\forall u)((g(z) = u) \leftrightarrow (\exists w)(w = f_2(u)\ \&\ z = f_1(w))$$

This procedure can be generalized. We can in fact easily replace predicate variables in the initial formula by variables for their characteristic functions. This extends the procedure so as to eliminate any formula-initial second-order existential quantifier albeit at the cost of introducing independence indicators (slashes). Moreover, this elimination can be applied to any unnegated existential quantifier in context, not just initial ones.

As to universal second-order quantifiers and negated second-order existential quantifiers, it suffices to point out that a universal second-order quantifier $(\forall f)$ prefixing a subformula $(\forall f) F[f]$ can be replaced by $\neg(\exists f)$ $\neg F(f)$. We can now eliminate $(\exists f)$ from the subformula $(\exists f)\neg F[f]$ in the way just indicated. The result does not contain second-order quantifiers (if we apply the reduction from inside out) but does normally contain contradictory negations $\neg$. It is therefore a FEIF logic (sub) formula.

When these eliminations are carried out step by step in a given second-order formula, moving from inside out, all the second-order quantifiers are ultimately eliminated. The procedure does introduce independence indicators and contradictory negations, which is to say that the result is a FEIF formula, but does not introduce any second-order quantifiers. This accomplishes the reduction of the entire traditional second-order logic to the first-order level. The reduct sentence is a first-order sentence: all its quantifiers range over first-order entities. However, it does contain contradictory negations also within the scope of quantifiers. The additional power of second-order logic is therefore due, not to its being second-order, but to its unlimited use of contradictory negation. This means essentially unlimited use of tertium non datur. In a sense, this vindicates Brouwer's idea that the excessive power of classical mathematics stems from the use of the principle of excluded middle.

The same reduction can apparently be used to translate logic of the order $n+1$ to the order n and hence ultimately to the first-order level. This possibility will not be discussed here, however.

This procedure reduces the traditional second-order to the logic of the first-order level. However, what remains to be explained is the semantics of FEIF logic. This semantics can be formulated in different ways. One transparent one is to use infinite methods. This means replacing in effect a quantified formula in the scope of $\neg$ by a conjunction or disjunction of its substitution instances with respect to the names of all the members of the given domain. These will be infinite if the domain is infinite.

For instance, $\neg(\forall x)A[x]$ is true iff the disjunction

(5) $\neg A[b_1] \vee \neg A[b_2] \vee \ldots$

is true, b_i being all the members of the domain. This suffices for the semantics in question.

This way of formulating a truth condition for second-order sentences helps to show in what sense the step from EIF logic to a logic based on unlimited use of tertium non datur means a step from elementary logic to a nonfinitistic logic.

However, we might want to have an explicit truth condition specified independently of any particular domain. Such a truth condition can be formulated by means of FEIF logic itself. In IF logic a natural truth condition asserts the existence of Skolem functions for S. This truth condition is obtained by replacing each existentially quantified formula $(\exists x)F[x]$ by $F[f(y_1,y_2,\ldots)]$ where f is a new (Skolem) function bound to an initial $(\exists f)$ and $(Qy_1)(Qy_2),\ldots$ are all the quantifiers on which $(\exists x)$ depends in S. We can do the same when S is a FEIF sentence, except for subformulas of the form $\neg F$. Here the analysis of the truth-condition of a contradictorily negated sentence presented earlier in this essay shows what can be done. There it was seen that $\neg F$ is equivalent to a Σ_2^1 formula. Hence a subformula of the form $\neg F$ can in a truth condition be replaced by a formula of the following form:

(6) $(\forall g_1)(\forall g_2)\ldots(\exists f_1)(\exists f_2)\ldots\neg F^*$

where $g_1, g_2,\ldots$ are the Skolem functions for F (i.e. strategy functions for the verifier) and $f_1, f_2,\ldots$ are the analogous strategy functions for the falsifier. The nesting of these functions is determined by the dependence relations between the different quantifiers in F. F^* is the result of replacing quantified variables by the appropriate function terms. The output is equivalent to an ordinary second-order sentence (assuming that atomic sentences obey the law of excluded middle). This output will have to satisfy certain conditions. The functions $g_1, g_2,\ldots,f_1,f_2,\ldots$ in (5) can have as their arguments only functions terms formed by means of these functions and the first function g_1 which is always a constant function. What this means is that the quantifiers in $\neg F$ are independent of all the quantifiers further outside. In linguistic terms this very nearly says that contradictory negation is a barrier for anaphora – a phenomenon that is in evidence in natural languages. This procedure eventually moves all occurrences of $\neg$ to positions where they have only atomic sentences within their scope and where they can be interpreted trivially. Thus the procedure can be thought of as specifying the meaning of $\neg$.

Thus for instance a (sub) formula of the form

(7) $\neg(\exists x)(\forall y)(\exists z)F[x,y,z]$

will be replaced in our reduction by a formula of the form

(8) $(\forall f_1)(\forall f_2)(\exists g)\neg F(f_1, g(f_1), f_2(f_1, g(f_1)))]$

(In this case the function f_1 is reduced to a constant.)

By repeated applications of this procedure, moving from outside in, we can formulate a second-order truth condition for each FEIF sentence. In the reduct, all contradictory negations $\neg$ occur in the negation prenexes of atomic formulas. Hence by the earlier reduction it is equivalent to a FEIF sentence. The functions $g_1, g_2, \ldots, f_1, f_2, \ldots$ deputize quantifiers in $\neg F$. These quantifiers in turn codify moves made by players in the game $G(\neg F)$ connected with $\neg F$. Hence, only variables occurring in the arguments of these functions can be variables bound to other quantifiers in $\neg F$.

In other words, by translating this second-order formula back to FEIF first-order logic we obtain for suitable FEIF languages a truth condition expressible in the same language.

Putting all this together, we can prove strictly the possibility of nominalism in the foundations of mathematics. This result is not only of philosophical interest. It has major implications for the foundations of mathematics in general and even for mathematics itself. First-order axiomatic set theory becomes redundant and so does in principle higher-order logic, except perhaps as a convenient shorthand. Our working logic will look more like general topology than conventional first-order logic or conventional set theory. I will leave the rest of the resulting revolution to my audience to carry out.

12

REFERENCES

Bernays, Paul, 1968, *Axiomatic Set Theory*, Amsterdam, North-Holland.

Ebbinghaus, Heinz-Dieter, 2007, *Ernst Zermelo,* Berlin, Springer.

Henkin, Leon, 1949, "The cCmpleteness of the First-order Fractional Calculus", *Journal of Symbolic Logic*, vol. 14, pp.159–166.

Hilbert, David, 1996 (original 1918), "Axiomatic Thinking", in: William B. Ewald (ed), *From Kant to Hilbert,* vol.2, Oxford, Clarendon Press, pp.1105–1115.

Hilbert, David, 1998 (original 1922), "The New Grounding of Mathematics, First report" in: William B. Ewald (ed), *From Kant to Hilbert*, vol.2, Oxford, Clarendon Press, pp.1115–1134.

Hilbert, David, and Paul Bernays, 1939, *Grundlagen der Mathematik*, vol.2, Berlin, Springer.

Hintikka, Jaakko, 1955, "Notes on Quantification Theory", *Societas Scientiarum Fennicae, Commentationes Physican Mathematicae*, vol.17, no.2.

Hintikka, Jaakko, 1996, *The Principles of Mathematics Revisited*, Cambridge, Cambridge University Press.

Hintikka, Jaakko, 2004(a), "What is the True Algebra of Logic?" in: Vincent Hendricks et al. (eds), *First-order Logic Revisited*, Berlin, Logos Verlag, pp.117–128.

Hintikka, Jaakko, 2004(b), "Independence Friendly Logic and Axiomatic Set Theory", *Annals of Pure and Applied Logic*, vol.126, pp.313–333.

Hintikka, Jaakko, 2006, "Truth, Negation and Other Basic Notions of Logic" in: J. van Benthem et al. (eds), *The Age of Alternative Logics*, Berlin, Springer, pp.195–219.

Hintikka, Jaakko, forthcoming(a), "Reforming Logic (and Set Theory)".

Hintikka, Jaakko, forthcoming(b), "The Past, Present and Future of Set Theory".

Hintikka, Jaakko and Jack Kulas, 1983, *The Game of Language*, (Synthese Language Library vol.22), D. Reidel, Dordrecht.

Hintikka, Jaakko, and Gabriel Sandu, 1999, "Tarski's Guilty Secret: Compositionality", in Jan Wolenski and Eckehart Köhler (eds.), *Alfred Tarski and the Vienna Circle,* Kluwer Academic, Dordrecht, pp.217–230.

Jónsson, Bjarni, and Alfred Tarski, 1951, "Boolean Algebras and Operators I", *American Journal of Mathematics,* vol.73, pp.891–939.

Jónsson, Bjarni, and Alfred Tarski, 1952 , "Boolean Algebras and Operators II", *American Journal of Mathematics,* vol.74, pp.127–162.

Väänänen, Jouko, 2001, "Second-order Logic and the Foundations of Mathematics", *Bulletin of Symbolic Logic*, vol.7, pp.504–520.

Zermelo, Ernst, 1908(a), "Neuer Beweis für die Möglichkeit einer Wohlordnung", *Mathematische Annalen*, vol.65, pp.107–128.

Zermelo, Ernst, 1908(b), "Untersuchungen über die Grundlagen der Mengenlehre", *Mathematische Annalen*, vol.65, pp.261–281.

13

PRESERVATION OF EMPIRICAL SUCCESS AND INTERTHEORETICAL CORRESPONDENCE: JUSTIFYING REALISM WITHOUT THE NO MIRACLES ARGUMENT

GERHARD SCHURZ
University of Düsseldorf

Abstract

This paper utilizes a logical correspondence theorem (which has been proved elsewhere) for a justification of a weak version of scientific realism which does not presuppose Putnam's no-miracles-argument (NMA). After presenting arguments against the reliability of the unrestricted NMA in sec.1, the correspondence theorem is explained in sec.2. In sec.3, historical illustrations of the correspondence theorem are given, and its ontological consequences are worked out in terms of the indirect reference and partial truth. In the final sec.4 it is shown how the correspondence theorem together with the assumption of 'minimal realism' yields a justification of the abductive inference from the strong empirical success of a theory to the partial truth of its theoretical part.

1 THE NO-MIRACLES ARGUMENT (NMA) AND ITS LIMITATIONS

It is a crucial property of scientific theories that they contain concepts, content, and/or models, which represent structures of objects which go beyond what is empirically observable, or 'pre-theoretically given' – so-called *theoretical* concepts, content, or models. This holds quite independently of how one draws the borderline between the observable and the non-observable (by the naked eye, by scientific measurement instruments, or by shared pre-theories). The 'theoretical superstructure' of scientific theories plays a crucial role in explaining and unifying the observable phenomena in the domain of the theory. The class of empirical consequences which follows from the theory (deductively or probabilistically) is called the *empirical* (or *pre-theoretical*) *content* of a theory. The empirical (or pre-theoretical) *success* of a theory is that part of its empirical content which is verified or confirmed by observations.

Scientific realism is the view that the empirical success of a theory is a reliable indicator of the (approximate) truth of the theory, including the truth of its theoretical superstructure. Thereby, the concept of truth is understood in the ordinary correspondence-theoretical sense, formally explicated in terms of semantical model-theory which goes back to Tarski. In contrast, *scientific instrumentalism* holds that the theoretical superstructure of a theory has merely the instrumental purpose of entailing the observed phenomena in a most simple and unifying way, but there is no reason to assume that this theoretical superstructure corresponds to an unobservable external reality. For example, according to the realistic interpretation of theoretical physics, electrons or quarks do exist, and what physical theories tell about them is approximately true, while according to the instrumentalistic interpretation, electrons and quarks don't exist, at least not literally, and what theories tell about them is not true, although it is a extremely economic way of unifying a variety of empirical phenomena.

The standard justification of scientific realism in the contemporary realism vs. instrumentalism debate is the *no-miracles* argument (NMA), which goes back to Putnam (1975, p.73), and has been used in various ways as a defense of scientific realism (cf. Boyd 1984). This argument says that the empirical success of contemporary scientific theories would be a sheer miracle if we would not assume that their theoretical superstructure, or ontology, is approximately true in the sense of scientific realism. More precisely, the best if not the only reasonable explanation of the continuous empirical success of scientific theories is the realistic assumption that their theoretical 'superstructure' (their non-observable part) is approximately true and, hence, their central theoretical terms refer to real though unobservable constituents of the world. However, there NMA is beset by two (at least) equally strong counterargument, one empirical counterargument and one theoretical counterargument.

The empirical counterargument is the *pessimistic meta-induction* argument (PMA), which goes back to Laudan (1981). The PMA points to the fact that in the history of scientific theories one can recognize radical changes at the level of theoretical superstructures (ontologies), although there was continuous progress at the level of empirical success. On simple inductive grounds, one should expect therefore that the theoretical superstructures (ontologies) of our presently accepted theories will also be overthrown in the future, and hence can in no way be expected to be approximately true.

The theoretical counterargument is the *no-speculation* argument (NSA), which has an old tradition in the philosophy of science. In Schurz (2008, §7) have tried to elaborate this argument in a defensible way. The NSA points out that for every possible observation one may construct *ex-post* and *ad-hoc* some speculative 'theory' which just entails ('explains') this observation, but has no other (logically independent) observable consequence. The empirical success of such speculative 'theories' is in no way a reliable indicator of their approximate truth. In the simplest case, a speculative explanation has the following structure:

> *Speculative 'explanation'-schema*
> (for particular and general phenomena):
>
> *Explanandum*: Something happened, or happens regularly.
> _____
> *Speculative 'explanans'*: Some kind of power wanted that this something to happen, or to happen regularly.

Speculative explanations of this sort have been applied by our human ancestors since the earliest times. All sorts of unexpected events can be explained by assuming one or several God-like power(s). Speculative pseudo-explanations do *not* offer a *proper* unification, because for every particular phenomenon E a special hypothetical 'wish' of the God-like power to create E has to be postulated (cf. Schurz/Lambert 1994, p.86). On the same reason, speculative pseudo-explanations are *post-hoc* and have *no predictive power* at all, because God's unforeseeable decisions can be known only *after* the event has already happened. Moreover, since the explanandum imposes no constraints on the hypothetical power except that it has created the explanandum in some unexplained (typically super-natural) ways, the same phenomena can be explained by a plentitude of different speculative explanations, which is historically illustrated by the fact that human mankind has invented a multitude of different religious stories about the genesis of the world (Wilson 1998, ch.11, estimates their number as 100.000).

In Schurz (2008, §7) the following criterion for demarcating speculative from scientifically worthwhile explanations (viz. theories) is proposed: while speculative explanations postulate for each new phenomenon a new kind of theoretical cause, scientifically worthwhile explanations introduce new theoretical entities only if they figure as common and unifying cause or explanations of *several* intercorrelated phenomena. It is of utmost importance that this unificatory potential of good scientific theories goes hand in hand with their potential to entail what we will call *strong* empirical success in sec.2: potentially novel predictions by which they can be tested *independently* from those phenomena to which they have been 'fitted' in an ex-post fashion.

2 THE CORRESPONDENCE THEOREM AND ITS CONDITIONS

The PMA and the NSA are strong counterarguments against the reliability of the NMA. Does there exists a justification of scientific realism which does not presuppose the dubious NMA? Even if such a justification does not exist, or exists only for a rather weak version of scientific realism, it would be advantageous to know, by an independent argument, under which conditions the NMA is reliable, and why it is unreliable if it is applied to theoretical speculations. In the remaining part I will propose such an argument. It is a logical argument which allows us to infer, under certain conditions, the partial truth of a theory from its empirical success, *relative* to a theory T^* which preserves T's empirical success and is assumed as true, or at least closer to the truth than T.

My argument is based on relations of *correspondence* between historically consecutive theories with increasing (or at least not decreasing) empirical success. Boyd (1984) and other philosophers of science have emphasized the existence of such relations of correspondence, which reflect that even on the theoretical level something is preserved through historical theory change and, thus, has a justified realist interpretation. Laudan (1981, pp.121, 126), however, has objected that there is no evidence for systematic relations of correspondence at the theoretical level − positive examples come mainly from the history of mechanics and have exceptional status. Laudan has given a much debated list of counterexamples − examples of scientific theories which were strongly successful at their time but whose ontology was incompatible with that of contemporary theories, from which Laudan concludes that these theories cannot possibly correspond to contemporary theories. In Schurz (2009) it is argued that Laudan is wrong: there are indeed systematic reasons for relations of theory-correspondence, which are based on the fact that under natural conditions the cumulatively

18

increasing empirical *success* of theories entails constraints on their theoretical superstructure from which one can obtain such relations of correspondence. Schurz (2009, §4) proves a correspondence theorem which presupposes the following conditions to be satisfied for the predecessor theory T and the successor theory T^* (both viewed as sets of sentences of an interpreted language):

(*Condition 1 on T and T**): The theories T and T^* share a common non-theoretical vocabulary in which their joint empirical (or non-theoretical) success is expressed, and they share a partitioned domain of application $A = A_1 \cup \ldots \cup A_n$, with $n \geq 2$, whose (disjoint) subdomains A_i are described by antecedent conditions A_i expressed by the shared non-theoretical vocabulary.

(*Condition 2 on T*): (2.1): The predecessor theory T has *strong potential empirical success* w.r.t. partitioned domain $A = A_1 \cup \ldots \cup A_n$, which means by definition that T entails a set of conditionals $S(T) = \{S_{i,j}: 1 \leq I \neq j \leq n\}$ of the form

$(S_{i,j})$ $(\forall x)$: $(\exists u)(A_i(x, u) \wedge \pm R_i[x, u]) \rightarrow (\forall u)(A_j(x, u) \rightarrow \pm R_j[x, u])$.
In words: If R_i has happened in circumstances A_i, then R_j will happen in circumstances A_j.

Notation: x and u are (sequences of) individual variables, x refer(s) to the system under consideration, u are non-theoretical auxiliary variables, e.g. the time variable (but possibly empty), the antecedent conditions A_i describe the conditions of the subdomains, the R_i describe typical reactions of the system x in the subdomain A_i expressed in the shared non-theoretical vocabulary and "$\pm$" means "unnegated or negated" (i.e., $\pm \in \{$emptystring, $\neg\}$). Round brackets "$A(v)$" indicate that formula A contains all of the variable(s) in v, while square brackets $R[v]$ mean that R may contain only some variables in v – this is needed for sufficiently flexible theory-reconstructions (see below). The conditionals (S_i) allow one to infer from what has been observed in one domain of application (namely $A_i \wedge R_i$) what will happen in a different domain of application (namely, if A_j, then R_j), without the system x having ever been put into conditions A_j before. Therefore, the conditionals (S_i) enable (potentially) *novel* predictions and, thus, serve as an example of *strong* empirical success. For example, when T is generalized oxidation theory, A_1 may describe the exposition of a metal to air and water and R_1 the end products of the reaction of oxidation, A_2 the exposition of a metal to hydrochloric acid and R_2 the end products of the reaction of salt-formation, etc.

(2.2): The strong potential empirical success $S(T)$ of T must have been *yielded* by a theoretical expression φ of T, which means by definition that T entails the set of bilateral reduction sentences $B(T, \varphi) = \{B_i: 1 \leq I \leq n\}$ of the form

(B_i): $(\forall x, u)$: $A_i(x, u) \rightarrow (\varphi(x) \leftrightarrow R_i[x, u])$.

In words: under empirical circumstances A_i, the presence of φ is indicated or measured by an empirical phenomenon or process R_i.

It is easily seen that $B(T, \varphi)$ entails $S(T)$. I understand bilateral reduction sentences, differently from Carnap, in a non-reductionist sense, as ordinary *measurement* conditions for theoretical expressions: (i) they are not analytically but synthetically true, (ii) they are usually *not* part of T's axiomatization, but are obtained as consequences of a suitably rich version of the theory, and (iii) their logical form covers all kinds of quantitative measurement laws (via the equivalence of "$\varphi(x) = r_i[x, u]$" with "$\forall z \in$ Reals: $\varphi(x) = z \leftrightarrow r_i[x, u] = z$") (for details cf. Schurz 2009, §3). The ontological interpretation of the role of φ as described by $B(T, \varphi)$ is the following: φ figures as a measurable *common cause* or *common explanation* of the observable regularities or dispositions $D_i := $ "if A_i, then R_i", in the sense that for all $1 \leq I \leq n$, $(\forall x, u)$: $(\varphi(x) \rightarrow (A_i(x, u) \rightarrow R_i[x, u]))$ (cf. Schurz 2008, §7.2).

(*Condition 3 on T^**): The strong potential empirical success of T, $S(T)$, must be entailed by T^* in a T^*-*dependent* way, which means by definition that for every conditional of the above form $(S_{i,j})$ which follows from T there exists a theoretical *mediator* description $\varphi^*_{i,j}(x)$ of the underlying system x such that $(\forall x)((\exists u)(A_i(x, u) \wedge \pm R_i[x, u]) \rightarrow \varphi^*_{i,j}(x))$ as well as $(\forall x)(\varphi^*_{i,j}(x) \rightarrow (\forall u)(A_j(x, u) \rightarrow \pm R_j[x, u]))$ follow from T^*. The need of condition 3 on T^* for the proof of the theorem is obvious, because in order to infer from the entailment of $S(T)$ by T^* something about a correspondence between T's and T^*'s theoretical part, we must assume that this entailment utilizes T^*'s theoretical part. The justification of condition 3 follows from the fact that $S(T)$ is a strong (potential) empirical success in the sense of novel predictions. From an empirical description of what goes on in domain A_i nothing can be concluded by means of empirical induction alone about what goes on in a qualitatively different domain A_j. For example, from observing the chemical reaction R_i of a given kind of substance (e.g. a metal) under the influence of oxygen (A_i), nothing can be concluded by empirical induction about the chemical reaction (R_j) of this substance under the influence of hydrochloric acid (A_j). For such an inference one needs a theoretical mediator description φ^* (e.g. the chemical structure of metals) which interpolates between ($A_i \wedge R_i$) and ($A_j \to R_j$).

(*Condition 4 on T and T**): The two theories T and T^* must be *causally normal* w.r.t. the partitioned domain $A = A_1 \cup \ldots \cup A_n$, which means by definition that: (a) the shared non-theoretical vocabulary of T and T^* divides into a set of independent and a set of dependent parameters (predicates or function terms), (b) the descriptions '$A_i(x)$' of the subdomains A_i are formulated solely by means of the independent parameters (plus logico-mathematical symbols), and (c) no non-trivial claim about the state of the independent parameters of a system x can be derived in T (or T^*) from a purely T (T^*)-theoretical and T (T^*)-consistent description of x. Again, this is a natural condition – for example, nothing can be concluded from the theoretical nature of a certain substance about what humans do with it, whether they expose it to hydrochloric acid or to heat or whatever. (*Remark:* for reasons of simplicity we use 'A' and 'A_i' both for an open formula and the set designated by the formula; the context makes it clear what is meant.)

Framed in the explained terminology, the correspondence theorem now asserts the following:

Correspondence theorem: Let T be a consistent theory which is causally normal w.r.t. a partitioned domain $A = A_1 \cup \ldots \cup A_n$ and contains a T-theoretical expression $\varphi(x)$ which *yields* a strong potential empirical success of T w.r.t. partitioned domain A.

Let T^* be a consistent successor theory of T (with an arbitrarily different theoretical superstructure) which is likewise causally normal w.r.t. partitioned domain A and which entails T's strong potential empirical success w.r.t. A in a T^*-dependent way.

Then T^* contains a theoretical expression $\varphi^*(x)$ such that T and T^* together imply a *correspondence relation* of the form

(C): $(\forall x)(\forall u): A(x, u) \to (\varphi(x) \leftrightarrow \varphi^*(x))$

In words: whenever a system x is exposed to the circumstances in one of the subdomains of A, then x satisfies the T-theoretical description φ iff x satisfies the T^*-theoretical description φ^*.

Remark: This implies that $\varphi(x)$ *refers indirectly* to the theoretical state of affairs described by $\varphi^*(x)$ – provided $\varphi^*(x)$ refers at all, which presupposes that T^* is at least partially true.

> *Corollary 1*: $B(T, \varphi) \cup T^*$ is consistent, and (C) follows already from $B(T, \varphi) \cup T^*$.
>
> *Corollary 2*: φ^* is unique in domain A modulo T^*-equivalence.

The proof of the correspondence theorem (details in Schurz 2009, §4) proceeds by showing that from T^*'s preservation of T's strong potential success plus condition 3 on T^* it follows that also T^* contains some expression φ^* whose designatum figures as a measurable common cause of the correlated regularities or dispositions "if A_i, then R_i". The requirement of T^*-theoretical mediators of condition 3 enables only the derivation of two unilateral reduction sentences from T^* (for each A_i), one for the positive test condition $(T^* \Vdash (A_i \to (\pi^* \leftrightarrow R_i))$ and one for the negative test condition $(T^* \Vdash (A_i \to (\mu^* \leftrightarrow \neg R_i))$. The causal normality condition 4 is then needed to prove that T^* entails $(\pi^* \leftrightarrow \neg \mu^*)$; whence π^* and $\neg \mu^*$ can be collapsed into the required T^*-corresponding concept φ^*. Thus, T^* entails the same set of bilateral reduction sentences as T entails for φ, or formally $T^* \Vdash B(\varphi, T)[\varphi^*/\varphi])$, where "$[\varphi^*/\varphi]$" denotes the operation of replacement of φ by φ^*.

While the conditions 1, 3 and 4 are rather mild, condition 2 on the predecessor theory T is a crucial constraint which excludes pre-scientific theoretical speculations. According to condition 2, the correspondence theorem applies to all and *only* those theoretical expressions φ of T which yield strong potential empirical success by way of bilateral reduction statements. (I speak of strong *potential* success $S(T)$ because the logical derivation of the correspondence theorem is independent from the factual truth values of the considered theories.) Condition 2 on T requires that (strictly) correlated empirical regularities or dispositions "if A_i, then R_i" are explained within T by an unobservable but measurable common cause or explanation φ. It was argued in sec.1 that it is exactly this *common cause* property which distinguishes *scientifically legitimate* theoretical explanations from speculative abductions. Indeed, the proof of the correspondence theorem would be impossible, if φ were characterized by only *one* disposition, i.e. one bilateral reduction sentence $A_1 \to (\varphi \leftrightarrow R_1)$. In Schurz (2009, §6) this is demonstrated by the example of Aristotelean physics which introduces a distinct cause for each kind of motion (cf. also van Fraassen

2006, p.281), whence no correspondence between Aristotelean and Newtonian physics can be established.

3 Ontological Interpretation and Historical Illustration of the Correspondence Theorem

It might seem to some readers that the result of the correspondence theorem is too good to be true. So we take pains to explain how the theorem works and to point to its weak spots. Implicit in corollary 1 is the possibility that the two theories T and T^* are mutually incompatible, at the theoretical level, or at the empirical level outside the domain of the shared empirical success. If T and T^* are incompatible, then it would, of course, be a trivial assertion that the union of T and T^* entails a correspondence relation (C), because in that case this union entails everything. Therefore, corollary 1 tells us that the correspondence principle follows in a non-trivial way from a certain part of T, namely $B(T,\varphi)$, which is *consistent* with T^*. Only this part of T, and not the whole of T, is preserved by the correspondence to T^*. In addition, our theorem takes care of empirical incompatibilities by restricting the correspondence between φ of T and φ^* of T^* to a given partitioned domain A, in which T was strongly successful. Outside of the domain A, T may have wrong empirical consequences which are not shared but corrected by T^*.

One example of a correspondence relation between theoretically incompatible theories is the *phlogiston theory* and the *generalized oxygen theory* of combustion. According to the phlogiston theory (developed by Becher and Stahl in the late 17th and early 18th century), every material which is capable of being burned or calcinated contains *phlogiston* – a substance different from ordinary matter which was thought to be the bearer of combustibility. When combustion or calcination takes place, the burned or calcinated substance delivers its phlogiston, usually in the form of a hot flame or an evaporating inflammable gas, and a dephlogisticated substance-specific residual remains. In the 1780s, Lavoisier introduced his alternative oxygen theory according to which combustion and calcination consists in the oxidation of the substance being burned or calcinated, that is, in the formation of a chemical bond of its molecules with oxygen. The assumption of the existence of a special bearer of combustibility became superfluous in Lavoisier's theory. In modern chemistry, Lavoisier's theory is accepted in a generalized and corrected form, in which the oxidizing substance need not by oxygen, but may be any electronegative substance.

Phlogiston theory was theoretically incompatible with oxygen theory because it assumed the existence of phlogiston which did not exist according to oxygen theory. Nevertheless phlogiston theory was strongly successful in explaining four domains of chemical reactions, namely (1.) the combustion of organic material, (2.) the calcination (roasting) of metals, (3.) salt-formation through the solution of metals in acids, and (4.) the inversion of calcination and salt-formation. In Schurz (2009) it shown that the theoretical concept which yielded phlogiston theory's strong success in these domains (in the sense of condition 2.2 in sec. 2) was not "phlogiston" itself – this term was empirically underdetermined – but, rather, the concepts of *phlogiston-richness* and *dephlogistication = release of phlogiston*. For these concepts, the following correspondence relation with generalized oxidation theory can be derived along the logical route of the correspondence theorem:

> *Phlogiston-richness* of a substance corresponds (and indirectly refers) to the *electropositivity* the substance.
> *Dephlogistication* of a substance corresponds (and indirectly refers) to the *donation of electrons* of substance's atoms to their electronegative bonding partner.

Let me turn to the *ontological interpretation* of the correspondence theorem. First of all, it is clear from the foregoing that the above correspondence relations do *not* preserve *all* of the meaning of 'phlogistication' or 'phlogiston-richness'. They cannot be regarded as an *analytic* truths, but have to be regarded as a *synthetic* statements which are true in the domain of applications in which phlogiston theory was empirically successful. Second, the correspondence relation (C) is *not* meant to say that whenever T's intended model (de-phlogistication) is realized, also T^*'s intended model (generalized oxidation) is realized – this would be a strange scenario of 'causal overdetermination'. Rather, (C) expresses the possibility of a φ-φ^*-*reference-shift:* instead of the reference assigned to φ in T's intended model M (e.g. phlogiston-richness, or dephlogistification), we can assign to φ the reference of φ^* in T^*'s intended model M^* (electropositivity, or donation of electrons, respectively). Such a φ-φ^*-reference shift will preserve the truth of $B(T, \varphi)$ (proof in Schurz 2009, §4).

It is important, thereby, that the expression φ which yielded T's strong success need not be a primitive term but may be a *composite* expression (and the same holds for the corresponding expression φ* of T*). Whenever T's expression φ corresponds to φ* of T*, but the ontology of the old theory T concerning the entities involved in φ is *incompatible* with the contemporary theory T^*, then it will be the case that φ is not a primitive but a *complex* expression of T, and T will contain certain theoretical assumptions about φ's *inner structure* or *composition* which from the viewpoint of T^* are false – for example, that 'dephlogistication' is a process in which a special substance different from ordinary matter, called 'phlogiston', leaves the combusted substance. While T has got a *right* model about φ's *outer structure*, i.e. the causal relations between the complex entity φ and the empirical phenomena, it has got a wrong model about φ's inner structure.

This situation is *typical* even for most advanced contemporary theories. For example, we are confident that protons exist because they are measurable common causes of a huge variety of empirical regularities. But concerning the hypothesis about the *inner composition* of protons consisting of *three quarks* things are different: physicists cannot measure quarks in isolation and, hence, are much more uncertain about their reality. In other words, the conception of realistic reference which is supported by the correspondence theorem is compatible with a certain amount of empirical underdetermination even in our most advanced theories. In Schurz (2009) it is argued that the notions of the outer and inner structure of a complex expression or entity φ reflect Worrall's (1989) distinction between 'structure' and 'content' in an ontologically unproblematic way: the 'structure' which is preserved is φ's *outer* structure, while the 'content' which is not preserved is φ's *inner* structure. Often, the preserved outer structure of a T-expression $φ_1$ does not only contain $φ_1$'s relations to observable phenomena, but covers also $φ_1$'s relation to other T-theoretical terms $φ_2$ for which a T^*-correspondence can *also* be established. In this sense, the relation between dephlogistication and phlogistication as inverse chemical reactions is preserved in modern chemistry.

The fact that the shifted interpretation of $B(T, φ)$ within T^*'s ontology forgets T's hypotheses about φ's inner structure and preserves only φ's outer structure implies that properly speaking, the preserved content-part $B(T, φ)$ has to be understood as a Ramsey-type existential quantification in which one quantifies over φ as a whole: if $B(T, φ)$ has the form $S(φ)$ where φ has the form $f(μ)$ (e.g. release-of-phlogiston), then what is preserved within T^*'s ontology is not $\exists X\, S(f(X))$ but the logically weaker $\exists X\, S(X)$. It follows from these considerations that the content-part of T which is preserved in T^* is a 'structural' (or quantificational) content-part of T in the explained sense, but not a simple *conjunctive* part of T's axioms. This contrasts with Psillos' 'theoretical constituents' (1999, pp.80f.), which are conjunctive parts of the given theory. The preservation of theoretical constituents in the sense of Psillos has been criticized by Lyons (2006), while the preservation of content-parts in my sense is not beset by Lyons' objections.

Two further applications of the correspondence theorem are illustrated in Schurz (2009, §5): one example is the caloric theory of heat, with the correspondence between the amount of caloric particles in a substance X and the mean kinetic energy of X's molecules, and the other example is Fresnel's mechanical wave theory of light, with the correspondence between the oscillation velocity of ether molecules and the oscillation strength of the electromagnetic field in Maxwell's account. In all these historical examples, there exists a *unique* correspondence concept φ^* in T^*. But not always is the situation so nice. T^* need not explain the correlated regularities "if A_i, then R_i" by postulating exactly one common cause (or explanation). It may also explain them by assuming a more complicated *net* of causes or hidden variables. This is the point where corollary 2 comes into play: if T^* may contain several causes $\varphi_1^*,\ldots,\varphi_k^*$ (with $k \leq n$) which correspond to φ in domain A, then corollary 2 tells us that in domain A all these causes are equivalent, i.e. (for all $1 \leq I \neq j \leq k$) $T^* \Vdash (\forall x, u): A \to (\varphi_i^*(x) \leftrightarrow \varphi_j^*(x))$. If we want to have a *unique* formal counterpart of φ in T^* in such cases, we should take the disjunction $\vee_{1 \leq i \leq k}\varphi_i^*(x)$. But this formal trick does not remove the possible ontological ambiguity. For the mutual equivalence of the φ_i^*'s which holds in domain A may fail to hold outside of domain A. It may happen that T^* contains several counterparts of φ, say φ_1^* and φ_2^*, which are not mutually identified by T^* because although they degenerate (extensionally) into one cause in domain A, they split up into two distinct causes outside of the domain A. An example of this sort which is analyzed by an early paper of Field (1973) is the correspondence between Newtonian mechanics and special relativity theory. Field shows that special relativity theory provides two counterpart notions to the Newtonian concept of mass m, (i) rest mass m_0 and (ii) relativistic mass

$$m_r := m_0/\gamma \ (\text{with } \gamma := \sqrt{1 - \frac{v^2}{c^2}}).$$

Since rest mass and relativistic mass are approximately identical in the domain in which Newtonian physics was empirically successful, this situation fits nicely with our correspondence theorem.

4 A JUSTIFICATION OF SCIENTIFIC REALISM WHICH DOES NOT PRESUPPOSE THE NMA

Under an additional assumption which I call 'minimal realism', the correspondence theorem justifies a weak version of scientific realism without presupposing the NMA or some other form of IBE (inference to the best explanation). Of course, the correspondence theorem alone justifies only a *conditional realism*: *if* one assumes the (approximate) realistic truth of the presently accepted theory T^*, then also outdated theories T (satisfying the conditions) will contain a (theoretico-structural) content-part which is indirectly and hence partially true. This conditional realism *weakens* Laudan's pessimistic meta-induction. But conditional realism *alone* is not sufficient to justify scientific realism. For someone who, on independent epistemological grounds, does not believe that contemporary or future scientific theories are approximately true, this conditional realism cannot tell anything about the partial truth of earlier theories.

But the situation changes if one makes the following assumption of *minimal realism* (MR):

> (MR) The observed phenomena are *caused* by an external reality whose structure can *possibly* be represented in an approximate way by an ideal theory T^+ which is causally normal, entails the observed phenomena in a T^+-dependent way, and whose language is in reach of humans' logico-mathematical resources.

(MR) is a *minimal* realistic assumption because it merely says that an approximately true theory describing the external reality in a humanly accessible language is possible – independent of whether humans will ever find this theory. The requirement that the T^+-language must be accessible by humans is necessary because otherwise we could not apply our correspondence theorem to this ideal theory T^+. The requirement of language-accessibility does not entail that the ideal theory T^+ itself must be graspable by humans. In the contrary, T^+ may be so complex that it can impossibly be understood by human brains, even if aided by super-computers.

Together with (MR), the correspondence theorem *entails* that the abductive inference from the strong empirical success of theories to their partial realist truth is *justified*. For if (MR) is true, then there exists an approximately true *ideal theory T^+*, which need not be known to us and preserves all of the (true) strong empirical success which our accepted theories have. So the correspondence theorem implies that every (theoretico-structural) content-part of our contemporary theories which satisfies condition 2 (plus 1 and 4) corresponds to a content part of the ideal theory T^+, and hence is indirectly true. In this way, my account provides an independent and non-circular justification of a weak version of the NMA, or of the abductive inference to the partial truth of strongly successful theories.

REFERENCES

Boyd, R. (1984): "The Current Status of Scientific Realism", in: J. Leplin (ed.), 1984, *Scientific Realism*, Berkeley: University of California Press, pp.41–82.

Field, H. (1973): "Theory Change and the Indeterminacy of Reference", *Journal of Philosophy* 70, 1973, pp.462–481.

Laudan, L. (1981): "A Confutation of Convergent Realism", reprinted in D. Papineau (ed.), 1996, *The Philosophy of Science*, Oxford: Oxford Univ. Press, pp.107–138.

Lyons, T.D. (2006): "Scientitic Realism and the Stratagemata de Divide et Impera", *British Journal for the Philosophy of Science*, 57, pp.537–560.

Psillos, S. (1999): *Scientific Realism. How Science Tracks Truth*, London and New York: Routledge.

Putnam, H. (1975): "What is Mathematical Truth?", in H. Putnam, *Mathematics, Matter and Method*, Cambridge: Cambridge Univ. Press, pp.60–78.

Schurz, G., and Lambert, K. (1994): "Outline of a Theory of Scientific Understanding", *Synthese* 101/1, pp.65–120.

Schurz, G. (2008): "Patterns of Abduction", *Synthese* 164, 2008, pp.201–234 (online http://dx.doi.org/10.1007/s11229-007-9223-4).

Schurz, G. (2009): "When Empirical Success Implies Theoretical Reference: A Structural Correspondence Theorem", *British Journal for the Philosophy of Science* 60/1, 2009, pp.101–133 (online: http://dx.doi.org/10.1093/bjps/axn049).

Van Fraassen, B. (2006): "Structure: Its Shadow and Substance", *The British Journal for the Philosophy of Science*, 57, pp.275–307.

Wilson, E.O. (1998): *Consilience. The Unity of Knowledge*, Alfred A. Knopf, New York.

Worrall, J. (1989): "Structural Realism: The Best of Both Worlds", *Dialectica*, 43/1–2, pp.99–124.

EMPIRICAL ADEQUACY AND RAMSIFICATION, II

JEFFREY KETLAND
University of Edinburgh

1. INTRODUCTION

1.1 Ramsey Sentences

This paper returns to the topic of Ketland 2004, which aimed to clarify the Newman objection to scientific structuralism. Several ways of formulating the propositional knowledge claims associated with scientific structuralism involve the appearance of a *Ramsey sentence*, in one form or another. Some structuralists "ramsify" the *linguistic formulations* of theories explicitly (e.g., Zahar 2001, Appendix), while others "ramsify" in a less obvious manner (e.g., the content of any "structural representation claim" seems to be a Ramsey sentence). However, there is a problem. In a 1928 review of Russell's structuralism, M.H.A. Newman pointed out that these "structural representation claims" reduce to *cardinality claims*. In 1985, Demopoulos and Friedman applied this criticism to argue that the truth of a theory's Ramsey sentence is equivalent to the theory's *empirical adequacy* plus a condition on the *cardinality of the world*. In particular, the "structural content" of a theory reduces to *cardinality content*. In Ketland 2004, the main result obtained was that a Ramsey sentence $\Re(\Theta)$ is true just if the theory Θ has an *empirically correct full model with sufficiently many objects*. Thus, not much more than empirical adequacy is required for $\Re(\Theta)$ to be true: so, structuralism collapses to *anti-realism* (cf., van Fraassen's constructive empiricism).

The notion of a Ramsey sentence first appears in Frank Ramsey's "Theories" (1929), discussing the role of *theoretical predicates* (*observational* predicates are supposed, via a "dictionary" or "correspondence rules", to "interpret" the theoretical predicates). Consider a statement of the form $\Theta(\mathbf{T}_1,\ldots, \mathbf{T}_n)$, with predicates $\mathbf{T}_1,\ldots, \mathbf{T}_n$ occurring in Θ. The corresponding Ramsey sentence has the form:

(1) There are relations $R_1,\ldots, R_n$ such that $\Theta(R_1,\ldots, R_n)$.

Syntactically, the Ramsey sentence replaces the predicates T_i with *second-order variables* R_i, and then prefixes the result with existential quantifiers for those variables. We say that the T_i have been "ramsified".[1] In effect, (1) expresses that the condition Θ is *satisfiable*. More generally, a Ramsey sentence has the form:

(2) There are relations R_1, ..., R_n on domain D such that
$\Theta(D, R_1, ..., R_n)$.

Example 1. Consider Max Born. The following is true:

(3) Max Born is the grandfather of Olivia Newton John.

Applying second-order ∃-I to the predicate "grandfather", (3) implies:

(4) There is a relation R such that Max Born bears R to Olivia Newton John.

This is the Ramsey sentence of (3). Call it $\mathfrak{R}(3)$. There is a sense in which the truth of $\mathfrak{R}(3)$ is nearly trivial. More exactly,

(5) $\mathfrak{R}(3)$ is *true* iff (3) is *satisfiable* on a domain containing Max and Olivia.

Example 2: Suppose L is a formalized language and Θ is an L-theory. Consider the claim,

(6) The theory Θ has a model with domain D.

This is equivalent to,

(7) There are relations $R_1, ..., R_n$ on D such that $(D, R_1, ..., R_n) \vDash \Theta$.

---

[1] "Ramsified" or "Ramseyfied"? As I understand the terminological use, the phrase "ramsified" is an allusion to Ramsey's discussion of Russell's *ramified* theory of types. Ramsey noted that the ramified theory of types is an unnecessary complication over the simple theory. And this observation has been expressed as a joke: "type theory needs *ramsification*, not ramification".

Thus, "Θ has a model" is, in effect, a *Ramsey sentence*.

Example 3. Suppose that **M** is a mathematical structure, as might crop up in the *mathematical* development of a scientific theory. For example, **M** might be the abstract 4-dimensional Minkowski spacetime, $(\mathbf{R}^4, \eta_{ab})$. Consider claims of the form:

Structural Representation Claims
(8a) **M** "represents" the world.
(8b) **M** is "isomorphic" to the world.
(8c) The world "exemplifies" **M**.
(8d) The world "instantiates" **M**.

It's unclear what this kind of claim means. One analysis of (8a)–(8d) seems to be the following:

(9) There are $R_1, \ldots, R_n$ on $D \subseteq$ the world, with $\mathbf{M} \cong (D, R_1, \ldots, R_n)$.

So, (8a)–(8d) are, in effect, Ramsey sentences. Under this analysis, *structural representation claims are Ramsey sentences*.

Example 4. Suppose that *Tim* is the set of temporal instants and *Bef* is the physical relation of time-ordering expressed, in English, by "t_1 is before t_2". Then a simple theory of time, Θ_T, may be expressed by the statement:

(10) $(Tim, Bef) \cong (\mathbf{R}, <_{\mathbf{R}})$.

One may "ramsify" Θ_T as follows:

(11) There is a set $X \subseteq$ the world and a relation S on X with $(X, S) \cong (\mathbf{R}, <_{\mathbf{R}})$.

Example 5. Maxwell's equations for electromagnetism may be written as follows:

(12) For any spacetime point p, $(\nabla \cdot \mathbf{B})(p) = 0$, and $(\nabla \cdot \mathbf{E})(p) = \rho(p)$, etc.

This is "ramsified" as follows:

31

(13) There exist vector fields $\mathbf{X}$, $\mathbf{Y}$, $\mathbf{Z}$ and a scalar field F, on space-time such that, for any spacetime point p, $(\nabla \cdot \mathbf{X})(p) = 0$, and $(\nabla \cdot \mathbf{Y})(p) = F(p)$, etc.

1.2 Structuralism

Throughout the 20th century, versions of *scientific structuralism* have been proposed by many philosophers of science, including Russell, Carnap, (G.) Maxwell, Sneed, Zahar, Worrall, Stegmüller, Redhead, French, Ladyman and others.[2] Simplifying somewhat, one school of scientific structuralism (Maxwell 1970, Worrall 1989, Zahar 2001, *et al.*) advocates an *epistemological* view, embodied by a slogan along the lines of "all we can *know* of the external world is its *structure*". Zahar and Worrall relate their arguments back to Poincaré, and further back to Kant. These views are usually motivated by epistemological considerations about what we can come to *know* about the world. For Poincaré, Zahar and Worrall, these considerations involve *theory change* in science.

It is probably sensible to begin with the version of epistemological structuralism given by Russell (Russell 1919, 1927), who wished to analyse the relation of cognition to the external world. In modern terminology, Russell's idea is that a "phenomenal structure" of some sort is built up in the mind on the basis of *perceptual experience*. This contains the percepts arranged in a *relational structure*. The mind is *directly acquainted* with this structure. But we are, on Russell's view, *not* directly acquainted with external reality. In a sense, we know it only by "description". To cash this out, Russell suggested, again with modern terminology, that the relation of this phenomenal structure to the world is that it is "*isomorphic*" to the world. For example, let the phenomenal domain P be the set of auditory pitches $\{Do, Re, Mi, Fa, So, La, Ti\}$, familiar to readers who have seen *The Sound of Music*. Let the distinguished relation H be the perceptual relation "has higher pitch than". Then the structure (P, H) is the corresponding phenomenal structure. Russell's idea is that *experience* brings us into *direct acquaintance* with a *phenomenal structure* $\mathbf{M}_{phen}$. Then our *scientific knowledge of the external world*, in general, takes the following form:

(14a) The world W exemplifies (or: instantiates) $\mathbf{M}_{phen}$.

---

[2] In addition, we have other forms of "structuralism", including Saussure in linguistics, Levi-Strauss in anthropology, and the more plausible *mathematical* structuralism of Shapiro and Resnik.

(14b) $\mathbf{M}_{phen}$ represents (or: is isomorphic to) the world W.

These are *"structural representation claims"* whose obvious analysis is a Ramsey sentence, thus:

(15) For some $D \subseteq W$, there are $R_1, \ldots, R_n$ on D with $(D, R_1, \ldots, R_n) \cong \mathbf{M}_{phen}$.

There is a connection between Russell's structuralism and a more recent position concerning the nature of theories, the "model-theoretic" conception of theories, which holds that a *scientific theory* is, or is to be "presented" as, a "class of mathematical structures" or a "class of models". The main problem with the model-theoretic conception of theories concerns its *repudiation of semantics*.[3] For, *if* a theory is a class of mathematical structures, it is extremely unclear what it means to say of a *theory* (a collection of structures) that it is *true*. There is no familiar sense in which *structures* are *truth-bearers*. In contrast, under ordinary Tarskian semantics, truth bearers are formulas of some interpreted language **L**. An interpreted language **L** may be construed as a pair $(L, \mathbf{M})$, where L is an uninterpreted language, and **M** is an L-structure (or interpretation). Then *truth* of a formula φ in **L** is precisely defined in the usual way. I.e., φ is true in **L** iff $\mathbf{M} \vDash \varphi$. Alternatively, truth bearers may be taken to be *propositions* (e.g., those expressed by sentences in an interpreted language). Indeed, in my view, scientific theories simply *are* collections of propositions. But models and structures are not truth-*bearers*.[4] So, what does it mean to say of a *structure* (or model) that it is "true"? For example, given a class Σ of structures (e.g., the models of Peano arithmetic; the countable dense linear orderings without endpoints, etc.), what could the following mean:

(16) The class Σ of structures is *true*?

Perhaps, (16) means something like:

---

[3] Ironically, the model-theoretic conception is sometimes called the "semantic view" of theories. But the central concepts of semantics are *truth*, *meaning* and *reference*. And there is no defined notion of a structure, or model, being "true".

[4] One *can*, in fact, define an auxiliary notion of an "interpretation" $\Im$ of a structure **M**. One can go on to define "**M** is correct, under $\Im$". But we lack the space here to discuss this.

(17) Some $\mathbf{M} \in \Sigma$ "represents" (or "is isomorphic to") the world.

This is a "structural representation claim" again, whose meaning is, presumably:

(18) For some $\mathbf{M} \in \Sigma$, there are $R_1,\ldots, R_n$ on $D \subseteq$ the world such that $\mathbf{M} \cong (D, R_1,\ldots, R_n)$.

Again, this is a Ramsey sentence. So, advocates of the model-theoretic conception of theories are committed to *ramsification*, but in a less obvious way. The model-theoretic conception of scientific theories tends to be associated with a certain *sub*school of scientific structuralism: "ontic structural realism" or "ontological structuralism" (see Ladyman 1998, French & Ladyman 2003, Brading & Landry 2005 *et al.*). Insofar as I grasp its claims, it appears to rest on two main lines of argument. First, there are certain arguments about *indiscernibility* in quantum theory and spacetime theory, alleged to have structuralist consequences; second, a preference for the model-theoretic conception of scientific theories. In contrast with the idea that our *knowledge* is *limited* to the world's "structure", the slogan is something like "*all there is is structure*" (Brading & Landry 2004). This is baffling. The standard conception of *structure* is the usual one from logic and mathematics: a *domain*, with some sequence of *distinguished relations*. So, does "all there is is structure" mean that reality has a *domain* and a *sequence of distinguished relations*? Is ontological structuralism the view that:

Reality is a Structure
(19) *Reality* itself is a structure, of the form $(W, R_1,\ldots, R_n)$?

If one makes this metaphysical assumption then the Newman objection discussed below does not apply. For, in that case, claiming that a given structure $\mathbf{M}$ is "isomorphic to the world" is then the claim that $\mathbf{M} \cong (W, R_1,\ldots, R_n)$. This is *non-trivial*. For example, suppose that reality, at bottom, has two basic distinguished 3-place relations, R_1 and R_2. Suppose our representing structure $\mathbf{M}$ is the usual field $(\mathbf{R}, +, \times)$ of real numbers. Then the claim that $(\mathbf{R}, +, \times) \cong (W, R_1, R_2)$ is highly non-trivial. However, if one does *not* make the "reality is a structure" assumption, the Newman objection *does* apply, and the structural representation claim "$\mathbf{M}$ is isomorphic to the world" is *equivalent* to "The world has cardinality at least $|\mathbf{M}|$". As things stand, I do not know whether or not advocates of ontological structuralism do or don't make this metaphysical assumption.

In contrast, the *epistemological* school of scientific structuralism tends to maintain that theories be identified with their linguistic formulations, holding the "cognitive content" of a theory Θ, expressed in an interpreted language **L**, to be given by its Ramsey sentence $\Re(\Theta)$ (see, e.g., Carnap 1956). The epistemological claim is that when a theory Θ satisfies certain conditions of epistemic warrant (predictive, explanatory success, etc.), one is justified in accepting that $\Re(\Theta)$ is true, or approximately true. This is meant to implement the vague idea that all we *know* of reality is its "structure", while its "nature" remains forever hidden.[5]

1.3 Newman's Objection

A central problem with structuralism, epistemological or ontological, is the objection given by the Cambridge mathematician M.H.A Newman in a short critical review (Newman 1928) of Russell's *Analysis of Matter* (Russell 1927). After quoting some examples of Russellian structural representation claims, Newman comments,

> [A]ll we can say is, "*There is* a relation R such that the structure of the external world with reference to R is **M**". Now I have already pointed out that such a statement expresses only a trivial property of the world. Any collection of things can be organised so as to have the structure **M**, provided there are the right number of them. Hence the doctrine that *only* structure is known involves the doctrine that *nothing* can be known that is not logically deducible from the mere fact of existence, except ("theoretically") the number of constituting objects. (Newman 1928, p.144; slight change in notation.)

So, *if* all that we know of reality is that it "instantiates" a structure **M**, then it follows that we know *nothing more* than a *lower bound on the cardinality of reality*. The mathematical point is this:

---

[5] Ramsey sentences crop up elsewhere, including Lewis's 1970 view concerning how to "define" theoretical terms, and versions of functionalism in philosophy of mind. (A *Lewis* sentence is stronger than a Ramsey sentence, as it contains *uniqueness* quantifiers.)

Basic Mathematical Point

The following statements are equivalent:

(a) There exists a structure $\mathbf{M}_W$ on some subset of W such that $\mathbf{M}_W \cong \mathbf{M}$.

(b) $|\mathbf{M}| \leq |W|$.

Consider again the structural representation claims of the sort associated with the model-theoretic conception of theories:

(20a) Minkowski spacetime $(\mathbf{R}^4, \eta_{ab})$ "represents" (or is "isomorphic" to) the world.

(20b) The world instantiates, or exemplifies, Minkowski spacetime $(\mathbf{R}^4, \eta_{ab})$.

Newman's objection is that these are *equivalent* to saying:

(21) The cardinality of the world is at least $2^{\aleph_0}$.

Thus, whether a class Σ of structures is "true" or not depends merely on the *cardinality* of the world.

For epistemological structuralism, the situation is more complicated. Consider a scientific theory Θ, expressed in an interpreted language $\mathbf{L}$ with domain W. Suppose first that *all* predicates are "ramsified". Then Newman's point tells us that,

(22) $\mathfrak{R}(\Theta)$ is true iff Θ has a full model with cardinality $|W|$.

So, the truth of $\mathfrak{R}(\Theta)$ reduces to a *satisfiability* condition, weaker than Θ's *truth*. However, perhaps some predicates, the "observational" ones, should *not* be ramsified. This is the standard approach, associated with Carnap, Maxwell, Worrall and Zahar. Does Newman's objection apply here? The first discussion of this scenario was given in an interesting and very important 1985 article by William Demopoulos and Michael Friedman, who summarize the application of Newman's objection in this case as follows:

> [I]f our theory is consistent, and if all its purely observational consequences are true, then the truth of the Ramsey-sentence follows as a theorem of set theory or second-order logic, provided our initial domain has the right cardinality – if it doesn't, then the consistency of our theory again implies the existence of a domain that does. (Demopoulos & Friedman 1985, p.635.)

The implications seem to be devastating:

(i) Epistemological structuralism reduces to a version of anti-realism (constructive empiricism, instrumentalism, or something similar).
(ii) Ontological structuralism reduces to the claim that every scientific theory can be re-expressed as *"the world has cardinality at least κ"*.

The main technical conclusion given by Demopoulos and Friedman – let us call it *DF* – has been endorsed by several authors in the recent literature on the scientific realism debate (e.g., Psillos 1999). My intention in Ketland 2004 was to clarify the matter by providing an appropriate framework for formalizing scientific theories and seeing how to prove *DF*. As it turns out, *DF* formulated as above is not quite correct: the main block in the proof is a kind of ω-inconsistency (see footnote 10 below for some details). However, with certain modifications to the formulation of *DF*, one gets closely connected results (see, e.g., Theorems 1, 4 and 5 below). The main result of Ketland 2004, using a 2-sorted formalization of the language of scientific theories, was:

$\mathfrak{R}(\Theta)$ is *true* iff Θ has a full model which is T-cardinality correct and empirically correct.

Thus, ramsification threatens to trivialize the content of scientific knowledge. *For structural claims are, in effect, cardinality claims*. Recently, there has been much further discussion of the Newman-Demopoulos-Friedman objection. The two most interesting discussions, in my view, are Cruse 2005 and Melia & Saatsi 2006. Melia and Saatsi propose to introduce into theory formulations certain higher-order modal relations between theoretical relations. I am not convinced that this approach will work. Cruse's points, concerning the observation-theory distinction, are more closely relevant to what is discussed below.[6]

---

[6] See Ainsworth 2009 for a clear survey of the main results, and some new ones, and an excellent discussion of some of the main lines of reply that have been given to Newman's objection.

2 FORMALIZATION OF SCIENTIFIC THEORIES

2.1 Empirical Adequacy and the O/T Distinction

Below, we introduce two formalization schemes for scientific theories. The notion of "empirical adequacy" has to be defined somehow. Trying to do this carefully, one notices two notions of *observationality* at play. First, the notion of *observable objects*; second, the notion of *observational predicates* (or *relations*). In light of this, one might argue that an *observational* predicate could, in principle, be true of *unobservable* objects (or could relate observable objects to unobservable ones, or even unobservable objects to unobservable ones). Consider the predicate "part of". Suppose we take "*part-of*" to be *observational*. Consider the following three statements:

(23a) My left thumb is a *part* of my left hand.
(23b) There are blood cells which are *parts* of my left thumb.
(23c) There are molecules which are *parts* of blood cells.

Statement (23a) involves a relation between observable objects; an *observable state of affairs*. Statement (23b) is *mixed*: the corresponding state of affairs involves a relation holding between an *unobservable* objects and an *observable* one. Statement (23c) concerns a relation holding between unobservable objects. So, does "part of" count as an observational predicate? Must an "observational" predicate apply *only* to observable *objects*?

If we say *No*, then the obvious 1-sorted way to formalize scientific theories leads to "observational" statements whose truth value depends upon the properties of *unobservable* objects. If we say *Yes*, then one *cannot* get a theorem of the kind that Demopoulos and Friedman were after *unless* one uses the 2-sorted formalization used in Ketland 2004. On the 2-sorted approach, we represent (23a)–(23c) as involving three distinct predicates, say "part$_O$", "part$_M$" and "part$_T$", depending on the observational status of their relata. So, the *empiricist* desire to impose an O/T distinction has forced us to "split" the *part-of* relation into three separate relations.[7] How-

---

[7] I described this "relation-splitting" objection to the O/T distinction in talks in 2002 (at LSE and Leeds); in Ketland 2004, I commented: "The technical framework described here ... is riddled with further problems ... [M]any scientifically significant relations and quantities will 'decompose' into three strangely distinct relations, depending upon the observational status of their relata" (Ketland 2004, p.289, footnotes 3 and 4.)

ever, on this 2-sorted approach, the observational predicates do only have *observable* objects as their relata; and one then obtains a correct *DF*-style result.

A less metaphysically artificial approach introduces either a distinction in the semantics (by supposing that some special subset *Obs* of the domain *W* of the intended interpretation consists of the observable objects) or by explicitly introducing into the theory-formulation language a primitive unary predicate *Obs*(*x*) meaning "*x* is an observable object", and defining the observationla statements by restricting quantifiers to *Obs*(*x*). (Cf., in set theory, one can restrict quantifiers to a given set, e.g., ω.) This is, in effect, a 1-sorted formalization, in which the observable objects are explicitly distinguished by some predicate. We shall briefly discuss this approach below, in Section 3. However, one *cannot* then get a *DF*-style result, because the relevant notion of "empirical adequacy" is *too weak* to entail the truth of the Ramsey sentence (see the remarks after Definition E below).

However, the *usual* approach, associated with Carnap, is to consider a 1-sorted theory-formulation language *L* with primitive predicates partitioned into "observational" and "theoretical" ones, saying nothing about the observational status of the *objects* to which these predicates apply. In particular, the domain *W* of the interpreted language may contain unobservables and the O-predicates are permitted to apply to these. On this approach, one may define a notion of "O-adequacy" and one obtains a *DF*-style result, "$\Re(\Theta)$ is true iff Θ is O-adequate". However, the problem is that "O-adequate" *doesn't mean what is intended*. For the quantifiers of *L* range over *all* elements of *W*, including *unobservables*. So, certain "observational" statements will be true/false in virtue of facts about unobservable objects.

2.2 One-Sorted Formalization

Scientific theories are to be formulated in a one-sorted, second-order, theory formulation language *L* with identity. Non-logical primitives of *L* are classified into two kinds: *observational* predicates, O_i, and *theoretical* predicates, T_i. The sublanguage of *L* from which the theoretical predicates and second-order variables have been deleted is called *L*'s *observational* sublanguage, denoted L_O. An *L*-theory Θ is a deductively closed set of *L*-sentences. We may identify a theory Θ with some axiomatization of it; if Θ is finitely axiomatizable, then we may identify Θ with a single formula which is the conjunction of the axioms. Suppose Θ is the single axiom for a finitely axiomatized L-theory. The Ramsey sentence $\mathfrak{R}(\Theta)$ is obtained by replacing, in Θ, each occurrence of a theoretical predicate $\mathbf{T}_i$ by a second-order variable X_i of the same arity, and prefixing the result with a string of existential quantifiers, one for each variable X_i that appears. Thus,

Definition A
$\mathfrak{R}(\Theta)$ is: $\exists X_1 \ldots \exists X_n \Theta(\mathbf{T}_1/X_1,\ldots, \mathbf{T}_n/X_n)$.

L is given a special partial interpretation $(W, \{O_i\})$, where W is the domain over which the quantifiers range and the O_i are the "observational" relations on W which interpret the observational predicates $\mathbf{O}_i$. We suppose that $W = Obs \cup Unobs$, where Obs is the set of "observable" objects and $Unobs$ is the set of "unobservable" objects. (Obs and $Unobs$ are assumed disjoint.) As discussed above, we allow "observational" predicates to apply to some *unobservable* objects. The semantics is standard Tarskian semantics.[8]

2.3 Two-Sorted Formalization

The language L is now a two-sorted, second-order, language with identity. The non-logical primitives of L are classified into three kinds: *observational*, $\mathbf{O}_i$; *mixed*, $\mathbf{M}_i$; and *theoretical*, $\mathbf{T}_i$. The sublanguage from which the theoretical and mixed predicates have been deleted is L's observational sublanguage, denoted L_O. If Θ is a finitely axiomatized theory in L, the Ramsey sentence $\mathfrak{R}(\Theta)$ is obtained by ramsifying the theoretical *and mixed* predicates. L has a special 2-sorted partial interpretation $((D_O, D_T), \{O_i\})$, where D_O is the domain of observable objects and D_T is the domain of unobservable objects. (These are disjoint.) The two sorts of variable range over these distinct domains.

---

[8] For second-order sentences of L, standard *full* semantics is assumed.

As noted above, the relevant notion of empirical adequacy is tricky to formulate on the 1-sorted formalization.

Definition B
The substructure $(Obs, \{O_i|_{Obs}\})$, generated by the subset Obs, is the *empirical substructure* of $(W, \{O_i\})$.

Definition C
An L-theory Θ is *weakly empirically adequate* iff all L_O-theorems of Θ are true in $(Obs, \{O_i|_{Obs}\})$.

Perhaps a better analysis of the notion of empirical adequacy requires an *embedding* of the empirical substructure into some model of Θ. That is:

Definition D
An L-structure $\mathbf{M} = (D, \{R_i^O\}, \{R_i^T\})$ is *empirically correct* iff there is an embedding $f: (Obs, \{O_i|_{Obs}\}) \to (D, \{R_i^O\})$.

Definition E
An L-theory Θ is *empirically adequate* iff Θ has a full model which is empirically correct.

Sadly, Definitions A-E are *pointless*. For the adequacy conditions on Θ given in Definitions C and E are too *weak* to imply the truth of $\Re(\Theta)$. As it turns out, *if* we want *DF*-style results, we *must* either move to the 2-sorted formalization or introduce a stronger notion, "O-adequacy":

Definition F
An L-theory Θ is *weakly* O-adequate iff all L_O-theorems of Θ are true.

Definition G
An L-structure $\mathbf{M} = (D, \{R_i^O\}, \{R_i^T\})$ is O-correct iff $(D, \{R_i^O\}) \cong (W, \{O_i\})$.

Definition H
An L-theory Θ is O-adequate iff Θ has a full, O-correct, model.

Next, assume the 2-sorted formalization.

Definition I
A 2-sorted L-structure $\mathbf{M} = ((D_1, D_2), \{R_i^{\mathrm{O}}\}, \{R_i^{\mathrm{M}}\}, \{R_i^{\mathrm{T}}\})$ is empirically correct iff $(D_1, \{R_i^{\mathrm{O}}\}) \cong (D_{\mathrm{O}}, \{O_i\})$.

Definition J
A 2-sorted L-structure $\mathbf{M} = ((D_1, D_2), \{R_i^{\mathrm{O}}\}, \{R_i^{\mathrm{M}}\}, \{R_i^{\mathrm{T}}\})$ is T-cardinality correct iff there is a bijection $f: D_2 \to D_{\mathrm{T}}$.

4 MAIN RESULTS

On the 1-sorted formalization, we first show that $\mathfrak{R}(\Theta)$ is true iff $(W, \{O_i\})$ can be expanded to a full model of Θ. Hence:

Theorem 1: $\mathfrak{R}(\Theta)$ is true iff Θ is O-adequate.

Note that O-adequacy (Definition H) is stronger than empirical adequacy (Definition E). So, $\mathfrak{R}(\Theta)$'s truth is *not* necessarily implied by Θ's empirical adequacy. Next, consider whether *weak* O-adequacy is sufficient for the truth of $\mathfrak{R}(\Theta)$. First, we can show,

Theorem 2: If Θ is O-adequate, then Θ is weakly O-adequate.

However, the converse is not true:

Theorem 3
There are *weakly* O-adequate theories Θ which are not O-adequate.

This occurs only when the intended domain W is *infinite*. We can fix things up a bit:

Theorem 4: Suppose W is *finite*. Then $\mathfrak{R}(\Theta)$ is true iff Θ is weakly O-adequate.[9]

---

[9] The proof uses the following lemma: Let L^* be a sublanguage of L. Suppose Θ^* is the set of L^*-theorems of Θ. Then any *finite* model of Θ^* can be expanded to a model of Θ.

This is the closest we get, on the 1-sorted formalization, to the original claim of Demopoulos & Friedman 1985, which spoke of the truth of "all purely observational consequences" (i.e., *weak* adequacy). Two comments are worth making. First, we must use the notion of "weak O-adequacy" rather than the notion of *weak empirical adequacy*; second, the domain W of the intended interpretation must be *finite*.[10]

On the 2-sorted formalization, we obtain,

Theorem 5
$\Re(\Theta)$ is true iff Θ has a full empirically correct and T-cardinality correct model.

In this framework, the truth condition for $\Re(\Theta)$ now involves *empirical adequacy*, not O-adequacy: this was the motivation for using this framework in Ketland 2004. However, Cruse 2005 has criticized my decision to ramsify the "mixed" predicates on the 2-sorted formalization. Cruse argues that *mixed* predicates should count as "observational" and thus *shouldn't* be ramsified. However, this definition of "observational predicate" becomes analogous to the notion of O-predicate on the 1-sorted approach. One can then give a definition of an "O-M correct" structure:

Definition K
An L-structure $((D_1, D_2), \{R_i^O\}, \{R_i^M\}, \{R_i^T\})$ is O-M correct iff
$$((D_1, D_2), \{R_i^O\}, \{R_i^M\}) \cong ((D_O, D_T), \{O_i\}, \{M_i\}).$$

A modification of the proof of Theorem 5 gives:

Theorem 6: $\Re(\Theta)$ is true iff Θ has a full model which is O-M correct.

---

[10] If we admit possible worlds containing an *infinity* of observables, resembling the natural numbers, then counterexamples to the original *DF* claim can be given. In Ketland 2004, one is given based on the ω-inconsistent Friedman-Sheard truth theory over Peano arithmetic, using results obtained by McGee 1985 and Halbach 1999. A similar counterexample can be given based on the ω-inconsistent, conservative extension of Peano arithmetic, based on Yablo's paradox, discussed in Ketland 2005. Another counterexample appeared in van Benthem 1978, based on the (r.e.) theory of $(\omega, <)$ extended by axioms saying "*there is* a T", but "$0 \notin$ T and, for all x, if $x \notin$ T, $s(x) \notin$ T". In each case, we obtain examples of theories which are *weakly* O-adequate (and have a model of the right *size*), but their Ramsey sentences are *not true*.

This is Theorem 1 in disguise. $\Re(\Theta)$'s truth condition now involves facts about unobservables. However, information about the *purely theoretical* relationships amongst unobservables has again been reduced to mere cardinality (encoded into the bijections required for O-M correctness). So, this response achieves little.

5 CONCLUDING COMMENTS

It seems to me that the results above confirm Demopoulos and Friedman's main conclusion that ramsification *"trivializes physics"* (Demopoulos & Friedman 1985, p.635); ramsification leads to what might be called *physics without physics*. That is, *purely structural content just is cardinality content*.[11] So far as I can see, if one wishes to avoid such conclusions, one must adopt a form of scientific essentialism or natural kinds realism:

Scientific Essentialism/Natural Kinds Realism
Nature has its own special *"natural kind"* structure; second-order variables only range over the relations that are *"natural"*.

Thus, Ramsey sentences should be understood as follows:

(24) There are *natural* relations $R_1,\ldots, R_n$ such that $\Theta(R_1,\ldots, R_n)$.

However, is scientific essentialism *consistent* with scientific structuralism? The structuralist, epistemological or ontological, must take the metaphysical notion of *"natural relation"* as an unreduced primitive in theorizing, and must assume from the outset that reality has a built-in natural kind structure.

REFERENCES

Ainsworth, P. 2009: "Newman's Objection". *B.J.P.S.* 60, pp.135–171.
Brading, K. and E. Landry. 2005: "Scientific Structuralism: Presentation and Representation". *Philosophy of Science* 73, pp.571–581.

---

[11] Roy Cook put it as follows: ramsification "reduces physics to *counting*".

Carnap, R. 1956: *The Philosophical Foundations of Physics*, edited by M. Gardner. New York: Basic Books. Reprinted as *An Introduction to the Philosophy of Science*, New York: Dover Books, 1995.

Cruse, P. 2005: "Ramsey Sentences, Structural Realism and Trivial Realization". *Studies in the History and Philosophy of Science* 36, pp.557–576.

Demopoulos, W and M. Friedman 1985: "Critical Notice: Bertrand Russell's *The Analysis of Matter*: Its Historical Context and Contemporary Interest", *Philosophy of Science* 52, pp.621–639.

Halbach, V. 1999: "Conservative Theories of Classical Truth". *Studia Logica* 62, pp.353–370.

Ketland, J. 2004: "Empirical Adequacy and Ramsification". *B.J.P.S.* 55, pp.287–300.

Ketland, J. 2005: "Yablo's Paradox and ω-Inconsistency". *Synthese* 145, pp.295-302.

Ladyman, J. 1998. "What is Structural Realism?", *Studies in the History and Philosophy of Science* 29, pp.409–424.

Lewis, D. 1970: "How to Define Theoretical Terms". *Journal of Philosophy* 67, pp.427–446.

Maxwell, G. 1970. "Structural Realism and the Meaning of Theoretical Terms", in S. Winokur and M. Radner (eds), *Analyses of Theories and Methods of Physics and Psychology*, Minneapolis, MN: University of Minnesota Press, pp.181–192.

McGee, V. 1985: 'How Truthlike can a Predicate Be? A Negative Result', *Journal of Philosophical Logic* 14, pp.399–411.

Melia, J. and J. Saatsi. 2006: "Ramseyfication and Theoretical Content". *B.J.P.S.* 57, pp.561–585.

Newman, M.H.A. 1928: "Mr Russell's Causal Theory of Perception". *Mind* 37, pp.137–148.

Psillos, S. 1999: *Scientific Realism: How Science Tracks Truth*. London: Routledge.

Ramsey, F.P. 1929: "Theories", in R.B. Braithwaite (*ed.*), 1931, *Foundations of Mathematics*, London: Routledge and Kegan Paul.

Russell, B.A.W. 1919. *A Mathematical Introduction to Philosophy*. London: Allen and Unwin.

Russell, B.A.W 1927: *Analysis of Matter*. London: Allen and Unwin.

van Benthem, J. 1978: "Ramsey Eliminability". *Studia Logica* 37, pp.321–336.

van Fraassen, B.C. 1980: *The Scientific Image*. Oxford: Clarendon Press.

Worrall, J. 1989: "Structural Realism: The Best of Both Worlds?". *Dialectica* 43, pp.99–124.

Zahar, E. 2001: *Poincaré's Philosophy: From Conventionalism to Phenomenology*. Chicago: Open Court.

ELIMINATING MODALITY FROM THE DETERMINISM DEBATE? MODELS VS. EQUATIONS OF PHYSICAL THEORIES

THOMAS MÜLLER
Utrecht University

This paper addresses a specific question of reductionism, viz., the question of whether modalities are basic for the notions of determinism and indeterminism, or whether one can do without them. I will argue that the current treatment of these notions within philosophy of science, which takes determinism and indeterminism to be properties of scientific theories rather than metaphysical theses about what the world is like, amounts to a reductionist stance with respect to modality for which no good reasons have been given. Furthermore, I will show that the current implementation of that treatment is not without problems: there is a discrepancy between the official definition of determinism and indeterminism, phrased in terms of the 'modally flat' collection of models of a theory, and the practice of assessing determinism[1] by looking at the possibly branching space of solutions to a theory's constitutive equations, which moves that practice much closer to a pro-modality stance.

Apart from commenting on use of models vs. equations in the determinism debate within philosophy of science, my paper is also an attempt at getting clear on the proper dialectics of the question of modal reductionism. I will thus also lay out my view as to how determinism and indeterminism or other modal notions should be addressed.

---

[1] And thus, indeterminism. In what follows I will often mention, for brevity's sake, just one of the notions when I am in fact concerned with both.

1 MODALITY AND THE METAPHYSICAL QUESTION OF DETERMINISM VS. INDETERMINISM

There are two ways to read the question of what the world is like. One, which may be called the everyday reading, points to a question that can be answered by straightforward empirical experiment and observation, e.g., by describing the breeding cycle of a population of penguins living in a particular region, by finding out about the crystal structure of diamonds, or, if you wish, by counting the occurrences of the letter "r" in this paper. As a philosopher, however, one is often concerned with another reading of the question of what the world is like – and one, it seems, that would still be open after all the empirical questions have been answered. This *metaphysical* sense of the question may be gestured towards by asking what the world is *really* like. Specific instances of the question of what the world is like taken in that sense are, e.g., about the reality of colour (is the world really such that objects have colour?), or about the nature of time (is there really a distinguished present?).[2] The question of whether the world is deterministic or not, which is perceived by many to have enormous consequences for our understanding of ourselves as free agents,[3] is also first and foremost a metaphysical one (and in fact it may be a very close cousin of the question about the nature of time);[4] determinism and indeterminism are metaphysical notions. They are not about what does or doesn't happen, but about what *can* or what *has to* happen and are thus built upon the modal notions of possibility and necessity. Since one can only experience that which is actual and not what is merely possible, empirical research cannot resolve questions of possibility and necessity directly.

It has become common to distinguish a number of different kinds of modality, e.g., to distinguish logical from metaphysical and physical possibility: after all, what is physically impossible (like going faster than the speed of light) may still be metaphysically possible. For the question of determinism, the pertinent notion of possibility is often taken to be physical possibility. This notion of possibility, being tied to the abstract concept of laws of nature, is however too far removed from our initial practical con-

---

[2] For arguments to the effect that this is how we should understand metaphysics, and for more about these specific examples, cf. Stroud [2000] and Fine [2005, pp.261–320].

[3] For an overview of the current state of the free will debate cf., e.g., the articles in Kane [2002].

[4] This connection has been explored, e.g., in the tradition of Prior's [1957] and [1967].

cerns about determinism. Those concerns, which provide our first motivation for being interested in the metaphysical notions of determinism and indeterminism, are not connected with abstract laws, but with concrete situations. The appropriate notion of possibility in discussing determinism is, therefore, what has been called *real* or *historical* possibility: possibility in a given, concrete situation.[5]

Even if one doesn't subscribe to the thesis of indeterminism, just by asking the question of whether determinism is true of false (and thus, whether indeterminism is false or true) one thus needs to take seriously the notion of real possibility, i.e., of an open possibility in a given concrete situation. My point is not that this proves the existence, or even just the relevance, of real possibility once and for all. But it determines where the dialectics of the argument has to start, since this is how the question, initially, makes sense to us. It may turn out that there are arguments against setting up the discussion in this way. Then, the discussion will have to be transformed. But first and foremost, determinism and indeterminism are based on real possibility.

One open real possibility is enough to prove indeterminism, and thus to disprove determinism. It is however clear from the metaphysical nature of the determinism/indeterminism question as laid out here that there can be no hope of answering that question empirically in any straightforward manner. Possibilities can be experienced only once they are actualized, by which time they have ceased to be open possibilities and have become real in the simple, empirical sense of that term.

This seems to create a problem for the approach to determinism that I am advocating. Determinism is true if and only if there is only one way that the future can (really) turn out to be, whereas indeterminism is true if there is at least one open real possibility. I have suggested that we understand that notion well enough, but I have also said that it is not empirically accessible, at least not in any straightforward sense. But is the question of determinism, on that reading, then really a genuine question and not just nonsense? The importance of the question for our practical lives in my view points strongly to its reality. This link can of course also be questioned. It is true that people are often enough caught up in superstitions,

---

[5] This notion of possibility has not been much discussed outside rather formal contexts; cf. Xu [1997], Belnap et al. [2001] and Placek and Müller [2007]. Historically, however, it is already invoked in Aristotle's famous argument about the sea-battle tomorrow in *De Interpretatione*.

viewing as practically important questions that cannot be answered and shouldn't even be asked – but this doesn't seem to be one of them.[6] Furthermore, the reality and importance of the question is corroborated by the fact that we acknowledge modal truths about most, if not all, ordinary things. Chances are you are reading this from a book (do the obvious substitution if you're reading from a different source). It is nothing out of the ordinary to claim that, as of your reading it in the concrete situation you are in, it is really possible that the book should still exist in 100 years' time (in fact you know how to make pretty sure, even if this may be costly and involve steel casing embedded in layers of concrete), and that it is also really possible that it shouldn't (the easier exercise). Real possibilities are nothing spooky or special, we live in a world full of them. This world we picture, at least intuitively, as a branching arrangement of possible histories.[7]

It is a curious fact that amongst philosophers, proponents of the commonsensical view of real modality appear to be a minority, while extreme positions such as Quine's or Lewis's are favored by a majority.[8] These extreme views are however revisionist, which means that the onus of proof is on their side: in order to adopt one of them one would seem to need good arguments. The general methodological point here is that "you start from where you are", not necessarily "you stay where you are". My further specific point is that in the case of determinism and indeterminism we should also stay where we are, because there aren't any good arguments to pull us away from there.

---

[6] This is a tangled issue, as anyone who has surveyed the current free will debate will acknowledge. There are numerous writers who try to convince one that the open future image of decision and action is a superstition that should be abandoned in the name of science. My point here is not to enter that debate, but to get clear on the dialectics of the argumentation. Even people who argue against the open future conception of indeterminism acknowledge that we do have such an image of the open future. My point is that, therefore, this is where the discussion should start: with the facts of what Strawson calls "descriptive metaphysics". Of course we could still be wrong – but strong arguments would be needed in order to prove this.

[7] Some people may prefer the "growing block" picture that one finds in Broad [1923]. For present purposes the difference doesn't matter much.

[8] Cf. Fine [2005, pp.214–231].

2 DEFINING DETERMINISM AND INDETERMINISM IN PHILOSOPHY OF SCIENCE

Above I have already given a rough and ready definition of determinism and indeterminism: determinism is true if and only if there is only one way that the future can (really) turn out to be, whereas indeterminism is true if there is at least one open real possibility. This is not the definition of determinism that is employed in the current discussion about determinism and indeterminism in philosophy of science. There, the focus is, on the contrary, exclusively on scientific – mostly, physical – theories, and determinism is defined as a property of such theories, i.e., of pictures we make of the world, not of the world itself. Roughly, a theory is said to be deterministic if and only if it describes a unique temporal evolution of each of the systems falling under it.

It is easy enough to imagine how it may have come about that the discussion shifted from the metaphysical question to one about properties of theories. (No specific historical claims intended.) Modal notions have poor empiricist credentials (if they have any at all), and current philosophy of science is a brainchild of the logical empiricism of the 1930s. The modalities can be circumvented – or so it seems – by moving the determinism discussion towards a study of physical theories: abstract and therefore modally innocent entities. (Never mind *their* empiricist credentials.) And it seems clear enough when one should call a specific scientific theory "deterministic" and when "indeterministic", via uniqueness of temporal evolution.

It took some ingenuity to spell out that idea in a succinct fashion. Earman [1986] relates the history and points out the crucial role of Montague [1962], who was the first to advance a model-theoretic definition of the notion of determinism. Basically, a theory is (future-)deterministic[9] if for any two of its models describing the possible temporal evolution of a system, coincidence of the state at one time brings with it coincidence at all times from then on, where "coincidence" is to be spelled out in terms of a suitable mapping. Montague in fact considered identity of states and pre-

---

[9] Here and in the following we will discuss the notion of future-determinism; there is obviously a temporal mirror image to all the definitions. Sometimes the term "determinism" is used to encompass both past- and future-determinism. Most fundamental physical theories are time reversal invariant and thus future-deterministic if and only if they are also past-deterministic.

supposed a time axis outside the models to be given. In this he is followed by Earman [2007]. Butterfield [2005] in his highly informative *Routledge Encyclopedia* article on determinism however points out that presupposing such an external meta-time "would be very questionable"[10] and instead bases his definition on a broader class of mappings, viz., isomorphisms "in the usual sense used by logicians".[11] Accordingly, he gives the following definition:

> [A] theory is deterministic if, and only if: for any two of its models, if they have instantaneous slices that are isomorphic, then the corresponding final segments are also isomorphic.

An instantaneous slice here comprises all the relevant information about the system in question at one point in time – its *state* at that time –, while the corresponding final segment comprises the whole future development of the state from that time on. Much depends on how much of the system the isomorphism in questions 'sees', or what the instantaneous state of the system – the information about the system available at an instantaneous slice – is taken to be. Obviously, if that state encodes information about the future evolution of the system (think of natural-language predicates such as "mortally wounded"), the system may be judged to be deterministic without good reasons; the same can happen if the state employed is too thin, missing out on crucial information (like calling a quantum system deterministic because total charge is conserved). Butterfield is explicit about the fact that the notion of state at issue does play this crucial role, and that there is no formal way to extract the relevant notion out of a theory – it is rather that considered judgment is called for. Earman [2007] supplants these caveats by pointing to difficulties with the notion of an *instantaneous* state in various space-time theories. In fact, addressing questions of determinism or indeterminism of theories tends to take one to the heart of con-

---

[10] It surely would be, and it should give rise to extensional differences between, e.g., Earman and Butterfield, *if the official model-theoretic definition were actually employed*. In section 3.2 below I will point out that this is not so.

[11] In logic, a function f is called an isomorphism between models A and B of a language if f maps the domain of A bijectively onto that of B and carries the respective interpretation along, so that, e.g., $f(c_i^A) = c_i^B$ for a constant symbol c_i, and $P_i^A(x)$ if and only if $P_i^B(f(x))$ for a one-place predicate symbol P_i. Note that in the discussion of determinism in philosophy of science the language in question is hardly ever made explicit, so that the notion of an isomorphism remains vague.

ceptual issues about these theories, a fact that Earman [2007] rightly emphasizes. Norton additionally points out that questions of determinism also tend to trigger questions of the *physicality* or otherwise of a model system, such as his famous dome [Norton 2008b].

In section 3, I will look at the actual practice of assessing the determinism of physical theories, i.e., at the way the above definition is put to use in philosophy of science. Before that, however, I would like to comment on the relation between the discussion about the determinism of theories and the primary metaphysical question of determinism addressed in section 1 above.

It is clear that the question about the determinism of theories is not the same as the primary, metaphysical one, and I have suggested that the discussion in terms of properties of theories was chosen intentionally because the other, metaphysical, discussion was viewed with suspicion (or worse). Still, it is that *metaphysical* notion of determinism that plays a role, or should play a role, e.g., in the free will debate. So what is the point of suggesting, as the use of the same terminology insinuates, that the same issues are addressed?

I see two motivations, both of which are in fact discernible in Butterfield [2005]. First, one may be convinced that the general metaphysical question makes no sense. I have tried to argue that it does make sense, but obviously sentiments differ. If the original metaphysical question makes no sense, it is a good idea to go for the next best thing, and that would indeed be the determinism or indeterminism not of the world, but of pictures we make of the world, e.g., physical theories. A second motivation is that investigating scientific theories may tell us something about the metaphysical question after all. The idea here is that if a scientific theory is deterministic, that means that the world, if the whole truth about it were described by that theory, would also be deterministic; and the same holds for indeterminism. Now since physics strives to give us ever more encompassing theories (some of which have historically been claimed, wrongly, to be the whole truth about the world) and may be hoped to approximate the true nature of our world (for whichever reason), assessing current physics as to determinism seems to be our reasoned best guess at the metaphysical question.

Both these motivational stories strike me as dubious. Against the first I have tried to argue that our methodological starting point needs to be our intuitive self-conception, which would answer the metaphysical question in favor of indeterminism – not as an unassailable fact, but as something against which one would need to argue. Saying that the metaphysical question is indeed metaphysical isn't an argument against it; it is just pointing to a possible epistemological problem. The second point strikes me as basically sound – of course we should listen to science. But I believe that the evidence that science gives on the issue of determinism is much richer than what is encoded in scientific theories. Scientific practice and the use of the experimental method seem to me to provide stronger arguments in favor of indeterminism than any specific theory could provide. That practice relies on the possibility of freely choosing initial conditions for experiments. Experiment isn't just observation, but observation after intervention. And intervention is a modal notion: it means to realize a (real) possibility in a concrete situation in which the normal course of things would have been otherwise. If one adjusts a setting of an instrument or pushes a button to start a run of an experiment, that is an intervention; it wouldn't have happened if it hadn't been for the experimenter. Furthermore, if one tries to find out about determinism or indeterminism by looking at currently championed scientific theories, one finds deterministic ones (special relativity theory and maybe some other space-time theories) alongside a number of indeterministic ones (arguably quantum theory, and certainly some space-time theories as well as Newtonian mechanics). Even for one and the same theory, the verdict as to determinism or indeterminism can depend on fine details of formulation or interpretation [Earman 2007] – determinism (or indeterminism) doesn't seem to be a stable property of a theory that one should expect to be preserved in historical succession. Therefore it does not seem that consensus on the determinism issue is anywhere in sight from the theoretical side. It is rather that the study of scientific theories provides us with toy models of what the world could be like if one such theory were the whole truth about everything, which we know it isn't.

To sum up my points here: I see no good arguments forthcoming that show the infeasibility of investigating a metaphysical notion of determinism and indeterminism. And even if one goes along with the sentiment that the answer to the question of determinism or indeterminism can only come from science, that does not prove that one should only look at scientific theories. In fact there are good reasons for not doing that. First, science is a human practice, and modern science relies on real possibilities in its central notion of experiment. And second, no consensus about determinism or indeterminism of current science – even of current physics – seems to be forthcoming.

The upshot of the above discussion seems to be the following: When it comes to assessing determinism, there are two camps disagreeing about whether the question makes sense as a metaphysical question about what the world is really like, or not. If one thinks that the metaphysical question does make sense, one's project would seem to be that of getting clear about our everyday conception of indeterminism and its role in agency, causation, and scientific practice. If one disagrees and holds the metaphysical question to be nonsensical – for which, as I stressed, a good argument would need to be given that I don't see to be forthcoming, but the discussion is tangled – then what one should do is to investigate, one after the other, specific scientific theories, and assess them as to their determinism and indeterminism; without much hope of arriving at a uniform verdict as to determinism or indeterminism viewed globally. And that is what is happening in philosophy of science, at a very high level of technical sophistication; witness again Earman [2007]: determinism and indeterminism are studied as properties of physical theories.

3.1 Physical Theories

It is not so easy to say what a physical theory is – physical theories can be viewed in many ways. According to the well established if somewhat tiresome opposition between a syntactic and a semantic view of theories, a theory can be specified syntactically, as a set of sentences in a specified (traditionally, logically regimented) language – or semantically, as a class of models, abstract mathematical structures. On both views the empirical significance of a theory thus specified has to be spelled out in a further step, commonly by labeling some part of the vocabulary as "observational" or by specifying a notion of isomorphism with structures having direct empirical significance.

If one looks at textbook accounts of physical theories or the way such theories are taught to students, one may wonder which form of representation one is witnessing. Surely a textbook contains a text with a syntactic structure, not an abstract mathematical object. But theories in such textbooks are hardly, if ever, formalized; they do not accord with the ideal of the syntactic view. Nor does one normally find in a textbook a method for constructing abstract classes of models. One does, however, often find something pretty close: Most theories are presented and studied via their constitutive equations, and solutions to these equations correspond to models of the theory in question. Thus, a semantic representation of a given physical theory can be obtained as the set of all solutions to the theory's constitutive equations. Such a set normally has a natural subdivision corresponding to the values of specific parameters like mass or charge. Initial values can also function as parameters.

In this way, a theory's constitutive equations determine its models as the space of their solutions.

3.2 Models vs. Equations in Assessing Determinism

The official definition of determinism agreed upon in current philosophy of science is the model-theoretic one expressed in the quote from Butterfield [2005] above: a theory is (future) deterministic if for any two of its models that have isomorphic instantaneous slices, the corresponding final segments are also isomorphic. This definition has a precise mathematical meaning.[12] It all boils down to investigating the separate models expressing the individual time courses of systems allowed by the theory. As such, this approach is completely modality-free:[13] give me the collection of models – extensional, set-theoretic structures –, and I give you back a verdict as to determinism or indeterminism. It may not be easy, and no verdict may be forthcoming in complicated cases (it is not claimed that there is a decision procedure that one could use), but *if* a verdict is forthcoming, this is how it works.

When one looks at what people actually do when they apparently implement the mentioned definition and check whether a specific theory is deterministic or not, however, the picture changes. Straightforward uses of the model-theoretically phrased definition in the philosophy of science lit-

---

[12] At least once the language of the theory has been described in sufficient detail, cf. note 11. A further point is that the precise meaning that that definition has may not be the *intended* meaning – there is a subtle issue about the quantification over isomorphisms ("isomorphic" is defined in terms of "there is an isomorphism ...") that also needs to be addressed; see below.

[13] At least if one discounts the remnants of modality in the phrase "allowed by the theory" as a mere metaphor which is to be resolved by extensionally quantifying over all mathematically existing models, without taking recourse to a notion of physicality. Again, this is a tangled issue; cf., e.g., the discussion about our reasons for preferring the retarded solutions to Maxwell's equations, as in Frisch [2008] vs. Norton [2008a], or the discussion of physicality in connection with Norton's dome [Norton 2008b].

erature are hard to find. Instead, it is common practice to look at the theory's defining equations and take recourse to results from mathematical physics that state whether, and under which circumstances, these equations have a unique solution. If these equations guarantee uniqueness of the solution for given initial values, the theory is declared to be deterministic, totally in accordance with the intuition behind calling a theory deterministic if it describes unique time courses of development for systems falling under it. This also makes practical sense: For the assessment of equations in that respect, mathematical physics has provided a large range of techniques and pertinent results;[14] there are no, or hardly any, comparable results phrased model-theoretically. Thus, studying the equations gives one a fair chance of answering the question of determinism vs. indeterminism of a specific physical theory. Furthermore, it seems that what one is doing is really just the same thing as what is demanded by the official definition, so that the move from models and isomorphisms to studying the equations is completely innocent. The move is made in passing, and no need for justification seems to be felt by those who make it.

The important question is whether this discrepancy between definition and method of assessment really makes no difference. It obviously wouldn't if the equivalence of the two approaches could be demonstrated, so that one would just be a reformulation of the other. And the equivalence is obviously presupposed by researchers working in the field. But whether it really holds depends on fine details that would need to be spelled out. In order to fix the notion of an isomorphism, the language of the theory would have to be made precise (cf. note 11 above), which hardly ever happens. And there is the further question of the intended type of quantification over isomorphisms (cf. note 12 above): is the definition to quantify over isomorphisms existentially (signaling determinism if for any isomorphic instantaneous slices there is *some* isomorphism identifying the final seg-

---

[14] Some of these results are technically quite involved; cf., e.g., Xia [1992] on the collision-free five-body problem in classical mechanics. As a simpler example, for differential equations, the typical form of constitutive equations of dynamical theories, it is often sufficient to study some structural properties in order to find out whether unique solutions are guaranteed. A case in point is the Picard-Lindelöf theorem stating that the initial value problem $dx(t)/dt = f(t, x(t))$ for given $x(t_0)$ has a unique solution around t_0 if f obeys certain conditions (Lipschitz continuity in x, continuity in t). Conversely, violations of these conditions allow for indeterministic time development. Norton's dome [Norton 2008b] is built on exactly this strategy.

ments) or universally (demanding agreement for all such isomorphisms), and may different isomorphisms be employed? To make these questions a little more precise, let A and B stand for two models of a theory T, let A_t and $B_{t'}$ be instantaneous slices (where the labels "t" and "t'" do not belong to the models themselves, nor to a meta-time, as stressed by Butterfield), and let $A_{>t}$ and $B_{>t'}$ be the corresponding final segments. Then the official definition clearly needs to be spelled out as follows:

> T is deterministic if, and only if: for any models A and B of T and for all their instantaneous slices A_t and $B_{t'}$, if there is an isomorphism f between A_t and $B_{t'}$, then there is an isomorphism g between $A_{>t}$ and $B_{>t'}$.

Thus, different isomorphisms may be used to identify the slices and the final segments. But shouldn't one demand that *the same* isomorphism f that identifies the instantaneous slices, also identifies the final segments? Furthermore, the quantification is existential, but it is not clear that this always gives the correct assessment. Thus, in a toy theory of discrete time radioactive decay pictured as a branching tree in Figure 1, in (A) an isomorphism identifying m_0 in history (model) h_0 with m_1 in history (model) h_1 can be extended to an isomorphism for the corresponding final segments (the end points of the respective histories) and thus threatens to signal determinism for the obviously indeterministic scenario. In (B) this even holds if one includes the whole past history of the system. In these cases, the overall assessment remains correct because the definition also forces one to look at the isomorphism between m_0 in h_0 and m_0 in h_1, for which no isomorphism between the corresponding final segments can be given. In a modified deterministic scenario of (B) with just the one history h_1, the assessment however becomes incorrect, as the isomorphism between m_0 and m_1 isn't accompanied by a corresponding isomorphism between the corresponding final segments and the definition thus signals indeterminism.

Obviously many responses are possible with respect to these toy models – e.g., I haven't specified a language either, nor shown that there is any serious physical content behind my pictures. I deliberately called them toy models. My point is just that if the official definition of determinism in terms of models and isomorphisms were actually employed, such cases, and more elaborate ones like them closer to actual physics, would have to be scrutinized in detail in order to check the tenability of the definition. This however does not happen – and since the question of determinism or indeterminism is really approached from the point of view of a theory's equations, these questions do not need to be answered, and no confusion threatens. A proper mathematical study of the equations is enough, there is sufficient context to identify cases in which the same state can be followed by different time courses of development.

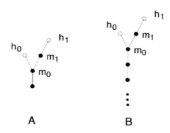

Figure 1: Toy model for radioactive decay in discrete time. Open circles indicate that the particle has decayed. (A) First time step specified, (B) backwards infinite time. See text for details.

3.3 Consequences for the Role of Modality in the Determinism Debate

Given that there is such a large discrepancy between official definition and actual practice of assessment when it comes to the determinism or indeterminism of theories, one may wonder how this situation could arise and why it is sustained. I will end this paper by trying to spell out my – rather speculative – diagnosis of this situation.

Historically, the model-theoretic tradition in which Montague worked certainly had an enormous and also a very beneficial influence on the discussion of the determinism of theories. Montague [1962] points out that the determinism debate may be trivialized unless one pays attention to a large number of fine details. The definition in terms of models and isomorphisms however seems to me to be preferred also for different, metaphysical reasons: it is extremely well suited to the general metaphysical outlook propounded by Lewis [1986].[15] According to Lewis, modality needs to be understood not as something inherent in the world we live in, but rather as based on counterpart relations between wholly separate and equally real "worlds". Thus, e.g., no two worlds can contain the same individual. In Figure 1 I pictured the time development of systems in terms of branching histories, i.e., a single past time development giving rise to different possi-

---

[15] Lewis is explicitly invoked, e.g., in Earman [2007].

ble future developments. This is in accord with what happens when one studies the time development of a system's state according to constitutive equations, and it is very close to the intuitive understanding of indeterminism as involving open real possibilities. But it is not in accord with a Lewisian outlook on modality, which demands wholly separate worlds between which isomorphisms may act as a counterpart relation.

The discrepancy between a model-theoretic definition of determinism and its assessment via a study of constitutive equations is thus interpretationally highly significant. Models are abstract and extensional creatures; quantifying over them, or over isomorphisms between them, can never amount to building up real modality. Giving a model-theoretic definition of determinism and indeterminism is thus in full accord with the project of reducing modalities away. The practice of assessing determinism via a study of constitutive equations however does not support this stance. Thus, even practitioners of an officially model-theoretic approach to determinism and indeterminism in philosophy of science should acknowledge the importance of real modality.

4 CONCLUSIONS

In this paper I have tried to argue that it makes good sense to view the question of determinism vs. indeterminism in the way in which that question initially presents itself to us: As a practically *and* theoretically relevant question about what the world is really like. Despite some epistemological worries, the notion of modality that I identified as lying behind the distinction between determinism and indeterminism, *real modality*, is sufficiently well understood.

This picture is apparently threatened by a manner of treating the issue of determinism vs. indeterminism that has strong currency in philosophy of science, and which seems to give a strong argument for the elimination of real modality from the determinism debate: As defined in philosophy of science, determinism and indeterminism are simply properties of physical theories that can be assessed purely extensionally, via a study of a theory's models. My reaction to this threat has been twofold. First, while agreeing with the slogan "go scientific", I have stressed that science as a human endeavor is more than just the production of abstract structures: it involves intervention in the course of nature via experiment, and real possibilities lie at the bottom of that practice. Second, I have tried to show that the modality-unfriendly outlook of the study of determinism in philosophy of science is at odds with the very method employed in that field: the model-theoretic definition is not implemented, but rather given up in favor of a much more modality-friendly way of looking at things, viz., the study of constitutive equations and the possibly branching space of their solutions. The diversity of results obtained by such studies furthermore strengthens my first reaction: given that no unique verdict as to determinism or indeterminism of scientific theories in general seems to be forthcoming, the impact of science on the question of determinism can only be weighed by considering the practice of science as a whole, not just one of the products of that practice.

Thus, science and the philosophical study of science do not pose a threat to the importance of real modality for the metaphysical question of determinism, nor do they provide arguments for a reductionist stance with respect to real modality.

ACKNOWLEDGEMENTS

I would like to thank the organizers of and my audience at the *31st International Wittgenstein Symposium*, Kirchberg, 13 August 2008. Thanks to Janneke van Lith and Sebastian Lutz for helpful comments on a previous draft. Support by the *Deutsche Forschungsgemeinschaft* is gratefully acknowledged.

REFERENCES

Belnap, N., Perloff, M., and Xu, M. [2001]. *Facing the Future. Agents and Choices in Our Indeterminist World.* Oxford: Oxford University Press.
Broad, C.D. [1923]. *Scientific Thought.* New York: Harcourt, Brace and Co.
Butterfield, J. [2005]. Determinism and Indeterminism. In Craig, E., editor, *Routledge Encyclopedia of Philosophy.* London: Routledge. Retrieved March 7, 2008, from http://www.rep.routledge.com/article/Q025.
Earman, J. [1986]. *A Primer on Determinism.* Dordrecht: Reidel.
Earman, J. [2007]. Aspects of Determinism in Modern Physics. In Butterfield, J. and Earman, J., editors, *Handbook of the Philosophy of Physics,* pp.1369–1434. Amsterdam: Elsevier.
Fine, K. [2005]. *Modality and Tense.* Oxford: Oxford University Press.
Frisch, M. [2008]. Causal Reasoning in Physics. Available at http://philsci-archive.pitt.edu/archive/00003820/.

Kane, R., editor [2002]. *The Oxford Handbook of Free Will*. Oxford: Oxford University Press.

Lewis, D. [1986]. *On the Plurality of Worlds*. Oxford: Blackwell.

Montague, R. [1962]. Deterministic Theories. In Willner, D., editor, *Decisions, Values and Groups*, pp.325–370. Oxford: Pergamon Press. Reprinted in *Formal Philosophy*, ed. R.H. Thomason, New Haven, CT: Yale University Press 1974, pp.303–359.

Norton, J. [2008a]. Is There an Independent Principle of Causality in Physics? A Comment on Mathias Frisch, "Causal Reasoning in Physics.". Available at http://philsci-archive.pitt.edu/archive/00003832/.

Norton, J. [2008b]. The Dome: An Unexpectedly Simple Failure of Determinism. *Philosophy of Science* 75(5), pp.786–798.

Placek, T. and Müller, T. [2007]. Counterfactuals and Historical Possibility. *Synthese*, 154: pp.173–197.

Prior, A.N. [1957]. *Time and Modality*. Oxford: Oxford University Press.

Prior, A.N. [1967]. *Past, Present and Future*. Oxford: Oxford University Press.

Stroud, B. [2000]. *The Quest for Reality: Subjectivism and the Metaphysics of Colour*. Oxford: Oxford University Press.

Xia, Z. [1992]. The Existence of Noncollision Singulatities in the *n*-body Problem. *Annals of Mathematics*, 135: pp.411–468.

Xu, M. [1997]. Causation in Branching Time (I): Transitions, Events and Causes. *Synthese*, 112(2): pp.137–192.

DETERMINISTIC VERSUS INDETERMINISTIC DESCRIPTIONS: NOT THAT DIFFERENT AFTER ALL?

CHARLOTTE WERNDL
University of Cambridge

1 INTRODUCTION

The guiding question of this paper is: *can we simulate deterministic descriptions by indeterministic descriptions, and conversely?* By simulating a deterministic description by an indeterministic one, and conversely, we mean that the deterministic description, when observed, and the indeterministic description give the same predictions.

Answering this question is a way of finding out how different deterministic descriptions are from indeterministic ones. Of course, indeterministic descriptions and deterministic descriptions are different in the sense that for the former there is indeterminism in the future evolution and for the latter not. But another way of finding out how different they are is to answer the question whether they give the same predictions; and this question will concern us.

Since the language of deterministic and indeterministic descriptions is mathematics, we will rely on mathematics to answer our guiding question. In the first place, it is unclear how deterministic and indeterministic descriptions can be compared; this might be one reason for the often-held implicit belief that deterministic and indeterministic descriptions give very different predictions (cf. Weingartner and Schurz 1996, p.203). But we will see that they *can* often be compared. The deterministic and indeterministic descriptions which we will consider are measure-theoretic deterministic systems and stochastic processes, respectively; they are both ubiquitous in science. To the best of my knowledge, our guiding question has hardly been discussed in philosophy.

In this paper I will explain intuitively some mathematical results which show that, from a predictive viewpoint, measure-theoretic deterministic systems and stochastic processes are, perhaps surprisingly, very similar. I won't go into the technical details (ergodic theory and the modern theory of stochastic processes); they can be found in Werndl (2009c and 2009d).

This paper is organised as follows. In section 2 I will introduce measure-theoretic deterministic systems and stochastic processes. In section 3 I will explain how, at a basic level, deterministic systems and stochastic processes give the same predictions. Section 4 will be devoted to more advanced results on the predictive equivalence of deterministic and indeterministic descriptions. I will argue that the results show that from a predictive viewpoint, measure-theoretic deterministic systems and stochastic processes are very similar.

2 INDETERMINISTIC AND DETERMINISTIC DESCRIPTIONS

Let us introduce the indeterministic and deterministic descriptions which will concern us. There are two kinds of indeterministic and deterministic descriptions: for *discrete* descriptions the time increases in discrete steps, and *continuous* descriptions involve a continuous time-parameter. We confine ourselves to discrete descriptions. For continuous descriptions similar but also slightly different results to the ones discussed here hold (cf. Werndl 2009d).

2.1 Stochastic Processes

The indeterministic descriptions we are concerned with are *stochastic processes*. Basically all the indeterministic descriptions in science are stochastic processes, which are thus ubiquitous in science. A stochastic process is a process that evolves according to probabilistic laws. That is, for a stochastic process there usually is some indeterminism: even if the initial state of the process is known, there are many possibilities the process might go to, and these possibilities are measured by probabilities. A sequence describing a possible evolution of the stochastic process over time is called a realisation.

Let me introduce stochastic processes in more detail.[1] Probability theory is concerned with probabilistic experiments. The set of all possible outcomes of a probabilistic experiment is denoted by Ω and called the *sample space*. It comes equipped with a *probability distribution Q* which

---

[1] All the seemingly mathematical definitions introduced in this paper are intuitive descriptions of measure-theoretic definitions which are given in Werndl (2009c, 2009d).

assigns probabilities to the subsets of Ω you are interested in. In applied problems you are usually interested in functions of the outcomes of a probabilistic experiment. Hence the concept of a random variable is introduced. A *random variable* is a function Z from a sample space Ω to a set E, called the *state space*, which assigns a value $Z(\omega)$ to each ω in Ω. An *event A* is a subset of the set E which you are interested in, and the *probability distribution* of the random variable Z is given by looking back to Q on Ω, i.e. $P := Q(Z^{-1}(A))$ defined for all events A of E. Finally, a *stochastic process (Z_t)* with *state space E* is a collection of random variables Z_t, where t is in an integer, defined on the same sample space Ω and taking values in E. The sequence $r(\omega) := (\ldots Z_{-1}(\omega), Z_0(\omega), Z_1(\omega) \ldots)$ for any ω in Ω is called a *realisation* of the stochastic process. Intuitively, t represents time; so that ω represents a possible history in all details, and $r(\omega)$ represents the description of that history by giving the 'score' at each t.

For instance, a *Bernoulli process* is a stochastic process where at each time point an N-sided die is tossed and the tosses are independent. That is, it is a stochastic process (Z_t) where (i) the state space is $\{e_1, \ldots, e_N\}$, and for any t the probability for outcome e_i is p_i where $p_1 + \ldots + p_N = 1$; and (ii) $P(Z_{i1} = e_{j1}, \ldots, Z_{in} = e_{jn}) = P(Z_{i1} = e_{j1}) \bullet \ldots \bullet P(Z_{in} = e_{jn})$ for any $e_{j1}, \ldots, e_{jn}$ in E and any integer-valued $i_1, \ldots, i_n$.

2.2 Deterministic Systems

A description is *deterministic* exactly if any two solutions which agree at one time agree at all times (Butterfield 2005). Hence for deterministic descriptions there is no indeterminism about the future evolution. A sequence describing the evolution of a deterministic description over time is called a solution.

We are concerned with measure-theoretic deterministic descriptions, in short *deterministic systems*. They are denoted by (X, T, μ) and consist of three components: a set X, called the *phase space*, which represents all possible states of the system; a bijective map $T: X \to X$ which describes how states evolve, namely every x in X evolves to $T(x)$ in one time unit and so to $T^t(x)$ in t time units. And μ is a *normalised measure*; intuitively, the subsets of X you are interested in are called *events*, and the measure assigns to all events a nonnegative size with total size one, i.e. $\mu(X) = 1$. As we will see, for connecting deterministic with indeterministic descriptions it is crucial that a measure is given on the phase space.

The *solutions* of a deterministic system are (... $T^{-1}(x)$, x, $T(x)$ ...) for any x in X. We will often be concerned with measure-preserving deterministic systems, which are deterministic systems where the measure is *invariant* under time-evolution, i.e. where $\mu(T(A)) = \mu(A)$ for all events A. There are various interpretations of invariant measures. For instance, according to the *time-average interpretation* the measure of an event A is the long-run proportion of time a solution spends in A and thus can be interpreted as probability. In what follows we make the common assumption that invariant measures can be interpreted as probability (cf. Werndl 2009a).

Deterministic systems, and measure-preserving deterministic systems in particular, are among the most important deterministic descriptions in science. To require that the measure is invariant is not very restrictive because for wide classes of deterministic systems invariant measures exist (cf. Werndl 2009c). For instance, all deterministic descriptions in Newtonian and statistical mechanics are measure-preserving deterministic systems.

When you observe a deterministic system a value is observed which is dependent on, but maybe does not uniquely encode the actual state. Hence observing the system can often be modelled by an *observation function*, i.e. a function $\Phi: X \to M$ where M contains all possible observed values.

The deterministic system of the *baker's system* will accompany us throughout this paper. States (x, y) in the unit square $X := [0, 1] \times [0, 1]$ are mapped to $T(x, y) := (2x, y/2)$ if $0 \delta x < 1/2$ and $(2x–1, (y+1)/2)$ otherwise. *Figure 1* shows the dynamics of the baker's system. For the standard volume (the Lebesgue measure) we obtain a measure-preserving deterministic system. It describes a particle bouncing on mirrors (Pitowsky 1995).

Figure 1: Dynamics of the baker's system

3. BASIC INDISTINGUISHABILITY OF DETERMINISTIC SYSTEMS AND STOCHASTIC PROCESSES

This section is about indistinguishability results which are *basic* in the sense that they answer the question whether, given a deterministic system, we can find *any* stochastic process which simulates the system, and conversely. In section 3.1 I will explain how stochastic processes can be simulated by deterministic systems; these results seem to be unknown to philosophers. In section 3.2 I will show how deterministic systems can be simulated by stochastic processes; here the basic idea is known to philosophers of physics (Butterfield 2005).

3.1 Deterministic Systems Simulated by Stochastic Processes

How can you simulate deterministic systems by stochastic processes? Contrary to deterministic systems, for stochastic processes there is usually indeterminism in the future evolution. But when you *observe* a deterministic system, you see only how the system moves from one observed value to another; and because the observation function can map two states to the same value, the same current observed value can lead to different future observed values. Hence only if you make the assumption that a deterministic system is observed with an observation function can you hope to simulate it by a stochastic process. But this assumption is unproblematic: deterministic systems in science typically have an uncountably large phase space, and scientists can only observe finitely many different values.

A deterministic system comes equipped with a probability measure. Hence when observing the system, you see the probability distributions of sequences of possible observations of the deterministic system; and the predictions you obtain are these probability distributions. A stochastic process is defined by the probability distributions over its realisations, and these probability distributions are the predictions you obtain. Consequently, when saying *that a stochastic process* (Z_t) *and a deterministic system, as observed with* Φ, *give the same predictions* we mean the following: *(i) the possible states E of the stochastic process are the possible observed values of the deterministic system, and (ii) the realisations of the stochastic process have the same probability distribution as the solutions of the deterministic system observed with the observation function.* Recall that we say that a deterministic system is simulated by a stochastic process, and conversely, exactly if the deterministic system, when observed, and the stochastic process give the same predictions.

Formally, *for any* (X, T, μ) *and any observation function* Φ, $(Z_t) :=$ $\Phi(T^t)$ *is a stochastic process and hence simulates the deterministic system observed with* Φ. But the question is, of course, whether this stochastic process is *nontrivial*. To stress the point, if Φ is the identity function, then although $\Phi(T^t)$ is formally a stochastic process, it is evidently equivalent to the original deterministic system. But several results show that we often obtain nontrivial stochastic processes. Let me mention one result which is shown in Werndl (2009c).

> **Proposition 1**. *Assume that a measure-preserving deterministic system is weakly mixing*[2]. *Then for any observation function with finitely many different values*[3] *the stochastic process* $(Z_t) := \Phi(T^t)$ *is nontrivial: there are observed values, that is, elements* e_i, e_j *of the state space* E *of the stochastic process such that* $0 < P(Z_{t+1} = e_i$ *given that* $Z_t = e_j) < 1$.

Let us assume that only finitely many different values can be observed. Most measure-preserving deterministic systems, including many systems in science, are weakly mixing (Halmos 1944). Hence *Proposition 1* says that *for most measure-preserving deterministic systems, regardless how you observe them, you always obtain nontrivial stochastic processes*. For instance, the baker's system is weakly mixing. Therefore, regardless of how you observe it, you obtain a nontrivial stochastic process.

3.2 Stochastic Processes Simulated by Deterministic Systems

How can a given stochastic process be simulated by a deterministic system? Again, simulating the behaviour of a stochastic process by a deterministic system will only work if you allow that the deterministic system is observed. As argued, this assumption is unproblematic.

Assume that a stochastic process (Z_t) is given. We can construct a deterministic system as follows: X is the set of all imaginable realisations of

---

[2] A measure-preserving deterministic system (X, T, μ) is weakly mixing iff for all events A, B
$$lim_{n \to \infty} 1/n \, (|\mu(A \cap B) - \mu(A)\mu(B)| + |\mu(T(A) \cap B) - \mu(A)\mu(B)| + \ldots + (|\mu(T^{n-1}(A) \cap B) - \mu(A)\mu(B)|) = 0.$$
[3] We assume that the observation function does not only take one value.

the stochastic process, i.e. the set of sequences $e = (\ldots e_{-1}, e_0, e_1 \ldots)$ where e_i are elements of the state space E of (Z_t). Let T be the map on X which shifts each sequence to the left, i.e. $T((\ldots e_{-1}, e_0, e_1 \ldots)) = (\ldots e_0, e_1, e_2 \ldots)$. Finally, (Z_t) determines a probability distribution on the realisations and hence a measure μ on X. Then (X, T, μ) is a deterministic system. Now assume you observe the 0th coordinate, i.e. you employ the observation function $\Phi(e) = e_0$. Clearly, the deterministic system (X, T, μ) observed with Φ simulates the process (Z_t). (X, T, μ, Φ) is called the *deterministic representation* of (Z_t). Thus we can conclude that *every stochastic process can be simulated by at least one deterministic system which, when observed, gives the same predictions, namely its deterministic representation.*

The deterministic representation is, from a philosophical perspective, a cheat because its states are constructed to encode the future and past evolution of the indeterministic process; also, the observation function is unnatural because scientists usually do not observe the 0th coordinate of a bi-infinite sequence. Still, it is important to see how, mathematically, stochastic processes can be simulated by the deterministic representation. There remains the question whether there are also other deterministic systems that simulate a stochastic process; we will return to it later (in section 4.1).

For instance, for a Bernoulli process with N different outcomes the deterministic representation is the following: the phase space is the set of all possible bi-infinite sequences of the N outcomes, the evolution equation shifts each sequence to the left, and the observed value is the 0th coordinate of the sequence. Generally, – and this definition will be important later – a *deterministic Bernoulli system* is a deterministic system which is probabilistically equivalent to the deterministic representation of a Bernoulli process, and hence (observed with specific observation functions) simulates a Bernoulli process.

Let me briefly comment on the philosophical significance of the above results. The guiding question of this article is: can we simulate deterministic systems by indeterministic processes which give the same predictions, and conversely? Our results show that stochastic processes can always be simulated by deterministic systems, and that many deterministic systems, when observed, can be simulated by nontrivial stochastic processes. *Therefore, from the perspective of predictive power, stochastic processes and deterministic systems are similar.*

69

4. ADVANCED INDISTINGUISHABILITY OF STOCHASTIC PROCESSES AND DETERMINISTIC SYSTEMS

This section is about indistinguishability results which are *advanced* in the sense that they concern the question whether it is possible to separate deterministic systems *in science* from stochastic processes *in science*.

4.1 Deterministic Systems Simulating Stochastic Processes in Science

We have seen that any stochastic process can be simulated by at least one deterministic system, namely its deterministic representation. However, the deterministic representation is artificial in the sense that scientists do not encounter it when modelling phenomena. So you might still guess that *the deterministic systems which simulate the stochastic processes in science, such as Bernoulli processes, are very different from the deterministic systems in science, such as Newtonian systems.*

Until the late 1950s it was widely believed that stochastic processes and deterministic systems are different in this way. More specifically, Kolmogorov conjectured that while the deterministic systems which simulate stochastic processes in science produce positive information, the deterministic systems in science produce zero information. Kolmogorov and Sinai introduced the *Kolmogorov-Sinai entropy* to capture the property of producing positive information; and this property was expected to be able to separate stochastic processes from deterministic systems. It was a big surprise when it was found that many deterministic systems in science, among them Newtonian systems, have positive Kolmogorov-Sinai entropy and thus produce positive information (Frigg and Werndl 2009; Sinai 1989, Werndl 2009b).

What is more, Bernoulli processes are often regarded as the most random stochastic processes because past outcomes are independent of future outcomes. And there are even deterministic systems in science which are deterministic Bernoulli systems; hence *there are deterministic systems in science which, when observed with specific observation functions, simulate a Bernoulli process.* For instance, to mention a few, dispersive billiard systems, the logistic map (for some parameter values) which models population dynamics and the climate, and the Hènon map which models weather phenomena (Lorenz 1964; Lyubich 2002; May 1976; Ornstein and Weiss 1991; Young 1997; see also Winnie 1998). Also the baker's system produces a Bernoulli process. Assume that you only see whether the state of the baker's system is to the left or to the right of the unit square, i.e. $\Phi((x, y)) := 0$ if $x < 1/2$ and 1 otherwise. This makes the system equivalent to a fair coin toss, viz. a Bernoulli process with outcomes 0 and 1 which have both probability $1/2$.

Hence even Bernoulli processes, often regarded as the most random stochastic processes, are simulated by deterministic systems in science when observed with specific observation functions. But then any attempt to separate such deterministic systems from the deterministic systems needed to simulate the stochastic processes in science must fail. The philosophical implication of this result is that the above guess is wrong, viz. *the deterministic systems which simulate the stochastic processes in science include deterministic systems in science. This indicates that from a predictive viewpoint, stochastic processes and deterministic systems are very similar.*

4.2 Stochastic Processes Simulating Deterministic Systems in Science at Any Observation Level

The deterministic systems which simulate the stochastic processes in science include deterministic systems in science. Still, you might conjecture that *only if* you employ *specific coarse observation functions* for such deterministic systems, do you obtain stochastic processes in science; and if you make observations of such deterministic systems which are precise enough, you will not any longer obtain a stochastic process in science or an observation of a stochastic process in science. Hence you might guess that stochastic and deterministic descriptions are different in the following way: *the stochastic processes which simulate deterministic systems in science at any observation level are very different from the stochastic processes in science.*

Let us introduce two natural ways of understanding the notion that stochastic processes of a certain type simulate deterministic systems at any observation level. In practice, for sufficiently small α_1, you cannot distinguish states of a deterministic system which are less than α_1 apart; and, for sufficiently small α_2, you won't be able to observe differences in probabilistic predictions of less than α_2, and you can thus neglect events of probability less than α_2. Assume that α is smaller than α_1 and α_2. Then a deterministic system and a stochastic process in practice give the same predictions if the solutions of the deterministic system can be put into one-to-one correspondence with the realisations of the stochastic process such that the state of the deterministic system and the corresponding outcome of the stochastic process are less then α apart except for states of probability less than α. Formally, this idea is captured by the notion of α-congruence (Ornstein and Weiss 1991). The deterministic system (X, T, μ) and the stochastic process (Z_t) are α-*congruent* exactly if there is a function $\Psi: X \to X$ such that (i) (Z_t) is the stochastic process $\Psi(T')$, and the deterministic representation of (Z_t) is probalistically equivalent to (X, T, μ), and (ii) x and $\Psi(x)$ differ by less than α for all x in X except for a set of measure smaller than α. Note that the notion of α-congruence *does not assume that the deterministic system is observed with an observation function.* But observation functions can, of course, be brought in: assume you make a coarse-grained observation of a deterministic system. Then the probabilistic predictions you obtain are essentially the same (differ at most by α) as the probabilistic predictions of the corresponding observed stochastic process, i.e. the process obtained by applying the observation function to the stochastic process which is α–congruent to the deterministic system. So we arrive at that a plausible meaning of the notion that stochastic processes of a certain type simulate a deterministic system at any observation level is that for any α > 0 there is a stochastic process of this type which is α-congruent to the system.

Another approach is to start with the idea that for sufficiently small α > 0, you won't be able to distinguish an observed deterministic system from a stochastic process if the stochastic process nearly simulates the deterministic system; i.e. if the deterministic system, when observed, and the stochastic process have the same outcomes, and their probabilistic predictions are either the same or differ by less than α. The following notion captures this idea: a stochastic process (Z_t) (α, Φ)-*simulates* a deterministic system (X, T, μ) observed with $\Phi: X \to M$ exactly if there is a function $\Psi: X \to M$ such that (i) (Z_t) is the stochastic process $\Psi(T')$, and (ii) Ψ has the same ranges as Φ and differs from Φ only on a set of measure < α (cf. Ornstein and Weiss 1991, p.95). Hence the notion of (α, Φ)-simulation captures the idea that in practice the observed deterministic system and the stochastic process give the same predictions. Unlike α-congruence, (α, Φ)-simulation *assumes that the deterministic system is observed with an observation function.* By generalising over α and Φ we obtain a plausible meaning of the phrase that stochastic processes of a certain type simulate a deterministic system at any observation level, namely: for every Φ and every α there is a stochastic process of this type which (α, Φ)-simulates the deterministic system.

For Bernoulli processes future outcomes are independent of past ones. In contrast, for deterministic systems in science future states are strongly constrained by its previous state. Thus, intuitively, *such deterministic systems cannot be simulated at every observation level by Bernoulli processes.* This intuition is correct. First, as shown in Werndl (2009c), for any deterministic system in science there is a $\alpha > 0$ such that no Bernoulli process is α-congruent to the deterministic system. Second, for any deterministic system there is an observation function and a $\alpha > 0$ such that no Bernoulli process (α, Φ)-simulates the deterministic system (Werndl 2009d). Despite these results, there remains the question whether deterministic systems in science can be simulated by other paradigm stochastic processes at every observation level.

To answer it, we have to introduce two paradigm stochastic processes, namely Markov processes and multi-step Markov processes. For a *Markov process* the probability distribution of the next state only depends on the previous state. That is, (Z_t) is a Markov processes exactly if (i) the state space consists of N states $e_1,\ldots, e_N$, and (ii) $P(Z_{t+1} = e_i$ given $Z_t, Z_{t-1},\ldots, Z_k) = P(Z_{t+1} = e_i$ given $Z_t)$ for any t and any k, $k \leq t$, in the integers and any i, $1 \leq i \leq N.$[4] We will be concerned with *irreducible* and *aperiodic* Markov processes. These are Markov processes which cannot be split into two separate processes and which have no periodicities, and they are generally regarded as the most random Markov processes.

Multi-step Markov processes generalise Markov processes. They consist of all Markov processes of order n, where n is a natural number. For a Markov process of order n the probability distribution of the next state only depends on the previous n states. That is, (Z_t) is a Markov process of order n exactly if (i) the state space consists of N states $e_1,\ldots, e_N$, and (ii) $P(Z_{t+1} = e_i$ given $Z_t, Z_{t-1},\ldots, Z_k) = P(Z_{t+1} = e_i$ given $Z_t,\ldots, Z_{t+n-1})$ for any t and k, $k \leq t$, in the integers and any i, $1 \leq i \leq N$. Again, we will be concerned with the most random multi-step Markov processes: namely those which cannot be split into two separate processes and which have no periodicities, called *irreducible* and *aperiodic* multi-step Markov processes.

Recall that deterministic Bernoulli systems are deterministic systems which are probabilistically equivalent to the deterministic representation of a Bernoulli process (section 3.2), and that many deterministic systems in science are deterministic Bernoulli systems (section 3). *It holds that several deterministic systems in science, namely all deterministic Bernoulli*

---

[4] We assume that the probability distribution of Markov processes and of Markov process of order n is independent of time.

systems, can be simulated at any observation level by paradigm stochastic processes, namely by Markov processes or by multi-step Markov processes. More precisely, for the first meaning of the phrase that deterministic systems are simulated at every observation level it holds that every deterministic Bernoulli system can be simulated at any observation level by irreducible and aperiodic Markov processes. For the second meaning of the phrase it holds that every deterministic Bernoulli system can be simulated at any observation level by irreducible and aperiodic multi-step Markov processes. It is not hard to see that any Markov processes of order n is an observed Markov process, i.e. a process which is obtained by assigning to some of the states of the Markov process the same value (Werndl 2009d).[5] Hence we rediscover a result which we already arrived at for the first meaning of simulation at every observation level, viz. that regardless how fine we observe a Bernoulli system, the outcomes could have resulted from an observed Markov process:

Theorem 1. *Let (X, T, μ) be a deterministic Bernoulli system. Then for every $\alpha > 0$ there is an irreducible and aperiodic Markov process which is α-congruent to the deterministic system* (Werndl 2009c).

Theorem 2. *Let (X, T, μ) be a deterministic Bernoulli system. Then for every observation function Φ and every $\alpha > 0$, there is an irreducible and aperiodic multi-step Markov process which (α, Φ)-simulates the deterministic system* (cf. Werndl 2009d).

Also, deterministic Bernoulli systems are the only systems in science which can be simulated at every observation level by multi-step Markov processes or by Markov processes. That is, a deterministic system where for every observation function and every α there is an irreducible and aperiodic Markov process which is α-congruent to the system is a deterministic Bernoulli system (Ornstein 1974, p.45). And a deterministic system in science where for every Φ and $\alpha > 0$ there is an irreducible and aperiodic multi-step Markov processes which (α, Φ)-simulates the system is a deterministic Bernoulli system (Werndl 2009d). For instance, the baker's system is a deterministic Bernoulli system. Thus it can be simulated by

---

[5] This follows because a multi-step Markov process can be reduced to a Markov process by considering the process whose state space consists of all possible n-tuples of the states of the Markov process of order n.

Markov processes or by multi-step Markov processes at any observation level.

Let me comment on the philosophical significance of these results. We guessed that the stochastic processes which simulate deterministic systems in science at any observation level are very different from the stochastic processes in science. *Clearly, the above results show that this guess is wrong because several deterministic systems in science can be simulated at any observation level by Markov processes or by multi-step Markov processes. This further underlines that from a predictive viewpoint deterministic systems and stochastic processes are very similar.*

Suppes (1993), Suppes and de Barros (1996) and Winnie (1998) are the only philosophical discussions about the results of this section I could find. They all discuss some results involving the notion of α-congruence. Suppes and de Barros (1996) and Winnie (1998) claim that the philosophical significance of some α-congruence results is that, at every observation level, you have a choice between a deterministic description in science and a stochastic description. However, this seems weak and hence misguided: that, at every observation level, you have a choice between a deterministic description in science and a stochastic description is already shown by the results in section 3.1, and these results were known much earlier. As argued, the real philosophical significance of the α-congruence results is that the stochastic processes needed to simulate deterministic systems in science at any observation level include paradigm stochastic processes (cf. Werndl 2009c).[6]

There remains, of course, the very important question: if we have a choice between a deterministic and a stochastic description, which one is better? Winnie (1998) criticises Suppes (1993) for arguing that in the case of the α-congruence results both descriptions are equally good. Winnie thinks that the deterministic description is preferable, and his argument goes as follows. Assume we have a Markov process which simulates the deterministic system for the current observation level. The observation level in the future may become so fine that we need to introduce another Markov process to simulate the deterministic system at the finer observation level. Hence the deterministic system is better. However, I think the situation is often not as clear as Winnie claims. For instance, suppose that in principle the states of the modelled phenomenon can never be distinguished beyond a certain level, e.g. because these states do not take infi-

---

[6] Furthermore, Suppes and de Barros (1996) and Winnie (1998) both do not really understand the meaning of α-congruence (see Werndl 2009d).

nitely precise values. Then it seems less clear what is preferable: the deterministic system or the stochastic process resulting from an observation function which assigns to any two states that can never be distinguished the same value. I think the question of whether the deterministic or stochastic description is better needs more careful consideration. For some thoughts see Werndl (2009d), and it is my hope that further work will be dedicated to this question.

5. CONCLUSION

Our guiding question has been: can we simulate deterministic systems by stochastic processes which give the same predictions, and conversely? I have first explained that many deterministic systems, when observed, can be simulated by nontrivial stochastic processes, and that every stochastic process can be simulated by at least one deterministic system. Yet you might still guess that the deterministic systems which simulate the stochastic processes in science are very different from the deterministic systems in science. I have shown this to be false since there is a class of deterministic systems, including several paradigm deterministic systems, which even produce the most random stochastic process of tossing a die. Given this, you might still guess that the stochastic processes which simulate the deterministic systems in science at every observation level are very different from the stochastic processes in science. I have explained that also this guess is wrong because there are many deterministic systems in science which can be simulated at every observation level by paradigm stochastic processes, namely by Markov processes or by multi-step Markov processes. I have argued that all these results show that from a predictive viewpoint, deterministic systems and stochastic processes are very similar.

ACKNOWLEDGMENTS

I am indebted to Jeremy Butterfield. Many thanks also to Cymra Haskell, Franz Huber, Thomas Müller, Amy Radunskaya, Peter Smith and the audience at the Wittgenstein Symposium 08 for valuable discussions. I am grateful to St John's College, Cambridge University, for financial support.

REFERENCES

Butterfield, J.N. (2005). 'Determinism and Indeterminism'. *Routledge Encyclopaedia of Philosophy*.

Frigg, R. and Werndl, C. (2009). 'Entropy and Probablities'. Forthcoming in: C. Beisbart and S. Hartmann (eds). *Probabilities in Physics*. Oxford: Oxford University Press.

Halmos, P.R. (1944). 'In General a Measure-preserving Transformation is Mixing'. *The Annals of Mathematics* 45, pp.786–792.

Lorenz, E.N. (1964). 'The Problem of Deducing the Climate from the Governing Equations'. *Tellus* XVI, pp.1–11.

Lyubich, M. (2002). 'Almost Every Regular Quadratic Map is Either Regular or Stochastic'. *Annals of Mathematics* 156, pp.1–78.

May, R.M. (1976). 'Simple Mathematical Models with Very Complicated Dynamics'. *Nature* 261, pp.459–467.

Ornstein, D. (1974). *Ergodic Theory*, Randomness, *and Dynamical Systems*. New Haven: Yale University Press.

Ornstein, D. and Weiss, B. (1991). 'Statistical Properties of Chaotic Systems'. *Bulletin of the American Mathematical Society* 24, pp.11–116.

Pitowsky, I. (1995). 'Laplace's Demon Consults an Oracle: The Computational Complexity of Prediction'. *Studies in History and Philosophy of Modern Physics* 27, pp.161–180.

Sinai, Y.G. (1989). 'Kolmogorov's Work on Ergodic Theory'. *The Annals of Probability* 17, pp.833–839.

Suppes, P. (1993). 'The Transcendental Character of Determinism', *Midwest Studies in Philosophy* 18, pp.242–257.

Suppes, P. and de Barros, A. (1996). 'Photons, Billiards and Chaos'. In: P. Weingartner and G. Schurz, eds., *Law and Prediction in the Light of Chaos Research*. Berlin: Springer, pp.189–201.

Weingartner, P. and Schurz, G., eds. (1996). *Law and Prediction in the Light of Chaos Research*. Berlin: Springer.

Werndl, C. (2009a). 'What Are the New Implications of Chaos for Unpredictability?'. *The British Journal for the Philosophy of Science* 60, pp.195–220.

Werndl, C. (2009b). 'Justifying Definitions in Mathematics – Going Beyond Lakatos'. *Philosophia Mathematica*, doi: 10.1093/philmat/nkp006.

Werndl, C. (2009c). 'Are Deterministic and Indeterministic Descriptions Observationally Equivalent?'. Submitted to: Studies in History and Philosophy of Modern Physics.

Werndl, C. (2009d). *Philosophical Aspects of Chaos: Definitions in Mathematics, Unpredictability and the Observational Equivalence of Deterministic and Indeterministic Descriptions*. Ph.D. thesis. University of Cambridge.

Winnie, J.A. (1998). 'Deterministic Chaos and the Nature of Chance'. In: Earman, J. and Norton, J., eds., *The Cosmos of Science – Essays of Exploration*. Pittsburgh: University of Pittsburgh Press, pp.299–324.

Young, L.-S. (1997). 'Ergodic Theory and Chaotic Dynamical Systems'. *XII-th International Congress of Mathematical Physics, Brisbane*. Cambridge, MA: International Press, pp.311–319.

THE "MULTIREALIZATION" OF MULTIPLE REALIZABILITY

HOLGER LYRE
University of Bielefeld

Abstract

Multiple Realizability (MR) must still be regarded as one of the principal arguments against type reductionist accounts of higher-order properties and their special laws. Against this I argue that there is no unique MR but rather a multitude of MR categories. In a slogan: MR is itself "multi-realized". If this is true then we cannot expect one unique reductionist strategy against MR as an anti-reductionist argument. The main task is rather to develop a taxonomy of the wide variety of MR cases and to sketch possible reductionist answers for each class of cases. The paper outlines some first steps in this direction.

1 SHORT INTRODUCTION

Multiple Realizability (MR) must still be regarded as one of the principal arguments against reductionist accounts of higher-order properties and their special laws. The MR argument, following Putnam (1967) and Fodor (1974), is widely known: higher-level properties M possess multiple lower-level realizers or instantiations. Since the realizers are "drastically hetero-geneous", no bi-conditionals between higher-level M-types and lower-level P-types can be established. But this means that the higher-order laws of the special sciences cannot be reduced to lower-level laws, since, following the classic account of theory reduction by Nagel (1961), the failure of M/P-biconditionals is equivalent to the non-existence of unique bridge laws between M and P. The upshot is that in the reducing science the unifying power of the higher-level law gets lost and that at best a generalization over an unsystematic disjunction of lower-level properties can be retained. Hence, type-reductionism fails.

The MR argument is indeed a remarkable argument. What really makes it remarkable is the curious fact that, given its simplicity and gen-erality, the argument came surprisingly late and entirely unexpectedly. In retrospect it seems almost unbelievable how it could have been overlooked for so long. Perhaps the argument was overlooked because, in a very elementary sense, the argument is bogus. This might also be the implicit reason why working scientists are usually not alarmed by this argument. Hence, the primary task of this paper is to uncover the bogus nature of the MR argument by showing that MR is not a unique phenomenon, but rather spans a variety of classes of MR cases. In a slogan: MR is itself "multi-realized". The paper aims to develop a taxonomy of the multiplicity of MR cases and to sketch corresponding possible reductionist strategies.

2 SHARED INTRINSIC PROPERTIES

MR cases are omnipresent. As a starter, let us consider an easy and apparently innocuous example: the case of water. Water is usually identified with H_2O. From a more fine-grained perspective, however, water molecules come in different varieties: hydrogen oxide ^1H_2O, deuterium oxide D_2O and tritium oxide T_2O, or, accordingly, regular water, heavy water and tritiated water. This three-fold distinction between the three types of water can of course be traced back to the distinction between the three isotopes of the hydrogen atom: protium ^1H, deuterium D and tritium T, where in the case of deuterium one and in the case of tritium two further neutrons are added to the proton of the regular hydrogen nucleus (hence, $D = {}^2H$ and $T = {}^3H$).

This setting already includes several MR scenarios: First, water is multiply realized as regular, heavy and tritiated water; second, water molecules are multiply realized as ^1H_2O, D_2O and T_2O; third, hydrogen is multiply realized by means of the isotopes protium, deuterium and tritium; and fourth, the hydrogen nucleus is multirealizable as one proton, the compound of a proton and a neutron, and the compound of a proton and two neutrons. While all this is well known, it seems pretty clear that no working scientist ever believed that because of these various MR cases there is a pressing problem with the reduction of molecular chemistry to atomic physics or the like. This is not to say that there might not very well exist problems in reducing chemistry to physics, but those problems do not, in any obvious manner, stem from the MR scenarios just mentioned.

For the sake of our argument, we may assume a bundle ontology point of view. We may describe the entities involved in MR scenarios as bundles of properties. The case of water is a particularly handsome case in this respect since we may simply identify the "nucleonic content" of the various isotopes with their basic properties, which we shall call the p-property and the n-property. To simplify things, let us neglect the oxygen nucleus and just concentrate on the hydrogen atoms. Hence, the n-property of ^1H_2O is 0, while for D_2O it is 2 and for T_2O it is 4. In contrast to this, the p-property of all isotopes is the same, namely 2. Now, most of the laws which govern the behaviour of water can be traced back to the p-property of the three water isotopes. Since the p-property of ^1H_2O, D_2O and T_2O is the same, the electromagnetic properties and, hence, most of the chemical properties are the same. Only in case where the n-property counts (e.g., when the mass of the atoms comes into play) do differences between the three realizations of water occur. In these cases, however, we are no longer facing an MR scenario, since we are not dealing with three instantiations of one kind, but rather with three different kinds. In contrast, in the true MR case, where we may consider water as one kind with laws quantifying over this water kind, the behavior of this kind and hence the water laws can be reduced to the p-property of the isotopes, which are the same for the different instantiations ^1H_2O, D_2O and T_2O.

It can of course easily be seen why the MR case of water isn't a problematic case at all. For in general, water laws quantify over p-properties. And hence, although water isotopes differ in n-properties, this difference doesn't count for the typical water properties, which are, as p-properties, one and the same for the three isotopes. Thus, from the p-property perspective, the MR scenario collapses. The more general upshot is that higher-level laws in many cases do not quantify over all the properties – the whole property bundle – of the higher-level entities but only over a suitable subset – a partial property bundle, perhaps only one property – thereof. This motivates to the following more general conclusion: *Higher-level laws quantify over causally relevant higher order properties of the supposed higher order entities only.* In many merely superficial MR cases it is therefore sufficient for a full-blown type-reduction (in a Nagelian schema of reduction or perhaps in a some more refined way) to reduce the reduction-relevant properties to causally relevant lower-level properties which the multiple realizers share. In the case of water such causally or reduction-relevant properties are the p-properties of the isotopes. Whether the realizers differ in other properties doesn't affect a successful type-reduction at all.

We've highlighted an important and at the same time innocuous category of MR cases: the class of shared intrinsic properties of the realizers. But of course there's more to come. Let us consider another kind of example. "Games" seem to provide an interesting case of MR as well – just think of soccer games, card games, Olympic games, children's games, gladiator's games etc. The examples also seem to instantiate "drastically heterogeneous" cases, a crucial ingredient not fulfilled in the case of shared intrinsic properties. However, as Wittgenstein has forcefully argued, "game" is a family concept: the members of a family show "… *a complicated network of similarities overlapping and criss-crossing*" (Wittgenstein 1953, §66), but there is no single property shared by all the members (cluster concepts are similar cases). Let's assume Wittgenstein is right on this. Insofar as the case of games provides a genuine MR case, it does obviously not belong into the MR-class of shared intrinsic properties. But we get a quick explanation at hand: while there is no single property shared by all the family members, there are nevertheless certain properties shared within certain member sub-classes. We must therefore simply restrict our shared-intrinsic-properties approach to such sub-classes to demystify family concept cases as MR cases.

This is actually the general strategy of David Lewis (1969) in his early reaction on Putnam. Lewis promotes a "restricted" type-type-identity theory allowing for domain-specific reductions. Take the case of "pain" as an infamous example of MR. Under Lewis' account the reductionist should rather restrict herself to certain subclasses or subtypes. From the same logic Lewis denies viewing pain as a natural kind. There may be pain-in-men, pain-in-dogs, pain-in-Martians, pain-in-robots, or what have you, but there is no such general kind as pain. So Lewis and Wittgenstein in a sense meet: the idea of domain-specific reductions harmonizes with the case of family types, since suitable sub-types may exactly be those which share certain lower-level properties. And, of course, such domain-specific cases then come out, again, as innocuous shared-lower-level-properties-cases.

The "Wittgenstein-Lewis-view" aligns with the empirical fact that apparently nobody is able to present non-trivial and interesting generalizations over the class of *all* pain or game realizers. There simply are no overall pain or game laws, but just laws about suitable subclasses. This echoes Wittgenstein's anti-essentialist attitude: lacking a shared – let alone essential – property, no law-like generalizations "all *F*'s are *G*'s" over "family types" F and G exist. Under Wittgenstein's idea of family resemblance it becomes plausible why we have pain and game *concepts* (and therefore perhaps mistakenly assume the existence of unanimous pain or game generalizations), but why we should at the same time not expect the existence of general pain or game *laws* – after all, over which property should they quantify?

4 THE EMPIRICAL NATURE OF MR, CAUSAL POWERS AND FUNCTIONAL REDUCTION

It might seem, however, that we have turned the logic of the MR argument on its head: we've argued for the impossibility of general pain or game laws under the presupposition that no shared intrinsic pain or game properties exists. But the MR argument is meant as an argument for the possibility of just the opposite: the possibility of law-like generalizations over drastically heterogeneous realizers. And one way to spell out drastic heterogeneity is to reject shared intrinsic properties. The systematic question behind all this is of course whether the MR argument should be considered an empirical or an a priori argument. Lawrence Shapiro (2000, 2004) has given a number of reasons in favour of the view that MR is a matter of nomological rather than logical possibility, but perhaps no deep metaphysical consideration is necessary here. Not only should it be obvious that we cannot infer about the MR status of the world from mere a priori considerations – the empirical nature of the MR thesis has also been made explicit in the statements of MR proponents themselves: *"These are not supposed to be knock-down reasons; they couldn't be, given that the question of whether reductionism is too strong is finally an* empirical *question. The world could turn out to be such that every kind corresponds to a physical kind … It's just that, as things stand, it seems very unlikely …"* (Fodor 1974, pp.102–103).

As so often in philosophy discourse the question is on which side of the debate the main burden of proof lies. But even if MR proponents accept the main burden, this wouldn't settle the issue because, as they see it, the empirical evidence is already on their side (cf. Fodor: *"as things stand"*). It seems therefore more promising to tackle the issue from another angle and to ask how to individuate the various allegedly existing kinds in an *empirical* science. Jaegwon Kim (1998, 2006) has argued that in order to be empirically dignified kinds the higher order kinds must be individuated by means of their causal roles. This is the key idea of Kim's account of functional reduction. His model involves two steps: firstly, to identify the causal role of the higher order M's and, secondly, to identify the lower-level realizers exactly by means of their causal role.

Note that under a more abstract description of this model to individuate something causally means to reconstrue it on purely relational grounds. Hence, a property defined by its causal role, and by its causal role alone, is a relational property only. We follow up on this point in the next section. But there are two important consequences from Kim's account of functional reduction. One is his well-known causal exclusion argument. The argument in brief is that there is no causal work left for the higher order entities, if we accept the otherwise convincing assumptions of the supervenience of M over P and the causal closure of P – and unless one is not willing to accept a systematic causal overdetermination. More precisely, under the assumption that higher-level tokens supervene on lower-level tokens and that any fundamental physical token has a sufficient fundamental physical cause, if it has a cause at all, the supposed extra-causal efficacy of higher-level tokens must be excluded. Functional reduction implies that, as Kim would have it, causation "drains down" from the allegedly causal power of the higher-level to the lower-level.

Another consequence concerns the widespread talk of "cross-classification". As many non-reductionists put it: higher order properties cross-classify the lower-level ones. But as Kim (1998, p.69) has pointed out, this can only reasonably be maintained if one is willing to give up supervenience. For in order for two taxonomies to cross-classify, the possibility is admitted that the higher-level taxonomic class makes causally effective distinctions not made by the lower-level class. And this is a clear failure of supervenience. Cross-classifying taxonomies define, as it were, conflicting causal profiles. Since, however, only non-reductionists of an explicit non-physicalist inclination are willing to give up supervenience in this sense, the talk of cross-classification turns out as rather loose talk not suited to spell out the consequences of MR. MR itself does not imply cross-classification. Intended as an anti-reductionist argument, the MR argument emphasizes the drastically heterogeneous nature of the realizers, but it does not imply any mysteriously conflicting causal profiles.

To sum up this interim section: MR must be understood as an empirical phenomenon. Both MR-proponents and opponents accuse each other not to have the empirical evidence on their side, but it is far less controversial to demand from those, who claim a higher-level autonomy, to indi-

viduate their thus claimed entities and properties by means of a scientifically dignified procedure, hence, to individuate entities and properties by
means of their causal roles. From this it can clearly be seen that MR does
not imply cross-classification but that properties may be individuated purely relationally. This point should be considered now.

5 SHARED RELATIONAL PROPERTIES

Let's take another MR example: the case of the harmonic oscillator. This is
actually a clear case of MR, harmonic oscillators are multi-realizable by a
plethora of physical systems: pendula, springs, atoms, electromagnetic os-
cillatory circuits and many more. Do all these realizers have certain properties in common? At least this isn't obvious. Generally speaking, a harmonic oscillator is a system where the restoring force is proportional to the
displacement from the equilibrium position. This can be captured by means
of an differential equation, the oscillator equation $d2/dt2\ x(t) + k\ x(t) = 0$.
The oscillator equation represents a higher-level law which unifies and
systematizes the harmonic behaviour of the lower-level realizers in a clean,
nice way. And we get interesting generalizations from it: whenever something obeys the oscillator equation, it works under a force proportional to
the displacement. Moreover, the realizers seem to be drastically heterogeneous. This is formally reflected by the fact that the equation leaves the
nature of the proportionality constant k open. In fact, the equation gives no
intrinsic but rather a purely relational or structural characterization of the
harmonic oscillator: all instantiations of a harmonic oscillator share the
same set of relational properties defined by the oscillator equation.

We have therefore discovered another class of MR cases, the class of
shared-relational-properties-cases, where the harmonic oscillator is a prime
example. Unlike the class of shared intrinsic properties this class seems to
provide more genuine cases of MR in the sense that structural laws allow
for interesting generalizations and that the realizers may differ drastically
in any intrinsic, albeit not relational properties. Because of their structural
commonalities, however, there is again nothing mysterious about such MR
cases.

Mention should be made at this point about the remarkable fact that
Structural Realism, a considerable movement in philosophy of physics
claiming to provide the most appropriate metaphysics of modern physics,
acknowledges primarily relational properties only on the most fundamental

level (French and Ladyman 2003, Lyre 2009). Physical laws it seems, even fundamental ones, prove themselves to a large extend as purely structural laws. It has often been a background assumption in the MR debate that the fundamental physical laws quantify over fundamental intrinsic properties. From the perspective of Structural Realism, however, physics includes basically relational properties and collections thereof. On such an account, higher-level properties, if reducible, will eventually be reducible to collections of lower-level relational properties only. This by itself already undermines the MR argument and is grist on the mills of the shared-relational-properties view. Unfortunately, it is beyond the scope of this paper to pursue this line of thought.

Let us rather consider a further example. Genes are sometimes said to be reducible to DNA segments. While this is certainly a gross oversimplification, we may nevertheless use it as an illustration in the sense that genes are multirealizable by means of DNA segments. On the one hand, this has to do with the degeneracy (redundancy) of the genetic code: almost all amino acids are encoded by more than one triplet of nucleotides (DNA codons). On the other hand it is possible to think of other biological substrates on which the genetic code acts. (In fact, when Watson and Crick discovered the genetic code they soon emphasized the fact that it is not the particular bio-substrate that counts but rather, being an information-processing code, the purely structural relations between the coding units.) By characterizing certain laws of molecular genetics as structural laws, we abstract from the intrinsic properties of the realizers (here: DNA segments) and emphasize the causally relevant relations in which they stand. Obviously, the pure structural web of relations can be multiply realized, while, *a fortiori*, the various realizations share just the proper set of relational properties which suffice to set up the intended structure. This can be generalized: the laws of the higher-level sciences, in many cases, do not pick out special heterogeneous kinds that cannot be traced back to more fundamental ones, as Fodor would have it, but typically highlight shared relational properties of lower-level realizers suited to set up a certain structure.

This conclusion also highlights the promising fact that functional properties can quite generally be reconstructed as relational properties by strictly individuating them by their causal roles – as pointed out in the preceding section and in accordance with Kim's account of functional reduction. Generally, for two entities to stand in a causal relation requires that whenever entity A occurs, B follows as its effect. That is to say, A and

B stand in an (asymmetric) relation R, where R is likewise to be considered a relational property of entities A and B (R is part of the property bundles of both A and B). Therefore, the different MR realizers will necessarily fulfil the same causal roles and, hence, *must possess at least one* relational property in common: the relational property connected with their common causal role.

6 FURTHER COMPLICATIONS AND DISCUSSIONS

6.1 Kinds by stipulation

Let's start over again with another example. Paying one's dues can be realized in various ways: by means of a bank transfer, by either cash or credit card payment, by sending a cheque, etc. A clear MR case. In the light of the above, the reductionist might use the following counter-strategy: payments are functionally defined. Their realizations may look as heterogeneous as they like, they nevertheless fulfill the same causal role in the web of economic relationships between different parties on a market. The causal effect of party A on party B – as far as A's dues and their repayment to B are concerned – is, *in economic terms,* the same for every particular realization of the payment. Economic laws do merely quantify over causal-relational properties like, for instance, the payment-relation between A and B and do not care about the particular instantiation of the payment.

While this is a first step to dissolve the case of payment as an MR example, there is perhaps more to it. The question is in fact why this example should be an alarming anti-reductionist example at all. Let's compare it to the case of pain. Admittedly, we have already argued that the case of pain is no genuine example because pain is most likely a family concept. But assume it is not, assume it were a genuine MR case. The crucial difference to the payment case is that pain is indeed a natural phenomenon. Hence, to assume pain as a higher-order classification is to assume a natural kind. Payments, however, are certainly no natural phenomena. Surely, economists treat payments as kinds in the sense that they use them in generalizations. But nevertheless payments do not occur in nature. Whether something figures as a currency or payment method is a matter of cultural stipulation and, hence, a convention. We must therefore carefully distinguish between genuine natural kinds and kinds by means of stipulation. Since we are free to declare any token whatsoever as a particular currency, we should not expect some intrinsic nature of the token to bring about its causal economic effects. Such effects are simply brought about by fiat. Not only are they functional, they are functional by convention.

6.2 Approximation cases, idealization cases and intertheory reduction

Temperature, at least in the case of gases, can be reduced to mean kinetic energy of the gas molecules. Consider the case of 1 mole of a particular gas. The number of molecules in such an amount of stuff is Avogadro's constant, which is of the order of 10^{23}, a truly gigantic number. Now, a certain macrostate of an ideal gas characterized by a particular value of the mean kinetic energy of its molecules may very well be instantiated by an equally gigantic number of microstates (we do not dispute about a few orders of magnitude more or less here), all of which in general include different individual molecule velocities which nevertheless lead to the same mean value of the molecules' kinetic energy. Hence, temperature, a property of the macrostate of a gas, is multirealizable by a vast number of microstates. While this is in a sense a truly dramatic MR case, this does not at all mean that the reduction of temperature to individual molecule velocities or kinetic energies is blocked. The different microstates belonging to one macrostate may differ in various properties (e.g. the individual molecule velocities), but as far as the relevant property is concerned – the mean kinetic energy of the molecules – these states are of one kind. Temperature laws may very well be reduced to laws about mean molecular kinetic energy despite the fact that the different microscopic realizations differ in various regards, since temperature laws do not quantify over the differing properties of the microscopic realizers, but only about the property in common. Hence, the temperature case belongs, just like the case of water, to our first innocuous MR class of shared intrinsic properties.

But there's a further complication involved. While in the case of water identifying water with H_2O (and its various isotopes) is quite straightforward, in the case of temperature identifying temperature with mean molecular kinetic energy draws essentially on an approximation. Literally speaking, there exists no such property as the mean kinetic energy. In fact, in any particular microstate the mean kinetic energy will in general be instantiated only by a tiny fraction (if at all!) of the gas molecules. We have a case here where the Nagelian bridge principles cannot be recovered as strict identities – neither for types nor for tokens!

So let's have a quick look at the issue of intertheory reduction. Ernest Nagel's (1961) classic account is based on the idea that reduction is a variant of deduction. In a nutshell: to reduce means to deduce laws. On such an account a higher-level theory T_{high} reduces to T_{low} if and only if the laws of T_{high} may be deduced from the laws of T_{low}. With laws as generalizations over property predicates, this leads to the necessity of establishing meaning relations between higher and lower-level predicates. Nagel therefore introduced bridge or correspondence principles stating that the laws of T_{low} in conjunction with the bridge principles logically comprise the laws of T_{high}.

Cases like our "temperature equals mean energy"-approximation obviously pose a problem for this approach, since generally and in fact in many cases T_{high}, from the more fundamental perspective of the lower theory T_{low}, turns out to be only merely approximately true though literally false. Hence, the very idea of reduction seems to be undermined and the threat of eliminativism is lurking. In order to cope with these problems, Schaffner (1967) and Hooker (1981) developed more elaborate accounts of reduction. Their basic idea is that to reduce means to formulate an analogous image I_{low} of T_{high} in the vocabulary of T_{low}. The trick is that by using the vocabulary of T_{low} only, reduction is accomplished without appeal to bridge principles or to worrisome token or type identities. On such an account the higher-level theory isn't entirely eliminated. There is instead a substitute provided by an analogous theory image. (Obviously, this account stands or falls with a proper account of what counts as "analogous").

So sometimes, indeed, higher-level entities or properties are introduced by means of idealization or approximation procedures. While Nagel's original account cannot cope with such cases, other reduction frameworks, most prominently the Schaffner/Hooker account, can. It is indeed a sad fact that in a majority of philosophy of mind discussions the Nagelian approach is often still the only one mentioned, while philosophers of science have discussed so many other options (starting already in the 50's with Kemeny, Oppenheim, Feyerabend, Schaffner, Sneed, Scheibe, Ludwig, to mention just a few). The upshot of approximation cases regarding the MR argument is that one must be very careful whether the allegedly multirealisable higher-level entities can be obtained from direct compositions of lower-level constituents or by means of approximations only. It is neither astonishing nor is it a deep problem that in such cases a naïve Nagelian approach of reduction fails, as long as the approximative or idealized nature of the higher level is acknowledged.

6.3 Higher-level realism, eliminativism, and bottom-up ontologies

The topic of the preceding section touches upon an important ontological issue, a full-blown discussion of which is certainly far beyond the scope of this paper. It should nevertheless be addressed here ever so briefly. It's the issue of the pros and cons of higher-level realism. Given the above MR class of approximation cases, it seems that, from a rigorous point of view, we end up with outright eliminativism: taken literally, mean energy, like other statistic concepts such as the mean woman with her mean number of 1.4 children (in the sad case of Germany), is a proper and instrumentally useful theoretical concept but it doesn't refer to any real property or entity. From the identification of a higher-level property such as temperature with a statistical quantity, the conclusion follows that the higher-level property, in our case temperature, also doesn't refer.

Take David Lewis' explanation of supervenience as another example: "*A dot-matrix picture has global properties – it is symmetrical, it is cluttered, and whatnot – and yet all there is to the picture is dots and non-dots at each point of the matrix. The global properties are nothing but patterns in the dots. They supervene: no two pictures could differ in their global properties without differing, somewhere, in whether there is or there isn't a dot*" (Lewis 1986, p.14). Do global patterns exist? Obviously, they are idealizations from dot distributions. In that sense they supervene on the lower-level dot distributions and are, the same time, multi-realizable by many distributions. The intriguing "realistic" nature of global patterns can best be seen from John Conway's infamous "Game of Life", a well-known example of a cellular automaton. From a set of perplexingly few and simple rules one gets a gorgeous complexity of patterns, a whole universe of "life forms". And it is more than compelling to describe the regular pixel distributions in the Game of Life as stable patterns, which themselves sometimes (again very perplexingly) obey higher-level regularities. Not only is it compelling, the pattern description seems to be the only appropriate description. Daniel Dennett (1991) has therefore pled for a moderate realism about higher-level patterns. For in order to cope with the otherwise overwhelming complexity we have no other choice than to describe the higher-level goings-on from the, as Dennett would have it, "design stance".

The philosophical consideration of such examples may trigger an endless debate about ontology. But whether one sticks with realism (moderate or full-blown), instrumentalism or outright eliminativism regarding higher-level patterns, isn't our primary concern. Our concern should be whether the evidence for patterns as lower-level approximations or idealizations is in accordance with reductionism or not. So here's a claim: *If for some higher-order entity or property there exists a bottom-up account that explains the entity or property if not literally but to any desired accuracy (for the purposes of higher-level observation and measurement), then that bottom-up account is sufficient for epistemic (let alone ontic) reduction.* It is, moreover, obvious that in such cases we have any reason to assume that the causal efficacy of the higher-order entities "drains down" to the lower level, to use Kim's terminology. It's not the mean woman that "does" anything in the world nor is it gas temperature as mean kinetic energy, it is the particular women and particular gas molecules in a microstate that act.

7 CONCLUSION

The paper's overall theme was that MR is no unique phenomenon, but that it is itself "multi-realized". Needless to say that this is not the same sense of multirealization as in MR itself, but rather a metaphorical use (hence the quotation marks). A variety of different classes of MR cases has been carved out in the paper. Here's again a list of them:

(1) Shared intrinsic properties
(2) Shared relational properties
(3) Functional properties
(4) Domain-specific sub-types
(5) Family concepts
(6) Kinds by stipulation
(7) Approximation cases

This list is probably not exhaustive nor is it meant to be clear-cut. In fact it were a serious misunderstanding to assume that the different MR classes are clear-cut. The point is that in many cases we need to combine different classes and their corresponding possible reductionist recipes! This shall be outlined here, on the fly I will also point out connections and similarities to more recent work in the field.

First we may distinguish "real" from "fake" cases. Real MR cases are either grounded in shared intrinsic (1) or relational (2) properties. Shared-intrinsic-properties-cases are in general innocuous (the case of water), whereas non-trivial cases quite often rely on functional properties

(3), which can, as we have seen, usually be reconstrued as cases of shared relational properties (2). In such cases the higher-level generalizations will be structural laws (the harmonic oscillator). As far as I understand him, the idea of structural laws also provides the background of Battermann's (2000) analysis, if only stated by means of the concept of universality.

The general idea to restrict attention in MR cases to the causally relevant, shared properties can also be found in Shapiro (2000, 2004) and Pauen (2002). Bickle's (2003) ruthless reduction of psychological phenomena to the molecular level can, I think, be understood as an attempt to ground psychological multirealizability in shared intrinsic molecular properties. Shapiro (2000) has moreover set up an interesting dilemma for MR proponents. His concern is about the empirical evidence of the MR thesis and the existence of truly interesting and genuine cases of MR. Shapiro argues that in the genuine cases the different realizers bring about the function in causally different ways. Hence we should not be concerned with property differences of the realizers which do not contribute to the function. In Shapiro's example: whether a corkscrew is made out of aluminium or any other steel doesn't really matter. However, the fact that here exist different mechanisms to realize a corkscrew – a winged mechanical device opposed to a gas injection device – is of interest. Shapiro's dilemma now is that either the realizers differ in the causal way they bring about the function or they do not. In the latter case we have no interesting case of MR at all, if they do, however, then they are really different kinds, because in that case only a few shared laws or generalizations will be left – laws or generalizations he attributes as "*numbingly dull*" (Shapiro 2000, p.649) such as "mouse traps are used to catch mice" or "eyes are used to see". While I basically agree with Shapiro's analysis, the emphasis is a bit different. If all mouse traps bring about the causal effect to catch mice then they share this very property and mouse trap "laws", as generalizations over exactly this property, are possible. Admittedly, such generalizations aren't very instructive, but the crucial point is that even "numbingly dull" generalizations subsist only on the basis of shared properties – if only, in the extreme, by sharing just one relational property. Of course, the fewer commonalities, the less useful the generalizations.

Classes (4) to (7) can in principle be combined both with each other and with classes (1) and (2). We have seen some examples already. Family concepts (5) will generally allow for domain-specific sub-types (4) on the basis of shared properties (1,2). Recently, Lewis' idea of domain-specificity was revived by Esfeld and Sachse (2007) in terms of "functional sub-types", i.e. a combination of (3) and (4) without, however, further analyzing (3) in terms of (1) or (2). Classes (6) and (7) are largely overlooked in the literature, though they most certainly play an eminent role, especially the class of approximations and idealizations (7), where, strictly speaking, MR proponents only mistakenly assume genuine multirealizable kinds.

I should finish with the remark that, admittedly, the paper has an ambitiously wide scope. It touches upon many deep philosophical issues which cannot all be addressed adequately in just one paper. However, since the issues are deeply intertwined, it is my firm belief that when we consider only single pieces of it alone important points will be missing. This is also intended by the term "multirealization" (in quotes): the many faces of the MR problem. And exactly because of the many faces there is no unique antidote against MR's supposedly anti-reductionistic force. But there is perhaps enough hope that all of the various "instantiations" of MR can be dismissed case by case (or class by class, respectively). So the paper should eventually be considered an outline of a prospective framework of how to deal with the MR problem (or "problems") from a strengthened (type) reductionist perspective.

REFERENCES

Batterman, R.W. (2000). Multiple Realizability and Universality. *British Journal for the Philosophy of Science* 51: pp.115–145.

Bickle, J. (2003). Philosophy *and Neuroscience: A Ruthlessly Reductive Account.* Dordrecht: Kluwer.

Dennett, D.C. (1991). Real Patterns. *Journal of Philosophy* 88(1): pp.27–51.

Esfeld, M. and Sachse, C. (2007). Theory Reduction by Means of Functional Sub-types. *International Studies in the Philosophy of Science* 21(1): pp.1–17.

Fodor, J. (1974). Special Sciences: Or the Disunity of Science as a Working Hypothesis. *Synthese* 28: pp.97–115.

French, S. and Ladyman, J. (2003). Re-modelling Structural Realism: Quantum Physics and the Metaphysics of Structure. *Synthese* 136(1): pp.31–56.

Kim, J. (1998). *Mind in a Physical World: An Essay on the Mind-Body Problem and Mental Causation.* MIT Press, Cambridge MA.

Kim, J. (2005). *Physicalism, or Something Near Enough.* Princeton University Press, Princeton.

Lewis, D. (1969). Review of Art, Mind, and Religion. *Journal of Philosophy* 66: pp.23–35.

Lewis, D. (1996). *On the Plurality of Worlds.* Blackwell, Oxford.

Lyre, H. (2009). Structural Realism and Abductive-Transcendental Arguments. In: M. Bitbol, P. Kerszberg and J. Petitot (eds.): *Constituting Objectivity: Transcendental Perspectives on Modern Physics*. Springer, Berlin.

Nagel, E. (1961). *The Structure of Science*. Routledge, London.

Pauen, M. (2002). Is Type Identity Incompatible with Multiple Realization? *Grazer Philosophische Studien* 65: pp.37–49.

Putnam, H. (1967). Psychological Predicates. In: W.H. Capitan and D.D. Merrill (eds.): *Art, Mind and Religion*. Pittsburgh University Press, Pittsburgh.

Shapiro, L. (2000). Multiple Realizations. *Journal of Philosophy* 97: pp.635–654.

Shapiro, L. (2004). *The Mind Incarnate*. MIT Press, Cambridge MA.

Wittgenstein, L. (1953). *Philosophical Investigations*. Blackwell, Oxford.

PESSIMISTIC META-INDUCTION AND THE EXPONENTIAL GROWTH OF SCIENCE[1]

LUDWIG FAHRBACH
University of Konstanz

1 SCIENTIFIC REALISM

This paper presents the outlines of a defense of scientific realism against the argument of pessimistic meta-induction (PMI for short). I will understand the position of scientific realism to consist of the claim that our current empirically successful scientific theories are probably approximately true. Examples of such theories are the atomic theory of matter, the theory of evolution or claims about the role of viruses and bacteria in infectious diseases. In what follows, I omit "probably" and "approximately" (as in "probably approximately true") and simply use "true." Furthermore, I use the term "theory" in a rather generous sense, so that it also denotes laws of nature, theoretical statements, sets of theoretical statements, and so on.

A theory is defined as being *empirically successful* at some point in time if there are sufficiently many cases of fit and no serious cases of non-fit between the known observational consequences of the theory and the observations gathered by scientists until that time. In contrast, if a consequence of a theory conflicts with some observations and scientists cannot find any other source of the error, e.g., they cannot blame an auxiliary statement, the theory is refuted and does not count as successful.

---

[1] For discussion and support, I would like to thank audiences in Manchester, Konstanz, Düsseldorf, Dortmund, Oldenburg, Bristol and Lissabon; and Christopher von Bülow, Franz Dietrich, Dorothee Fahrbach, Claus Beisbart, Berna Kilinc, Ari Duwell, Anna Kusser, Luca Moretti, Kyle Stanford, Luc Bovens, Stephan Hartmann, Erik Olsson, Bernward Gesang, and especially Gerhard Schurz. My research was supported by a stipend by the Alexander von Humboldt Foundation, the Federal Ministry of Education and Research and the Program for the Investment in the Future (ZIP) of the German Government through a Sofja Kovalevskaja Award.

2. WEAK PMI AND STRONG PMI

There are several different versions of PMI. I only deal with some of them here. I will use the expression "PMI" in a generic way to denote the common idea of the different forms of pessimistic meta-induction discussed here. Stated generally, PMI starts from the premise that the history of science is full of theories that were accepted for some time but were later refuted and replaced by other theories, where these changes in theories occurred even though the refuted theories were empirically successful while they were accepted. This premise has a strong and a weak reading. The strong reading is that *most* successful theories in the history of science were later refuted. The weak reading is that at least *a significant fraction* of all successful theories accepted in the history of science were later refuted. The qualification "at least" is used here in order to make the weak premise logically weaker than the strong premise, so that it is easier to provide support for it from the history of science. To illustrate, "most" may be taken to mean "90 percent" and "a significant fraction" may be taken to mean "20 percent". Instead of the cumbersome term "significant fraction", I will also use the term "some". Thus, the weak premise states that *some* successful theories accepted in the history of science were later refuted.

In accordance with the two premises, there are two versions of PMI; a strong version and a weak version.[2] The strong version invites us to infer from the *strong* premise that *most or all* of our current successful theories will be refuted at some time in the future. The weak version of PMI invites us to infer from the *weak* premise that at least *some* of our current successful theories will be refuted at some time in the future. The weak PMI deserves its name, because its conclusion is compatible with some or even the majority of our current successful theories' being true.

The two PMIs are naturally associated with two forms of antirealism, one strong and one weak. The strong form uses the strong PMI to predict that most or all current successful theories will be refuted and therefore recommends believing that they are false (compare Ladyman 2002, p.231). An example of the strong form is Kuhn's account of science of changing paradigms. One plausible interpretation of his perspective is that he believed that "all paradigms are doomed to fail eventually" for the reason that "the world is just so *complicated* that our theories will always run into trouble in the end." (Peter Godfrey-Smith 2003, p.177, his empha-

---

[2] The distinction between strong and weak PMI was put forward to me by Gerhard Schurz.

sis). The weak form of anti-realism uses the weak PMI to predict that at least a significant fraction of our current best theories will be refuted. It recommends agnosticisms about these theories offering as reason that even if some of them are true, we do not know which ones are the true ones.

As stated, the two PMIs are cases of enumerative induction. They can be understood as being instances of the argument schema that projects the relative frequency of As among *observed* Bs to the relative frequency of As among *unobserved* Bs. (The As are the refuted theories and the Bs are the successful theories.) However, if we examine them more closely, we quickly see that in several respects, they are more complicated affairs and more fraught with difficulties than it seems at first. So, let us examine them more closely with the help of some idealizing assumptions. This will also help us to clarify what both arguments are actually stating. Let us assume for the moment that scientific fields are defined in such a way that in each one, exactly one theory is accepted at any time, and that scientific fields neither merge nor split. Let the number of scientific fields be N, and the number of successful but refuted theories from science's past be R. N is also the number of theories that are held today. Then the total number of all successful theories in the past is $R + N$. The ratio of refuted theories to all successful theories of the past is represented by the number $R/(R + N)$. The strong PMI states that if this ratio is not far from one, then most or all currently successful theories will be refuted in the future. Its premise can be taken to mean that on average there were several theory changes per scientific field in the past. For example, assuming that there are 100 scientific fields, and that on average every field experienced three theory changes, then $R/(R + N)$ is $300/400 = ¾$. The conclusion of the strong PMI can then be taken to be that most or all scientific fields will experience further theory changes in the future. Given the premise, this seems to be a reasonable conclusion.

The weak PMI states that if the fraction $R/(R + N)$ is "significant", then we should expect at least "some" changes among our current best theories. The premise can be taken to mean that at least "some" scientific fields have experienced one or a few theory changes in the past, and its conclusion can be taken to say the same thing about the future. However, it is not so clear how to make the inference more precise. One may wonder whether one should project the fraction $R/(R + N)$, the relative frequency of refuted theories among all successful theories of the past, or the fraction R/N, the average number of refuted theories per scientific field, as a lower bound for the expected fraction of refutations among our current best theories. Fortunately, for small R, the two ratios do not differ much. For example, if 33% of all fields experienced one theory change in the past, while 67% did not experience any theory changes, then R/N is 33%, while $R/(R + N)$ is 25% (because in that case of all successful theories of the history of science, 25% were refuted).[3]

Both PMIs are sensitive to additional considerations. For example, assume again that 33% of all fields experienced one theory change in the past, while 67% did not experience any theory changes, i.e., R/N is 33%. On the one hand, one might think that the fact that 33% of theories have been refuted shows that some of the fields with non-refuted theories probably also have unstable theories, only it did not show until now; as a result, this line of interpretation would continue, we should expect that more than 33% of current theories will be refuted. On the other hand, one might think that since the 33% figure implies that the theories of the majority of disciplines have been stable, this shows that stable theories will probably remain stable and, what is more, that some of the current theories in the bad disciplines will also remain stable in the future, because scientists have hit on the true theories, so less than 33% of current theories will be refuted. Which one of these projections is more plausible depends on one's background assumptions. These are only some of the problems and complications that one encounters when attempting to make meta-induction more precise. Further problems quickly crop up, e.g., how to individuate theories, how to determine the reference class (i.e., the set of all successful theories in the history of science), and how to do justice to the fact that theories often have parts that one may want to deal with separately. To my mind, all of this shows that it makes little sense to try to formulate PMIs with any higher degree of precision than that of the words "most" and "some".

The premises of both PMIs require evidence. Larry Laudan (1981) famously presented a long list of theories (which I will not repeat here), all of which were once successful, and all of which are now considered to have been refuted. An example discussed especially often in the literature is the sequence of theories of light in the 18th, 19th and early 20th centuries, see Figure 1. Many philosophers have considered Laudan's examples to be impressive evidence for the premise of PMI where the premise is usually understood in the strong way. If the strong PMI is correct, scientific realism is refuted, as the latter holds that our current successful theories are probably true. However, scientific realism is also refuted by the weak PMI,

---

[3] The numbers $a = R/N$ and $b = R/(R+N)$ are related by $a = b/(1–b)$ and $b = a/(a+1)$.

which concludes that at least some of our current successful theories are false. This is significant, because it is considerably easier to provide evidence for the premise of the weak PMI than the premise of the strong PMI.

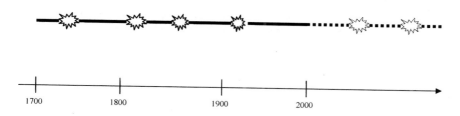

Figure 1: The sequence of theory changes in the case of theories of light and the projection of that sequence into the future

3 REFINEMENTS OF PMI

There are further ways to refine PMI. The premises of both PMIs average over all scientific fields, in the sense that all theory changes of all scientific fields are pooled disregarding any possible differences between the fields. To do this is not unreasonable, as Laudan's examples of refuted theories come from many different scientific disciplines such as physics, chemistry, biology, medicine, etc. Still, theory changes may not be distributed so evenly among scientific fields, as some fields may suffer from more theory changes than others do. This is the case, for example, if the premise of the weak PMI but not the premise of the strong PMI is true – i.e., if theory changes occurred in some, but not all, scientific disciplines or fields. Furthermore, even if theory changes are distributed evenly, the future stability or instability of a theory from a certain scientific field may be taken to depend on the specifics of that field, e.g., its subject matter or its methods, while the past stability or instability of theories of *other scientific fields* may not be taken as indicative of the future fate of theories *in that field*. Hence, one may want to refine PMI in such a way that the projection of theory changes is made relative to specific scientific fields. Every such PMI is then a localized "contextualized" inference. Some fields may then give rise to weak PMI, while others give rise to strong PMI. These field-relative forms of PMI can be made more precise in different ways, e.g., by specifying how broadly the respective scientific field is to be understood. At one extreme, a field may be defined such that it consists of only one theory at every point in time. At the other extreme a field may be defined as encompassing an entire scientific discipline such as biology or chemistry, or it may even be understood as encompassing all of natural science.

As an example of the application of a field-relative form of PMI consider the field of clinical studies. In a recent meta-study, 49 highly cited (i.e., cited more than 1000 times) original clinical studies claiming that a drug or other treatment worked were examined. It turned out that subsequent studies of comparable or larger sample size and with similarly or better-controlled designs contradicted the results of 16% of the earlier studies and reported weaker results for another 16%. This means that nearly one-third of the original results did not hold up.[4] For example, the refuted studies had seemingly shown that hormone pills protect menopausal women from heart disease and that vitamin A supplements reduce the risk of breast cancer. An argument very similar to a field-relative form of PMI may then be used to infer that at least the same percentage of currently non-refuted clinical studies will not hold up in the future. Such a projection is akin to a weak form of PMI, because what is projected is not that *most or all* of these studies are false, but only that *some* of them are (where we do not know which ones). Finally, relativizing PMI to the field of clinical studies makes it possible to enrich and improve PMI by taking into account additional factors, such as the quality and size of the clinical studies.

Field-relative forms of PMI provide the basis of some forms of anti-realism. These forms of anti-realism state that many successful scientific fields have experienced theory changes in the past, and that if a field has experienced theory changes in the past, then we should, because of the respective strong or weak field-relative PMI, disbelieve or be agnostic about the current successful theories of that field. Such a field-restricted form of anti-realism may recommend, for example, that we not believe our current best theory of heat (roughly, that heat is mean kinetic energy) because several incompatible theories of heat were successful and accepted at different times in the past. Kyle Stanford's (2006, Ch.8) form of anti-realism seems to be a version of this field-restricted form of anti-realism. He essentially recommends that although we may believe *some* predictions of the best theories of unsteady fields, we should not believe many other predictions of those theories, especially those about new kinds of phenomena, again for the reason that the respective field-restricted PMIs should make us ex-

---

[4] Paraphrased from John Ioannidis (2005) and Lindey Tanner (2005)

pect that some of those theories will eventually fail empirically at some future time.

Figure 1 suggests a further idea regarding how to understand PMI. Assume once again for a moment that the notion of a scientific field is defined such that scientists of that field accept just one theory at any given moment in time. If the theory changes in such a field show a regular pattern, we can extrapolate that pattern along the timeline into the future, similar in kind to the extrapolation of a time-dependent regular curve of a certain form along the timeline into the future.[5] In the same vein, we can extrapolate *some chosen feature* of the pattern of past theory changes in such a field into the future. For example, a possible feature for projection suggested to me by Gerhard Schurz is to the "mean survival time" of theories of the respective scientific field. Let us call this form of PMI "the dynamic PMI". It is obviously a version of field-restricted PMI. Furthermore, we may understand the notion of scientific field in broader ways, e.g. as sets of theories. Thus understood, one possibility is to extrapolate how the frequency of theory changes per time developed over time where the frequencies are obtained from the whole scientific field: this frequency may have increased, decreased, or stayed the same, and this development is projected into the future. Then earlier theory changes have less of a bearing on the extrapolation than later theory changes do. Such extrapolations that are based on sets of patterns of theory change in broader scientific fields will also count as dynamic PMI. In general, the premise of any dynamic PMI is a statement about a feature of the set of time-dependent patterns of theory change in some scientific field in the past, and its conclusion is the statement that the same field will exhibit that feature in the future. I will call this focus on the pattern of theory changes "the dynamic understanding of the history of science". The dynamic PMI is also an instance of enumerative induction, although of a more complicated sort.

In discussions of PMI, the dynamic understanding is usually not mentioned explicitly, although it is lurking in the background and adds to the intuitive plausibility of PMI. The difference between the strong/weak PMI and the dynamic understanding is that the former completely abstracts from the timing of the theory refutations and theory changes, while for the

---

[5] The step-function which takes time points t as arguments and natural numbers as values where the value of the step-function at t is the number of theory changes up to t in the given scientific field encodes the pattern of theory changes in that field. If it has some regular form, that form can be extrapolated into the future.

latter, the distribution of the points of time of the theory changes are relevant.

What could the rationale for the dynamic PMI be? One might think that it has no rationale, because the points in time of the theory refutations are irrelevant for the projection of theory changes into the future; the timing of the refutations and their distribution seem to have no epistemic significance. Still, a preference for the nearer past over the more distant past may be justified by claiming that science is constantly changing for the better in several respects – methodologically, for example (Devitt 2005, p.787) – but most importantly, in the amount and quality of evidence that scientists have accumulated (compare Gerald Doppelt 2007). To this, one might reply that the increase in evidence and the increase in success of the theories do not really make much of a difference, as this is the same kind of success and nothing qualitatively new (compare Stanford 2006, Section 1.2). However, we will see in a moment that the dynamic understanding of the history of science, if developed further in the right direction, has more to it than meets the eye.

4 REFUTATION OF PMI

Let us now turn to developing the argument against PMI. Consider the amount of scientific work done by scientists in different periods of time, and how that amount increased over time. Here, "scientific work" means such things as making observations, performing experiments, constructing and testing theories, etc. It is plausible to assume that the amount of scientific work done by scientists during some period can be measured by the number of journal articles published in that period. Over the last few centuries, this number has grown exponentially. The doubling rate of the number of journal articles published every year has been 15–22 years over the last 300 years (see Figure 2). This is a very strong pattern of growth. As is shown in the appendix, these doubling rates imply that at least 95% of all scientific work ever done has been done since 1915, and that at least 80% of all scientific work ever done has been done since 1950.

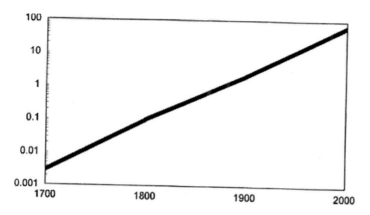

Figure 2. The growth in the number of scientific journal articles over the last 300 years. The vertical axis shows the cumulative number of scientific journal articles measured in millions. It has a logarithmic scale; hence, the straight line represents exponential growth. Note the small bend in the curve. Note also its thickness, demonstrating the uncertainty of the data. (From Brian C. Vickery 2000, p.xxii).

Let us examine how the exponential growth of science affects the different forms of PMI. Let us first consider the premise of PMI in its intuitive form: the history of science is full of theories that were once successful and accepted but were later refuted. As we saw earlier, proponents of PMI support it by offering numerous examples of such theories. Now, however, given the exponential growth of science, we have to recheck whether these examples are really evidence for the premise of PMI. If we do so, we get a very different idea of the matter. Inspecting Laudan's list, we see that all entries on that list are theories that were abandoned more than 100 years ago. This means that all corresponding theory changes occurred during the time of the first 5% of all scientific work ever done by scientists. As regards the example of theories of light, all changes in those theories occurred before the 1930s, whereas 80% of all scientific work ever done has been done since 1950. The same holds for practically all examples of theory changes offered in the philosophical literature. Thus, it seems that the set of examples offered by proponents of PMI is not representative and cannot be used to support the premise of PMI. If this is right, the premise lacks support and PMI does not work.

To this argument, one might object that the intuitive understanding of the premise is misleading. We should use the premise as it is understood in the weak and strong PMI. Both of these state only relative frequencies (namely, of the appearance of refuted theories among those that were successful in the past). They abstract from the periods of time at which the theories were accepted and the points in time at which they were refuted, and rightly so (according to this objection), because neither has any epistemic significance. The only thing that is relevant for PMI is that the refuted theories were successful. Hence, Laudan's list is a representative sample of refuted theories after all, and it can serve to support the premises of the strong or weak PMI.

In response to this objection, I want to show that it is actually the premises of relative frequency that are not adequate as premises for meta-induction. I will do so by elaborating on the dynamic PMI. The dynamic PMI states that certain features of the pattern of refutations and stability in the past of science are to be projected into the future. But how exactly is the projection to be accomplished? Consider Figure 1, where the x-axis is weighted in a linear fashion such that equal lengths of time are represented by intervals of equal length on the x-axis. With the exponential growth of science in mind, a second weighting suggests itself: the x-axis could be weighted in such a way that the length of any interval on the x-axis is proportional to the amount of scientific work done in that interval; see Figure 3. I will call these two ways of weighting the x-axis the linear weighting and the exponential weighting.

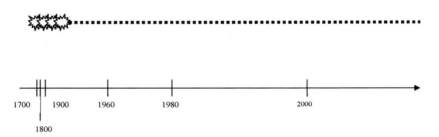

Figure 3: Exponential weighting of the x-axis and the sequence of theories of light.

Both weightings could be used in the premises of the dynamic understanding of PMI. Which one should be used? If we want to project the past development of science into the future, which weighting is the right one? The exponential weighting is more plausible for the following reasons. If we want to determine how stable or unstable the best scientific theories have been in the past, we should look at the amount of scientific work done by scientists, because the amount of scientific work can be expected to be very roughly proportional to the amount and quality of empirical evidence compiled by scientists to confirm or disprove their theories. More concretely, but still on a very general level, more scientific work results in the discovery of more phenomena and observations, which, in turn, can be used for more varied and better empirical tests of theories. More varied and better empirical tests of theories, if passed, result in greater empirical success for theories. Although it is certainly not plausible that *all* scientific disciplines profited from the increase in scientific work in this way, it is even less plausible that *no* scientific disciplines and *no* scientific theories profited from the increase in scientific work in this way, and it is obviously the latter–the disciplines and theories that did profit–that realists want to focus on.[6] This consideration is a good reason to adopt the exponential weighting of the x-axis in the premise of the dynamic PMI.

Although this consideration offers a prima facie strong case for the exponential weighting, it clearly is in need of further elaboration. However, in order to develop it more fully, we would need a better worked-out notion of the degree of success of scientific theories. Such a notion has to be developed in future work. The main tasks are then, first, to establish a sufficiently strong connection between the amount of scientific work (as measured by the number of journal articles) and the degree of success of the best scientific theories, and second, to show that such a connection can be exploited for a more fully developed argument against PMI. From now on, I will proceed using the assumption that such a connection can be established.

The assumption implies that the exponential weighting of the x-axis is the correct weighing. It also implies that the premises of the strong and the weak PMI, which make statements exclusively about frequencies, are inadequate: in projecting the past development of science into the future, it is not appropriate to abstract from the times at which the theories were accepted or changed. Time matters because different periods differ very strongly in terms of the amount of scientific work done in them, and because the amount of scientific work is linked with the degree of success of the best theories. Hence, the two premises leave out relevant information and should therefore not be used in an inductive argument; it follows that neither the weak PMI nor the strong PMI are cogent arguments.

---

[6] This focus is, of course, a form of field-restriction.

Let us proceed by examining what the exponential weighting implies for the dynamic PMI. Our observation from the beginning of this section, that all examples of theory changes discussed in the philosophical literature are rather old, shows that this set of examples is not representative and therefore cannot support the premise of the dynamic PMI. Based on this set of examples, nothing can be inferred about the future change or future stability of scientific theories. This is illustrated in Figure 3. Thus, we need to come up with a more representative sample set. We should examine the last 50 to 80 years. Only then can we decide whether the premise of the dynamic PMI is plausible. So, let us look at this period. Moreover, as we just observed, we should focus on the *best* (i.e., most successful) scientific theories. If we do so, it quickly becomes clear that virtually all of our best scientific theories have been entirely stable in the last 50 to 80 years. Despite the very strong rise in the amount of scientific work, refutations among them have basically not occurred. Here are some examples of such theories (remember that the realist endorses the *approximate* truth of those theories):

- The theory of evolution
- There are 92 natural chemical elements
- The conservation of mass-energy
- Infectious diseases are caused by bacteria or viruses
- $E = mc^2$
- The brain is a net of neurons
- There are billions of galaxies in the universe.
- Sound consists of air waves
- In the Earth's past, there were many ice ages
- And so on

Proponents of PMI will have a hard time finding even one or two convincing examples of similarly successful theories that were accepted for some time during the last 50 to 80 years but were later abandoned (and one or two counterexamples could be tolerated because, after all, we are dealing with inductive inference here). This does not mean that there were no theory changes in the last 50 to 80 years, which there clearly were; of course the large amount of scientific work done in the recent past has also brought with it a lot of refutations. It only means that there were practically no theory changes *among our best (i.e., most successful)* theories. For example, the highly cited clinical studies mentioned earlier, which were partly or wholly refuted later on, constitute theory changes; still, every such study is just *one single study*, which is clearly insufficient for one to count its result as belonging to the most successful theories.

At this point, one might object that the notion of "the most successful theory" is intolerably vague; it can neither be used to delineate a set of theories, nor for the statement that the most successful theories have been stable. A satisfactory reply to this objection would have to rely on a better elaboration of the notion of success, a task that, as noted earlier, has to await another occasion. In this paper, I have to appeal to our intuitive understanding of it and trust that it is not too vague to serve my purposes here. However, as a preliminary reply to this objection, I want to offer the following argument.

The argument is meant to defend that even if the notion is rather vague, the claim of the stability of our current most successful theories is quite plausible. Consider Laudan's list once again. Although the set of *theory changes* on Laudan's list is not representative for projection, it is plausible to assume that the set of *scientific fields* of those theories form a representative set of scientific fields for projection. These fields belong to many different scientific disciplines: astronomy, chemistry, biology, medicine, geology, etc. When we examine the currently accepted descendant theories of the theories on Laudan's list, that is to say, those theories that are about the same subject matter as Laudan's theories and that are accepted today, then we observe that most of them can be regarded as being among our current most successful theories. At this point, the objection was that the notion of a "most successful theory" is dangerously vague and should not be used to describe the past of science. However, it turns out that it does not matter that this notion is rather vague, because *all* of the descendent theories have been entirely stable for the last few decades (and most of them for a far longer time). This is the case for the descendant theories of phlogiston theory, the crystalline spheres of ancient and medieval astronomy, the effluvial theory of static electricity, both theories of heat, and the theory of circular inertia. (For some theories on the list, it is not clear which current theories to count as descendant theories, because they are too general or too unspecific – for example, the humoral theory of medicine and the vital force theories of physiology.) Thus, for a representative set of theories, the vagueness of the notion "most successful" does not matter.

What follows from all this for the dynamic understanding of PMI? As we saw, the dynamic understanding of the history of science is the right understanding of the history of science for any instance of meta-induction, but it also turned out that the premise of this version of the dynamic PMI was false (if restricted to the set of our current best theories). We already concluded above that neither the weak nor the strong PMI is a cogent argument. Thus, no form of PMI considered in this paper, neither the weak PMI nor the strong PMI nor the dynamic PMI, is a cogent argument. Their conclusions that some, most or all of our current best scientific theories will fail empirically in the future is therefore not supported by the history of science. Hence, PMI in any of these forms is refuted.

The refutation of PMI has two consequences. First, field-relative forms of PMI are not cogent for fields involving our current best theories. Hence, Stanford's form of anti-realism is not tenable for those theories (although it may be tenable for theories of less successful scientific fields such as the field of clinical studies). Second, scientific realism, the claim that our current most successful theories are true, is saved from being undermined by PMI.

5 APPENDIX

1. In the main text, I use the number of scientific journal articles published in some period as a statistical quantity to measure scientific work in that period. As is the case for any statistical quantity (and, actually, any scientific quantity generally), we can distinguish two main tasks, the task of definition and the task of determination, where both tasks come with their specific difficulties. First, we have the conceptual task of providing sufficiently precise and fruitful definitions of the respective statistical quantities, in this paper the notion of a scientific journal article. The accompanying difficulty is that usually, several different ways to define any quantity are possible, and often, no definition is clearly superior to all other definitions. Furner writes, "If we are to count 'publications,' ... should we count monographs, or serials, or both? If we are counting serial publications, should we count yearbooks and technical reports, in-house organs and newspapers, as well as journals? Should we count journal titles, or journal articles, or pages, or words? How, moreover, should we define 'scientific'?" (Furner, 2003, p.9) Second, we have the empirical task of determining values of the quantity, i.e., the number of journal articles per year. Here, the difficulty is that whatever definition of "journal article" we choose their number at any point in time is not easy to ascertain. Especially

for centuries earlier than the 20th century, Bibliometricians can only yield estimates with limited accuracy. In any case, neither kind of difficulty threatens our project here because all we need are rough estimates; for this, what Bibliometricians offer is entirely sufficient. Different definitions of "journal article" and different estimates of their numbers by Bibliometricians do not lead to significantly different results as far as the aims of the paper are concerned.

2. We have to show that of all scientific work ever done, at least 95% has been done since 1915, and at least 80% has been done since 1950. Consider the following list of the number of scientific journal articles during different periods[7]:

1600 till 1900	2 million
1901–1915	1 million
1950s	4 million
1960s	600 000–900 000 annually
1600 till 1970	20–25 million
1600 till 2010	60–80 million

As for the first claim, adding the first two entries of the table and comparing the sum with the last entry, we observe that at most 5% of all scientific work ever done was done before 1915. As for the second claim, the upper bounds of the last two entries show that at most 25 million out of the total 80 million articles ever published were published before 1970. Around 6–9 million articles were published in the 1960s, and at least 4 million were published in the 1950s, leaving at most 15 million articles before 1950, which is less than 20% of 80 million. We obtain a similar number if we use the lower bounds of the last two entries. Because the last two entries in the table are not independent from each other, we need not consider the combination of the upper bound of the second to last entry with the lower bound of the last entry. Apart from the last assumption, my calculations are mostly rounded in such a way that if they err, they err to my disadvantage.

We obtain the same results when we use the doubling rate (the length of time in which the number of journal articles doubles). Because we only

---

[7] The numbers are taken from Vickery (1990, 2000, p.xxii, see figure 2), Meadows (2000, p.89) and Furner (2003). See also Mabe/Amin (2001, pp.145–5). Numbers before 1600 can be neglected. This is especially obvious for the time before the invention of movable type printing by Gutenberg around 1450.

need a low level of precision, we can assume that the number of publications per year follows an exponential function $f(t) = a \cdot \exp(\lambda t)$, where a is a normalization factor (which disappears in the results), and λ is the growth rate. Let d be the doubling rate. The doubling rate has been between 15 and 22 years over the last 300 years. λ and d are related by $\lambda d = \ln 2 = 0{,}7$ (because $f(t+d) = a \cdot \exp(\lambda(t+d)) = a \cdot \exp(\lambda t) \cdot \exp(\lambda d)$ and $f(t+d) = 2 \cdot f(t) = 2a \cdot \exp(\lambda t)$). For example, a doubling rate of 20 years corresponds to a growth rate of 3.5% per year. The number of publications between two points in time is given by the integral of $f(t)$ between those two points in time. For example, the number of publications from the beginning of science until time T is given by

$$\int_{-\infty}^{T} f(t)\,dt = a \cdot 1/\lambda \cdot \exp(\lambda T).$$

This integral is a measure of overall scientific work done in that period.

We are interested in how many of all publications ever published were published after a certain year T. Let r denote this ratio. Let S denote the present time, and n be such that $n = (S - T)/d$ (n measures how often the number of publications doubles between T and S.). Then

$$
\begin{aligned}
r \quad &= \quad \int_{S-nd}^{S} f(t)\,dt \; / \; \int_{-\infty}^{S} f(t)\,dt \\
&= \quad a \cdot 1/\lambda \, (e^{\lambda S} - e^{\lambda S - \lambda nd}) \; / \; a \cdot 1/\lambda \; e^{\lambda S} \\
&= \quad 1 - e^{-\lambda nd} \\
&= \quad 1 - 1/2^{n}
\end{aligned}
$$

For example, assume that we want to know what fraction of all scientific articles ever published were published between 1970 and 2010. Let us assume a doubling rate of 20 years. Then $n = 2$ and $r = 1 - ¼ = 75\%$. Hence, the answer is that of all articles ever published 75% were published between 1970 and 2010. Here are some values of r for different years and for doubling rates of 20 and 22 years. (Judging from the literature, a doubling rate of 22 years is too high an estimate, and here serves merely as an upper bound.)

T	1810	1873	1918	1953
r for d = 20 years	99,9%	99,1%	95,9%	86,1%
r for d = 22 years	99,8%	98,7%	94,9%	83,4%

We see once again that around 95% of all journal articles ever published have been published since 1915, and more than 80% have been published since 1950.

REFERENCES

Devitt, M. (2005), "Scientific Realism", In *The Oxford Handbook of Contemporary Analytic Philosophy, Frank Jackson and Michael Smith*, eds. Oxford: Oxford University Press, pp.767–791.

Doppelt, Gerald (2007). "Reconstructing Scientific Realism to Rebut the Pessimistic Meta-induction", *Philosophy of Science*, Vol.74, pp.96–118.

Furner, J. (2003). "Little Book, Big Book: Before and After Little Science, Big Science: A Review Article, Part II", Journal of Librarianship and Information Science, Vol.35, No.3, pp.189–201.

Godfrey-Smith, P. (2003). *Theory and Reality: An Introduction to the Philosophy of Science*, The University of Chicago Press, Chicago.

Ioannidis, John P. A. (2005). "Contradicted and Initially Stronger Effects in Highly Cited Clinical Research" *Journal of the American Medical Association*, July 13, 2005; 294: pp.218–228.

Ladyman, James, (2002). *Understanding Philosophy of Science*. London: Routledge

Laudan, L. (1981) "A Refutation of Convergent Realism", Philosophy of Science, 48 March, pp.19–49.

Mabe, M. and M. Amin, (2001). "Growth Dynamics of Scholarly and Scientific Journals", Scientometrics. Vol.51, No.1, pp.147–162.

Meadows, J. (2000). "The Growth of Journal Literature: A Historical Perspective" in: The Web of Knowledge: A Festschrift in honor of Eugene Garfield Edited by Blaise Cronin and Helen Barsky Atkins ASIS&T Monograph Series, Information Today, Inc., Medford, New Jersey.

Stanford, P. Kyle (2006). *Exceeding Our Grasp: Science, History, and the Problem of Unconceived Alternatives*. Oxford University Press.

Tanner, Lindey (2005). "Review of Medical Research Turns Up Contradictory Results", The Associate Press, July 13, 2005.

Vickery, B.C. (1990). "The Growth of Scientific Literature, 1660–1970", in: The Information Environment: A World View, Studies in Honour of Professor A.I. Mikhailov, Elsevier Science Publishers B.V. North-Holland.

Vickery, B.C. (2000). *Scientific Communication in History*, The Scarecrow Press, Lanham, Maryland.

WEAK PHYSICALISM AND SPECIAL SCIENCE ONTOLOGY

JAMES LADYMAN
University of Bristol

> "While still at school our children get taught that water *consists* of the gases [sic] hydrogen and oxygen, or sugar of carbon, hydrogen and oxygen. Anyone who doesn't understand is stupid. The most important questions are concealed." Ludwig Wittgenstein, *Culture and Value*, p.71

> "In science there is only physics; all the rest is stamp collecting." Ernest Rutherford

1 INTRODUCTION: THE CONFLICTING IMAGES OF COMMON SENSE, THE SPECIAL SCIENCES AND PHYSICS

Arthur Eddington (1928, pp.ix–x) famously cast the problem of the relationship between the manifest image and the scientific image in terms of the two tables of common sense and of science respectively. They have seemingly incompatible properties and so it is natural to wonder whether both really exist. Prima facie the two images conflict. There are two broad strategies that we can take in response.

(1) The images really are in conflict so we must abandon one of them:
eliminativism about the manifest image; or,
eliminativism about the scientific image.

(2) The images are not really in conflict so we can retain them both:
reductionism about the manifest image; or,
non-reductive physicalism according to which the scientific image is ontologically primary but the entities of the manifest image supervene on the entities of the scientific image.

Even if one was happy to abandon the manifest image because it is anthropomorphic and the product of the peculiarities of our perception, Eddington's problem generalizes because the special sciences each have their own distinctive ontologies:

> *Fundamental physics*: particles, fields, spacetime, strings,…
> *Physics as a special science*: phonons, forces, quasicrystals,…
> *Chemistry*: molecules, ions, chemical bonds,…
> *Biochemistry*: lipids, proteins, nucleic acids,…
> *Biology*: cells, genes, species,…
> *Ecology*: producers, consumers, decomposers,…
> *Psychology*: minds, beliefs, desires,…
> *Sociology*: groups, structures, classes,…
> *Economics*: money, markets, economies,…
> *Geology*: plates, faults, intrusions,…
> *Astronomy*: planetary nebulae, main sequence stars, galactic clusters,…
> *Cosmology*: the universe(s), M-branes, dark energy,…

Some metaphysicians dispute the reality of many of these entities. They think about objecthood in terms of the issue of which mereological sums of simples are bona fide wholes. There are three common positions.

> *Nihilism*: there are only simples.
> *Unrestricted composition*: all sums of simples are genuine objects.
> *Restricted composition*: only some sums of simples are genuine objects.

All these are blind to the way science comes to posit new ontological commitments, and to scientific accounts of the how higher level ontology arises dynamically out of lower level stuff. Even if there are simples, it is clear that the way parts combine to form wholes is in general different for the entities of the different sciences. Stars do not combine to form galaxies in the same way that cells combine to form multicellular organisms. There is no reason to suppose that there is a single composition relation in the different sciences. The above are also all synchronic conceptions of composition. In science, it is the interaction of parts over time that forms higher level entities. Furthermore, in science there is in general no interesting cause versus constitution distinction, rather in most cases to say how the parts causally interact is to say how the whole is constituted by them. Naturalists should take these facts at face value and reject the conception of object, part and whole in analytic metaphysics. Science should determine our ontology and philosophy should look outwards when considering the relationship between the objects of physics and those of the rest of science (and manifest objects).

Jonathan Lowe says:

> ... [R]eality is one and truth indivisible. Each special science aims at truth, seeking to portray accurately some part of reality. But the various portrayals of different parts of reality must, if they are all to be true, fit together to make a portrait which can be true of reality as a whole. No special science can arrogate to itself the task of rendering mutually consistent the various partial portraits: that task can alone belong to an overarching science of being, that is to ontology. (2006, p.4)

If we naturalize this conception of the distinctive task of metaphysics then we get something close to what Wilfrid Sellars said the philosopher's aim should be, namely "knowing one's way around with respect to the subject matters of all the special [scientific] disciplines" and "building bridges" between them (1962, p.35).

2 PHYSICALISM

But naturalized metaphysics still faces the problem of the apparent conflict between the images of the special sciences and physics. Physicalism is commonly a commitment of naturalists. Physicalism is the heir of materialism. However, ironically materialism was killed by science, in particular by physics. Materialism has positive and negative components. The former is the ontological commitment to matter, the latter is the denial of the existence of mental or spiritual substance. The latter is retained in physicalism. There are various kinds of Physicalism:

Ontological imperialism: everything is physical
Causal closure: the physical world is causally closed – all physical events are determined or have their chances determined by physical causes.
Causal exclusion: the only genuine causes are physical causes.[1]

Ontological Imperialism is expressed by Philip Pettit when he says the world "contains just what a true complete physics would say it contains" (1993, p.213). This kind of physicalism conflicts with naturalism (if current physics is supposed to be a reasonable guide to true complete physics). This claim is not warranted by taking science as a whole seriously.

All forms of physicalism face Hempel's Dilemma: however physicalism is defined some content must be given to the term 'physical'; then physicalism will be either trivially true, if 'physical' is taken to refer to the content of idealized future physics, or false if 'physical' is taken to refer to the content of our best current physics.[2]

2.1 The Completeness of Fundamental Physics

Ladyman and Ross (2007) offer a new characterization of fundamental physics as the only science such that measurements at all scales and at all locations in spacetime are potential falsifications or confirmations of it. However, fundamental physics may not exist other than as a limiting ideal (if there is no fundamental level). (Many parts of physics are special sciences.) Fundamental physics aspires to a kind of completeness in so far as it is never permitted to invoke entities or processes from the special sciences in an explanation of the behaviour of the fundamentally physical. Physics is therefore analytically complete in so far as it is the only science that by its nature cannot be left incomplete. On the other hand, the incompleteness of the special sciences is a trivial fact about them. In all the special sciences it is acceptable to invoke entities and processes from more fundamental sciences in explanations. For example, the economy may be affected by the weather, living systems may be affected by radiation, chemical reactions may be affected by magnetic fields, and so on. Hence,

---

[1] In his paper Jerry Fodor characterized physicalism as the view that 'only matter has causal powers'.

[2] Brown and Ladyman (2009) offer a way out of Hempel's Dilemma and give references to the recent literature on characterizing physicalism.

there is a fundamental asymmetry between physics and the special sciences.

2.2 The Primacy of Physics Constraint (PPC)

Naturalists ought only to accept a form of physicalism that is motivated by reflection on the history of science and the nature and practice of contemporary science. Ladyman and Ross argue that this justifies nothing more than the PPC (a methodological form of physicalism):

> "Special science hypotheses that conflict with fundamental physics, or such consensus as there is in fundamental physics, should be rejected for that reason alone. Fundamental physical hypotheses are not symmetrically hostage to the conclusions of the special sciences." (2007, p.44)

This leaves it open to the naturalist to believe both that the entities posited by the special sciences exist, and that the causal relations posited by them are genuine.

2.3 Causation and Physics

The asymmetry in the PPC may be expressed by the claim that the physical world is causally closed, i.e. that all genuine causes of physical events are physical causes. But now, if special science entities are not reducible to physical entities, then this form of physicalism also conflicts with naturalism since the special sciences prima facie describe all manner of causal relations between special science entities and physical events. Furthermore, if one takes causal efficacy as a necessary condition for something to be counted as real (the Eleatic principle/Alexander's Dictum); then eliminativism about the ontologies of the special sciences follows.

3 THE CAUSAL EXCLUSION ARGUMENT

3.1 Causal Exclusion and Mental Causation

Jaegwon Kim's (1998, 2005) uses the following argument as a reductio of non-reductive physicalism about the mind:

> Mental states are not reducible to (identical with) physical states.
> Mental states are realised by physical states and supervene on them.
> Effects are not generally overdetermined by causes.
> The physical world is causally closed (there is some set of physical causes that are sufficient for any physical event (or at least sufficient to fix its objective chance).
> Mental states can cause other mental states and physical states.

The last premise contradicts the rest of the premises. Since Kim thinks that we must hold on to the reality of mental causation, and since the second premise is weaker than the first and the third and fourth premises are supposed to be independently plausible, Kim therefore concludes that we should deny the first premise and accept that mental states are reducible to physical states. It follows that mental causal relations are real just because they are reducible without residue to physical causal relations.

3.2 The Causal Exclusion Argument Generalised to Causes in the Special Sciences

Many critics (Baker 1993, Bontly 2002, Burge 1993, Fodor 1991) have argued that Kim's argument generalises to one with the conclusion there is no macrocausation at all. This is then regarded, for example by Block (2003), as showing that the original causal exclusion argument is unsound, if it is taken for granted that there is macrocausation and that interesting causal relations are described by the various special sciences. However, Kim agrees that there is mental and other forms of causation, he just thinks that reductionism must also be true. These critics do not diagnose where the argument goes wrong.

3.3 The Nature of Causation and the Causal Exclusion Problem

Kim thinks of causation as a physical phenomenon (2005, p.55, note 22). He defends a conception of causation as essentially connected with the spatial distribution of physical objects. It is not clear whether this notion of causation can survive the transition to a conception of the fundamental nature of the world that dispenses with spatiality as we know it and also with time as standardly construed as absolute. Many philosophers of science, following Russell (1913), deny that there is any causation in fundamental physics (c.f. Price and Corry (2007) and especially Norton (2007)). Whether or not they are right about this it is clear that causal exclusion is simply not an issue for a Humean view of causation. Whether causal relations are construed in terms of counterfactuals and then reduced to Humean facts about relations between possible worlds, whether concrete or abstract, or thought of as at best secondary qualities, there is no reason to think that underdetermination is problematic. Kim's arguments need only concern those who adopt a theory of generative or productive causation, or some kind of non-Humean approach.

4 WEAK PHYSICALISM AND SPECIAL SCIENCE ONTOLOGY

4.1 Weak Physicalism

If it cannot be assumed that there is causation in fundamental physics then physicalism cannot be defined in terms of the causal completeness of physics. Here is a characterization of a weak form of physicalism that makes no reference to causation:

- Global supervenience (asymmetric)
- The PPC
- Ideal physics is analytically complete in its own domain but no other special science is.
- Theoretical reductions may or may not exist in particular cases, but do not exist in general.
- In general, no collection of fundamental objects is identical with the objects of the special sciences (such as the futures market in oil or the taxa *Felis silvestris catus*).

Of course, philosophers who worry about what they call 'fundamental ontology' are inclined to deny the existence of taxa and markets, but then many of them deny the existence of tables too, or hold that tables only exist because every arbitrary sum of fundamental objects exists. According to the proposed weak physicalism high level entities are not even token identical with aggregates of lower-level ones pace mereological accounts of composition. (Hence, the problem of the many is a pseudo-problem.) This is explained in the next section.

Here is a hypothesis that adds a further defeasible and a posteriori methodological component to the weak analytic completeness of physics above and the PPC: no new entities or processes will ever be introduced into fundamental physics solely to account for mental phenomena, and fundamental physics will never posit entities that have mental, intentional or spiritual properties. The history of science to date, in particular the failure of research programmes that posited vital forces and spiritual fluids and substances, supports this hypothesis.

Note that weak physicalism is compatible with there being no fundamental level, and note also that Kim thinks that the causal exclusion argument only works if the level of genuine causation is closed and complete (1998). The causal exclusion argument begins to seem less compelling once the token identity of higher level objects with collections of fundamental physical ones is denied.

4.2 Fundamental Physics and Special Science Objects

Hawthorne (forthcoming) distinguishes between two views of the relationship between the objects of fundamental physics and those of the special sciences. A conservative one involves the identification of the macro or manifest objects with fundamental objects or aggregates of them, while a liberal one posits additional objects that 'float over the fundamental layer'. However, this is a false dichotomy. A third position asserts that the macro or manifest objects are patterns in the structure of the fundamental objects that are neither free floating nor identical with those objects (Wallace 2003). A fourth position adds that there is no fundamental layer at all, and that the allegedly fundamental objects are themselves patterns in the structure of some deeper level of reality (Ladyman and Ross, 2007). (A fifth position is agnostic about whether there is a fundamental level.)

Note that in science one is only interested in recovering the statistical properties of low-level entities when tracking high level ones: for example, information about exact microstates is not relevant in thermodynamics. It is plausible to generalize and suppose that coarse-graining and approximation are necessary for all or almost all special science ontologies to emerge from fundamental physics. This explains why even token identities do not obtain between say a cat and its constituent atoms. A cat is coarse-grained with respect to atomic theory; it is not that there are many possible exact collections of atoms that might be identical with a given cat, it is rather that no exact collection of atoms could be identical with the cat because no such collection has the right properties, since all the properties are defined at the higher level and are themselves coarse-grained with respect to lower level properties. In the special sciences one is usually interested in 'universal' forms of behaviour, where 'universal' means independent of microphysical or lower level constitution. The identification of universality and the appropriate descriptive categories for tracking it is one of the principle tasks of the special sciences.

This leads to what Ladyman and Ross (2007) call 'the scale relativity of ontology', namely the thesis that the existence of special science (and everyday) objects is relative to particular time and length scales (and relatedly to energy scales in particle physics). Tables and cats do not exist at very short or very long time or length scales. This idea is similar to what Sokal and Bricmont call the 'renormalization group view of the world' (Sokal 2008): the renormalization group describes transformations that allow the number of degrees of freedom in the Hamiltonian of a system to be massively reduced while still recovering the critical behaviour of the system. On the other hand, fundamental physics alone aspires to a scale-free ontology but it may never get there.

The special sciences are possible because the world is to some extent algorithmically compressible. At certain levels of description it is possible to use much less information to predict the behaviour of systems described in an approximate and probabilistic way, than would be needed to describe their microstates; for example, Kepler's laws, the ideal gas laws, the Hardy-Weinberg law, and so on. In fact almost all laws in the special sciences are like this. The special sciences rely upon reduction in the degrees of freedom of the system. There are real patterns in the world that are only visible at the right scales of resolution and degrees of approximation. If you don't see them you are missing something about reality and that is good enough to allow us to say that the objects, properties and processes described by the special sciences are real.

Many philosophers will think that the above may all be taken as an account of the epistemological short-cuts that are necessary in describing the world, but that only the fundamental ontology is real and that all the higher level stuff is just necessary for pragmatic reasons. Of course, if there is no fundamental level then on such a view nothing is real except perhaps the whole universe. Either way, such a view leaves unanswered all the interesting questions about the relationship between the ontologies of fundamental physics and the special sciences. Supposing there is a fundamental level that will one day be described by fundamental physics, it remains to be decided whether epistemological irreducibility and indispensability is sufficient for genuine ontological commitment. The best answer to this question is to ask how else we are to mark the distinction between spurious ontological commitments of special sciences and genuine ones other than by assenting to the existence of the latter and not the former. This will not persuade those who think there is a special metaphysical sense of 'exists'.

It can also be questioned whether high-level properties are determined by low-level ones. It is not obvious that global supervenience entails this. Consider Laplace's demon: it is usually said that the demon would know everything about the future but is this correct? Of course the demon would know everything about the positions of all the particles but does it follow that it would know what you had for breakfast? Not if there is no type-type identity. What if high level objects and properties are only apparent if one makes exactly the right approximations and coarse-grainings?

Metaphysicians often operate with what Ladyman and Ross (2007) call 'domesticated physics' and deploy in their metaphysical theorizing what Lakoff and Johnson (1980), 'the containment metaphor': The world is supposed to be 'made of' myriad 'little things' in roughly the way that (some) walls are made of bricks. Unlike bricks in walls, however, the little things are in motion, and the paradigm of causation is the little things hitting each other. Hence, the causal structure of the world imagined by the domesticating metaphysicians is a network of 'microbangings'. The preoccupation with the search for 'genuine causal oomph' or 'biff' to settle the competition between different levels of reality derives from this conception of causation and microbanging. This is profoundly unscientific and does not fit with contemporary physics.

Note however, that if there are no causal powers in fundamental physics this does not imply that there are none in the special sciences. Harold Kincaid (2004) describes how the special sciences seek laws and theories of causal processes particular to their domains. Russell presupposes a conception of causation as "invariable uniformities of sequence" (1913, p.178), and he is right that causation in this sense is not a feature of the scientific image of the world. However, the distinction between Humeanism and a notion of productive or generative causation that is based on an outdated model of the physical world is not exhaustive.

4.4 Functionalism about all Ontology

The above discussion motivates consideration of an information theoretic approach to ontology according to which 'to be is to be a real pattern' in the sense of a compressible set of data according to the relevant level of description (c.f. Dennett (1991)). This is a deflationary approach to ontology and a form of ontic structural realism (Ladyman (1998)).

4.5 Causation in the Special Sciences

Robin Hendry and Paul Needham argue that "[i]f molecules are ontologically reducible to their physical bases, then they ought to have no causal powers other than those conferred by those physical bases." (assuming causal completeness of physics) (2007, p.342). The argue that the acidic behaviour of HCl is due to its asymmetric shape and this shape is not conferred by its physical basis. However, we must ask what 'conferred by' means here. The shape of the molecule is surely supervenient on the physical because one cannot countenance two molecules with different shapes without there being a difference in the state of underlying physical entities. On the other hand, it is true that the shape is causally important and that the shape is not attributable to anything other than the whole molecule. There is an analogy with plural reference. Consider the sentence: 'the army surrounded the castle'; it is not possible to reduce this sentence to a claim about individual soldiers. Each one is only doing what they do because the others are there too. Similarly with a baseball breaking a window. This is not the aggregate of causal relations between minimal parts of the ball and minimal parts of the window. None of the minimal parts in each case is causally necessary for the effect. Each could be doing something slightly different and it wouldn't matter.

Causation in the special sciences is a relation between entities that are coarse-grained with respect to fundamental physics. Only probabilistic/

statistical facts about the underlying realms must be correctly described at the higher level. Difference making only obtains with respect to individual properties and objects at the coarse-grained level. After all, there are many changes to microproperties in the backwards lightcone of an event as described by a special science, for example, the erosion of a river valley, that make no difference to whether or not it occurs.

The general point made by Hendry and Needham is well taken: since there is (probably) no causation in fundamental physics and there is causation in the special sciences then all causal powers are likely to be emergent. This is even more clear when we are talking about population level causal claims in biology. However, since the fundamental physical level (if it exists) is either causally closed or nomologically complete, any instance of downwards causation is an instance of overdetermination and therefore harmless to physicalism.

5 CONCLUSION

The problem of emergent objects and properties and higher level causation is based on two misconceptions:

- There is a fundamental physical level of substantial objects with intrinsic properties.
- There is causal power at this level.

Rather the situation is this: ontology as pattern obtains all the way down and there is probably no causation at or below the level of current fundamental physics. There may be no fundamental level at all, and even if there is it will not consist of a set of simples. Hence, the causal relations tracked by the special sciences and common sense, and the ontologies that they relate are fully ontologically respectable. Sometimes at least: 'philosophy leaves everything as it is'.

REFERENCES

Baker, L.R.(1993), "Metaphysics and Mental Causation", in John Heil and Alfred Mele (eds.), *Mental Causation*. Oxford: Clarendon Press, pp.75–95.
Block, N. (2003), "Do Causal Powers Drain Away?", *Philosophy and Phenomenological Research* 67: pp.133–150.

Bontly, T. (2002), "The supervenience argument generalizes", *Philosophical Studies* 109: pp.75–96.

Brown, R. and Ladyman, J. (2009), 'Physicalism and the Fundamental Level', *The Philosophical Quarterly*, 59: pp.20–38.

Burge, T. (1993), "Mind-Body Causation and Explanatory Practice", in J. Heil and A. Mele (eds), *Mental Causation*. Oxford: Clarendon Press, pp.97–120.

Dennett, D. (1991), "Real Patterns", *Journal of Philosophy* 88: pp.27–51.

Eddington, A. (1928). *The Nature of the Physical World*. Cambridge: Cambridge University Press.

Fodor, J. (1991), "Making Mind Matter More", in *A Theory of Content and Other Essays*. Cambridge, MA: MIT Press, pp.137–159.

Hawthorne, J. (forthcoming), "A Metaphysician Looks at the Everett Interpretation", to appear in S. Saunders, J. Barrett, A. Kent and D. Wallace (eds), *Everett at the Crossroads: the Many-Worlds Interpretation of Quantum Mechanics* Oxford: Oxford University Press.

Hendry, R. and Needham, P. (2007), "Le Poidevin on the Reduction of Chemistry", *The British Journal for the Philosophy of Science*, 58: pp.339–353.

Kim, J. (1998), *Mind in a Physical World*. Cambridge, MA: MIT Press.

Kim, J. (2005), *Physicalism or Something Near Enough*. Princeton: Princeton University Press.

Kincaid, H. (2004), "There are Laws in the Social Sciences", in C. Hitchcock, ed., *Contemporary Debates in Philosophy of Science*. pp.168–185. Oxford: Blackwell.

Ladyman, J. (1998). What is Structural Realism? *Studies in History and Philosophy of Science* 29: pp.409–424.

Ladyman, J., and Ross, D. (2007), *Every Thing Must Go: Metaphysics Naturalised*. Oxford: Oxford University Press.

Lakoff, G. and Johnson, M. (1980), *Metaphors We Live By*. Chicago: University of Chicago Press.

Lowe, E.J. (2006). The Four-Category Ontology: A Metaphysical Foundation for Natural Science. Oxford: Oxford University Press.

Merricks, T (2001), *Objects and Persons*. Oxford: Oxford University Press.

Norton, J. (2007), "Causation as Folk Science", in Price and Corry (eds.) (2007), pp.11–44.

Pettit, P. (1993). "A Definition of Physicalism", *Analysis* 53: pp.213–223.

Price, H. and Corry, R. (eds) (2007), *Causation, Physics and the Constitution of Reality*. Oxford: Oxford University Press.

Russell, B. (1913 [1917]), "On the Notion of Cause", in B. Russell, *Mysticism and Logic*, pp.173–199. London: Unwin.

Sellars, W. (1962). "Philosophy and the Scientific Image of Man". in R. Colodny ed., *Frontiers of Science and Philosophy*, pp.35–78, Pittsburgh: University of Pittsburgh Press.

Sokal, A. (2008). *Beyond the Hoax: Science, Philosophy and Culture*, Oxford: Oxford University Press.

Wallace, D. (2003a). "Everett and Structure". *Studies in History and Philosophy of Modern Physics* 34: pp.87–105.

ARE NATURAL KINDS REDUCIBLE?

ALEXANDER BIRD
University of Bristol

1

We talk as if there are natural kinds and in particular we quantify over them. We can count the number of elements discovered by Sir Humphrey Davy, or the number of kinds of particle in the standard model. Consequently, it looks at first sight at least, that natural kinds are entities of a sort. In the light of this we may ask certain questions: is the apparent existence of natural kinds real or an illusion? And if real, what sort of entity are natural kinds? Are they *sui generis*? Or can they be identified with or reduced to some other kind of entity? In this essay I shall look at possible reasons for asserting that either kinds are no sort of entity, or, if they are entities, their existence is equivalent to some fact not involving kinds.

Richard Boyd seems to take the view that the apparent existence of natural kinds is an illusion.

> [W]hat is misleading about formulations in terms of the "reality" or "unreality" of kinds, or of the "realism" or "antirealism" about them, is that they wrongly suggest that the issue is one regarding the metaphysical status of the families consisting of the members of the kinds in question – considered by themselves – rather than one regarding the contributions that reference to them may make to accommodation. Issues about "reality" or "realism about" are always issues about accommodation. (Boyd 1999: p.159)

What Boyd means by 'accommodation' is the ability of our theories to support effective inductive inferences. So when we say that a certain natural kind is real, we are not engaging in ontology, discussing the existence of some entity. Instead we are declaring that the use of the natural kind term in our theories is conducive to the inductive power of those theories.

Boyd's statement is perhaps ambiguous on this point, since he talks of 'the contributions that reference to them may make'. If natural kinds can be referred to, then they exist. That suggests a second interpretation of Boyd's comment: that while natural kinds exist, their existence amounts to precisely the fact that the use of natural kinds terms in our theories is inductively fruitful.

The first interpretation itself may subdivide into two views. The first says that the apparent talk of natural kinds is syntactically misleading. The true logical form of statements containing natural kind terms is not one in which those terms appear as singular terms. The second view concedes that the apparent syntactic form is the true syntactic form, but maintains that this is misleading in so far as the propositions thereby asserted are nonetheless false. That is, we do indeed use singular terms that would refer to entities that are natural kinds, but these terms do not in fact refer (they are empty singular terms), because the entities in question do not exist. Thus we may distinguish three views:

(I) In so far as statements appear to employ natural kind terms as singular terms, those statements are syntactically misleading. The true logical form of those statements is such that they contain no purported referring kind terms.

(II) Statements employing apparently referring natural kind terms are not syntactically misleading, since that is indeed the syntactic function of those terms. But the statements are semantically misleading in the sense that we use them as if they were true, whereas they are in fact false. That is because such terms are empty – there are no entities that are natural kinds to which they can refer.

(III) Natural kind terms are (sometimes) successfully referring terms. So natural kinds do genuinely exist. But the existence of the kinds is in some sense nothing more than the fact that employing the terms in our theories is conductive to inductive success.

While I suspect that Boyd intends (I) with his assertion, there remains a question as to which of these views, if any, is correct.

2

If we adopt view (I), then we are under some obligation to suggest what the true logical form of a statement containing a natural kind term is. Consider a standard kind of statement about a chemical element, such as:

(S) Mercury is a chemical element, with atomic number 80, and is among the transition elements; it has a melting point of 234K, a boiling point of 623K, and a density of 13.5 g.cm^{-3}.

How should we eliminate the use of the apparently singular, referring term, 'mercury'? A natural alternative to suggest is that statements such as (S) are disguised universal quantifications. Instead of a natural kind referring expression we have a natural kind predicate, so that in general, statements of the (apparent) form:

(S0) $\Phi(K)$

should be given reducing equivalents of the form:

(R0) $\forall x(Kx \rightarrow \Phi x)$.

Let us call the claim under consideration, that every statement of the form (S0) has an equivalent of the form (R0), the 'reducibility claim'. Thus, according to the reducibility claim, the statement:

(S1) Mercury boils at 623K,

which is a component of (S), receives the reduction:

(R1) $\forall x(x$ is a sample of mercury $\rightarrow x$ boils at 623K).[1]

It is worth mentioning, however, that there are technical reasons why (RI) cannot be equivalent to (S1). One is the phenomenon of superheating. Superheating, which is not uncommon with water heated in a microwave, occurs when a sample of a liquid is heated above the boiling point for that substance. Now this might be thought to be merely a technical quibble. Perhaps the 'correct' replacement for (R1) is something like:

(R1') $\forall x(x$ is a sample of mercury $\rightarrow$ (x is in a container with sufficient nucleation sites and at a pressure of 1 bar $\rightarrow x$ boils at 630K)).

The additional detail that (R1') contains, consists of additional facts that can be known only from a knowledge of the physics of boiling. Consequently the transition from (S1) to (R1') cannot be a purely syntactic trans-

---

[1] One might wonder whether it is strictly true that 'mercury has a boiling of point of 623K' and 'mercury boils at 623K' mean exactly the same. If not, the reductive account here under consideration is in even more difficulty.

formation. Thus, not only is the reducibility claim strictly false, it does not appear as if any other general description of an appropriate syntactic reformulation is viable.

Even if we can give (S1) a fairly obvious reductive equivalent, it is less clear that the same is true for:

(S2) Mercury is a transition element.

This statement refers to the position of mercury within the periodic table of elements. One plausible way of understanding (S2) is as asserting of one kind, mercury, that it belongs to a higher-order kind, the transition elements. The higher-order kind is a kind whose instances are themselves kinds. A higher-order kind is thus a different sort of thing from just a more inclusive kind.[2] According to the reducibility claim, the reducing equivalent to (S2) is:

(R2) $\forall x(x$ is a sample of mercury $\rightarrow x$ is a transition element).

But that is clearly false, since samples of stuff do not have positions in the periodic table. The transition elements are also known as the 'd-block elements', because they are those elements whose atoms have an incomplete d sub-shell. So instead of (R2) one might try:

(R2') $\forall x(x$ is an atom of mercury $\rightarrow x$ has an incomplete d sub-shell).

But the proposal that (R2') is the correct reduction for (S2) is open to two objections. First, the content of (R2') cannot be analytically equivalent to (S2) since it is an a posteriori discovery that the transition elements are those whose atoms have an in- complete d sub-shell. Secondly, the form of (R2') shows a significant deviation from (R0), because the quantification in (R0) is over samples of the kind, where as the quantification in (R2') is over atoms of the kind. Thus the reducibility claim fails if it is considered as a general recipe for reduction. This objection and that of the preceding

---

[2] A set theoretic analogy is the distinction between set A having set B as a member, $B \in A$, and set A being a superset of B, $B \subset A$. However, a more appropriate analogy might be with the theory of types, in which case the claim that (S0), when Φ is a higher-order kind predicate, always has an equivalent (R0), finds its analogue in the much-reviled axiom of reducibility.

paragraph suggest that we are unable to find reductions that are systematic, and that one reason for this is the fact that the best reductions require the auxiliary use of a posteriori knowledge specific to the nature of the predicate 'Φ'.

Even if we accept that the reductions provided by (R1') and (R2') are individually unproblematic, a further worry arises from the fact we need a form of reduction that will work simultaneously for supposedly different uses of the kind term. We have seen that the reductions of (S1) and (S2) have different forms, one involving quantification over samples, and the other over atoms. Now let us return to (S). After the semi-colon we have assertions about mercury whose reductions must be in terms of samples of mercury, whereas before the semi-colon we have assertions which can only be reduced to assertions about atoms of mercury. The semi-colon itself must be understood as a conjunction, as is shown by the anaphoric 'it', immediately following the semi-colon. 'Mercury is a transition element with a boiling point of 623K' is perfectly well-formed.[3] But there is no way of providing a reduction for this sentence, since there is no domain of quantification that it suitable for both predicates simultaneously.

It must be concluded, therefore, that (I) in Section 1 is not a viable option. Which is to say that we must understand natural kind terms as syntactically genuine referring terms. That conclusion is consistent with their in fact failing to refer. And so the next option to consider is that natural kind terms are empty singular terms.

3

There are natural kind terms that are, we can all agree, empty: 'phlogiston', 'caloric', 'celestial sphere', 'quintessence', 'N-ray'. Option (II) proposes that all natural kind terms are like these. However, the reason why we are convinced that the terms mentioned fail to refer is that the scientific theories hypothesizing the existence of the kinds have been shown to be false. That clearly does not apply across the board. The philosophy of mathematics provides an analogy: we have specific reasons for thinking that certain mathematical singular terms fail to refer, e.g. 'the largest prime number'.

---

[3] If in doubt consider the following statement: 'With a boiling point of 623K and low vapour pressure, mercury is a vapour at a lower temperature than any other d-block element, and as such is a suitable substance for the principal component of flourescent lamps.'

Usually, as in this case, the reason is a proof that the corresponding entity cannot exist. But we may also have general reasons for thinking that none of our mathematical terms refer: e.g. metaphysical arguments that mathematical entities could not exist, or that if they do exist, we cannot succeed in referring to them (for example, because we cannot interact with them causally).

Are there any arguments parallel to the mathematical ones, for thinking that singular natural kind terms must fail to refer? Here the burden is on those who wish to make such an argument. The obvious analogues to the mathematical parallel do not furnish such reasons. For example, while it may be true that mathematical entities, if they exist, are causally inert, the same, it would appear, is not true for natural kinds. And in many cases at least, ostensive definition of a kind term is paradigmatic of reference fixing through causal interaction.

However, matters may not be so clear. What are natural kinds? Are they particulars, or universals, sets, *sui generis* entities? Until we can answer questions of this sort, we are not in a position to be confident either way as regards our ability to interact with kinds causally or to refer to them. If we hold, as Quine (1969) did, that kinds are the sets of their members, then they are abstract entities of a sort similar to mathematical ones. They may then face the same disabilities as such entities when it comes to causal interaction and reference (though we may also note Penelope Maddy's (1990) argument that impure sets can be causal in virtue of the causal efficacy of their members). If kinds are universals, then we are in the arena of the debate between realists and nominalists, given that one argument of the nominalists is that universals are beyond cause and reference. It would be unproductive to pursue this issue further in the absence of further research on the nature of natural kinds. While there has been much consideration of whether there are natural classifications of the world, little has been written on the topic of what, if anything, natural kinds *are*. (The exception to this being the debate over whether species are individuals or kinds.)

Thus the position for kinds is different from that for mathematical entities. In the case of the latter, we can be reasonably confident that if they exist at all, they are abstract objects. The issues concerning the (im)possibility of reference to such objects arises immediately. In the case of kinds, matters are different; we do not know what such entities would be, and so we do not know whether parallel concerns arise or not. However, when we consider various proposals for the nature of natural kinds, we will be able to see whether such a proposal does raise such worries (as does the proposal that kinds are sets). Consequently one of the considerations in play when assessing any such proposal will be whether or not it leads to problems of this sort. That it does so would count against the proposal. It would be premature, therefore, to predict that our best theory of natural kinds must imply that kind terms all fail to refer. On the contrary, there is a good chance that our best theory will not have that implication, simply because not having that implication will be one criterion of being a good theory. As a result, I think we are under no current obligation to regard attempts to refer to natural kinds as failing systematically.

4

The final option we must consider, (III), is that while natural kind terms do refer, their success in so doing is in some sense a reflection of facts in which natural kinds take no part. Again we may turn to a mathematical analogue. According to the neo-Fregean (neo-logicist) position promoted by Wright (1983) and Hale (1987), statements about the identity of numbers are equivalent to statements about the equinumerosity of concepts, encapsulated in Hume's principle:

> (N) the number of Fs = the number of Gs iff the Fs and the Gs may be put into 1-1 correlation.

Hume's principle does not provide a means of eliminating use of numerical referring expressions, although it does allow us to prove Peano's postulates, with the consequence that the theorems of Peano arithmetic are deducible from second order logic plus (N). Since the numerical expressions cannot be eliminated, (N) does not strictly provide for any kind of reduction – it is more a matter of deflating the commitment to kinds. It would thus be wrong to think of (N) as implying that 'the number of Fs = the number of Gs' is a notational variant on 'the Fs and the Gs may be put into 1-1 correlation'. As a result we must regard 'the number of Fs' as a genuine referring expression, and 'the number of Fs = the number of Gs' as a genuine identity claim. The truth of (N) guarantees that some such identity claims are true and so that some numerical referring expressions succeed in referring.

Could we employ a similar approach for natural kinds? Just as facts about the identity of numbers reflect or are shadows of (but are not identical to) facts about equinumerosity, facts about natural kinds would reflect facts concerning some equivalence relation on instances of a kind. For example, some kind of similarity relation might ground identity of natural kinds. Putnam's (1973: pp.702–703) discussion of water suggests something along those lines:

(K) The kind to which **a** belongs = the kind to which **b** belongs iff **a** and **b** are related by a same-kind relation.[4]

The 'same-kind' relation must be one that is not equivalent to 'belongs to the same kind as', for then (K) would be uninformatively tautologous. The problem is to find something that will fill this role. It is a problem for two reasons. First, it is unclear that any relation will do for all natural kinds. For chemical kinds one might think that sameness of micro-constitution will do. But this will not work for biological kinds. Secondly, if kinds are defined by this same-kind relation, that would imply that there is at most only one kind to which any individual can belong, whereas there can be nested kinds, and even cross-cutting ones.

One response to such problems is to regard (K) as providing a schema for more specific abstraction principles. So:

(C) The chemical compound of which **a** is an instance = the chemical compound of which **b** is an instance iff **a** and **b** share the same molecular structure,

and:

(B) The species to which **a** belongs = the species to which **b** belongs iff **a** and **b** are both members of the same breeding population,

might be first passes at abstraction principles in chemistry and biology. Furthermore, different equivalence relations from the same science may define different kinds, allowing for one item to be a member of several different kinds.

---

[4] Putnam says 'same liquid' but that clearly will not do, since a phase difference does not imply a kind difference.

The last suggestion does raise a possible problem in the opposite direction, that we might have too many kinds. Does any equivalence relation on natural objects define a natural kind? Presumably not; this is the analogue to Alan Weir's (2003) 'embarrassment of riches' problem for neo-Fregeanism. To avoid this problem scheme (K) must be supplemented by a principle which states which equivalence relations may legitimately be substituted for the 'same-kind relation' of (K). As the quotation from Boyd suggests, we want the use of our kind terms to reflect and underwrite our inductive and explanatory practices. So the appropriate principle is one that restricts the substitutable relations to those that will give inductive and explanatory power to kinds. (C) is legitimate, for example, because molecular structure is inductively and explanatorily powerful in chemistry. There will be natural similarities between objects, such as colour, which will support some inductions, but not enough to base a natural kind. Thus the concept of natural kind captured by (K) will be vague.

5

We have considered three ways in which natural kinds might, in some sense, be reduced. The first suggested that statements containing singular natural kind terms are syntactically misleading and that such statements are equivalent to statements not containing such terms. Such a suggestion fails, since their is no systematic way of eliminating the relevant terms for all statements, including complex ones in which several different predications are made with the same natural kind term in subject position. The second possibility was an elimination of natural kinds, considering all natural kind terms to be semantically empty. Such a view can be neither substantiated nor refuted without further investigation of what sort of entities natural kinds would be if they do exist. But as it stands, natural kinds do seem to be capable of being referred to and any account of their existence that denied this would be prima facie implausible. Finally we considered a neo-Fregean approach. This seems the most promising avenue. But it is also the least reductive. On this view, natural kinds do exist. It is reductive only in that there is a conceptual tie between facts about the identity of kinds and facts about equivalence relations among their instances. Furthermore, such a view is also consistent with a more robust view of what natural kind existence is. It is also consistent with natural kind essentialism. As such the neo-Fregean view offers only the weakest kind of support for a reductive view. That is, it is consistent with taking the view that kind identity is analytically equivalent to or in some sense constituted by the equivalence relation among kind-instances; in that sense it deflates the existence of kinds. Can we make sense of this in a way that will satisfy the reductionist impulse behind comments such as Boyd's? In the philosophy of mathematics the status of (N) in this regard is a matter of debate (see e.g. Boolos 1987, 1990; Wright 2001). Given the falsity of option (I) and the prima facie implausibility of (II), we have to regard the left hand sides of instances of (K) as successfully referring to entities that are kinds. But how then can the left hand sides be mere reflections of the contents of the right hand sides, in which no reference to kinds is made? On the other hand if the right hand sides have a hidden commitment to the existence of kinds, then although the left hand sides may be equivalent (making the commitment to kinds explicit), (K) cannot now be used to deflate the existence of kinds to mere reflection of inductive similarity among instances. In the light of this, it is uncertain even that the deflation of kinds via (K) is successful.

REFERENCES

Boolos, G. 1987. The Consistency of Frege's Foundations of Arithmetic. In J. Thomson (Ed.), *On Being and Saying: Essays in Honor of Richard Cartwright*, pp.3–20. Cambridge, MA: MIT Press.

Boolos, G. 1990. The Standard of Equality of Numbers. In G. Boolos (Ed.), *Meaning and Method: Essays in Honor of Hilary Putnam*, pp.261–277. Cambridge: Cambridge University Press.

Boyd, R. 1999. Homeostasis, Species, and Higher Taxa. In R.A. Wilson (Ed.), *Species: New Interdisciplinary Essays*, pp.141–185. Cambridge: MIT Press.

Hale, B. 1987. *Abstract Objects*. Oxford: Blackwell.

Maddy, P. 1990. *Realism in Mathematics*. Oxford: Oxford University Press.

Putnam, H. 1973. Meaning and Reference. *Journal of Philosophy* 70: pp.699–711.

Quine, W.V. 1969. Natural Kinds. In *Ontological Relativity and Other Essays*, pp.114–138. Columbia University Press.

Weir, A. 2003. Neo-Fregeanism: an Embarrassment of Riches. *Notre Dame Journal of Formal Logic* 44: pp.13–48.

Wright, C. 1983. *Frege's Conception of Numbers as Objects*. Aberdeen: Aberdeen University Press.

Wright, C. 2001. Is Hume's Principle Analytic? In B. Hale and C. Wright (Eds.), *The Reason's Proper Study*, pp.307–333. Oxford: Oxford University Press.

ONTIC GENERATION: GETTING EVERYTHING FROM THE BASICS

PETER SIMONS
Trinity College Dublin

1 NATURALISM WHAT

Properly executed, metaphysics consists in part of painstaking ontological detail and in part of grand systematic speculation. The distinction between these two aspects is not new: it is inspired by Wolff's distinction between *metaphysica generalis sive ontologia* and *metaphysica specialis*, Husserl's distinction between formal and regional ontology, and finally D.C. Williams's distinction between analytic ontology and speculative cosmology.[1] The detail concerns the basic kinds of entity and the ways in which they are discerned, analysed, fitted together and wielded in explanation. In this, analytic philosophy excels, but it cannot take place in a speculative vacuum. The speculation concerns hypotheses for which evidence is partial and inadequate to ground them without demur or risk. The classic metaphysical positions of Platonism, Aristotelianism, Cartesian dualism, Leibnizian monism, and Hegelian idealism all unabashedly adopt such metaphysical speculations. Analytic philosophers have tried generally to steer away from grand speculation because it got a bad name with Hegel and because it tends to undermine their self-sought credentials as "scientific". The upshot has been that their cosmological positions have been largely tacit or shamefaced: commonsense ordinary-language Moorean realism, Carnapian disavowal, Wittgensteinian quietism. But several significant twentieth century philosophers have been unafraid to speculate: Alexander, Whitehead, Quine and Lewis being examples. In my view it is part of a metaphysician's – nay any philosopher's – responsibility, to articulate the speculative hypothetical framework within which his or her detailed work takes its place.[2]

---

[1] This second terminological distinction comes from Williams 1953, p.3. It is no accident that Williams studied and was influenced by Husserl.

[2] When philosophers shrink from this responsibility, the vacuum is willingly filled by others.

I do not shrink from this responsibility, I welcome it. So here is my first grand speculative hypothesis: for better or worse, I call it *naturalism*. It consists in the view that nothing, no thing, that exists, is outwith the single spatio-temporal-causal framework within which we have our place and with which we uphold our everyday commerce. This separates into two partial hypotheses. *Energism* holds that everything is capable of playing a role in causation. *Localism* holds that all is spatiotemporal. The two go together if it is assumed, as I think is correct, that causation and spacetime are intrinsically interwoven. This being a framework hypothesis, I neither seek nor attempt here to defend it in detail. I think it can be defended, but that is a matter for elsewhere. Of course naturalism is neither new nor original, nor untested: presaged by Greeks including Epicurus, its archdefender was Hume. Its many prominent modern adherents include Armstrong, Bunge, Dawkins, and Dennett.

The primary evidence for naturalism comes from the ongoing success of the natural sciences. More and more phenomena prove themselves amenable to explanation through the natural sciences, from physics to geology to evolution to genetics to neuroscience. I regard this inductive and progressing success as a bald and uncontestable historical fact. Nevertheless I distinguish naturalism, as an ontological hypothesis about what there is, from physicalism, as a methodological or linguistic hypothesis about what kind of language is suitable to articulate our knowledge. Physicalism, as I understand it here, is the view that the apt vocabulary for adequately describing the world may be drawn exclusively from physics: if not today's physics, then a better or perhaps a completed physics. I regard physicalism in this sense as a cosmologically incompletable and hopeless position. Firstly, the vocabulary of physics is by design partial, intended to serve solely the science of physics, with its focus on basic forces and forms of energetic interaction, and not the manifold other disciplines of natural, biological, social, cultural and mathematical science, nor the myriad items and concerns of everyday life, from the price of bread or lack of confidence in the stock-market to trends in the performance of Baroque music. Secondly, although according to my version of naturalism everything is touched positively by the vocabulary and theory of physics, that does not mean everything true can be stated in terms of that vocabulary. This entails me taking a particular position with regard to physicalist reductionism, of which more below.

The consequences of adopting naturalism as a framework hypothesis are not anodyne: they are radical and far-reaching. If naturalism is correct, then a host of variously popular metaphysical positions are ruled out: these include Platonism, the view that there are abstract or ideal entities which are acausal and alocal; psychophysical dualism, according to which there are souls or states of consciousness which are not also inherently physical and spatial; and theism, according to which there is an eternal deity outside space and time but nevertheless affecting it. Briefly and provocatively, naturalism enjoins a "no magic" position, according to which there are no spooky entities having spooky relationships to ordinary real entities. Having thus alienated the sympathies of a good proportion of my readership, I press on undaunted.

2 ONTIC GROUNDING

The second speculative hypothesis concerns what I call ontic grounding. It consist in the belief that there are entities which are ontically basic, and that everything else that exists is ultimately a combination of ontically basic entities, according to basic modes of combination (which are therefore themselves also basic). This rules out an infinite descending sequence of ever more basic entities. As with naturalism, this hypothesis goes well beyond the evidence, and is upheld according to the principle of inference to the best explanation. Massive inductive evidence for it is supplied by the continuing success of the sciences in accounting for the behaviour of many things, from quarks to organisms to stars. Ontic grounding would be wrong if the world consisted of at least some things which consisted of different types of things which consisted of different types of things and so on ad infinitum down. So it's a speculative hypothesis but not unreasonable.

Between them, naturalism and ontic grounding provide reasons to be a certain kind of reductionist, but what kind of reductionism they support is something that will take me a little while to explain. In a sense what I am trying to do is to outline a general ontological framework within which everyday scientific reduction can be at home.

The two principal rivals to or enemies of monistic naturalism are various dualisms or other pluralisms on the one hand, and emergence on the other. But only certain kinds of emergence. I do not rule out explanatory, *epistemic* emergence. On the contrary, it is to be expected. Explanations at different levels of scale and granularity, for example neurophysiological and evolutionary-behavioural explanations of animal behaviour, will be different in kind, so we should not expect meso- and macroscopic phenomena to be described or explained solely in terms of the language describing their contitutive parts and their characteristic operations. The kind of emergence that naturalism cannot accept is *ontic* emergence, the appearance of radically new types of entity. Ontic emergence is its own kind of magic, dosed magic with preconditions, perhaps requiring supervenience, perhaps not, but magic nonetheless. Even so prominent and indeed notorious an emergentist as Samuel Alexander appears at one point to reject ontic emergence. Here is what Alexander says in a sub-section of *Space, Time and Deity* entitled "Identity of Mental with its Neural Process":

> Correlation is … an inadequate and misleading word to describe the relation of the mental to the corresponding neural process […] In truth, according to our conception, they are not two but one.[3]

This is in truth the very first Australian identity theory, though of course by the time he wrote *STD* Alexander had been in England for many years.

All the money in the rejection of ontic emergence is on what it means to be radically new, and that is where the notion of ontic generation comes in. So let's put a bit more detail into the various ideas of emergence.

3 EMERGENCE, VARIETIES OF [4]

An emergent entity E is one which is in some way "new" or "surprising" with respect to a (comprehensive)[5] basis of other entities B. Now 'surprising' is an epistemic category, so one way of thinking of emergence is with respect to our knowledge. An entity E is *epistemically* emergent with respect to a basis B if no knowledge of B and their principles of combination and operation is sufficient to explain or predict E. This can be further refined. If the knowledge with respect to which E is surprising is the knowledge we *actually* have, then this is *weak* epistemic emergence. It may turn

---

[3] Alexander 1920, p.5. Alexander is a slippery customer however: there are other passages where he does appear to accept metaphysically novel emergent properties. Small wonder that his stance on emergence remains controversial.

[4] Emergence is a vague and equivocal notion: it has many variants, a complex history, and has proven difficult to formulate clearly. On the history and variations, see O'Connor and Wong 2009. For my own attempt to get a foothold in this slippery terrain see Simons 2008.

[5] On why the basis needs to be comprehensive, see the following section.

simply on contingent or factical gaps in our knowledge. This is not a particularly theoretically interesting concept because our ignorance may turn on contingent matters unconnected with the nature of the entity E, for example lack of funding for research. If E is still inexplicable or unpredictable with regard to knowledge we *could* have in respect of B, then we have *strong* epistemic emergence. Strong epistemic emergence is a much more theoretically interesting condition than weak, because it does not turn on what knowledge we as a matter of fact have but on what knowledge we could have of a given domain, whether we have it or not.

The alternative description of an emergent entity as "new" hints at another way of defining emergence. We say an entity E is *ontically* emergent with respect to entities B if E does not naturally arise out of the entities B themselves. By this we mean that whatever operations and forms of combination entities B sustain are themselves fail to give rise to E. Again we can distinguish a weak, factical concept, according to which E as matter of fact fails to arise out of B, and a strong concept according to which E not only does not but *cannot* arise from B. Again, clearly only the modally strengthened concept is of central theoretical interest. So from now on when we speak of epistemic or ontic emergence we shall mean in each case the strong concept only. It is important that the idea of ontic emergence is in no way tied to matters of knowledge: it has to do with how the entities themselves comport and consort. This is important because ontic emergence and (strong) epistemic emergence are frequently run together. Whether the concepts turn out to be coextensional or not, which is another matter, they are not cointensional. The assumption that ontic and epistemic emergence (or their opposites, reducibility) coincide is based on an assumption which I question and indeed believe is wrong, namely the assumption of a thoroughgoing harmony between the way our knowledge works and the way the world works. If we think for a moment that the world's ways might be in some respect inherently inscrutable to us, then we have slipped a blade between ontic and epistemic emergence, because entities might for all we do or could know be emergent, but as a matter of fact arise naturally from their base in ways we cannot fathom or track.

4 GENERATION

Our characterization of "arising naturally" is imprecise and needs more work. Pushing the difficulties back but only one step, I say that an entity arises naturally from others if it is generated from or constituted by entities from B via combinations and operations characteristic of B, where by 'combinations' I mean the relations that naturally obtain among B, that belong naturally to the ontological repertoire of B; and by 'operations' I mean the characteristic modes of (inter)acting that occur naturally among entities B. In short I will say that an entity E so constituted is (naturally) *generated* from or out of B. I am very conscious that this alleviates the terminological and conceptual fog only a little, though I find the switch from negative talk of irreducibility to positive talk of generation useful, and the articulation of generation into relational and operational components also worth making. Nevertheless it may be that generation is something that cannot be fully explained or defined by anything more simple: we run that risk.

A brief word is in order on the qualification 'naturally' above. It is again probably a slippery concept, but here is the idea. If we consider William Paley's famous thought-experiment of a watch found on a beach, most people would accept the idea that a watch is simply not the sort of thing that could have arisen naturally among the minerals of an inorganic planet acting among themselves according to natural processes. Pebbles, rivers, mountains, lakes, are so conceivable, but not a pocket-watch. That indeed is part of the point of Paley's example. It takes an extrinsic agency, that of human designers and craftspeople, to produce the watch. The watch is not a natural but an artificial, i.e. intentionally designed and made, object. However, there is another, post-Darwinian sense, in which the watch indeed is natural. Though still designed and made by human agency, on a naturalistic interpretation of the origins and characteristics of humankind, such abilities have arisen naturally, spontaneously, yet over a long time and with extreme complexity, through the process of evolution by natural selection. The natural processes by which the watch arose involve a massive detour away from metallic and silicate minerals through animal consciousness and the rise of technology. It is the length and complexity of that detour which lends credence to the reasonable but not unbreachable distinction between natural objects and artificial ones. A theist who considered human consciousness and the ability to make artifacts like the watch a divine gift rather than something which could have arisen spontaneously in mere matter goes a crucial step further in denying naturalness to the watch than our Darwinian, for whom it is natural via a long detour.

Returning summarily to the idea of ontic emergence: an entity E is ontically emergent with respect to a basis B if it could not be or have been generated from B. On the basis of our definition, there will be cases of emergence that arise trivially or as side-effects of an inappropriate or merely idiosyncratically chosen basis *B*. Life is emergent with respect to non-metals, because life-chemistry requires some metallic elements, but no one would say this is an important form of emergence, interesting though it is that organisms are mainly non-metallic in composition, since metals and non-metals jointly go to make up the inorganic basis of life. When considering emergence we will and should always consider the most comprehensive basis, and that is the point of the qualification at the beginning of the previous section.

5 MEREOLOGY: AN IMPOVERISHED BASIS

One of the most common statements made about emergence and reduction is that an entity *E* is reducible to entities *B* if it is composed solely of entities from *B*. The idea is that if an entity *E* with parts from *B* is "more than the sum of its parts" then it must be emergent with respect to *B*. The near-ubiquity of such mereological interpretations of emergence may best be explained by recalling how successful micro-reductive explanations have been in the last centuries. So many explanations of the observable features of macroscopic things, like the way ice floats on water or the way rain and sun produce rainbows, turn on accounts of the behaviour of the small parts of material things, that it is natural to think that where such an explanation is not forthcoming, we are confronting an emergent phenomenon. Indeed the idea of something's being other than the sum of its parts has sometimes been taken to *define* the concept of emergence. This leads to some strange consequences however, and makes the concept of emergence too wide in certain cases. For example, a travelling water wave is a macroscopic phenomenon constituted by the many concerted small circular motions of successions of ensembles of water molecules. It has features which the molecules and their motions do not have: an amplitude, a wavelength, endurance through time, a propagational velocity, the ability to travel long distances. But a wave is clearly generated by the motions of the water molecules. The weight of a complex body is readily construed as the sum of the weights of its (mereologically disjoint) small parts, whereas the body's shape arises from the distribution of these parts, which is not a sum in any straightforward sense, yet is clearly a property explicable in terms of the properties of and relations (in this case spatial) among the small parts.

More often the idea has been fleshed out to say that an entity E made of parts B is emergent if some features or behaviour of the whole E are untraceable to, unpredictable, or *inexplicable* in terms solely of the relationships among and behaviour of the parts B. In this regard, while a wave has novel characteristics by comparison with the water molecules whose motion constitute it, the water, its parts and their motions clearly do suffice to explain the wave's features, this novelty notwithstanding. However the notions of predictability and explicability are clearly epistemic ones: how things in themselves are, which would be evident to a divine observer, may not be accessible via prediction or explanation even in principle to a finitely endowed observer. If some features of composite individuals or systems are too complicatedly dependent on the behaviour of their parts to be predictable or explicable, that does not mean they cannot arise naturally.

From an ontological point of view, a solely mereological approach to emergence and reduction is simply too narrow: it lets far too much count as emergent. If an emergent complex whole is one which is not merely the sum of its parts, then understanding the term 'sum' in its purely mereological sense means that arguably very few natural wholes are sums in this sense, which would mean that nearly all wholes are emergent.[6] The need for a less restricted notion of a generated or reducible wrehole is recognized in the move from merely novel features of wholes to inexplicable novel features. This epistemic addition broadens the effect of a basis, but not with ontic means alone. For a sensible *ontic* characterization of emergence, we need additional help from elsewhere.

6 WHAT MORE IS AVAILABLE

The example of the shape of a macroscopic body used earlier indicates one area in which we need more ontological resources: we need to invoke the conceptual scheme of location, in space, time, spacetime, or indeed more generally at a "place" in a structure (for example at a certain position in a crystal or in a DNA molecule). The notion of being located at, and its terms, occupant and locus, are a very general, indeed in my view a *formal* ontological notion, on a par with part/whole, applicable *partout* in a domain-neutral way.[7] The extended family of concepts associated with location, including the broadly geometric notions of relative location and rela-

---

[6] Cf. Simons 2006.
[7] Simons 2004.

tions among locations, add to the ontological resources we need in any case to use in talking about objects and their features and relationships, so let us add them to the repertoire of descriptors for objects alongside mereological concepts.

Taking the cue from the two previous examples, when we find a family of interrelated ontological concepts which we either know or surmise to be domain-neutral and further consider indispensable to ontology at large, then we should add them to our basis forthwith. Another obvious example concerns the plurality and numbers of items. Systems consist not of one but of several or many objects, consorting together. We can and must use the idea of a natural plurality or collection of things in addition to that of a single individual. This is not a controversial addition, since number is often taken as a logical concept and so already part of the logical background which we can always bring to bear on our ontological descriptions. Whether difference, identity, plurality, collection, number, sevenness, infinity, and many other cognate concepts are ultimately logical or ontological or indeed both is perhaps not as easy to decide as might at first appear, but it matters little if we assume we can have them in our descriptive repertoire.

Another family of concepts which are more unambiguously ontological this time are those concerning the notions of ontological dependence and independence. This family has been recognized and exploited in ontology since its inception: we find them in Aristotle, the Scholastics, Descartes, Leibniz, Husserl, Ingarden and others. At one time it seemed to me that dependence of various kinds could be defined in modal terms, but it now seems that Fine, Lowe and Correia are correct in taking dependence and cognates to be a family not definable in terms of other formal concepts.[8] Whether that it right or not is again not so important as the decision to add them to our basis.

Many of the data that scientists use to explain natural phenomena are quantitative in form: they concern such things as mass, electromagnetic charge, velocity, distance, angle, luminosity, temperature, energy, density, and the like. These many kinds of physical quantity are discovered empirically and their comparisons and measurement are part of the job of empirical science, but again behind them are a family of formal structures, which render the various such quantities apt for representation through mathematical number systems. These structures vary in detail from case to case, but they have a common formal core which makes them all quantities. The

---

[8] Fine 1995, Lowe 2005, Correia 2005.

family of concepts going to describe quantity in general is arguably not reducible to anything else we have considered, so for ontological completeness we should add them to the basis.

We have left out so far the concept or conceptual family most frequently invoked in connection with arguments pro and contra reduction in many a given sphere, and that is causality. Sometimes indeed emergence is characterized simply in terms of what is called "downwards causation". An entity is emergent if it *qua* whole can cause changes in its parts, that are not changes caused by other parts. This assumes that we can talk about different levels of entity, and that higher-level entities which in their own right (not via their parts) influence lower-level entities do so via downwards causation as distinct from lateral causation. I must confess I have persistently been unable to make clear sense of this notion of downwards causation, so I shall not make it part of my definition of emergence. Be that as it may, causation is certainly in view in most cases when the talk is of explanation for the behaviour of objects and systems in respect to the behaviour of their parts. So without causation in our ontological repertoire, we shall definitely be working with too impoverished a basis in which to assess questions of what generates what. The energy transmitted by a water wave, for example, is explained in terms of the kinetic energy of many water molecules moving in concerted ways being transmitted in the direction of wave propagation, as molecule tugs and pushes at molecule.

I am here assuming that causation is something that applies to the real world, and not a conceptual convenience or merely methodological principle. That is of course not a neutral position, but there is no space to argue for it here. At its most blunt and basic, causation is about some things' happening making other things to happen. This much is mere common sense, though there is subtlety to the notion of "making", exposed by Hume, which I acknowledge only to duck. It is a more delicate question as to whether causation is part of formal or material ontology. I happen to think it is formal, and is actually slightly more general as such than the simple billiard-ball event-causation idea just alluded to. The more general notion, of which causing is a prime but not the only instance, is that of determining: one thing's being like this determining or ensuring that another thing is like that. There might pehaps be determination which is not causal, for example a spontaneous (uncaused) event of nuclear fission determines the extinction of a material possibility of the nucleus continuing to exist. Determining is what gives time its asymmetry: the present at any location is the boundary or limit of indetermination. So with determination (causation) and location we generate the distinction between local past and local present, though what material principles govern this is a matter not for ontology but for empirical investigation. The ontologist should not overstep her remit. Another putative case of determination which fails to fit the event-causation model is the way in which a planet orbits the sun, because the continuous change of direction and the continuous change of line of application of gravitational attraction go together. Russell pointed this out long ago, and notoriously concluded that the notion of causation was as outmoded as the monarchy, and should be replaced by that of functional correlation.[9] But the less sceptical and I believe correct conclusion is that this is a case of continuous determination.

7 A MORE ADEQUATE BASIS

Let us review the formal ontological concept-families that we have introduced into the basis for description of entities. We have for a start the part/whole family, as studied in mereology. In addition there are the concepts associated with number and its cognates, location and its cognates, quantity and its cognates, dependence and its cognates, and determination and its cognates. These various families are investigable separately but in any actual instance they apply together, since formal ontological concepts are domain-neutral, go-anywhere concepts. Perhaps there are other families, perhaps not. It would be good to have a definitive list but for the purposes of making my point it is not necessary. The first point to make is that when mereology is enriched by all these other families, the formal mechanisms for describing combinations and operations are multiplied manyfold, which has the effect that ontic generation appears capable of generating a much wider range of entities from a given basis. Ontic emergence becomes as it were more expensive, and also more dramatic. The second point is that these formal families provide only the formal ontological framework for reductionistic or generational accounts of complex phenomena. Any actual object or phenomenon to be examined falls not only under formal but also under material or substantive concepts: it has to do with real taxa of things such as electrons, water, planets, nuclear fusion, pyroclastic flow, osmosis, cell membranes, meiosis, demographics, wars, or whatever. Without an adequate supply of material taxa, the provision of which is no part of the ontologist's job, description and therefore explanation of real

---

[9] Russell 1913.

phenomena cannot get started. This may seem obvious but it is important not to lose sight of it in the drive to give a formal account of what is involved in emergence or generation.

Finally, ontological concepts and material taxa are not enough for our descriptive and scientific needs. We need a range of logical, mathematical and perhaps other concepts to enable us to carry through our scientific tasks, from negation, quantification and modalization in logic through differentiation and integration in mathematics to probabilistic and statistical concepts in applications. In describing matters of experience, society and culture we are perhaps forced to rely on phenomenological, folk-psychological and semantical concepts. We typically rely throughout science on abstractions, idealizations and simplifying models. Yet although these concepts are humanly necessary for us to pursue our cognitive and scientific goals, it does not follow that they enrich the ontological basis, nor that they point to irreducible phenomena or realms of entities outside the naturalistic domain. Mathematics, modality, mind, and morality have often been considered to provide the hardest tests for naturalism. That naturalism should be able to withstand these tests is part of our initial metaphysical speculation.

8 SUBSIDIARY SPECULATION

On the basis of a widened repertoire of formal ontological tools with which to categorize and describe the relationships among entities, the naturalistic speculative claim is that there are material taxa of entities which are securely naturalistic, the combinations and operations of which generate all we experience, including life, mind and culture, including the phenomenal as well as the physical. There is no ontological magic, whether it be the global magic of a pluralism of realms, at least one of which is not naturalistic, nor the local magic of carefully prepared emergence of new naturalistically ingenerable, irreducible kinds of entity. This lack of ontic emergence from natural kinds is perfectly compatible with and indeed tends to call for a richly epistemic emergence of inexplicably and unpredictably novel entities. Ontic generation may be graspable in its simplest forms, but it is almost certainly humanly inscrutable in all its gory detail.

I accept with Kant that for knowledge to be humanly possible we must deploy a range of basic concepts that we cannot do without. Unlike Kant but like Aristotle, I consider that some of these concepts are classificatory of reality as it is in itself, they "cut nature at the joints". Call such basic concepts *ontic categories*. They include the formal concepts of part, number, location, determination etc. mentioned above. That a certain aggregate of matter that we call the earth's crust is part of the earth is a fact expressed using the formal concept of part, but its truth depends on there being an objective material difference between the crust and other parts which enables us to differentiate it from cases of arbitrary or gerrymandered "parts" such as Switzerland. The ontic categories – whichever ones they are – make up the ontologist's basic tools for analysing or assaying putatively emergent entities. If an entity *E* cannot be plausibly taken to be generated from some basic entities *B* by their characteristic modes of combination and operation, analysed employing *B* and the ontic categories, then we have two choices: deny that *E* exists, or accept that it exists but is irreducible to *B*, whether it is emergent with respect to *B* or primitive.

Among his categories Kant reckoned not just ontic concepts like substance or causation but also such logical constants as negation, universality, implication and necessity. We would be cognitively deeply impaired without the ability to deploy these. But that does not mean there are negative, universal, conditional or modal facts in addition to simple or atomic facts. Wittgenstein was right: the logical constants do not represent anything. Their use however significantly *assists* us in our cognitive endeavours. For that reason I call such concepts *auxiliary* categories. In addition to employing logical auxiliaries, our minds busily fabricate cognitive tokens which do not stand for objects, but which we manipulate as if they do. We could call them cognitive fictions. Some such fictions are generated by recurrent and seemingly natural types of cognitive operation. For example, as Locke pointed out, all humans naturally abstract. They do so under salient equivalence relations, some so self-evident we don't even notice them, for example we abstract out under manifold changes and unperceived ongoing constitutive processes the invariant continuants which we call physical bodies. In treating the cognitive tokens (terms and concepts) thereby deployed as standing for their own entities humans *hypostatize*. Hypostatization may well be a human cognitive invariant. One familiar and exhaustively investigated form of abstraction is that of cardinal number: under the equivalence relation of equinumerosity we abstract out the cardinals. But weights, heights, lengths, angles, masses, incomes, are all abstracta with a more or less obvious base of concreta and a simple equivalence relation. More complex cases may be found in geometry, where we abstract over four-, six- and eight-place relations having analogous logical properties to two-place equivalence relations. Some hypostatizations are either so outrageous or so obviously deliberate that they generate controversy from the moment they are publicized: Meinong's nonexistent objects and Lewis's possible worlds both arouse widespread disbelief. Other cognitive operations are so familiar they pass notice: predication and judgement for example. Yet the assumption that they somehow correspond to items in the world – attributes (properties and relations), and propositions respectively – is one which is not and can not be unquestioned. Deciding which cognitive operations correspond to entities and which do not is obviously a significant part of the metaphysical enterprise.

The utility of auxiliary categories is undeniable, but they do not contribute to the world's store of entities. It is ontic categories alone that structure ontology and provide the framework for the systematic variety of things. Only they can figure in the argument whether or not an entity E is generated by entities B.

10 REMARKS ON METAPHYSICAL METHOD

Metaphysical hypotheses are, I claim, not irrefutable stances. They are no more immune from refutation by counterexample than normal scientific hypotheses. A counterexample to our naturalistic reductionism is perfectly imaginable, indeed for all I know is sitting out there and recognized by those less wedded to naturalism than I am. It is common to cite mind and consciousness as the most likely recalcitrant phenomena troubling a naturalistic standpoint. Aside from the fact that we are probably decades if not centuries away from gaining enough knowledge to hazard a good guess as to whether this is true, my own view is that mind and consciousness will probably tumble to naturalistic reduction, provided we or our successors live long enough. A more worrying potential counterexample I think comes from mathematics, which may (epistemically may) turn out to be seriously irreducible by any plausible account, so that one would have to live with a form of platonism. That I think is less worrying than psychophysical dualism. The steps to a naturalistic account of mind are well under way; a deflationary account of the apparent indendence of abstract mathematica stands on much shakier ground. It would be deeply disturbing to the thrust of the centuries of progress in natural science if dualism were correct, whereas platonism by its nature stands more aloof from the march of science. Either way, even the broadest and most reasonable-seeming metaphysical speculations are prone to abandonment under the weight of evidence, and that goes for naturalism too. So when Franz Brentano proposed among his *Habilitation* theses that the true philosophic method is no different from that of natural science,[10] he was proposing a truth.

In the days when metaphysics was being rehabilitated after the passing of positivism, it was standard in analytical philosophy to pursue metaphysics and ontology by a logico-linguistic method, whether cleaving more closely to ordinary language or to the sanitized language of formalized science. The problem with this approach is that there is slack between linguistic and ontological facts which is taken up by semantics, and it turns out that semantics is pliable enough to bend with the varying ontologies pairable with a single syntax. Quantifying predicate variables only ontologically commits one to properties or sets if quantification is interpreted in a certain way, for example. Metaphysical facts cannot be dependent on such vagaries. A more autonomous, naturalistic approach characterizes later analytic metaphysics in for example Armstrong and Lewis, but has its genealogical antecedents in Anderson, Alexander and Whitehead. This of course has its risks: uncoupled from logico-linguistic constraints, metaphysics can and indeed recently often has become more fanciful and extreme, with such positions as genuine modal realism, presentism, subjective idealism, panpsychism and Parmenidean monism being reintroduced as respectable options. Finding the right balance between Moorean descriptive fidelity and plausible speculative boldness is not easy, but it has to be ventured.

---

[10] Brentano's fourth habilitation thesis ran: "Vera philosophiae methodus nulla alia nisi scientiae naturalis est." Brentano 1929, 137.

REFERENCES

Alexander, S. 1920. *Space, Time and Deity.* London: Macmillan.
Brentano, F. 1929. *Über die Zukunft der Philosophie: nebst den Vorträgen: Über die Gründe der Entmutigung auf philosophischem Gebiet. Über Schellings System, sowie den 25 Habilitationsthesen.* Leipzig: Meiner, 1929, repr. 1968.
Correia, F. 2005. *Existential Dependence and Cognate Notions.* Munich: Philosophia.
Fine, K. 1995. Ontological Dependence. *Proceeding of the Aristotelian Society* 95, pp.269–290.
Lowe, E.J. 2005. Ontological Dependence. In E. Zalta, ed., *The Stanford Encyclopedia of Philosophy.* URL = <http://plato.stanford.edu/archives/fall2008/entries/dependence-ontological/>.
O'Connor, T. and Hong Yu Wong 2009. Emergent Properties. In E. Zalta, ed., *The Stanford Encyclopedia of Philosophy* (Spring 2009 Edition), URL = <http://plato.stanford.edu/archives/spr2009/entries/properties-emergent/>.
Russell, B. 1913. On the Notion of Cause. *Proceedings of the Aristotelian Society* 13, pp.1–26
Simons, P.M. 2004. Location. *dialectica* 58, pp.341–347.
Simons, P.M. 2006. Real Wholes, Real Parts: Mereology without Algebra. *The Journal of Philosophy* 103, pp.597–613.
Simons, P.M. 2008. The Emergence of Intentionality. In T. Botz-Bornstein, ed., *Culture, Nature, Memes: Dynamic Cognitive Theories.* Newcastle upon Tyne: Cambridge Scholars Publishing, pp.78–87.
Williams, D.C. 1953. The Elements of Being. *Review of Metaphysics* 7, pp.3–18, 171–192.

WHAT REDUCTIONISTS BELIEVE IN

Christian Kanzian
University of Innsbruck

> "We have been told by popular scientists that the floor on which we stand is not solid, as it appears to common sense, as it has been discovered that the wood consists of particles filling space so thinly that it can almost be called empty. This is liable to perplex us ... Our perplexity was based on a misunderstanding; *the picture* of the thinly filled space *had been wrongly applied*." (Wittgenstein, *Blue Book*, 45.46, *emph.* CK)

1 INTRODUCTION

Ontological reductionism is normally motivated by a skeptical view on what people in ordinary life assume to be the case in their ordinary world: on things like cars, sheep and human beings having properties, being related to one another, and remaining the same even if they undergo changes. Reductionists want to protect us from taking such a naive access to reality as *ontologically* serious. Ontology should not reflect upon that what normal people mean, but what the basic structure of our world *really* is. And science – natural science of course – tells us what this basic structure really is. Thus the noblest aim of ontology is to reduce the objects in one's everyday world to the basics presented to us by natural science; respectively to reconstruct these objects from this basis. This is the only way to get a real scientific ontology in the context of a rational world-view.

In this article I try to examine ontological reductionism with a little bit more scrutiny. The question is how we could understand reductionism and its consequences. More philosophically speaking: I am going to ask what "reductionism" may refer to, look for common premises shared by the different reductionistic positions, and try to discuss them. My result will be that "scientific" ontologies stick to strong premises – believes, I am inclined to say. This is problematic, because these premises can be called into question: on the one hand by reason of ontological and on the other hand of methodological – as I would prefer to say meta-ontological – arguments.

2 WHAT IS REDUCTIONISM?

2.1 As far as I can see there is no fixed or technical usage of the term "reductionism" in ontological contexts. Sometimes "ontological reductionism" stands for a specific ontological position. I will call this position "reductionism in the narrow sense". Sometimes "reductionism" is used to refer to a general label under which various different positions can be subsumed. That is "reductionism in the broader sense". However, I start with the latter, ontological reductionism in the broader sense.

The next question should be the following: What makes a position suitable to be subsumed under this label "reductionism"? – I think it is a claim, which can be expressed by the scheme:

E has to be replaced by B

"To be replaced by" could be made more precise by adding "in an ontological context" or "as commitment of an ontological theory", or such kind of phrases. It is not decidable in this phase of investigation whether "replacement" stands for a relation in a technical sense or not. Take it simply as what it sounds: something must be introduced into an ontological theory instead of something other.

"E" does not denote a single object, but a type of objects, like things as the before mentioned cars, sheep, or human beings. And it is accordingly asserted by reductionism that the tokens of the E-type are excluded from belonging to the structure of reality, to which an ontological theory commits. "E" stands, in an open or pre-theoretical sense for "epiphenomenon". A famous Australian philosopher recently called E's as "ontological free lunch"[1]; German-speaking friends of neologisms would translate this into: "Epiphänomene existieren nicht wirklich." We will examine what these metaphorical phrases could mean.

"B" also does not refer to single objects, but to a type of objects. B, the basis of E, belongs to the ground structure of reality. B is that to what a really ontological theory commits. "B" is no "free lunch", and neither a cheap one. *Die Basis existiert wirklich.*

---

[1] Armstrong 1997, 12f.

To remain at my example: One instantiation of the reductionist scheme would be: "Things, like cars, sheep, and human beings have to be replaced in an ontological theory by something other, by real basic entities." These real basic entities should be introduced into an ontological theory instead of the mentioned things. Things have a mere epiphenomenological status. Despite their seeming to they "do not really" exist.

2.2 With the mentioned scheme we have a first clue to an understanding of the label "ontological reductionism". How to put flesh on the bones? – We can differentiate various positions within the label of ontological reductionism: first, according to the status of E; second, according to the strength of replacement; and third, according to the nature of B. I am sure that we can make the matter always more difficult, but for the beginning we can help ourselves with the following: Concerning the third way of distinguishing, the relevant literature presents us with prominent candidates for basic-categories: processes (Whitehead, 1978), atoms, thing-like simples (Van Inwagen, 1990) or quality-like tropes (Campbell, 1990), normally understood as material entities.

Concerning the second way, the extremes are, on the one hand, the replacement of E in favour of B can be explained with nomological strength; on the other hand, the replacement of E in favour of B can be explained, at least in principle, but without any prospect of nomological regularity.

Concerning the first level of distinguishing positions, we can identify views which regard E as neglectable as well as for everyday use as for every ontological context. I would call them *eliminativist* views with respect to E. Then there are E-theoreticians who defend the relevance of E for everyday use, but deny its theoretical relevance for ontology at all. Such a position comes near to that what I called above "ontological *reductionism* in a narrow sense". Finally there are "reductionists in a broader sense" who defend E as indispensable both for the explanation of our everyday world, and, at least partially, for some theoretical contexts. *Supervenience*-theoreticians are prominent holders of the last view concerning E.

Thus, under the label of reductionism in a broader sense, there may be included the positions holding that our everyday objects can be replaced – without any loss for theoretical ontology and for our everyday phenomenology – with nomological stringency to – lets say – material processes. This would be nomological eliminativistic process-ontologies. In addition there may also be included under the label of reductionism positions holding that our middle-sized things must be ultimately replaced by some kinds of atoms, simples or tropes. However, because of their indispensability in everyday life and for some theoretical contexts, as well as the a-nomological character of the putative replacement we have to take a non-eliminative and non-reductionistic (in a narrow sense) replacement view: things supervene on some kinds of atoms. These seem to be the extremes: there are, according to my scheme, a lot of possible theories between them.

2.3 At the beginning I mentioned that I primarily will not look for the differences, but for the common premises shared by reductionistic positions. What have eliminativists in common with supervenience-theoreticians, process-ontologists with tropists and other atomists? – I think, they share basically three premises – believes, as I said at the beginning polemically.

The first is the assumption of the *ontological priority of the bottom*, the basis, as I called it in my scheme above. That does not mean that they have the same understanding of how strong this priority must be interpreted, how great the difference between the prior and the posterior has to be assumed. But, if an ontologist denies the priority of the basis in comparison with the non-basic phenomena, there remains no reason for the replacement claim, which is indeed essential for reductionism.

The second premise, which is inseparable from the first, is that all reductionists must rely on the success of any *bottom up-strategy*. It must be, at least in principle, possible to reconstruct the things of our ordinary world from the assumed bottom or basis. Otherwise replacement, however considered, cannot work. It must be possible to reconstruct Susan, the sheep on the grass, from the atoms or the processes to which it is pretended that she can be reduced to.

Finally, the third premise is (according to non-idealistic reductionism and idealistic reductionism we leave aside here) that the basis must be discovered and described to the ontologists by the others, normally physicists or quantum mechanicians. Ontology is an *a posteriori-discipline*, as a prominent reductionist recently urged.[2] Ontology has to look first to that what the others say and must take their results as the preliminary findings of its own theorising. (I don't deny inner-ontological replacement-claims, for instance concerning universals, which should be replaced by concrete properties, according to "inner-ontological reductionism". But these claims should not be mixed up with reductionistic replacement-claims as they are discussed here.)

---

[2] Simons 1998, p.251.

I call these premises the *reductionist-triangle* which is characteristic for every reductionistic theory. With the use of this metaphor I do not only maintain that every angle, i.e., every premise, is indispensable for reductionistic ontology; but also, that if one of them can be rejected, then the triangle collapses, resulting in the refutation of the core idea of reductionism.

3 IS REDUCTIONISM TRUE?

3.1 One standard way of criticism is to attack premise one because of its *counter-intuitive* consequences. We intuitively accept the inhabitants of our ordinary world as real units, "real" in a stable sense. We especially like to regard ourselves as self-remaining entities in spite of the various changes we undergo. – This kind of criticism, whether true or false, leads to a dead-end of the debate because reductionists normally do not intend to theorize in accordance with intuition. As another important reductionist succinctly pointed out: "Unnaturalness in philosophy is all right."[3]

Another way of criticism would be to doubt the success of a premise two-strategy. I am convinced that this really refers to a hard problem for reductionism. In fact, as far as I can see, there is no widely accepted theory of reconstruction of at least some phenomena of our macro-world from the basis of a physical micro-world. – The reductionist's reply is normally immunizing. It does not matter that we, today, have no theory of the reconstruction, for instance of our sheep Susan from its subatomic basic constituents. But *in principle* we can develop one and future generations of scientists surely will provide it. – However, controversies about futurabilia cannot be resolved. This is why I am going to focus especially on the third angle of the reductionist's triangle: the premise that ontology is an a posteriori discipline which has to start with the given results of physical world-descriptions. This kind of argumentation is methodological or meta-ontological as I called it at the beginning.

The intended meta-ontological debate can and should be led from the most fundamental level: What is ontology, and what are natural sciences? With regard to reductionism: What understanding of these sciences and their relation must someone presuppose who regards ontology as an a posteriori enterprise in the sense of the third reductionistic angle? – Ontology must be considered as a kind of natural science with all of its consequences; a discussion of which would lead us too far away from our topic.

---

[3] Quine 1994, p.93.

Another level of the debate could be how ontological descriptions, explanations, and theories can be related to, e.g., physical ones. What is the epistemic status of the first, what of the latter? Are there differences, and how can they be explained? To what understanding of this matter does the third reductionistic angle commit? – According to reductionism, no differences in principle, for example concerning verification/falsification should be allowed between ontological and physical theories.

3.2 On this occasion I do not intend to discuss the mentioned fundamental questions. I rather want to make aware of one concrete point, which allows illustrating the methodological or meta-ontological difficulty of the reductionistic premise three. According to the third reductionistic angle, ontology has to start with the results of physics. Let us ask, what these results, in which our reductionistic colleagues are interested, actually are? – The uninterpreted bare empirical data are not interesting. No ontologist starts with a look into an electronic microscope. And even if he would, he could not understand what he sees. What philosophers need are *interpretations*. And the first level of interpretation contains *models* physicists use to come to theoretical explanations of the given data. – *Simple material elements* for instance (and it does not matter if they call them actually atoms, or electrons, quarks, or sub-sub-quarks) are such models. And it seems to be the case that successful physical theorizing relies on such models. – The problem is that our colleague-philosophers, in their effort to start with the results of physics, import such models and take them, and this is the decisive point, as ontological hard facts. To remain with the example we can state that they regard material simples (some actually call them atoms, some other simply "simples", some "tropes") as the basic units of reality and give them genuine ontological characteristics like "primitiveness", "undividability", and so on. The result is an atomistic ontology: material simples, called "atoms", "simples", or "tropes" are taken as primitive and undividable basic units of reality. They are regarded as the basic category of entities, from which all the macroscopic phenomena can be reconstructed. – The case of material simples is just one example – we also can take processes, "space-time worms", or something else – but a very interesting and influential one; because it has given rise to one mainstream of reductionistic ontology. I repeat the point: What they seem to do is to hypostasize or to ontologize physical models or "pictures". In fact there do not *exist*, in a stable sense, simple, primitive, undividable material units (however you call them).

"Atoms do not exist" seems to be a rather dangerous thesis. – And I try to be careful, and insist on the differentiation, that I, of course, do not deny the usefulness of models for interpreting the empirical data we have from the basic levels of material reality. But to repeat it, I deny that we should convert models into entities. "Atom" may be a useful concept for a model in physics, but not for an ontological entity – if it should refer to material simples.

3.3 I would be ready to defend this view, not only because of meta-ontological reasons, but also because of ontological arguments. I briefly sketch two of them. The first one: considered ontologically, the concept of a material simple is – I say it cautiously – gravely defective. Materiality necessarily implies extension, and something extended cannot be simple in the sense atomistic ontologists suppose. The second: identity. According to his reductionistic bottom-up postulate, the reductionist must be able to reconstruct the identity of middle-sized objects from the identity of the basic entities. That presupposes that he must be able to say in what the identity of the latter consists. He must provide *informative* conditions of their identity. How should we reconstruct our middle-sized objects and their identity without positive knowledge about the identity of the bottom items? – But: as we can learn from John Locke, Jonathan Lowe, and other important philosophers in between, informative conditions of identity always refer to the *constituents* of the entities in question.[4] (Heaps of sand are identical iff their grains are; organisms are identical iff their life-functions are …) Simples have no constituents. That is why we cannot give informative conditions for their identity. Thus, they are no plausible basic-elements for the reconstruction of cars, sheep, humans, and their identity. (Therefore perhaps, Locke, Lowe, and some other philosophers are no re-ductionists.)

If it is not possible to reconstruct the identity of middle-sized objects from the identity of material simples (however you call them), or if these simples are no entities at all, ontological reductionism pretending that they are the only entities of a real scientific world-description is definitively false. Beginning with premise three of the reductionistic triangle we can knock the bottom out of premise one, and in consequence that of premise two. – What can we do now? Are there alternatives to reductionism? – Yes, I think, there is one, and this is:

---

[4] Locke 1975, book II, chapter XXVII, §3. Lowe 1989, chapter VII.

Finally I will try to give an outline of some core-assumptions of a non-reductionistic ontology. In contrast to the premise one of reductionism, a non-reductionistic ontology asserts the ontological *priority of the units of our ordinary world*: macro-things like cars, sheep, and human beings. It does not matter whether you add also the properties of these units and their changes to your ontology or not; neither whether you are ready to make ontological differentiations within the thing-world (artefacts – living beings) or not – the prior beings are the units of our macro-world. One possibility of being non-reductionistic in this sense would be to stick to an Aristotelean-like substance-ontology.[5]

But what is with the reductionist's basis, the micro-world, what is its place in a non-reductionistic theory? – The non-reductionistic strategy to analyse macro-things in comparison to the micro-world is not, as the reductionistic premise two indicates, bottom up, but *top down*. And, in contrast to the reductionist premise three, as non-reductionists we are obliged to differentiate between the *ontological* top-down program and the procedures of the different natural sciences. Of course, there are several possible genuinely ontological top-down strategies. One of them is the Aristotelean-like analysis of the inner constitution of our complex macro-things; holding that this complexity is constituted by an individual material-aspect and an individual form-aspect: *What* a thing is made of and *how* the components are built into a complex unity. Both, the what-, and the how-aspect are irreducible to each other in their functions for the constitution of the whole complex thing.

In contrast to ontological top-down analysis there may be a wide range of other methods of top-down investigations into a complex macro-thing. One of them, of course a rather interesting and important one, is a physical investigation into the material aspect of such a thing. And the results of such a physical investigation may be very informative physical theories, making use of illustrative models, like the above-mentioned atoms, protons, quarks, and – if you want – sub-sub-quarks.

What is with the ontology of the micro-world, the reductionist may critically throw in? – Non-reductionistic ontology is open for every kind of investigation into the material aspect of our basic units – that is the proper

---

[5] For some new approaches to "substance", but also for new critical arguments against substance-ontologies, see Trettin 2005; for a historical summary of the substance-debate see Gutschmidt (ed.) 2008.

task of natural sciences – and for efforts to integrate the results of natural sciences *as such* into a philosophical theory of the basic structures of reality – that would be the aim of philosophy of nature. Non-reductionistic ontology gratefully receives the results of philosophy of sciences reflecting on the differences between the methods in natural science and in ontology, and examining seriously the relevance of physical models for an understanding of the material aspect of our basic units of reality.

Non-reductionistic ontology does not the job of the others. It is an open project. As non-reductionistic ontologists we are open for the results of the others, but we let them be the others and strictly refuse to ontologize their conceptualized metaphors or to "apply wrongly" their "pictures", as Wittgenstein once exposed one of the methodological premises of the reductionistic fallacy in his *Blue Book*.

REFERENCES

Armstrong, D. 1997: *A World of States of Affairs*. Cambridge University Press, Cambridge.
Campbell, K. 1990: *Abstract Particulars*. Blackwell, Oxford.
Gutschmidt, H. (ed., together with Lang-Balestra, A., Segalerba, G.) 2008: *Substantia – Sic et Non*. Ontos, Heusenstamm.
Locke, J. 1975: *An Essay concerning Human Understanding*. Ed. by P.H. Nidditch. Clarendon Press, Oxford.
Lowe, J. 1989: *Kinds of Beings*. Blackwell, Oxford.
Quine, W.V.O. 1994: *Stimulus and Science*. MIT Press, Cambridge (Mass.).
Simons, P. 1998: Farewell To Substance: A Differentiated Leave-Taking, in: *Ratio* (new series) 11, pp.235–252.
Trettin, K. (ed.) 2005: Substanz. *Neue Überlegungen zu einer klassischen Kategorie des Seienden*. Klostermann, Frankfurt a. M.
Van Inwagen 1990: *Material Beings*. Cornell University Press, Ithaca NY.
Whitehead 1978: *Process and Reality*. Ed. by D.R. Griffin & D.W. Sherburne. MacMillan, New York.
Wittgenstein, Blue Book: *The Blue and Brown Books*, Basil Blackwell, Oxford 1958.

SUPERVENIENCE AND MORAL REALISM

ALISON HILLS
University of Oxford

1 INTRODUCTION

According to objective moral realism, there exist moral properties that are not dependent on our beliefs or our attitudes about them. In Mackie's famous first chapter of his book *Ethics*, he gives three arguments against this theory. His first argument is that the nature and quantity of moral disagreement gives us reason to deny that there are any objective moral properties. His second argument is that the very nature of putative objective moral properties or moral facts – as essentially motivational (or perhaps, essentially normative) – is reason to doubt that any such thing could exist. Moral realists have not been too impressed by these arguments, however. It is perfectly clear that moral properties can coexist with widespread and persistent disagreement about their nature. In response to the queerness argument, moral realists have either opted for naturalism, trying to show that moral properties are not really peculiar at all – in fact they simply are natural properties – or they have conceded that moral properties are non-natural and that at least to that extent they are queer, but have argued that this is not a sufficient reason to deny that they exist.

The third argument, concerning supervenience, has been comparatively neglected, however, though it was taken up by Simon Blackburn, with responses from a variety of moral realists. In the following sections I will make the supervenience argument against moral realism more precise, showing that it must be directed at non-naturalist forms of moral realism. I will consider one possible response to the argument: I will look at the possibility of denying that supervenience is true.

2 THE SUPERVENIENCE ARGUMENT

It is widely, perhaps even universally believed that moral properties necessarily depend on other properties. To be more specific (but still quite rough):

> Supervenience: there can be no difference in moral properties without a difference in the natural properties.[1]

Supervenience in one form or another is accepted by a range of philosophers who otherwise have quite different meathetical views, including G.E. Moore, R.M. Hare, Blackburn, Shafer-Landau, and Ridge. Some of these philosophers accept moral realism, others do not. But according to Mackie's supervenience argument, moral realists cannot comfortably accommodate Supervenience. The problem is not that Supervenience is actually *inconsistent* with moral realism, rather that Supervenience generates an *explanatory demand* which moral realism cannot meet but certain versions of non-realism can. If the argument succeeds, moral realism is at a considerable disadvantage to a theory like Blackburn's non-cognitivism.

We can distinguish between different versions of Supervenience. I will assume that the necessity at stake is metaphysical:[2]

---

[1] What are the natural properties? It is well-known that "the natural" is difficult to define. Typically philosophers understand the "natural" properties as something like: those properties that are studied by science (or perhaps those that would be studied in a future, complete science). Do mental properties – being happy, being in pain, having a desire or intention, deciding to act – count amongst the natural? One might say no, they do not, and deny Supervenience on that basis. Do supernatural properties – being prescribed or proscribed by God – count as natural properties? Again, one might say no, and deny Supervenience for that reason. But I will assume for the purposes of this paper that the "natural" can be defined sufficiently clearly and sufficiently broadly that supervenience is a plausible claim.

[2] Alternatively, Supervenience could be primarily a semantic thesis about the meaning of moral terms (or the requirements on a competent user of moral terms), with reference to analytic necessity. In Blackburn's presentation of the supervenience argument, he seems to be discussing analytic necessity, and requiring a moral realist to explain why it is part of our concept of morality that there can be no moral changes without accompanying changes in natural properties. However, it seems to me more difficult for the moral realist to explain the metaphysical connection between the moral and the natural (at least, this is a difficulty for a non-naturalist moral realist), so I will focus on the metaphysical supervenience claim.

Metaphysical Supervenience: it is metaphysically impossible for there to be a difference in moral properties without a difference in natural properties.

But we can distinguish a stronger and a weaker claim, depending on whether we are talking about differences within one world, or between worlds:

Strong Metaphysical Supervenience: it is metaphysically impossible for there to be a difference in moral properties (between any two possible worlds) without a difference in natural properties.

Weak Metaphysical Supervenience: it is metaphysically impossible for there to be a difference in moral properties (within one possible world) without a difference in natural properties.

That there is a dependence between moral and natural properties is not itself inconsistent with moral realism. But a necessary connection between two kinds of property is the sort of thing that calls for explanation and it is cost to a theory if it is committed to such a connection without being able to explain it. The problem for moral realists is that they have not offered an adequate explanation – in fact in many cases they have offered no explanation at all – of why this dependence should hold. There seems to be a particular difficulty in explaining why weak supervenience is true, if strong supervenience is not. Suppose that in World 1, natural property N1 underlies moral property M, so that there is never a change in property M without a change in N1 in that world. And suppose that in world 2, natural property N2 underlies moral property M, so that in world 1, there is never a change in property M without a change in N2. According to weak supervenience, there can be no "mixed worlds" in which a change in M is sometimes accompanied by a change in N1 and sometimes by N2. But why not?[3] Moral realists have some explaining to do.

---

[3] Blackburn thinks that his non-cognitivism can explain this better, because on that view the function of moral discourse is to praise, recommend or condemn actions, states of affairs etc in terms of their natural properties, in order to regulate our behaviour. So it is clear why weak supervenience is true, given non-cognitivism. But since there is no single best way of carrying out this function, strong supervenience is not true. There is nothing mysterious to explain.

According to some moral realists, moral properties simply are natural properties. So it is obviously true that necessarily, there can be no change in moral properties without a change in natural properties – a change in moral properties is a change in natural properties. In which case there is no need to offer a special explanation for the supervenience of the moral on the natural.[4]

But non-naturalist moral realism is in a more difficult position. According to non-naturalists, moral properties are not natural properties: the two are distinct. So why is there a necessary connection (either strong or weak) between the two? Non-naturalists need not offer a naturalist explanation for this connection (they need not commit themselves to what has been called "superdupervenience").[5] But it remains true that they think that there is a metaphysically necessary connection between two distinct kinds of properties, natural and moral, and it is not unreasonable to expect this sort of connection to be explicable.

The non-naturalist might simply bite the bullet and refuse to give any explanation at all. It is simply a brute fact, she might say, that there is this necessary connection between moral and natural properties. This rejection of the demand for explanation is not very appealing, but the non-naturalist might bolster her position by claiming that others are in an equally difficult place. For example, she might cite other topics where realists have accepted supervenience theses, including the thesis that mental properties de-

---

[4] Naturalist moral realists can claim that there are analytic connections between moral and natural predicates, but more typically they deny this, claiming that moral terms cannot be analysed in natural terms, but nevertheless they refer to natural properties (on an analogy with the identity between water and H_2O – water cannot be analysed as H_2O, but nevertheless water necessarily refers to H_2O). Analytic naturalism is not very plausible, since it has not proved possible to provide naturalistic analyses of moral terms; the non-analytic version is more appealing. However, there are serious questions over whether the semantics of moral terms really are similar to those of natural kind terms and it is not obvious that either type of naturalism is sustainable.

[5] Superdupervenience is "ontological supervenience that is robustly explainable in a materialistically explainable way." (Horgan 1993 p.566). This is more than a moral realist needs to accept, unless they are committed to naturalism. But of course, if they accept non-natural moral properties and they accept a necessary connection that is not naturalistically explicable, they violate naturalism twice over. But if naturalism is false, as the non-naturalist believes, two departures from naturalism are no worse than one. So it is not a compelling objection to a non-naturalist moral realist that she has no naturalistically respectable explanation for supervenience.

pend on physical properties, that chemical properties depend on atomic properties, that colour properties depend on physical properties. It is rare for anyone to offer explanations for the proposed necessary connections between these sets of properties. Yet philosophers advocating these supervenience theses are often realists about the supervening properties. So a moral realist who accepts an unexplained dependence between the moral and the natural is no worse off than these.

This defence of moral realism is vulnerable, however, to someone prepared to be sceptical about all these topics – or rather, someone who would be sceptical about an unexplained necessary connection between the mental and the physical, for example. They might insist that we must be either (type) identity theorists, or irrealists about the mental. In which case, an appeal to "companions in guilt" will not save the moral realist.

4 Denying supervenience

We have seen that the Supervenience Argument fails against naturalist moral realism – for they can explain the dependence of the moral on the natural easily, because moral properties are natural properties. Non-naturalist moral realism (which was Mackie's original target anyway) does not fare so well.

I want now to consider a radical option for non-natural moral realism in response to the Supervenience Argument. Shafer-Landau describes this response as "extreme" and no one to my knowledge has taken it sufficiently seriously even to explore it. This response is to deny supervenience.[6]

Supervenience, whether strong or weak, is a modal claim. It states that there could be no moral difference (within one possible world, or at all) without a natural difference. I suggest that a non-naturalist realist might deny this modal claim and make a much weaker claim about the actual world:

Constant conjunction: in the actual world, there are no differences in moral properties without differences in natural properties.

---

[6] There are other responses open to a non-naturalist, for example Shafer-Landau (2003, pp.80–115). For criticism of this defence of non-naturalism, see Ridge (2007).

In other words a moral difference is constantly conjoined, in the actual world, with a difference in natural properties. But there is no implication that this is so necessarily, or that it must be so in every possible world.

There is a danger that constant conjunction as stated here is a trivial truth. For after all, it is plausible that no two distinct actions have exactly the same natural properties – one must be at a different time, or in a different place, or carried out by a different agent. But there may be a more interesting class of natural properties – such as those connected with welfare or happiness – such that in the actual world there is no difference in moral properties without a difference in those natural properties. This revised version of constant conjunction, that is not trivially true, I will consider as a rival to Supervenience.

> *Constant conjunction (revised)*: in the actual world, there are no differences in moral properties without differences in (some interesting subset of the) natural properties.

The benefits to the non-naturalist of denying supervenience are obvious. There is no metaphysical necessity to explain. The Supervenience Argument must fail. Of course, you might say that there is no point in a non-naturalist moral realist denying supervenience when they are already willing to depart from naturalism by advocating "queer" non-natural properties, and more generally, they are prepared to take on the commitments of common sense morality even at the expense of considerable metaphysical concerns. But even if in general you think that common sense morality can trump metaphysics, in the sense that we should accept the existence of "queer" non-natural properties because common sense morality is committed to them, it does not follow that you should shoulder extra metaphysical burdens when you could just as easily refuse them. And it is quite clear that accepting extra necessary connections is an extra metaphysical cost.

If there is only constant conjunction between two distinct sorts of property, however, and no necessary connection at all, why has everyone thought that there is one? We might appeal to Hume, writing in a very familiar way about a similar problem. According to Hume, we see that cause and effect are constantly conjoined, but we do not see any necessary connection between the two. Nevertheless, we think that there is a necessary connection:

"after a repetition of similar instances, the mind is carried by habit, upon the appearance of one event, to expect its usual attendant, and to believe that it will exist." (Hume, *Enquiries*, p.75).

We have a feeling of determination, of expectation at seeing the effect when we have seen the cause, that is the explanation of our belief that cause and effect are joined by a necessary connection.

Perhaps we can give a similar explanation of our commitment to the supervenience of the moral and the natural. We see that the moral and the natural are constantly conjoined, so that we come to expect to see a difference in the interesting natural properties when we see a moral difference. It is the feeling of expectation that explains our belief that there is a necessary connection between the two. In fact, there may be no necessary connection at all.

But it is not obvious that we can borrow a Humean explanation of our belief in necessary causal connections to explain our commitment to Supervenience. There are important differences between the two. In the first place, we can conceive of causal connections failing to hold. We can imagine that one billiard ball hits the other, and the second explodes, or changes colour, or bursts into flame. But it is not so clear that we can conceive of moral differences without natural differences. And indeed this feature of moral properties has been used in an argument in defence of Supervenience. I will assess this argument in the next section.

5 CONCEIVABILITY

Though many philosophers seems to accept Supervenience in one form or another, arguments for it are rather thin on the ground, perhaps because many people have found the claim so obvious as to not need one (and because no one has seriously argued against it). Blackburn merely says that the supervenience of the moral on the natural is "widely held" and later that to deny it would be a logical mistake. (Blackburn 1993 pp.114, 116, see also p.137.)

Mike Ridge does offer something more in defence of supervenience (his account of supervenience is called S, which in our terms is a version of strong metaphysical supervenience):

(S) is extremely plausible, to the point that someone who denied it would thereby betray incompetence with normative concepts. To deny (S) would be to allow, for all that has been said so far, that it could have been the case that the world was exactly like the actual world in all of its non-normative and descriptive features, yet Hitler's actions were not wrong. Since all the non-normative and descriptive facts are the same in this possible world it will still be true that Hitler killed the same people, had the same intentions, etc. Such bare normative differences seem *inconceivable*. (p.335).[7]

There are plenty of ways that this argument could be questioned. First, one could deny supervenience without accepting that any natural property could be associated with any moral property. So one might deny supervenience without accepting that there is a possible world in which what Hitler did was morally right. But then one would have to explain why this natural property could not be associated with moral rightness, and we have taken on a different but not obviously easier explanatory burden. So I will not question that premise of the argument.

What I really want to look closely at is the connection between conceivability and possibility, or rather on inconceivability and impossibility. I think that this is at the root of many people's acceptance of supervenience, so if the non-naturalist can cast doubt on that connection in this context, she will have made good progress towards denying supervenience.

The connection between possibility and conceivability is notoriously problematic. But rather than talk about general issues, I want to focus on the specific link between conceiving of moral properties and impossibility. The first problem is that it is not at all clear what it is to conceive of a possible world with or without certain moral properties, for example, what exactly is it to imagine that Hitler's actions are or are not morally wrong in some world? If we cannot make good sense of conceiving of moral properties, or failing to conceive of them, the conceivability argument for supervenience obviously fails.

For the purposes of argument, however, I will assume that we can make sense of conceiving that moral properties exist or do not exist in a world. Nevertheless, it is well-known that there are interesting and puzzling issues surrounding conceiving of moral properties. In particular, we seem to find unusual difficulties in imagining that what we believe to be morally wrong is (in some world) morally right. These go under the title

---

[7] Ridge's (S) is his own version of Supervenience: (S) Necessarily: Two entire possible worlds cannot differ in their normative properties without also differing *either* (a) in their non-normative properties or (b) in their descriptive properties. The differences between this thesis and the ones I have set out are not relevant for our purposes, and so I will not be discussing them.

"puzzles of imaginative resistance" and are typically focussed on a discussion of fiction. Whilst some of the puzzles raise issues specific to fiction (such as questions about the authority of a fictional narrator), some of them are more general, puzzles about imagining worlds that need not be fictional in the sense of being explicitly part of a fictional narrative.

Can you imagine Hitler's actions (or actions that are naturalistically identical to Hitler's) being morally right? Probably not. Similarly, you probably cannot imagine that it is morally right to kill a baby because it is a girl, or that genocide and slavery are morally acceptable.

The key question for us is: what is the explanation of this inconceivability? One answer is precisely that we cannot imagine these because they are impossible. Walton explains the issue as follows:

> Moral properties depend or supervene on 'natural' ones ... being evil rests on, for instance, the actions constituting the practices of slavery and genocide ... This ... accounts ... for the resistance to allowing it to be fictional that slavery and genocide are not evil ... Our reluctance to allow moral principles we disagree with to be fictional [that is: true in the world of some fiction] is just an instance of a more general point concerning dependence relations of a certain kind[8]

And further:

> We need an explanation of why we should resist allowing fictional worlds to differ from the real world with respect to the relevant kind of dependence relations. My best suspicion ... is that it has something to do with ... an inability to understand fully what it would be like for them to be different (Walton, 1994, p.46).

We are struggling to imagine something that we think is impossible, that what Hitler did was morally right. We simply cannot understand how that could possibly be true.

If this explanation of our imaginative failure is right, we have some evidence that we are committed to a metaphysically necessary connection between the moral and the natural. Whether this commitment is evidence that there *is* such a connection is a separate question, one that I will not pursue here. Instead I want to consider, drawing on work by Tamar Gendler, whether there is a very different explanation for our imaginative failure.

---

[8] Walton (1994, pp.43–46).

Gendler suggests that, in general, it is possible to imagine that necessarily false propositions are true. But most important is her positive account of the source of the imaginative failure:

> Classic imaginative resistance arises when a reader can't imagine a certain moral claim being true in a story (Imaginative Barriers) because she won't bring herself to adopt the requisite set of generation principles governing the use of moral appraisals (Imaginative Impropriety). So classic imaginative resistance arises when we can't because we won't. (Gendler, 2006, p.164).

Gendler suggests that we think there is something wrong with engaging in an imaginative way with the possibility that murder, genocide and slavery are right, for example. Imagining is different from merely supposing (for the sake of argument), which itself can be somewhat distasteful when what we are asked to suppose is something that we regard as very wrong. Imagining requires more engagement than supposing, however, and is therefore more problematic.

Why don't we want to imagine that something that we think is morally wrong is in fact right? Gendler does not really give an account, but there are a number of possibilities. Perhaps we think it is somehow contaminating to engage with the possibility that it is acceptable to commit mass murder, for example. Or perhaps we think that thoughts and emotional responses associated with morality are habit-forming, and we should not risk forming bad habits. These reasons do not seem to be very strong, but it is quite possible that the desire not to imagine these things is very powerful, even though the reasons for that desire are weaker. [9]

I suggest that support for the "desire" account of resistance comes from reflection on different false moral claims. Consider something at issue between two of the major ethical theories, for example,

---

[9] Is the desire not to imagine that what Hitler did was right sufficient to explain our inability to imagine it? Gendler herself is tempted by a complication. She suggests that we may think that moral claims are metaphysically necessary, so if we think a claim is false, it is impossible. Hence there are two sources of resistance: a desire not to imagine that it is true and an inability to imagine in detail how it could be true (she thinks that the desire not to do so may lead us to notice the incoherence of the claim itself). But this doesn't seem to be an essential part of her explanation of imaginative resistance, and she herself is not sure that it should be a part (at least of all cases of imaginative resistance): "isn't it because I'm not willing to let myself imagine this that I can't see a way for it to be true?" (Gendler, 2006, p.171).

The benevolent lie: Mary told Peter that his prognosis was good, even though she knew that it was not, in order to make him happier in his last days.

Suppose that you think (like the utilitarian) that it is not always wrong to tell a benevolent lie of this kind. Can you imagine that it is always wrong (as the Kantian believes), that it is a failure of respect for that person not to tell them the truth? Surely you can. Similarly, if you believe that the Kantian is right about this, you can imagine that she is not.

But if so, then you can imagine two worlds with the same natural facts (someone tells another a proposition that they believe to be false in order to make her happy), one in which it is morally wrong, one in which it is morally acceptable. Perhaps in one world utilitarianism is true, in another Kant's moral theory is true.

There are two aspects to the benevolent lie example which make it easy to imagine: first, there are well-known moral theories supporting different sides, so it is quite easy to see how this particular claim would fit into a wider theory. Secondly, you may think that it is not always wrong to tell a benevolent lie of this type, but it is not so very far off the mark to think that it is always wrong – certainly not so far off the mark as thinking that what Hitler did was morally acceptable. The more mistaken the moral claim is that we are asked to imagine, the more resistance we feel to doing so.

So there is certainly no problem in supposing for the sake of argument that Kant's moral theory is true, and very little problem in imagining that it is true. And the same for utilitarianism. It is by contrast very difficult to imagine that Hitler was right and not that easy to suppose for the sake of argument that he was.

These are cases in which you are imagining that something you believe to be morally wrong is really morally right (or acceptable). But you can imagine actions that you believe to be morally acceptable are morally wrong too. Suppose that you think that early abortion is morally acceptable. Can you imagine that it is not? I think so – quite easily. Suppose that you think that eating animals is morally acceptable. Can you imagine that it is not? Again, this seems to be quite easy to do. There is no resistance.[10]

---

[10] There are, I think, some difficulties in imagining that something totally morally neutral – like turning on your computer – is morally wrong, partly because it is hard to see how it would fit in with an overall moral theory. But supervenience is not required to explain this.

If the "impossibility" explanation of imaginative resistance were true, it ought to be as difficult to imagine the benevolent lie being always wrong as to imagine that Hitler's actions were right – for both are metaphysically impossible (and both violate strong supervenience, if in this world Hitler's actions were wrong and benevolent lies are sometimes right). Since it is harder to imagine some of these examples than others, the "desire" account should be preferred.

A defender of the "impossibility" interpretation might respond by giving an account of how some things that are metaphysically impossible are easier to imagine than others. I don't think that it is out of the question that we could give such an account – but even if we could, it would still follow that the bare fact of something's being metaphysically impossible does not explain our resistance to imagining it. Imaginative resistance is not explained by our commitment to supervenience as such.

In the absence of this sort of explanation, the "unwillingness" account of why we are resistant to imaging different moral properties associated with the same natural properties is more compelling. In which case, it is not legitimate to cite the impossibility of conceiving of this as grounds for its being impossible. In the first place, as in the benevolent lie example, we can conceive of this. Secondly, in cases when we cannot, the best explanation seems to be that we are unwilling to do so, rather than that to do so is impossible. So we have no grounds for thinking that it is impossible. This argument for strong supervenience fails.

So far we have set out a thought experiment against Strong Supervenience – the claim that if N1 underlies M1, it does so in every possible world – not Weak supervenience – the claim that if N1 underlies M1 in one possible world, it always does so in that world. Consider a possible world in which there are two benevolent lies. Can we suppose for the sake of argument that first utilitarianism is true and the first lie is morally acceptable, then that there is a change in distribution of the moral properties so that Kant's moral theory is true and the second lie is morally wrong? Can we imagine that this is true? I think that, with the background of non-naturalism, this is imaginable. If this is right, then this is reason to think that the conceivability argument does not support weak supervenience either.

I have argued that a non-naturalist moral realist should consider responding to the supervenience argument by denying supervenience, that is, by denying that there is any necessary connection between moral and natural properties. In the last section, I showed that one of the main arguments for supervenience – that it is not conceivable that there might be a change in natural properties without a change in moral properties, therefore it is impossible for there to be such – is not compelling. It does not of course follow that supervenience is false; there might be some strong argument for it that I have not considered (though there are other arguments for supervenience in the literature, I think that the conceivability argument is the strongest that there is). I am not suggesting that supervenience is false because we can imagine a change in moral properties without a change in natural properties – for we may be able to imagine things that are in fact impossible. But given that there is a good explanation of our imaginative failure (when it occurs) that does not appeal to supervenience, the conceivability argument for supervenience fails and we have, as yet, no good reason to accept it. Without any such reason, a non-naturalist moral realist can simply that there is a necessary connection between (what she regards as) two distinct properties.

So are there any reasons for a non-naturalist moral realist not to accept the constant conjunction account? There are a number of objections that might be raised to it and I will consider two here. First, you might wonder whether the constant conjunction (in this world) between (certain) natural properties and moral properties needs explanation. If it does need an explanation, then the non-naturalist moral realist may not have been made any better off by accepting the constant conjunction account over supervenience.

The basic constant conjunction claim, that there happens to be no change in moral properties in this world without a change in natural properties is likely to be a trivial truth, for any two actions will have different natural properties (at least in terms of the time they take place, where they occur and the identity of the agent and those affected by the action). Clearly a trivial truth like that requires no explanation. Suppose that we restrict our attention to an interesting subset of the natural properties. Do we need an explanation for why there happens to be no change in moral properties without a change in those natural properties in this world? I do not think that a mere regularity, with no implications that the connection is necessary, does require an explanation. It is simply a brute fact, admittedly one that makes a certain kind of moral reasoning and moral argument possible. But a brute fact that does not require explanation nonetheless.

The second problem is potentially more serious. Is the constant conjunction account consistent with moral epistemology? What is the point of thought experiments for example, if you are not finding out about a necessary connection between properties? How could reflection on moral problems possibly be a reasonable strategy if you are not reflecting on a necessary connection?

It is certainly true that reflection and thought experiments play an important role in moral epistemology. But experience also plays an important role; it is sometimes true that one cannot appreciate whether an action is right or wrong without being the agent or the victim. And when one is acquiring moral beliefs in the first place, testimony from one's parents and guardians, friends and peers is very important.

According to constant conjunction accounts, when you are reflecting on moral problems or considering thought experiments, you are making use of a regularity that exists in this world between moral and natural properties. This regularity you may first discover through experience or through the testimony of others. Then you can use your knowledge in thought experiments to consider possible situations that you have not met – just as an experienced engineer might be able to use reflection or a thought experiment to tell you whether a bridge would stand up if it were built.

Of course there remain significant questions of moral epistemology for a non-naturalist moral realist, in particular, they need to offer an explanation of how we can ever discern non-naturalist moral properties or facts. But this is plainly a serious difficulty for a non-naturalist moral realist whether she accepts supervenience or constant conjunction. So the constant conjunction account does not raise any significant problems of moral epistemology, over those that the non-naturalist already has.

7. CONCLUSION

A non-naturalist moral realist could accept that (a certain subset of) the natural properties are constantly conjoined with the moral properties, rather than that there is a necessary connection between the two. So there is no argument against non-naturalist moral realism on the basis of supervenience.

REFERENCES

Blackburn, S. 1993. *Essays in Quasi-Realism*. Oxford: OUP.

Gendler, T. S. 2000. "The Puzzle of Imaginative Resistance" *The Journal of Philosophy*, 97.2, pp.55–81.

Gendler, T.S. 2006. "Imaginative Resistance Revisted", S. Nichols ed. *The Architecture of the Imagination*. Oxford University Press, pp.149–173.

Horgan, T. 1993. "From Supervenience to Superdupervenience: Meeting the Demands of a Material World" *Mind* 102, pp.555–586.

Hume, D. *Enquiry Concerning Human Understanding*, in *Enquiries Concerning Human Understanding and Concerning the Principles of Morals*, edited by L.A. Selby-Bigge, 3rd edition revised by P.H. Nidditch, Oxford: Clarendon Press, 1975.

Mackie, J.L. 1977. *Ethics: Inventing Right and Wrong*. New York: Penguin Books.

Ridge, M. 2007. "Anti-reductionism and Supervenience" *Journal of Moral Philosophy*, 4.3, pp.330–348.

Shafer-Landau, R. 2003. *Moral Realism: A Defence*. Oxford: OUP.

Walton, K. 1994. "Morals in Fiction and Fictional Morality/I," *Proceedings of the Aristotelian Society*, Supplementary Volume 68, pp.27–50.

ALTERNATIVE REDUCTIONS FOR DYNAMIC DEONTIC LOGICS

ALBERT J.J. ANGLBERGER
University of Salzburg

Abstract

A recent approach to deontic logic – the logic of permission, obligation and prohibition – places deontic logic into a dynamic framework. In dynamic logics we differentiate between actions and assertions. For every action term α, an execution operator '$[\alpha]$…' is introduced, which is read as 'every execution of α leads to a state in which … holds'. Enriching our language by a violation constant V, allows us to reduce deontic predicates in two obvious ways: (i) An action is forbidden iff every execution leads to a violation, (ii) an action is forbidden iff at least one execution leads to a violation. Both reductions lead – besides being somewhat coarse grained – to implausible theorems. In our paper we will address the question: where and how one may find more sophisticated reductions.

1 INTRODUCTION: STANDARD DEONTIC LOGIC AND ANDERSONIAN REDUCTIONS

In the standard systems of deontic logic – the logic of obligations, permissions and forbiddances, originating from [von Wright 1951] – the language of propositional logic is extended by (at least one of) the normative operators 'O', 'P' and 'F' for 'it ought to be the case that', 'it is permitted that it is the case that' and 'it is forbidden that it is the case that', respectively. At least one of these operators is primitive in those systems. Taken 'O' as primitive, the other operators are usually introduced via the definitions

    (DF) $F\varphi \leftrightarrow O\neg\varphi$, where φ is an arbitrary formula

and

    (DP) $P\varphi \leftrightarrow \neg O\neg\varphi$, where φ is an arbitrary formula.

A system of deontic logic is said to have the property of strong interdefinability iff (DP) and (DF) hold in it. Furthermore we call a deontic logic *re-*

ductive iff every formula containing a deontic operator is equivalent to a formula without deontic operators. In a reductive deontic logic normative operators can therefore be eliminated.

The proof theory of the simplest deontic logic is the modal logic D and its semantics therefore a Kripke-semantics with serial frames. Additionally it contains (DP) and (DF). From now on we shall call this logic the *standard system of deontic logic* (short: *SDL*). Hence, we may call SDL non-reductive, and SDL has the property of strong interdefinability.

In [Anderson 1958] Alan Ross Anderson presented a reduction of deontic logic to alethic modal logic. He enriched the modal base language by the propositional constant 'S', which he interpreted as occurrence of a sanction. His reduction was

(AR) $O\varphi \leftrightarrow \Box(\neg\varphi \to S)$,

meaning that it ought to be the case that φ iff it is necessary that $\neg\varphi$ implies a sanction. The other deontic operators were introduced via (DF) and (DP). Obviously, Anderson's deontic logic is reductive and has the property of strong interdefinability.

(AR) may be criticized for several reasons. E.g. the formula

(PR) $P\varphi \leftrightarrow \Diamond(\varphi \land \neg S)$

can be derived from (AR), (DP) and its modal base logic. In words: It is permitted that φ iff it is possible that φ but no sanction occurs. (PR) suggests a very weak notion of permission, maybe a notion too weak. However, it can be shown that

(PA) $Op \to \Box Op$

and

(PA*) $\Box(p \to q) \to (Op \to Oq)$

are theorems in Anderson's logic too. (PA) excludes obligations that are not necessary and (PA*) yields the (in)famous *Good Samaritan Paradox*. Additionally, Anderson's deontic logic contains *SDL*, and with it all its paradoxes. This shows – as it has been argued – that the reduction (AR) was not successful.

In 1950 a similar reduction has already been proposed by Stig Kanger in an unpublished manuscript. Kanger discusses in [Kanger 1971] his reduction

$$(KR) \; O\varphi \leftrightarrow \Box(Q \to \varphi),$$

where 'Q' is a propositional constant stating what is morally prescribed. (KR) hence reads 'φ ought to be the case iff it is necessary that the morally prescribed implies φ'. Defining 'Q' as '$\neg S$', Kanger's reduction (KR) turns out to be equivalent to Anderson's reduction (AR).

The implausible theorems depend on the specific reduction and on the modal base logic. Is it possible to avoid them in a different framework? In the next sections we will explore more recent approaches to such reductions. These reductions are formulated in a different formal language, hence, in a different base logic: in the language of a dynamic logic.

2. DYNAMIC DEONTIC LOGICS: KNOWN REDUCTIONS

2.1 Dynamic Logics: Execution Operators

In the language of a dynamic logic we differentiate between *action terms* and *assertions*. The language of propositional logic is extended by the undefined *execution operator* '[..]...' which applied to an action term α and a formula φ yields the formula

'$[\alpha]\varphi$'

which reads: 'every execution of α leads to a state in which φ holds'.

The dual operator '$\langle\alpha\rangle\varphi$' is defined as '$\neg[\alpha]\neg\varphi$', which reads 'there is an execution of α that leads to a state in which φ holds'. Instead of '$[\alpha]\varphi$' it is sometimes said that α *leads* to φ, and '$\langle\alpha\rangle\varphi$' is also read as '$\alpha$ *may* lead to φ'.

With the operator '$\langle..\rangle...$' we can elegantly define that an action is possible in a certain state: An action is possible iff there is a way to execute that action such that after its execution a tautology holds. In our formal language:

$$(DPoss) \; Possible(\alpha) \leftrightarrow \langle\alpha\rangle\mathsf{T},$$

where 'T' represents an arbitrary tautology. In its simplest form, the proof theory of '[..]...' is the modal logic K, extended by special axioms for complex actions.

2.2 Dynamic Logics: Actions

We start with a denumerable set of *atomic action terms*. A very natural way to interpret actions is to assign to each atomic action a set of ordered pairs of states (i.e. possible worlds). The first element of such a pair is a *start state*, the second element a *result state*.

On the basis of atomic actions we may construct several *complex actions*, for example

(Negation)	$\sim\alpha$	... not-α
(Choice)	$\alpha\cup\beta$	... α or β
(Conjunction)	$\alpha\&\beta$	... α and β
(Sequence)	$\alpha;\beta$	... α followed by β

One natural way to interpret these complex actions is as *set theoretic complement (w.r.t. to the set of all ordered pairs of possible worlds), union, intersection and relative product,* respectively. Depending on what kind of complex actions are allowed in the language, we get different proof theories. Unfortunately, a proof theory for & interpreted as intersection gets already very complicated (because & interpreted as intersection is not modally definable, see [Balbiani 2003]). Moreover, the question of how to interpret action negation remains a field of research in its own right (see for example [Broersen 2004]).

2.3 Dynamic Deontic Logics: Reductions

Looking back to the beginning of dynamic logic, Krister Segerberg has already developed a reduction of deontic logic to a dynamic logic in [Segerberg 1980]. Segerberg defined

(SR) $P\alpha \leftrightarrow [\alpha]OK,$

where '*OK*' is a propositional constant, expressing that a state is "deontically satisfactory". (SR) therefore calls an action permitted iff every execution of that action leads to a state which is deontically satisfactory.

Nevertheless, the first systematic contribution to dynamic deontic logic is to be found in Meyer's famous paper [Meyer 1988]. Meyer enriched the dynamic base language by the propositional constant V – standing for *violation* – which is said to be true in a state iff a violation occurs in that state. He then proposed the following reduction:

(R1) $F\alpha \leftrightarrow [\alpha]V$,

which calls an action α forbidden iff every execution of α leads to a violation. Additionally, we find the strong interdefinabilities

(DOD) $O\alpha \leftrightarrow F\sim\alpha$ and
(DPD) $P\alpha \leftrightarrow \neg F\alpha$

in Meyer's deontic logic PD_eL. (R1), (DOD) and (DPD) imply that PD_eL is reductive too. (R1) and (DPD) lead – together with some basic principles of dynamic logic – to

(MP) $P\alpha \leftrightarrow \langle\alpha\rangle\neg V$,

meaning that it is permitted to do α iff there is a way to execute α that leads to a state in which no violation occurs. (MP) and (R1) look very similar to Anderson's reduction (AR), and (PR). This justifies calling (R1) – as Meyer did himself – an *Andersonian reduction*. The crucial question now is: Does the shift from a "classical" modal base logic to a dynamic logic prevent all implausible theorems – usually called *paradoxes* – from being provable? Meyer had great hopes in his reduction. He claims that "reducing deontic logic to dynamic logic kills two birds with one stone. Most importantly, in this way we get rid of most (if not all) of the nasty paradoxes that have plagued traditional deontic logic." [Meyer 1993, p.11] Unfortunately, it was shown by R. van der Meyden in [vd Meyden 1990] and [vd Meyden 1996], and by myself in [Anglberger 2008], that some pretty nasty paradoxes are provable in PD_eL. Van der Meyden showed that the paradoxical formula

(vdM) $\langle\alpha\rangle P\beta \rightarrow P(\alpha;\beta)$

is a theorem in Meyer's logic. For its proof only (R1) and some basic principles of dynamic logic are needed. (vdM) has the highly implausible instantiation:

(vdMi) If there is an execution of shooting the president after which it is permitted to remain silent, then it is permitted to shoot the president followed by remaining silent.

In [Anglberger 2008] I was able to prove another implausible theorem in PD_eL, the formula

(T3) $F\alpha \rightarrow [\alpha]F\beta$.

(T3) says that after a forbidden action has been done, any arbitrary action is forbidden. (T3) may be regarded as the dynamic pendant of the *Paradox of Derived Obligation* (since $F\beta \leftrightarrow O{\sim}\beta$). This last paradox also has consequences for the treatment of contrary to duty imperatives, see [Anglberger 2008, p.430]. Additionally, if we extend Meyer's logic with the dynamic pendant of the axiom **D**

(Dd) $O\alpha \rightarrow P\alpha$

from classical deontic logic (which may be desired), we will be able to derive a theorem stating that no possible action is forbidden (see [Anglberger 2008, p.432]). But van der Meyden's paradox still seems to be the more interesting one. This is because in (T3)'s proof Meyer's full action algebra (and of course the dynamic base logic) was needed. The preconditions of (vdM)'s proof are therefore logically weaker and show with much more distinctness that (R1) needs to be given up, if we want to keep the dynamic framework.

In his paper [Broersen 2004] on action negation, J. Broersen proposed a different reduction. His reduction was

(R2) $P\alpha \leftrightarrow [\alpha]\neg V_p,$

where V_p is a propositional constant representing a special kind of violation ("permission-violation"). Broersen gave up strong interdefinability, he rather suggested a separate reduction for each deontic predicate. But his logic is still reductive; every deontic predicate can be eliminated. Furthermore, if 'OK' is defined as '$\neg V_p$' Broersen's 2004 reduction (R2) is equivalent to Segerberg's 1980 reducion (SR).

It was observed by Broersen himself that (R2) presupposes a special reading of actions. (R2) implies

(R2T) $P\alpha \rightarrow P(\alpha \& \beta)$,

which at first sight looks highly implausible. But under the so-called *open reading of actions* (R2T) becomes valid. The open reading of actions means that, whenever we talk about an action, we talk about *every way to perform* this action. Since $\alpha \& \beta$ is a way to perform α, $P(\alpha \& \beta)$ is implied by $P\alpha$. This validates (R2T). However, there definitely is a reason, why (R2T) looks paradoxical. Though quite interesting and elegant, the open reading of actions is simply not the one used in our ethical and juridical discourse. That is why, from an intuitive point of view, nearly everyone would immediately reject (R2T). Should not a deontic logic somehow model our (or at least: *one* of our) usage(s) of deontic expressions? Since a deontic logic is designed to be applied in ethical and juridical discourse, it seems justified to look for more "sophisticated" reductions.

3 ALTERNATIVE REDUCTIONS

3.1 A Bit of History

The paradoxes of classical deontic logics are usually regarded as a touchstone for any new system of deontic logic. As quoted above, Meyer hoped that his system would be able to solve all (or nearly all) of these paradoxes. However, when working out a solution for – as he calls it – "the deepest paradox in deontic logic" (i.e. the Good Samaritan Paradox) in [Meyer 1987], he recognized that his simple reduction was not sophisticated enough. He had to introduce more than just one violation constant. Therefore he extended the language of the dynamic base logic by n many violation constants $V_1, V_2, ..., V_n$ where the index i $(1 \leq i \leq n)$ of V_i indicates a violation of the i-th degree. Furthermore, he proposed n new reductions of the form

(R1n) $F_i(\alpha) \leftrightarrow [\alpha]V_i$, where $i = 1, 2, ..., n$.

With (R1n) he was able to express certain *degrees of forbiddance*: '$F_1(\alpha)$' was interpreted as 'α is forbidden to degree one', '$F_3(\beta)$' as 'β is forbidden to degree three' etc. In this example β is thus "more forbidden" than α. But this reduction is not able to solve the problems mentioned above: (R1n) is simply (R1) for every level $i = 1, 2,\ldots, n$. It is therefore possible to prove the aforementioned paradoxical formulae on every level. But in our opinion, it hints at a possible way for constructing new reductions.

3.2 New Reductions

3.2.1 Ordering violations

Let $L_{dyn(n)}$ be a language of dynamic logic extended by a finite number n of violation constants $V_1, V_2,\ldots, V_n$. V_n is true in a state iff a violation of the n-th degree occurs in this state. Interestingly, at the end of his paper [Meyer 1987] Meyer discusses the possibility of ordering these violations:

> The extension of the number of propositional variables related to sanctions also raises the question whether it is meaningful to put an ordering (e.g. a partial ordering) on them. $V_i \leq V_j$ for instance, would then express that sanction j is more severe than sanction i. Perhaps even $V_j \supset V_i$ [in our terminology: $V_j \to V_i$] can be chosen as an ordering. In this case, $[\alpha]V_j \wedge V_i \equiv [\alpha]V_j$ [in our terminology: $[\alpha]V_j \wedge V_i \leftrightarrow [\alpha]V_j$], since V_j comprises V_i entirely. [Meyer 1987, p.89]

Meyer did not work out this stimulating thought, though it opens up very interesting possibilities. In fact, we will use Meyer's own suggestion – the ordering of violations – as our only axiom for violations:

(AxV) $V_i \to V_{i-1}$, for all i ($1 < i \leq n$), where n is the number of violation constants in $L_{dyn(n)}$.

This axiom may be motivated along various lines. For example, consider the following a bit more concrete application: V_n expresses that one has to stay in prison for n days – a possible measure of a violation. If one has to stay in prison for n days, one also has to stay in prison for $n-1$ days. In this application (AxV) is obviously valid. In general: Whenever a state is "bad" to a certain degree, it also is "bad" to every degree below.

To achieve model theoretic validity of (AxV) we just have to postulate the according condition in the definition of a Kripke-model $\langle W, R, I \rangle$. In addition to the usual requirements on W (the set of possible worlds), R

(interpretation of actions) and I (valuation) the following condition has to be met:

(CAxV) $I(V_i) \subseteq I(V_{i-1})$, for all violation constants V_i ($1 < i \leq n$)

3.2.2 Evaluating the deontic status of actions

Consider the following situation: An airplane is about to crash because of some technical failure. Its pilot cannot prevent the airplane from crashing. Suppose further, that only two actions are available to the pilot: The first option is to crash-land the plane and by that maybe saving some people, the second option is to refrain from crash-landing the plane and by that killing all passengers with certainty. Though both actions would lead to an undesirable state of affairs – to a violation –, we would intuitively only call the second one *forbidden*. The reason for this is quite simple: In judging actions we usually relate them to other available options; if we intend to blame a person for having done something, we ask beforehand, what *she could have done instead*. Relating to our "airplane example": If the pilot tried to crash-land the plane, we could not blame her for having done something wrong, because it was the best action among its alternatives (actually, there was only one alternative to the crash-landing).

Summing this up: When evaluating the deontic status of an action we usually relate this action to other available alternatives. A (realistic) deontic logic should also somehow consider this idea. At this point one question naturally arises: Can this be expressed within the language $L_{dyn(n)}$ of a dynamic (deontic) logic?

3.2.3 Introducing new reductions

In dynamic logic an action can easily be compared with one of its alternatives: We just have to compare an action with its negation. Of course, what exactly is compared here depends on how action negation is modelled. If action negation is modelled as set theoretic complement – as mentioned above – it is not clear, whether it is useful in ethical and juridical discourse (for a more extensive critique see [Broersen 2004]). So this model of action negation does probably not suit our purposes. But there is a more realistic account: Broersen's relativized action negation from [Broersen 2004] models refraining from an action. Within Broersen's account doing $\sim\alpha$ means refraining from doing α. And refraining from doing α is a choice among (all) other available actions, i.e. (in a way) α's alternatives. With Broersen's relativized action negation we can express the comparison needed. This leads to the question: In what respect do we have to compare α with $\sim\alpha$? In our formal language we can compare them with respect to their *outcomes* (i.e. result states). Consider the formula

$$[\alpha]V_3 \wedge [\beta]\neg V_3.$$

The ordering implies that this formula expresses that doing β never leads to a greater violation than V_2 (otherwise the right conjunct would have to be false). This in turn means that every execution of α is worse – i.e. leads to a greater violation – than every execution of β. Furthermore, when comparing two actions, the ordering of violations allows us to measure the upper bound of their outcomes w.r.t. violations. E.g. the formula

$$\exists k([\alpha]V_k \wedge [\beta]\neg V_k)$$

expresses that there is a certain degree of violation such that every execution of α leads to that violation whereas every execution of β does not. The index k is the upper bound of these violations that may be led to by α (but not by β). The existential quantifier is justified by the fact that only finitely many violation constants are allowed in $L_{dyn(n)}$. There is no need for quantification over propositional variables as developed in [Shilov 1997] – it is a mere technical convenience: Let's suppose the number of violation constants is n. The formula above may then be rewritten (without the existential quantifier) as

$$([\alpha]V_1 \wedge [\beta]\neg V_1) \vee ([\alpha]V_2 \wedge [\beta]\neg V_2) \vee \dots \vee ([\alpha]V_n \wedge [\beta]\neg V_n)$$

i.e. a disjunction of n conjunctions.

Substituting '$\sim\alpha$' for 'β' in the above formula, we get the formula

$$\exists k([\alpha]V_k \wedge [\sim\alpha]\neg V_k),$$

which says that $\sim\alpha$ leads necessarily to a better state than α – every execution of α leads to a greater violation than every execution of $\sim\alpha$. One might now suggest the following reduction:

(NR1) $F\alpha \leftrightarrow \exists k([\alpha]V_k \wedge [\sim\alpha]\neg V_k),$

which calls an action α forbidden iff $\sim\alpha$'s outcome is always better than α's outcome. This seems to be too strong. A more useful concept could be defined by

(NR1*) $F\alpha \leftrightarrow \exists k([\alpha]V_k \wedge \langle\sim\alpha\rangle\neg V_k)$.

(NR1*) defines an action α as forbidden iff $\sim\alpha$ *may lead* to a better state than every execution of α. Consider our "airplane example" once again: There is an execution of refraining from doing nothing – e.g. crash landing the plane – which *may lead* to a better state (some people may be saved) than every "execution" of doing nothing (all people are going to die with certainty). That is why we would call the "action" of doing nothing forbidden. A second relevant factor seems to be, that, if an action α is forbidden, $\sim\alpha$ has to be possible (the meaning of an action being possible was defined above). This is a version of the *Principle of Alternate Possibilities* (= PAP) and – at least in the dynamic formalization with strong interdefinabilities – a version of the *Ought Implies Can Principle*. This leads to a second and better reduction:

(NR1**) $F\alpha \leftrightarrow Possible(\sim\alpha) \wedge \exists k([\alpha]V_k \wedge \langle\sim\alpha\rangle\neg V_k)$

However, there is still one relevant condition missing: If we call an action α forbidden, it may lead to a violation. If every execution of α leads solely to states where no violation whatsoever occurs, α would not be called forbidden. One natural way to express this is the formula

$\langle\alpha\rangle (V_1 \vee V_2 \vee \ldots \vee V_n)$.

Though it is a sound formalization of this thought, the formula still contains redundancies. Since we may use our ordering axiom, we can easily verify that

$\langle\alpha\rangle V_1$

is a shorter but equivalent formulation. This leads us to our final proposal:

(NR1F) $F\alpha \leftrightarrow \langle\alpha\rangle V_1 \wedge Possible(\sim\alpha) \wedge \exists k([\alpha]V_k \wedge \langle\sim\alpha\rangle\neg V_k)$

In a nutshell, (NR1F) calls an action α forbidden iff the following conditions are satisfied:

(i) α may lead to a violation,
(ii) it has to be possible to refrain from doing α,
(iii) if one refrains from doing α, we may end up in a better state than what is reachable by doing α.

This reduction is much more complex than (R1) and (R2), and obviously the mentioned paradoxes vanish. Whether (NR1F) leads to new paradoxes has to be further investigated. Anyway, (NR1F) seems to be a more realistic concept of *forbiddance*. A fact that justifies our hope of (possible) implausible theorems not exceeding a certain (reasonable) extent.

3.3 Further Research

The language $L_{dyn(n)}$ can easily be extended. For example, we could add m *reward constants* $R_1, ..., R_m$ to $L_{dyn(n)}$. A similar idea was already suggested by Meyer in his paper [Meyer 1988, p.125], though Meyer had only one reward constant in mind. The method developed in our paper – measuring the upper bounds of outcomes – makes it possible to define several concepts of *praiseworthiness*. This would also allow us to make a distinction between actions that ought to be done and actions that are praiseworthy. Praiseworthy actions are "better" than obliged actions; an action might be too good to be obliged.

REFERENCES

[Anglberger 2008] Anglberger, A.J.J.: Dynamic Deontic Logic and its Paradoxes. In: *Studia Logica* 89 (2008), pp.427–435.
[Anderson 1958] Anderson A.R.: A Reduction of Deontic Logic to Alethic Modal Logic. In: *Mind* 67 (1958), pp.100–103.
[Balbiani 2003] Balbiani et al.: PDL with Intersection of Programs: A Complete Axiomatization. In: *Journal of Applied Non-Classical Logics* 13, No.3–4 (2003), pp.231–276.
[Broersen 2004] Broersen, J.: Action Negation and Alternative Reductions for Dynamic Deontic Logics. In: *Journal of Applied Logic* 2 (2004), pp.153–168.
[Kanger 1971] Kanger, S.: New Foundations for Ethical Theory. In: Føllesdal D., Hilpinen R. (eds): *Deontic Logic: Introductory and Systematic Readings.* Dordrecht : D. Reidel Publishing Company, 1971, pp.36–58.

[Meyer 1987] Meyer, J.-J.C.: A Simple Solution to the "Deepest" Paradox in Deontic Logic. In: *Logique et Analyse* 117–118 (1987), pp.81–90.

[Meyer 1988] Meyer, J.-J.C.: A Different Approach to Deontic Logic: Deontic Logic Viewed as a Variant of Dynamic Logic. In: *Notre Dame Journal of Formal Logic* 29 (1988), pp. 109–136.

[Meyer 1993] Meyer, J.-J.C.: Deontic Logic: A Concise Overview. In: Meyer, J.-J.C., Wieringa, R.J. (eds.): *Deontic Logic in Computer Science*. Chichester: John Wiley and Sons Ltd., 1993, pp.3–16.

[Segerberg 1980] Segerberg, K.: Applying Modal Logic. In: *Studia Logica* 39 (1980), pp.275–295.

[Shilov 1997] Shilov, N.V.: Program Schemata vs. Automata for Decidability of Program Logics. In: *Theoretical Computer Science* 175 (1997), pp.15–27.

[vdMeyden 1990] Meydern, R. van d.: The Dynamic Logic of Permission. In: *Proc. 5th IEEE Conf. on Logic in Computer Science*, Philadelphia (1990), pp.72–78.

[vdMeyden 1996] Meyden, R. van d.: The Dynamic Logic of Permission. In: *Journal of Logic and Computation* 6 (1996), Nr.3, pp.465–479.

[von Wright 1951] Wright, G.H. von.: Deontic Logic. In: *Mind* 60 (1951) pp.1–15.

II.
Abstraction

THE METAPHYSICS AND
EPISTEMOLOGY OF ABSTRACTION[*]

CRISPIN WRIGHT
University of St. Andrews & New York University

1

Paul Benacerraf famously wondered[1] how any satisfactory account of mathematical knowledge could combine a face-value semantic construal of classical mathematical theories, such as arithmetic, analysis and set-theory – one which takes seriously the apparent singular terms and quantifiers in the standard formulations – with a sensibly *naturalistic* conception of our knowledge-acquisitive capacities as essentially operative within and subject to the domain of causal law. The problem, very simply, is that the entities apparently called for by the face-value construal – finite cardinals, reals and sets – do not, seemingly, participate in the causal swim. A refinement of the problem, due to Field, challenges us to explain what reason there is to suppose that our basic beliefs about such entities, encoded in standard axioms, could possibly be formed reliably by means solely of what are presumably naturalistic belief-forming mechanisms. These problems have cast a long shadow over recent thought about the epistemology of mathematics.

Although ultimately Fregean in inspiration, Abstractionism – often termed 'neo-Fregeanism' – was developed with the goal of responding to them firmly in view. The response is organised under the aegis of a kind of linguistic – better, propositional – 'turn' which I suggest it is helpful to see as part of the content of Frege's Context Principle. The turn is this. It is not that, *before* we can understand how knowledge is possible of statements referring to or quantifying over the abstract objects of mathematics, we need to understand how such objects can be given to us as objects of acquaintance or how some other belief-forming mechanisms might be sensitive to them and their characteristics. Rather we need to tackle directly the ques-

---

[*] This is a shortened version of Bob Hale's and my "The *Metaontology* of Abstraction" – Hale and Wright (2009). My thanks to Oxford University Press for permission to publish the present paper here.
[1] in Benacerraf (1973).

tion how propositional thought about such objects is possible and how it can be knowledgeable. And this must be answered by reference to an account of how meaning is conferred upon the ordinary statements that concern such objects, an account which at the same time must be fashioned to cast light on how the satisfaction of the truth-conditions it associates with them is something that is accessible, in standard cases, to human cognitive powers.[2]

Abstraction principles are the key device in the epistemological project so conceived. Standardly, an abstraction principle is formulated as a universally quantified biconditional – schematically:

$$(\forall a)(\forall b)(S(a) = S(b) \leftrightarrow E(a, b)),$$

where a and b are variables of a given type (typically first- or second-order), 'S' is a term-forming operator, denoting a function from items of the given type to objects in the range of the first-order variables, and E is an equivalence relation over items of the given type.[3] What is crucial from the abstractionist point of view is an epistemological perspective which sees these principles as, in effect, stipulative implicit definitions of the S-operator and thereby of the new kind of term formed by means of it and of a corresponding sortal concept. For this purpose it is assumed that the equivalence relation, E, is already understood and that the kind of entities that constitute its range are familiar – that each relevant instance of the right hand side of the abstraction, $E(a, b)$, has truth-conditions which are grasped and which in a suitably wide range of cases can be known to be satisfied or not in ways that, for the purposes of the Benacerrafian concern, count as

---

[2] For efforts to develop and defend this approach, see Wright (1983), ch.1; Hale (1987), chs.1,7; Hale & Wright (2001), Introduction sect.3.1, Essays 5,6; Hale & Wright (2002)

[3] More complex forms of abstraction are possible – see, for example, Hale (2000), p.107, where positive real numbers are identified with ratios of quantities, these being defined by abstraction over a four-term relation. One could replace this by a regular equivalence relation on ordered pairs of quantities, but this is not necessary – it is straightforward to extend the usual notion of an equivalence relation to such cases. It is also possible – and possibly philosophically advantageous, insofar as it encourages linking the epistemological issues surrounding abstraction principles with those concerning basic logical rules – to formulate abstractions as pairs of schematic introduction- and elimination-rules for the relevant operator, corresponding respectively to the transitions right-to left and left-to right across instances of the more normal quantified biconditional formulation.

unproblematic. In sum: the abstraction principle explains the truth conditions of S-identities as coincident with those of a kind of statement we already understand and know how to know. So, the master thought is, we can now exploit this prior ability in such a way as to get to know of identities and distinctions among the referents of the S-terms – entities whose existence is assured by the truth of suitable such identity statements. And these knowledge possibilities are assured without any barrier being posed by the nature – in particular, the abstractness – of the objects in question (though of course what pressure there may be to conceive of the referents of terms introduced by abstraction *as* abstract, and whether just on that account or for other reasons, is something to be explored independently[4].)

2

There are very many issues raised by this proposal. One might wonder, to begin with, whether, even if no other objection to it is made, it could possibly be of much interest merely to recover the means to understand and know the truth value of suitable examples of the schematised type of identity statement, bearing in mind the ideological richness displayed by the targeted mathematical theories of cardinals, real numbers and sets. The answer is that abstraction principles, austere as they may seem, do – in a deployment that exploits the collateral resources of second-order logic and suitable additional definitions – provide the resources to recover these riches – or at least, to recover theories which stand interpretation as containing them.[5] There then are the various misgivings – for example, about "Bad Company" (differentiating acceptable abstraction principles from various kinds of unacceptable ones), about Julius Caesar (in effect, whether abstraction principles provide for a sufficient range of uses of the defined terms to count as properly explaining their semantic contribution, or justifying the attribution of reference to them), about impredicativity in the key (second-order) abstractions that underwrite the development of arithmetic

---

[4] See Hale & Wright (2001), Essay 14, sect.4, for discussion of an argument aimed at showing that abstracts introduced by first-order abstraction principles such as Frege's Direction Equivalence cannot be identified with contingently existing concrete objects.
[5] At least, they do so for arithmetic and analysis. So much is the burden of Frege's Theorem, so called, and work of Hale and, separately, Shapiro. For arithmetic, see Wright (1983), ch.4; Boolos (1990) and (1998), pp.138–141; Hale & Wright (2001), pp.4–6; and for analysis, Hale (2000) and Shapiro (2000). The prospects for an abstractionist recovery of a decently strong set theory remain unclear.

and analysis, and about the status of the underlying (second-order) logic – with which the secondary literature over the last twenty-five years has mostly been occupied. For the purposes of the present discussion, I assume all these matters to have been resolved.[6] Even so, another major issue may seem to remain. There has been a comparative dearth of head-on discussion of the abstractionist's central *ontological* idea: that it is permissible to fix the truth-conditions of one kind of statement as coinciding with those of another – 'kind' here referring to something like logical form – in such a way that the overt *existential* implications of the former exceed those of the latter, although the *epistemological* status of the latter, as conceived in advance, is inherited by the former. Recently however there have been signs of increasing interest in this proposal among analytical metaphysicians. A number of writers have taken up the issue of how to "make sense" of the abstractionist view of the ontology of abstraction principles, with a variety of proposals being canvassed as providing the 'metaontology' abstractionists need, or to which they are committed.[7] I shall here describe what I regard as the correct view of the matter.

3

In what follows, I shall try to address two questions, one metaphysical and one epistemological, – questions that some may feel need answering before abstractionism should even be considered to be a competitive option. The metaphysical question is:

---

[6] Since the 'noise' from the entrenched debates about Bad Company, Impredicativity, etc., is considerable, it may help in what follows for the reader to think in terms of a context in which a first order abstraction is being proposed – say Frege's well known example of the Direction Principle:

Direction(a) = Direction(b) iff. a and b are parallel

in which range of 'a' and 'b' is restricted to concrete straight lines – actual inscriptions, for example – and of the listed concerns, only the Caesar problem remains. The pure ontological problems about abstraction – if indeed they are problems – arise here in a perfectly clean form.

Previous discussions of the more purely ontological issues are to be found in Wright (1983), chs.1–3; Hale (1987); Hale & Wright (2001), Essays 1–9 and 14.

[7] In particular, Eklund (2006), Sider (2007), Hawley (2007), and Cameron (2007) all discuss the abstractionist's (alleged) need for a suitable 'metaontology'.

(M) What does the world have to be like in order for (the best examples of) abstraction to work?

And the associated epistemological question is:

(E) How do we know – what reason can be given for thinking – that the transition, right to left, across the biconditional in instances of (the best examples of) abstraction is truth preserving?[8]

Very different conceptions are possible of what it is to give a satisfactory answer to question (E); that is, to justify the thought that a good abstraction is truth-preserving, right-to-left. One such conception, which I reject, has it, in effect, that it is, in some sense, *possible*[9] – something we have initially no dialectical right to discount – for any abstraction to fail right-to-left unless some relevant kind of independent, collateral assurance is forthcoming from the metaphysical nature of the world. There are, that is to say, possible situations – in some relevant sense of 'possible' – in which an abstraction which actually succeeds would fail, even though *conceptually*, at the level of explanation and the understanding thereby imparted, everything is as it is in the successful scenario. Hence in order to make good that the right-to-left transition of an otherwise good abstraction is truth-preserving, argument is needed that some relevant form of metaphysical assurance is indeed provided. This is, plausibly, the way that the metaphysicians who call for a suitably supportive 'metaontology' are thinking about the issue. The 'possible' scenario would be one in which not everything that could exist does exist – in particular, the denoted abstracts do not exist. And the requisite collateral assurance, to be sought within the province of metaphysics, would be that this 'possibility' is not a genuine possibility – because, for instance, maximalism[10] is true (and is so, presumably, as a matter of metaphysical necessity.) Although the idea is by no means as clear as one would like, I reject this felt need for some kind of collateral metaphysical assistance. The kind of justification which I acknowledge *is* called for is precisely justification for the thought that no such collateral assistance is necessary. There is no hostage to redeem. A (good) abstraction *itself* has the resources to close off the alleged (epistemic metaphysi-

---

[8] I will hence generally omit the parenthetical qualification "the best examples of". But except where stated otherwise, it is to be understood.

[9] – perhaps this modality is: *epistemically* [*metaphysically possible*]!

[10] See Eklund, op, cit. n.7

cal) possibility. The justification needed is to enable – clear the obstacles away from – the recognition that the truth of the right-hand side of an instance of a good abstraction is *conceptually* sufficient for the truth of the left. There is no gap for metaphysics to plug, and in that sense no 'metaontology' to supply. This view of the matter is of course implicit in the very metaphor of *content* recarving. It is of the essence of abstractionism, as I understand it.

4

Question (M) is: What does the world have to be like in order for (the best examples of) abstraction to work? A short answer is that it is at least necessary that the world be such as to verify the associated *Ramsey sentences*: the results of existential generalisation into the places occupied by tokens of the new operators. So for any particular abstraction,

$$(\forall a)(\forall b)(S(a) = S(b) \leftrightarrow E(a, b))$$

the requirement is that this be true:

$$(\exists f)(\forall a)(\forall b)(f(a) = f(b) \leftrightarrow E(a, b))$$

More generally, the minimum requirement is that each equivalence relation suitable to contribute to an otherwise good abstraction be associated with at least one function on the members of its field that takes any two of them to the same object as value just in case they stand in the relation in question.

A world in which abstraction works, then – a world in which the truth values of the left-and right-hand sides of the instances of abstraction principles are always the same – will be a world that displays a certain ontological richness with respect to functions. Notice that there is no further requirement of the existence of values for these functions. For if 'S' is undefined for any element, c, in the field of E, then the instance of the abstraction in question, $S(c) = S(c) \leftrightarrow E(c, c)$, will fail right-to-left. This brings us sharply to the second question, (E). To know that the transition right to left across an otherwise good abstraction principle is truth-preserving, we need to know that the equivalence relation in question is indeed associated with a suitable function. Here is George Boolos worrying about the latter question in connection with Hume's principle ("octothorpe" is a name of the symbol, '#', which Boolos uses to denote the cardinality operator, "the number of ..."):

> ... what guarantee have we that there is such a function from concepts to objects as [Hume's Principle] and its existential quantification [Ramsey sentence] take there to be?
>
> I want to suggest that [Hume's Principle] is to be likened to "the present king of France is a royal" in that we have no analytic guarantee that for every value of "F", there is an object that the open definite description[11] "the number belonging to F" denotes ...
>
> Our present difficulty is this: just how do we know, what kind of guarantee do we have, why should we believe, that there is a function that maps concepts to objects in the way that the denotation of octothorpe does if [Hume's Principle] is true? If there is such a function then it is quite reasonable to think that whichever function octothorpe denotes, it maps non-equinumerous concepts to different objects and equinumerous ones to the same object, and this moreover because of the meaning of octothorpe, the number-of-sign, or the phrase "the number of." But do we have any analytic guarantee that there is a function which works in the appropriate manner?
>
> Which function octothorpe denotes and what the resolution is of the mystery how octothorpe gets to denote some one particular definite function that works as described are questions we would never dream of trying to answer.[12]

Boolos undoubtedly demands too much when he asks for "analytic guarantees" in this area. But the spirit of his question demands an answer that at least discloses some reason to believe in the existence of a function of the relevant kind. So: what, in general, is it to have reason to believe in the existence of a function of a certain sort?

If, as theorists often do, we think of functions as *sets* – sets of pairs of argument-tuples, and values – then standard existence postulates in set theory can be expected to provide an answer to Boolos's question in a wide range of cases: there is whatever reason to believe in the existence of the functions required by abstraction principles as there is to believe in the existence of the relevant sets. But that is, twice over, not the right kind of way to address the issue for the purposes of abstractionism. For one thing,

---

[11] The reader should note Boolos' ready assimilation of "the number belonging to F" to a definite description – of course, it *looks* like one. But the question whether it is one depends on whether it has the right *kind* of semantic complexity. The matter is important, and we will return to it below.

[12] Boolos (1997), p.306

abstractionism's epistemological objectives require that the credibility of abstraction principles be *self-standing*. They are not to (need to) be shored up by appeal to independent ontological commitments – and if the abstractionist harbours any ambition for a recovery of set-theory, especially not by appeal to a prior ontology of sets. However there is a deeper point. Abstraction principles purport to introduce *fundamental* means of reference to a range of objects, to which there is accordingly no presumption that we have any prior or independent means of reference. Our conception of the epistemological issues such principles raise, and our approach to those issues, need to be shaped by the assumption that we may have – indeed that there may be possible – no prior, independent way of conceiving of the objects in question other than as the values of the relevant function. So when Boolos asks, what reason do we have to think that there is any function of the kind an abstraction principle calls for, it is to skew the issues to think of the question as requiring to be addressed by the adduction of some kind of evidence for the existence of a function with the right properties that takes elements from the field of the abstractive relation as arguments and objects of some independently available and conceptualisable kind as values. If the best we can do, in order to assure ourselves of the existence of a relevant function or, relatedly, of the existence of a suitable range of objects to constitute its values, is to appeal to our independent ontological preconceptions – our ideas about the kinds of things we take to exist in any case – then our answer provides a kind of assurance which is both insufficient and unnecessary to address the germane concerns: insufficient, since independent ontological assurance precisely sheds no light on the real issue – viz. how we can have reason to believe in the existence of the function purportedly defined by an abstraction principle, and accordingly of the objects that constitute its range of values, when proper room is left for the abstraction to be fundamental and innovative; unnecessary since, if an abstraction can succeed when taken as fundamental and innovative, it doesn't need corroboration by an independent ontology.

5

Let us therefore refashion question (E) as follows:

(E′) How do we know – what reason have we to think – that the transition, right to left, across the biconditional instances of abstraction principles is truth preserving, once it is allowed that the means of reference it introduces to the (putative) values of the (putatively) defined function may be *fundamental*, and that no antecedently available such means may exist?

An answer to (E′) in any particular case must disclose a kind of reason to believe in the existence of a suitable function which originates simply in resources provided by the abstraction principle itself, and independent of collateral ontological preconceptions. Those resources must pertain to what an abstraction can accomplish as an implicit definition of its definiendum – the new term forming operator. Allow, at least pro tem, that an abstraction principle, laid down as an implicit definition of its abstraction operator, may at least succeed in conferring on it a *sense*. So much is tacitly granted by Boolos when he writes in the passage quoted above:

> If there is such a function then it is quite reasonable to think that whichever function octothorpe denotes, it maps non-equinumerous concepts to different objects and equinumerous ones to the same object, and this moreover because of the meaning of octothorpe ... But do we have any analytic guarantee that there is a function which works in the appropriate manner?

For it is, after all, by its stipulated role in the relevant version of Hume's principle that the meaning of octothorpe is fixed. So the question is: what, for functional expressions – one standard practice calls them *functors* – needs to be in place in order for possession of sense to justify ascription of reference?

For Frege, functors are to be conceived as an instance of the more general category of *incomplete* expressions: expressions whose 'saturation' by a singular term results in a further complex, object-denoting term. So let's ask in the first instance: is there something general to be said about what justifies the ascription of reference to an incomplete expression? And what, in particular, is the role played by sense? I am not, in posing this question, taking it as uncontroversial that incomplete expressions as a class should be credited with a potential for reference as well as sense. The question is rather: for a theorist not already inclined – because of nominalist scruple or whatever reason – to deny reference to incomplete expressions across the board, what should justify the ascription of reference in any particular case?

Let's try the case of simple predicates. Take it that in order to assign a sense to a predicate, it suffices to associate it with a sufficiently determinate satisfaction-condition: to fix under what circumstances it may truly, or falsely, be applied to an item in some appropriate assigned range. And take it that the question whether it has a reference amounts to whether we have thereby succeeded in associating it with a genuine property. Then there is a contrast between two broad ways of taking the question. On one way of taking it, the relevant notion of genuine property is akin to that in play when we conceive it as a non-trivial question whether any pair of things which both exemplify a certain set of surface qualities – think, for example, of a list of the reference-fixers for 'gold' given in a way independent of any understanding of that term or an equivalent – have *a property in common*. When the question is so conceived, the answer may be unobvious and negative: there may be 'fool's' instances of a putative natural kind, or there may even just be no common kind underlying even normal cases of presentation of the qualities in question. Theorists who think of *all* properties in this way – sometimes termed "sparse" theorists – will recognise a gap between a predicate's being in good standing – its association with well-understood, feasible satisfaction conditions – and its hitting off a *real worldly property*. However this conception stands in contrast with that of the more "abundant" theorist, for whom the good standing, in that sense, of a predicate is *already* trivially sufficient to ensure the existence of an associated property, a (perhaps complex) *way of being* which the predicate serves to express.[13] For a theorist of the latter spirit, predicate sense will suffice, more or less,[14] for predicate reference. The sparse theorist, by contrast, will view the relationship as very much akin to that which obtains in the case of complex singular terms: the sense of – the satisfaction condition of – a predicate will aim at an underlying property fit to underwrite in some appropriate manner the capacity of an object to meet that satisfaction

---

[13] The terminology of abundant and sparse properties originates in Lewis (1986). The general distinction is in Armstrong (1979). See also Bealer (1982) and Swoyer (1996) For a useful overview see Mellor and Oliver (1997).

[14] "More or less" because the abundant theorist may still want to deny reference to certain significant predicates – for instance, those associated with inconsistent satisfaction conditions, or which embed empty terms ("That car is *my dog's favourite colour*").

condition, and the predicate will have reference only insofar as there is indeed such a property provided by the world. Whether that is so will then depend in turn on one's metaphysics of worldly properties.[15]

It is clear enough that the two conceptions of property need not be in competition: it is perfectly coherent to work with both simultaneously. What do compete, however, are the two associated views of predicate reference since no-one inclined to admit both conceptions of property is going to wish to maintain, presumably, that in the case when a predicate is associated with properties of both kinds, it somehow divides its reference over them both, or something of the sort. The natural compatibilising view will be, rather, that it is for the abundant properties to play the role of *bedeutungen* in semantic theory, and the sparse ones to address certain metaphysical concerns.[16]

For predicates at least, then, there is *a* good conception of reference such that to confer a sense is, more or less, to confer a reference. Do these ideas suggest a way of responding to Boolos's question, and thence to question (E′), for the target case: the functors introduced on the left hand side of instances of abstraction principles? Well, there are evident disanalogies. Any predicate associated with a (sufficiently) determinate satisfaction condition is, ceteris paribus, assured of reference to an abundant property. But it seems there should be room for a would-be functor to have sufficient sense to be associated with a determinate condition on any function that is to qualify as presented by it and yet fail to present one. Setting aside any issue about the existence of a range of suitable *arguments* for the purported function in question – as we may in the case of abstraction principles – there are two ways this can happen. One is if a relation can meet the condition in question and yet not be functional – not *unique*, i.e. many-(or one-) one. And the other is precisely if there are no objects suitable to constitute *values* for the purported function in question in the first place. The sense assigned to a putative functor may precisely carry sufficient information to enable us to show that the associated relation is not many-one (nor one-one) or that it fails to correlate the intended range of arguments with anything at all. Functors generally may have sense yet fail to present any function – so fail to have reference – if these conditions, of uniqueness and existence, are not met.

---

[15] For example, versions of both Aristotelian and Platonic conceptions of property are consistent with sparseness. For discussion of varieties of sparseness see Schaffer (2004).
[16] Cf. Schaffer op. cit.

Ok. So the question is whether a significant doubt is possible about whether they are met in the case of the functors introduced by (the best) abstractions. Might uniqueness be open to reasonable doubt in such a case? Here is a consideration that strongly suggests not. In order to entertain such a doubt, one needs to associate the relevant functor – 'S' – with an underlying *relation* and then to think of 'S(*a*)' as purporting to denote what is the only object so related to *a*. Uniqueness fails just when there more than one such object. But is there in general any conception of such a relation somehow conveyed as part of the sense that is attached to an abstraction operator by its implicit definition via the relevant abstraction principle? Take the case of Hume's principle and the associated cardinality operator, glossed as "the number of". In order to raise a meaningful doubt about uniqueness, we need to identify an associated relation such that the sense of "the number of Fs" may be conceived of as grasped *compositionally*, via grasping this relation plus the presumption of uniqueness incorporated in the definite article. The issue of uniqueness will be the issue of the many-oneness of this relation, – something which might ideally admit of proof. It is very doubtful however whether there is any good reason to think of the sense assigned to the cardinality operator by Hume's principle as compositional in this particular way[17]. And if not – if the operator is best conceived

---

[17] The issue is not uncontroversial. MacFarlane (forthcoming), like Boolos above, canvasses the view that numerical terms having the surface form 'the number of *F*s' are Russellian definite descriptions, presumed constructed using an underlying relational expression '*x* numbers the *F*s' – so that a sentential context '*A*(the number of *F*s)', with the definite description having wide scope, gets paraphrased as '∃!*x*(*x* numbers the *F*s ∧ *Ax*)'. On this view, at least as MacFarlane presents it, numerical terms are not genuine singular terms at all but a kind of quantifier. One could still enquire whether the postulated numbering relation is functional – i.e. whether, for any *F*, there always exists a unique *x* which numbers *F*. This would now be a substantial question, both as regards existence and uniqueness. This is not the place for detailed criticism of MacFarlane's proposal (for a response, see Hale & Wright (forthcoming)). But it is worth briefly separating some issues. One, obviously, is whether MacFarlane's proposal is viable at all. If Hume's Principle works as an implicit definition in the way we propose, it defines a certain functor – the number operator – *directly*. There simply is no underlying relational expression, from whose sense that of the functor is composed. One can of course define a relational expression, '*x* numbers *F*', to mean '*x* = N*y*:*Fy*' – but this relational expression is evidently compositionally *posterior* to the number operator. The question, for the viability of MacFarlane's proposal, must therefore be whether '*x* numbers the *F*s' can be defined independently, without presupposing prior understanding of numerical terms. It is certainly not obvious that it can. But even if it can, the more important issue for present purposes is not whether one could introduce the number operator on the basis of an underlying relation, but whether one can, as we

as semantically atomic – then there is no scope for a significant doubt about uniqueness of reference, since there is no associated condition which more than one item might satisfy.[18]

It is, on the other hand, by no means as evident that there is no room for a significant doubt about existence.[19] The abstraction operator refers (to a function) only if the singular terms it enables us to form refer (to objects.) What reason is there to think that (any of) these terms so refer?

To fix ideas, think of the routine ways in which one might satisfy oneself that *any* singular term refers. Suppose, for instance, you take it into

---

contend, introduce it as semantically atomic – if so, then there is, for the reasons noted in the main text, no scope for a significant doubt about *uniqueness* of reference for terms formed by its means.

[18] Lest there be any misunderstanding, this concern needs sharply distinguishing from the concern about uniqueness raised by Harold Hodes in Hodes (1984). Hodes' concern is based on the fact that one can, consistently with the truth of Hume's Principle, permute the references of terms formed by means of the number operator, provided one makes compensating adjustments elsewhere (e.g. to the extension of the <-relation). Thus besides the 'standard numberer' which takes empty concepts to 0 as value, singly-instantiated concepts to 1, doubly-instantiated concepts to 2, and so on, there are many non-standard numberers – e.g. one which coincides with the standard numberer except in its values for empty and singly-instantiated concepts (1 and 0, respectively), compensating with a non-standard <-1 relation which coincides with standard < except that we have $1 < 0$. Hodes grants, at least for the sake of argument, that the number operator, as introduced by Hume's Principle, will denote a function – the trouble, he thinks, is that there is no unique, privileged such function that it can succeed in defining; rather, there are infinitely many such functions, between which it is powerless to discriminate. The problem is not that it is open whether "the number of" succeeds in picking out any operation whose values are, as required by functionality, unique but that it is unsettled whether it succeeds in picking out any unique such operation. This kind of doubt is not at issue in the text, and demands a quite different response. The crux is whether Hodes succeeds, as he claims, in demonstrating that a special, distinctively recalcitrant type of indeterminacy afflicts numerical terms as introduced by Hume's Principle – i.e. that we have something worse that the kind of permutational indeterminacy that can be engineered for expressions of any type, and is not confined to those purporting reference to abstracta. See Hale (1987), pp.220–224 for some further discussion.

[19] To be sure, one kind of doubt about existence *is* pre-empted by the same point. There can be no doubt whether certain items stand in a relevant underlying relation to anything if there is no relevant underlying relation – if there is no prior relation R such that 'the □ of A" is constrained to stand, if for anything, then for the unique B such that $R(A, B)$. But those anxious about the existential consequences of abstraction principles will probably not be quickly persuaded that any proper doubt about existence here has to assume this pattern.

your head to try to show that "Bin Laden" is the name of a real man, rather than, say, the focal point of an elaborate fiction, promulgated by the CIA. There are various courses of action you might undertake to try to settle the matter, at least to your own satisfaction. But ultimately, what you need to do is gather evidence which is arguably sufficient for the truth of an *identity statement*, 'q = Bin Laden', for some 'q' whose reference to a real man is not in question. In this, 'q' might be a compendious definite description of the words and actions ("the man who said and did all of these things: …") of an unquestioned real man; or it might be a token demonstrative for the robed, bearded figure standing before you at the entrance to a cave in the Tora-Bora mountain range and revealed only after many days blind-folded travelling on the back of a donkey. The point generally is that verification of the existence of a referent for a term N is verification of a statement of the form: $(\exists x)(x = N)$. And the premium method for doing that is to verify an identity, $q = N$, where the existence of a referent for 'q' is not in doubt.

But this model exactly presupposes, of course, that the term in question is not *fundamental*. What about the case when N is a term purporting to stand for a new kind of object for which it is understood that no anterior means of reference need exist in the language – so that it is a given that there need be no suitable 'q'? In these circumstances verifying that N refers cannot be a matter of verifying that it co-refers with any expression, even a demonstrative, whose reference is not in doubt. So what can it be?

The only possible answer appears to be that such a feat of verification must consist in verifying – if not an identity statement linking the term in question with another whose reference is assured – then *some* form or forms of statement embedding the term in question whose truth *requires* that it refer: a statement, or range of statements, in which the term in question occupies a *reference-demanding* position. Such will be afforded by provision of the means to verify some form of *atomic* statement configuring such terms. Identity contexts are one kind of atomic statement. So abstraction itself – as a characterisation of putatively canonical grounds for the verification of such identity contexts – supplies a paradigm means, indeed an example it seems of the only foreseeable broad kind of means, for accomplishing the assurance required. If it is not acceptable, what would be acceptable instead?

There is a parallel here with material world scepticism. Imagine a situation in which we have only one means of reference to material objects – demonstratives, say, perhaps qualified by a sortal predicate: "that man", "this tree", and so on (*material demonstratives*). And suppose we are challenged to produce a reason to think that *any* uses of such expressions succeed in referring. Once again, any such reason would have to be reason to think that certain statements – "that man is running", "that tree is tall" – embedding material demonstratives in reference-demanding ways are, in their context of use, true. And that in turn will demand a conception of what justifies taking such a statement to be true. Such a conception, so says the Sceptic, will be that of the occurrence of a certain pattern of experience – a pattern which might be fully described in terms of appearances, without commitment to entities of the kind in question. Since the evidence may be so described, independent assurance is wanted that successful referential use of the relevant expressions is possible in the actual world – a fortiori that there are middle sized physical objects out there to be referred to at all – before we may justifiably take such evidence to establish the truth of the appropriate type of statements.

Responses to this kind of scepticism about material objects are of course various. They include denying the 'neutralist' (Lockean) conception of experience it exploits, and allowing that conception but denying that any need is thereby entailed for *independent* corroboration of a material world ontology before experience can carry the evidential significance customarily accorded it. Abstractionism, in so far as it reads an ontology of abstracta into the commitments of the right-hand-sides of abstractions, stands comparison with the former (direct realist!) line. But the question I would press on the anxious metaphysician is this: if one is not content to acquiesce in a sceptical view of the referential aspirations of material demonstratives, how is it relevantly different with the terms introduced by abstraction?

6

The friend of abstraction may take some satisfaction in the dialectical situation just suggested. But it is actually very much *not* where I want – or promised – to end up. If the best that can be done with an obdurate doubt about the truth-preservingness of the transitions right to left across the instances of an abstraction is to make good an analogy with the relation between experience and material world claims as viewed by a Sceptic, then I have precisely not made good on what I characterised as of the essence of abstraction: the contention of the conceptual sufficiency of the truth of the right-hand sides for the truth of the left. The whole point was to be that there *is* no metaphysical hostage in the transition, no need for an 'assist' from the World, and therefore no scope for doubt, even Sceptical doubt, that the requisite assistance is to hand. The best response to (E′), therefore, cannot rest upon a comparison between doubt about the inference, right to left, across an instance of an abstraction principle and scepticism about the reality of ordinary material objects. Rather, it has to be to make out a perspective from which abstraction actually involves nothing akin to the element of epistemological *risk* which scepticism finds in our purported cognitive commerce with the external world.

Let's step back. To ask, with Boolos, how we know that there is any function – hence, any objects to constitute its range of values – that behave as an abstraction principle demands is, in effect, to view the principle as proposed in a spirit of *reference fixing*: as imposing a condition, viz. association with the elements in the field of the abstractive relation in a fashion isomorphic to the partition into equivalence classes which it effects, which it is then up to the world to produce a range of objects to satisfy. This is the conception of the matter articulated in the following passage:

> What did Locke realise about 'gold'? Effectively, that there is an element of blind pointing in our use of such a term, so that our aim outstrips our vision. Our conception fixes what (if anything) we are pointing at but cannot settle its nature: that is a matter of what's out there. One image of the way [Hume's Principle] is to secure a reference for its terms shares a great deal with this picture.[20]

On this conception, we 'point blindly', using the sortal concept and terms explained by an abstraction principle, in the hope of *hitting off* reference to a range of entities qualified to play the role that the principle defines, and it is accordingly readily intelligible how the process might fail – it goes with the model that it must be at least initially intelligible that a principle proposed in this spirit fails to hit off reference to *anything*. It cannot just be a given that reference is secured, even if it is – let alone that it is secured to entities of which the principle states a necessary truth. Rather, this is something which needs to be verified as a by-product of our, so to say, *finding* a range of objects 'out there' to which the conception embodied in the principle is (necessarily) faithful. And of course if that is to be possible, the ob-

---

[20] Sullivan and Potter [1997], pp.145–146, quoted in Potter & Sullivan (2005).

jects in question must first be given to us under some *other* mode of presentation.

It is pointless to deny that it is *possible* to regard abstraction principles in this fashion. One can always ask, with respect to any particular domain of objects, whether there are any that are so related to the elements of the abstractive domain that identity and distinctness among them is tracked by the obtaining, or non-obtaining, of the relevant equivalence relation on pairs from that domain. It may be that in a particular case, the answer is not only affirmative but necessarily so – and in that case, the abstraction principle too will state a necessary truth, even when understood in the reference-fixing spirit. But this spirit – necessary for an 'anxious metaphysical' stance – is simply in flat tension with the abstractionist conception of the matter; indeed, it is to view abstraction principles in a manner inconsistent with their capacity to serve the process of abstraction itself. Properly viewed, the very stipulative equivalence of the two sides of an instance of an abstraction principle is enough to ensure both that it is not to be seen as proposed as part of a project of reference-fixing and that there *is no significant risk of reference failure.*

How can there be no such risk? In order to understand this, we need to be mindful again of the distinction between sparse and abundant properties and the role it can play in the semantics of predicates. For in general terms, the abstractionist metaphysics of abstract objects, and of reference to them – sometimes called *minimalism* – stands to the conception of the matter that underwrites the reference-fixing model as an abundant conception of properties stands to a sparse one. The analogy admittedly needs some care. On the most generous version of 'abundance' theory, there is for predicates, as remarked, no gap between sense and reference: the association of a predicate with a sense – a determinate satisfaction-condition, even if a necessarily unsatisfiable one – is enough to ensure the existence of a property – a way of being – to play the role of the reference of the predicate. It is not, by contrast, part of the minimalist view of the reference of singular terms introduced by abstraction to conceive of reference as bestowed purely by sense. But nor, according to the minimalist view, is reference secured by the abstraction's merely serving to introduce a conception of a kind of object whose exemplification requires a form of worldly co-operation going beyond anything that can be assured by the laying down of an abstraction principle which is in good standing by normal criteria – and so in particular features a *bona fide* equivalence relation. Anyone should agree that a justification for regarding a singular term as having objectual reference is provided just as soon as one has justification for regarding as true certain atomic statements in which it functions as a singular term. According to the abundant – "neo-Fregean" – metaphysics of objects and singular reference, such a justification is provided by the very manner in which sense is bestowed upon abstract singular terms, which immediately ties the truth conditions of self-identities featuring such terms to the reflexivity of the relevant relation. As with the abundant conception of properties, there is no additional gap to cross which requires "hitting off" something on the other side by virtue of its fit with relevant specified conditions, as the property of being composed of the element with atomic number 79 is hit off (or so let's suppose) by the combination of conditions that control our unsophisticated use of 'gold'. But nor is it the case that reference is bestowed by the possession of sense alone. The latter view, for singular terms, is Meinongianism. The abstractionist view agrees with the reference-fixing conception that it takes, over and above the possession of sense, the truth of relevant contexts to ensure reference. But it diverges from the reference-fixing conception in what it holds has to be accomplished before those contexts may justifiably be taken as true, and in how straightforward it views the accomplishment as being.

Can we make this clearer? On the abundant view of properties, predicate sense suffices for reference. But it is not the abstractionist view of singular terms that sense suffices for reference – the view is that the truth of atomic contexts suffices for reference. However everyone agrees with that. The controversial point is what it takes to be in position reasonably to take such contexts to be true. The point of analogy with the abundant view is that this is not, by minimalism, conceived as a matter of hitting off, Locke-style, some 'further' range of objects. We can perfect the analogy if we consider not simple abundance but the view that results from a marriage of abundance with Aristotelianism. Now the possession of sense by a predicate no longer suffices, more or less, for reference. There is the additional requirement that the predicate be true of something, and hence that some atomic statement in which it occurs predicatively is true. That is a precise analogue of the requirement on singular terms that some atomic statement in which they occur referentially be true. And abstractionist minimalism with respect to objects and singular reference is the exact counterpart of Aristotelian abundance with respect to properties and predicate reference. The Lockean conception, by contrast, is to be compared to the position of the 'sparse' opponent of the abundant Aristotelian who construes the relevant range of predicates as purporting reference to sparse properties. On that view there is scope for a doubt whether a relevant predication is true, even when the subject meets the working satisfaction-conditions assigned to the predicate – for there may be no genuine property associated with meeting those conditions. Likewise on the Lockean view, there is scope for a doubt whether an abstract-identity is true even though the appropriate equivalence relation holds between the relevant elements in its field – for there may be no, as it were, 'sparse' – metaphysical Worldly – objects suitable to serve as the referents of the relevant abstract terms. The abstractionist conception of the truth of the right-hand sides of instances of good abstractions as conceptually sufficient for the truth of the left-hand sides precisely takes the terms in question out of the market for 'hitting off' reference to things whose metaphysical nature is broadly comparable to that of sparse properties, and assigns to them instead a referential role relevantly comparable to that of predicates as viewed by the abundant Aristotelian.

Let me begin to draw things together. Aside from the earlier, rather obvious remarks about the requirement of the truth of the corresponding Ramsey sentences, we have been rather neglecting question (M):

> What does the world have to be like in order for (the best examples of) abstraction to work?

What, in the light of the foregoing discussion, should now be said in answer? First, for each equivalence relation which is to underpin an abstraction – for all we have said, indeed, for *every* equivalence relation – there has to be an associated function taking each of the elements which are equivalent under the relation to a common object and no two inequivalent elements to the same such object. Second, the existence of such a function will of course require the existence of a properly behaved range of values. The anxious metaphysician and the abstractionist can agree thus far. Their disagreement concerns what it takes for that to be so. The anxious metaphysician thinks of the issue on the analogy of the existence of a sparse property: just as a predicate's being semantically well-behaved and even featuring in true atomic predications is no assurance that it refers to one of the real properties characteristic of the divisions in the metaphysical World, so the fact that the terms introduced by an abstraction behave as singular terms should and feature in what, if the abstraction is accepted, are well understood and often verified contexts, is no assurance that they refer to any of the real objects in the metaphysical World. One who subscribes to this way of thinking then has to take a decision about whether they refer at all, with the minimalist conception of objects and singular reference on offer to play a role in a positive answer counterpart to that of abundant Aristotelian conceptions of property and predication. If the offer is spurned, the metaphysician will have to deny that abstractions can ever be simply stipulatively true. For the abstractionist, by contrast, there is no well-conceived objection to the unqualified stipulation of (the best) abstractions – if it seems otherwise, it is only because one is trying to combine their stipulative character with a reference-fixing conception of them – and the abundance of the entities thus recognised is simply the objectual counterpart of the abundance of abundant properties.

These remarks are not a *defence* of minimalism but merely a reminder – since it seems that one may be needed – of the kind of background thinking about objects and ontological commitment which undergirds the abstractionist view. Perhaps this background thinking constitutes a 'metaontology'. If so, then there is much more to say about the spirit of this metaontology – especially about the sense, if any, in which it is happily described as 'platonist'. But if it is accepted, the answer to question (M) could not be simpler: a world in which abstraction works is a world in which there are equivalence relations with non-empty fields.

REFERENCES

David Armstrong (1979) *A Theory of Universals*, Cambridge: Cambridge University Press.

George Bealer (1982) *Quality and Concept*, Oxford: Oxford University Press.

Paul Benacerraf (1973) 'Mathematical Truth' *Journal of Philosophy* 70, pp.661–680.

George Boolos (1990) 'The Standard of Equality of Numbers' in George Boolos ed. *Meaning, and Method: Essays in Honor of Hilary Putnam* Cambridge: Cambridge University Press 1990, pp.261–277; reprinted in Boolos (1998), pp.202–219.

George Boolos (1997) 'Is Hume's Principle Analytic?' in Richard G. Heck, Jr., ed. *Logic, Language, and Thought* Oxford: Oxford University Press 1997; pages references are to the reprint in Boolos (1998), pp.301–314.

George Boolos (1998) *Logic, Logic, and Logic* Cambridge, Mass.: Harvard University Press, 1998.

Ross Cameron (2007) 'Truthmakers and Ontological Commitment: Or How to Deal with Complex Objects and Mathematical Ontology without Getting into Trouble' http://www.personal.leeds.ac.uk/%7Ephlrpc/research.htm.

Matti Eklund (2006) 'Neo-Fregean Ontology' *Philosophical Perspectives* 20, pp.95–121.

Bob Hale (1987) *Abstract Objects* Oxford: Basil Blackwell

Bob Hale (1994) 'Is Platonism Epistemologically Bankrupt?' *Philosophical Review*, Vol.103, 2, pp.299–325.

Bob Hale (2000) 'Reals by Abstraction' *Philosophia Mathematica* (3) Vol.8, pp.100–123, reprinted in Hale & Wright (2001).

Bob Hale (forthcoming) 'Neo-Fregeanism and Quantifier-Variance: Chairman's Remarks' (forthcoming in *Proceeedings of the Aristotelian Society*).

Bob Hale & Crispin Wright (1994) 'A reductio ad surdum? Field on the contingency of mathematical objects' *Mind* Vol.103, No.410, pp.169–184.

Bob Hale & Crispin Wright (2001) *The Reason's Proper Study: Essays towards a Neo-Fregean Philosophy of Mathematics* Oxford: Oxford University Press.

Bob Hale & Crispin Wright (2002) 'Benacerraf's Dilemma Revisited' *European Journal of Philosophy* Vol.10, No.1, pp.101–129.

Bob Hale & Crispin Wright (2009) "The *Metaontology* of Abstraction" in David Chalmers, David Manley and Ryan Wasserman, eds., *Metametaphysics: New Essays on the Foundations of Ontology*, Oxford: Oxford University Press

Bob Hale & Crispin Wright (forthcoming) "Focus Restored", reply to MacFarlane (forthcoming) in Øystein Linnebo, ed. Special Issue of *Synthese* on the Bad Company Problem.

Katherine Hawley (2007) 'Neo-Fregeanism and Quantifier Variance' *Aristotelian Society Supplementary* Volume LXXXI, pp.233–249.

Eli Hirsch (2002) 'Quantifier Variance and Realism' *Philosophical Issues* 12, *Realism and Relativism*, pp.51–73.

Harold Hodes (1984) 'Logicism and the Ontological Commitments of Arithmetic', *Journal of Philosophy* Vol.81, pp.123–149.

David Lewis (1986) *On the Plurality of Worlds*, Oxford: Basil Blackwell.

John MacFarlane (forthcoming) 'Double Vision: Two Questions about the Neo-Fregean Programme' in Øystein Linnebo, ed. Special Issue of *Synthese* on the Bad Company Problem.

D.H. Mellor & Alex Oliver (1997) 'Introduction', in *Properties*, Oxford: Oxford University Press, pp.1–33.

Michael Potter & Peter Sullivan (2005) 'What Is Wrong With Abstraction?', *Philosophia Mathematica* 13, pp.187–193 .

Chris Swoyer (1996) 'Theories of Properties: From Plenitude to Paucity', *Philosophical Perspectives* 10, pp.243–264 .

Jonathan Schaffer (2004) 'Two Conceptions of Sparse Properties', *Pacific Philosophical Quarterly* 85, pp.92–102.

Stewart Shapiro (2000) 'Frege Meets Dedekind: A Neo-logicist Treatment of Real Analysis' *Notre Dame Journal of Formal Logic* Vol.41, pp.335–364.

Theodore Sider (2007) 'Neo-Fregeanism and Quantifier Variance' *Aristotelian Society Supplementary Volume* LXXXI, pp.201–232.

Peter Sullivan and Michael Potter (1997) 'Hale on Caesar', *Philosophia Mathematica* 5, pp.135–152.

Alan Weir (2003) 'Neo-Fregeanism: An Embarrassment of Riches' *Notre Dame Journal of Formal Logic*, 44, pp.13–48.

Crispin Wright (1983) *Frege's Conception of Numbers as Objects*, Aberdeen: Aberdeen University Press.

Crispin Wright (1990) 'Field and Fregean Platonism' in A.D. Irvine, ed. *Physicalism in Mathematics*. Dordrecht/Boston/London: Kluwer, reprinted as Essay 6 in Hale & Wright (2001).

Crispin Wright (1999) 'Is Hume's Principle Analytic?' *Notre Dame Journal of Formal Logic*, 40, pp.6–30; reprinted in Hale & Wright (2001).

HOW ABSTRACTION WORKS

LEON HORSTEN and HANNES LEITGEB
University of Bristol

Abstract
In this paper we describe and interpret the formal machinery of abstraction processes in which the domain of abstracta is a subset of the domain of objects from which is abstracted.

1 ABSTRACTION IN THE HISTORY OF PHILOSOPHY

Plato distinguished the world of ideas or forms from the world of experience. His distinction has been with us ever since. Plato's theory of the orderly world of forms was a first description of what we would now call the abstract realm.

The question about the ontological relation between the abstract realm and the realm of the given proved to be very difficult. One famous bone of contention was the issue of ontological dependence. Plato held that the existence of abstract entities is in some sense independent of the sensory realm. Indeed, he thought that the existence of the world of experience is dependent on the abstract realm: the sensory world consists of "shadows" of ideas. Aristotle riposted that it is rather the other way round. The existence of the forms depends on the sensory objects in which they are realized; the forms only exist in the sensory objects.

Aristotle added that on the cognitive side there is a constructive mental process associated with the relation between forms and objects. The human mind actively abstracts or extracts forms from the objects in which they are realized. This is done by "forgetting" some aspects of objects and focussing on others. Note that Aristotle does not say much about how relations (rather than properties) are abstracted: his was a monadic instead of a polyadic point of view.

A standpoint intermediate between Plato and Aristotle can be adopted. One can hold with Aristotle and against Plato that the existence of an abstraction somehow depends on the given, and at the same time hold with Plato and against Aristotle that an abstraction does not exist *in* the objects from which it is abstracted. In other words, abstract objects are not multiply instantiated—they do not exist in space and time. But their existence depends on the objects from which they are abstracted nonetheless. This is sometimes called a "light" conception of abstract objects.[1] This is the viewpoint that we shall adopt.

Note that we do not wish to imply that all abstract objects can be viewed in this way. Modern set theory, for instance, seems at least on the face of it to postulate many more abstract entities than can stand in some sort of abstraction relation with the given. But, again, the thought that there may be too many abstract objects to leave a direct signature or mark in the given is a modern thought. We confine our attention in this article to the abstracta which are somehow reflected in a fairly direct way in the given.

Another modern observation is that this dependence of abstract objects on the objects from which they are abstracted can be relativized. The given on which an abstractum depends does not have to consist of sensory objects. One can start from concepts, for instance, and abstract from them. Or one can start with mathematical entities, and abstract from them.

2 TO MATHEMATICS AND BACK AGAIN

The idea of abstraction has at some time migrated from philosophy to mathematics. A method of abstraction has been and continues to be fruitfully applied in all areas of mathematics. We are of course talking about the method of introducing new objects by *taking equivalence classes.* You are given a class of mathematical entities G. (These are already abstract entities.) And you are given an equivalence relation R on G. R will partition G into equivalence classes. Each equivalence class can be regarded as an element of a new class of mathematical entities A. The elements of A are regarded as abstracted from G through R. The class of new entities A is disjoint from the old class G and is totally and immediately determined by it through the equivalence relation R.

Examples abound. Here are a few:

EXAMPLE 1
1. *G is a collection of straight lines; R is the relation of parallelism; A is a collection of directions.*
2. *G is the collection of pairs of integers (with 0 excluded from the second coordinate); R is the relation of being an integral multiple of*

---

[1] We owe this term to Øystein Linnebo.

(for both nominator and denominator); A is is the set of rational numbers.

Often the new entities in A are regarded as constituting a mathematical domain in their own right on which more structure can be defined. Some of this structure is typically "lifted" from the underlying domain G to the new domain A.

Note that in these cases mathematicians typically do not say that the objects of A exist only "in" objects of G. So this aspect of the Aristotelian viewpoint is not adopted. But the elements of A are in some sense dependent on those of G. And, also in accordance with Aristotle, there is a constructive flavour to this. A is in a sense *generated* from G. Hence the anthropomorphic phraseology.

Frege was one of the first philosophers to realize the importance of the method of taking equivalence classes for philosophy. He, and Carnap after him, sought to apply it in philosophy. Especially Carnap also sought to bring the method of equivalence relations to bear on the empirical realm (in his *Aufbau*). Thus abstraction returned from its mathematical journey to where it was born in the days of Aristotle.

Here are some examples of attempts to apply the method of equivalence classes to philosophy:

EXAMPLE 2
1. *G is a collection of letter tokens; R is the relation of having the same shape; A is a collection of letters (types).*
2. *G is a collection of sentences; R is the relation of synonymy; A is a collection of meanings (fine-grained propositions).*
3. *G consists of monochromatic colour experiences; R is the relation of perceptual indiscriminability; A is a collection of colour shades.*

In many cases (such as in the last of these examples) it is not clear that the relation R that is involved is an equivalence relation: often it is a similarity relation that is not transitive. Carnap was clearly aware of this: he explicitly sought to apply the method of taking equivalence relations to the situation where there is no suitable equivalence relation at hand. We shall leave this development aside here. Instead, we return to Frege.

Frege did not respect the modern requirement that the domains G and A must be disjoint. He explored abstraction mechanisms that require that $A \subseteq G$. Thus he short-circuited the method of taking equivalence classes. He takes adequacy conditions for such abstraction processes to be given by so-called *level two* abstraction principles. Frege's two most famous examples are [Frege 1884]:

> EXAMPLE 3
> 1. *(Law V)* $\{x \mid Fx\} = \{x \mid Gx\} \leftrightarrow \forall x\colon Fx \leftrightarrow Gx$
> 2. *(HP)* $n(F) = n(G) \leftrightarrow F \equiv_{card} G$

Russell showed that Basic Law V is inconsistent. It has been shown that Hume's Principle *(HP)* is consistent. So the abstraction principles that Frege has in mind are inherently risky.

Abstraction principles regulate identities and differences between presented abstracta. In the method of taking equivalence classes, the abstracta never play a role in evaluating an instantiation of the right-hand-side of the relevant abstraction principle. Thus all identities and differences between presented abstractions are settled in one go. Let us say that an abstractum has been generated when all identities and differences involving presentations of it have been settled. Then the method of taking equivalence classes generates abstracta in one swift movement. Of course we know from the Julius Caesar problem that abstraction principles by themselves do not settle the question what the objects of a given kind are. But given an abstraction principle which involves an equivalence relation on an underlying domain, we have a uniform way of generating abstract entities satisfying that principle: the method of taking equivalence classes.

In Frege's case of numbers, the identity conditions of presented abstracta involve other identities and differences between presented abstracta. So our question becomes: *can we come up with a general method for generating abstracta when the equivalence relation itself involves the abstract entities already?* There is a fear, because of the circularity, that the process of generating abstracta never gets off the ground. But if an Archimedean starting point can be found, then in some cases all the identities and differences can be settled over the course of a series of stages.

Boolos informally describes Frege's numerical abstraction process in [Boolos 1990, pp.248f.]:

For how does Frege show that the number 0 is not identical with the number 1? Frege defines the number 0 as the number belonging to the concept *not identical with itself*. He then defines 1 as the number belonging to the concept *identical with 0*. Since no object falls under the former concept, and the number 0 falls under the latter, the two concepts are, by logic, not equinumerous, and hence their numbers are, by Hume's Principle, not identical [...] 2 arises in like manner: Now that 0 and 1 have been defined and shown different, form the concept *identical with 0 or 1*, take its number, call it 2, and observe that the new concept is coextensive with neither of these concepts *because the distinct objects 0 and 1 fall under it*. Conclude by Hume's Principle that 2 is distinct from both 0 and 1.

So there is an ontological dependence of identities and differences between concepted abstracta on identities and differences between other concepted abstracta. Especially the differences are important.

4 ABSTRACTION MODELS

We will now sketch a general framework for describing the dependency relation that is involved in Fregean self-reflexive abstraction processes, as we may call them. The framework is implicit in [Leitgeb 2005]. We are going to give a somewhat simplified description of the framework. Then we shall illustrate it on the basis of three examples.

Roughly, the idea is this. The identities and differences between some presented abstracta do not depend on identities and differences between presented abstracta at all. These will be our Archimedean starting points. But many identities and differences will only be determined once certain other identities and differences are settled. Thus the identity and difference conditions of presented abstracta can depend on other identities and differences. Identities and differences are no longer settled in one go, but are determined in stages. At some point, this "settling process" gives out.

The objecthood of an abstractum presupposes that the abstractum has been given determinate identity conditions. In Quinean terms: *no entity without identity!* Thus the objecthood of abstracta can depend on the objecthood of other abstracta. (This is of course a thoroughly un-Aristotelian idea.)

If at the end of the process all identities and differences have been settled, then all presentations present abstract objects with an associated determinate identity relation. If not, then matters are less clear.

Let $L_\equiv$ be a formal language that contains the relation symbol $\equiv$. We will consider models M^i for the language $L_\equiv$ that differ in what they assign to $\equiv$. We shall assume that all nonlogical symbols except $\equiv$ receive the same interpretation in all models M^i. Every model M^i interprets $\equiv$ as an equivalence relation, and for every equivalence relation R there is an M^i that interprets $\equiv$ as R. The domain of the models consists of presentations of abstracta. The aim is to arrive at reasonable answers to questions of the form: *does presentation p present the same abstractum as presentation q?* This will be done by systematically and successively revising the interpretation of $\equiv$. If two presentations stand in the relation $\equiv$ according to a model M^i then the model "judges" these presentations to present the same abstractum; if not, then it judges them to present different abstracta.

Let $\Phi(x, y)$ be a formula that is interpreted as an equivalence relation by all models M^i. The formula $\Phi(x, y)$ which figures on the right-hand of abstraction principles will be the engine for revising the interpretation of $\equiv$. The ground model M_0 is the model where $\equiv$ is interpreted as the identity relation. This is done in order not to prejudge identity and difference questions.

5 THREE APPLICATIONS

Rather than describing and investigating self-reflexive abstraction processes in general terms, we shall now present three concrete examples of self-reflective abstraction.[2] These examples will convey how such abstraction processes unfold.

5.1 Truth

We let $L_\equiv$ be the language of first-order arithmetic plus the equivalence symbol $\equiv$. The arithmetical vocabulary is interpreted in the standard way. Note that this means that this language contains both a symbol standing for *real* identity ($=$) and a symbol standing for an equivalence relation which does not in all models stand for real identity ($\equiv$).

The domain consists of codes of sentences, which are regarded as presentations of truth values; we denote codes by using quotation marks.

---

[2] The framework is studied in more generality and detail in [Horsten, Leitgeb, Linnebo in prep.].

We consider the following abstraction principle:

$$\text{``}\varphi\text{''} \equiv \text{``}\psi\text{''} \leftrightarrow (\varphi \leftrightarrow \psi)$$

Call this the *Tarski Abstraction Principle*. Then

$$x \equiv \text{``}0 = 0\text{''}$$

can be interpreted as a self-reflexive truth predicate.

5.2 Numbers

We let $L_\equiv$ be the language of second-order logic (without the identity symbol) plus the equivalence symbol $\equiv$. We consider only full second-order models.

The domain is taken to consist of codes of open formulas with one free variable, which are regarded as "concepts". We regard these concepts as presentations of numbers.

We consider the following abstraction principle:

$$\text{``}\varphi(x)\text{''} \equiv \text{``}\psi(x)\text{''} \leftrightarrow (\varphi(x) \equiv_{card} \psi(x))$$

This is *Hume's Abstraction Principle*. The right-hand-side expresses the second-order notion of standing in one-to-one onto correspondence. Since we do not have equality in the language, the role of identity in the right-hand-side of Hume's Principle must be played by the equivalence relation expressed by $\equiv$. In other words, we are *counting* objects using an equivalence relation on the underlying domain that may not coincide with the real notion of identity.

5.3 Events

We let $L_\equiv$ be the language of first-order logic (without the identity symbol) plus a causality relation symbol C plus the equivalence symbol $\equiv$.

The domain consists of presentations of events, and C is some sort of similarity relation indicative of causality. This is our abstraction principle:

$$e \equiv f \leftrightarrow \forall x[(\exists y: x \equiv y \wedge C(y, e) \rightarrow \exists y: x \equiv y \wedge C(y, f)) \wedge$$
$$(\exists y: x \equiv y \wedge C(e, y) \rightarrow \exists y: x \equiv y \wedge C(f, y))]$$

Let us call this *Davidson's Abstraction Principle*. It says, roughly, that a presentation *e* presents the same event as a presentation *f* if and only if the event(s) presented by *e* and *f* have the same causes and effects.

6 ABSTRACTION UNFOLDED

The intended interpretation of the equivalence relation symbol $\equiv$ is: *presents the same abstractum*. At the beginning of the process, in order not to prejudge any identities and differences, this interpretation is taken to be the identity relation on the underlying domain of presentations. But this choice will typically judge some presentations to present diffferent abstracta even though in reality they present the same abstractum. So the aim is to improve on this initial choice in stages. This is done in the following way.

An abstraction process is a sequence $\langle E_\alpha \rangle_{\alpha \in On}$ with for each α, $E_\alpha = \langle E_\alpha^+, E_\alpha^- \rangle$. E_α^+ contains "settled" identity facts; E_α^- contains "settled" difference facts. The sequence $\langle E_\alpha \rangle_{\alpha \in On}$ is defined by a recursion over the ordinals that we will now describe.

> DEFINITION 1 *An equivalence relation E is E_α-respecting if and only if:*
> $$E_\alpha^+ \subseteq E,$$
> $$E \cap E_\alpha^- = \varnothing.$$

The idea is that putative identity relations always have to respect the identities and differences that have already been settled in the process. Since the models in an abstraction process only differ by their interpretation of the equivalence symbol E, such models can be denoted as M^E. Let P be the set of presentations (pairs $\langle d_1, d_2 \rangle$ below will be members of $P \times P$).

> DEFINITION 2
> $$E_\alpha^+ = \varnothing.$$
> $$E_\alpha^- = \varnothing.$$
> $$E_{\alpha+1}^+ = \{\langle d_1, d_2 \rangle \mid M^E, \langle d_1, d_2 \rangle \text{ satisfy } \Phi(x, y) \text{ for all } E_\alpha\text{-respecting } E\}.$$
> $$E_{\alpha+1}^- = \{\langle d_1, d_2 \rangle \mid M^E, \langle d_1, d_2 \rangle \text{ satisfy } \neg\Phi(x, y) \text{ for all } E_\alpha\text{-respecting } E\}.$$
> $$E_\lambda^+ = \cup_{\alpha < \lambda} E_\alpha^+ \text{ for } \lambda \text{ a limit ordinal.}$$
> $$E_\lambda^- = \cup_{\alpha < \lambda} E_\alpha^- \text{ for } \lambda \text{ a limit ordinal.}$$

Clearly the successor step in such a process corresponds to van Fraassen's notion of supervaluation. All abstraction processes are constant from some $\lambda \in On$ onwards. For the first such ordinal λ, $E_\lambda = \langle E_\lambda^+, E_\lambda^- \rangle$ is the fixed point of the abstraction process. E_λ consists of the *grounded identities and differences*.

In the case of truth, this process generates (roughly) the least super-valuation fixed point of Kripke's theory of truth [Leitgeb 2005]. In the case of the numbers, at the first stage the number 0 is differentiated from all other abstracta, at the next stage the number 1 is differentiated from all other abstracta, and so on. In other words, the abstraction process unfolds in exactly the way in which it was described in the passage from [Boolos 1990] that was quoted earlier. In the case of events, it all depends what ground model (collection of event presentations with a causality relation defined on it) we start from. In some cases, all identities and differences will be grounded, in other cases this will not be so [Horsten 2009].

7 ABSTRACT OBJECTS

There are cases in which in the least fixed point all identities and differences are settled. Indeed, this is precisely what happens in the case of Hume's Principle. In such cases, all identities and differences are grounded. Then E_λ will be an equivalence relation on the domain of presentations of abstracta. And we can simply apply the method of taking equivalence classes, whereby a collection of abstract objects is generated.

But it can also happen that at the least fixed point not all identities and differences are settled. Indeed, this is what happens in the case of truth. In the least fixed point it is determined that the abstractum presented by "$0 = 0$" is different from the abstractum presented by "*it is true that* $0 = 1$". But it is not determined whether the abstractum presented by "$0 = 0$" is numerically identical with the abstractum presented by the liar sentence that says of itself that it is not true.

It is not immediately clear what to say in such cases. For in the case of truth, for instance, this would mean that identity conditions of the truth value presented by "$0 = 0$" (i.e., the truth value *True*) have not been fully determined. If we interpret the Quinean dictum *no entity without identity* in the strictest terms, then we should probably say that in such cases no realm of abstracta is generated.

Nevertheless, in a weaker sense the Quinean dictum might still be satisfied at least for many cells in E_λ^+. We would like to consider as generated abstracta *some* maximal subsets A of E_λ^+, such that for each a, b of the underlying domain which occur in some identity facts in A, the identity fact $\langle a, b \rangle$ itself belongs to A. It might be necessary to apply the supervaluation idea once more in order to determine such maximal sets.

REFERENCES

[Boolos 1990] Boolos, G. *The Standard of Equality of Natural Numbers.* Reprinted in: William Demopoulos (ed.), *Frege's Philosophy of Mathematics.* Harvard University Press, 1995, pp.234–254.

[Frege 1884] Frege, G. *Grundlagen der Arithmetik. Eine logisch mathematische Untersuchung über den Begriff der Zahl.* W. Koebner, 1884.

[Horsten 2009] Horsten, L. *Impredicative Identity Criteria.* Forthcoming in Philosophy and Phenomenological Research.

[Horsten, Leitgeb, Linnebo in prep.] Horsten, L., Leitgeb, H., Linnebo, Ø., *Abstraction, Dependence, and Groundedness.* In preparation.

[Leitgeb 2005] Leitgeb, H. *What Truth Depends on.* Journal of Philosophical Logic 34 (2005), pp.155–192.

THIN OBJECTS

Øystein Linnebo
University of Bristol

1 Introduction

Kant famously argued that all existence claims are synthetic. An existence claim can never be established by conceptual analysis alone but will always require some appeal to intuition or perception, thus making the claim synthetic. This view is rejected in Frege's *Foundations of Arithmetic*, where Frege defends an account of arithmetic which combines both platonism and logicism. Frege's platonism consists in taking arithmetic to be about real and independently existing objects. And his logicism consists in taking the truths of pure arithmetic to rest on just logic and definitions and thus be analytic. Most philosophers now probably agree with Kant in this debate: the existence claims of Frege's platonism cannot be established on the basis of logic and conceptual analysis alone.

However, the disagreement between Kant and Frege is alive and well in a somewhat different form. Forget the problematic analytic-synthetic distinction. Can there be objects which are "thin" in the sense that very little is required for their existence? A classic example is the view in the philosophy of mathematics that the mere consistency or coherence of a mathematical theory suffices for the existence of the objects that the theory purports to describe. This view has been held by many leading mathematicians and continues to exert a strong influence on contemporary philosophers of mathematics. A more recent example is the neo-Fregean view that the equinumerosity of two concepts is conceptually sufficient for the existence of the number that specifies the cardinality of both concepts. For instance, the fact that the knives on the table can be one-to-one correlated with the forks on the table is said to be conceptually sufficient for the existence of a number that specifies the cardinality both of the knives and of the forks.[1]

If the defenders of thin objects are regarded as heirs to the Fregean view that there are analytic existence claims, then there are also lots of heirs to the contrasting Kantian view. For instance, Hartry Field has at-

---

[1] See for instance Wright (1983) and the essays collected in Hale & Wright (2001).

tacked views according to which mathematical objects are thin, sometimes mentioning the Kantian origin of his criticism.[2] Like the original Kantian view on analytic existence claims, the contemporary view that there can be no thin objects strikes many people as highly plausible. Appeals to thin objects often come across as attempts to pull rabbits out of a hat.

The goal of this article is to explain, defend, and demystify the idea of thin objects. I will refer to the view that there are thin objects as *meta-ontological minimalism* or *minimalism* for short. Let me explain the label. Ontology is of course the study of what there is. Meta-ontology, on the other hand, is the study of these key concepts of ontology, such as the concepts of existence and objecthood. Meta-ontological minimalism is accordingly the view that the key concepts of ontology have a minimal character. Not surprisingly, this view tends to result in very generous ontologies. For the less that is required for existence, the more objects there will be.

However, it is important to note that minimalists do not claim that *all* objects are thin and that their existence thus makes only some minimal demand on reality. Their claim is that the notion of an object itself is thin and thus *allows for* thin objects. But they happily admit that many kinds of objects are thick. For instance, elementary particles are thick because their existence makes some substantive demand on reality. But the minimalists insist that the thickness of elementary particles derives from what it is to be an elementary particle, not from what it is to be an object.

This paper is structured as follows. First I review some considerations in favor of thin objects. Next I describe the neo-Fregean approach to thin objects and outline some problems that this approach faces. Then I outline my own version of this approach, which is better equipped to answer the problems. This approach ties the notion of an object to that of a semantic value and make crucial use of a principle of compositionality for semantic values.

---

[2] See Field (1989), pp.5 and 79–80.

Meta-ontological minimalism appears to enjoy a number of appealing features. For instance, it promises a way to accept face value readings of discourses whose ontologies would otherwise be philosophically problematic.

Arithmetic provides a good example. The language of arithmetic contains a variety of proper names which (it seems) are supposed to refer to certain abstract objects, namely the natural numbers. The language also contains quantifier phrases which (it seems) are supposed to range over the natural numbers. Moreover, a great variety of theorems expressed in this language appear to be true. For a lot of such theorems are asserted in full earnest by educated lay people as well as professional mathematicians. And since the arithmetical competence of these people is beyond question, there is reason to believe that most of their arithmetical assertions are true. But if these theorems are true, then their various subexpressions must succeed in doing what they are supposed to do. In particular, their singular terms and quantifiers must succeed in referring to and ranging over natural numbers. And for this kind of success to be possible, there must exist abstract mathematical objects.

This is a powerful argument. But is it sound? Since all I did was to observe that the premises *appear* to be true, they can of course be challenged. However, it is *prima facie* attractive to take these appearances at face value, since this will save us the difficult task of showing how both lay people and experts can be deceived about something they take to be obviously true. And when the premises are taken at face value, the argument shows that there must exist abstract mathematical objects.

However, this ontology of abstract objects is often found to be philosophically problematic. One well-known worry concerns epistemic "access" to such objects. Since perception and all forms of instrumental detection are based on causal processes, these methods cannot give us access to abstract objects such as the natural numbers. How then can we acquire knowledge of them?[3] Another worry is the sheer extravagance of postulating such huge ontologies. How can we postulate an infinity of new objects with such a light heart? No physicist would so unscrupulously postulate an infinity of new physical objects. Why then should mathematicians get away with it? Philosophers are notoriously divided over how serious these

---

[3] This worry was made famous by Benacerraf (1973). For discussion and improvements, see Field (1989) and Linnebo (2006).

worries are. But any successful account of mathematical objects needs to have some response to the worries, even if only to explain why they are misguided.

Thin objects offer an extremely promising strategy for responding to the worries. The vast ontology of mathematics may well be problematic when it is understood in a thick sense. If mathematical objects were pretty much like elementary particles except for being abstract, then there would indeed be good reason to worry about epistemic access and ontological extravagance. But perhaps mathematical objects need not be understood in this way. If there are such things as thin objects, then the existence of mathematical objects need not make much of a demand on the world. It may for instance suffice that the theory purporting to describe the relevant mathematical objects is coherent. And although facts about the coherence of mathematical theories are still inadequately understood, they are less problematic than thick mathematical objects would be. It is at least not a complete mystery how we can have epistemic access to facts about the coherence of mathematical theories. And since this account of mathematical objects sets the bar to existence extremely low, it is not at all surprising that an extravagant ontology should result.

3 AN ABSTRACTIONIST APPROACH TO THIN OBJECTS

One approach to thin objects is found in the neo-Fregean philosophy of mathematics developed by Hale and Wright. The neo-Fregeans seek to provide a logical and philosophical foundation for classical mathematics on the basis of so-called *abstraction principles*. These are principles of the form

$$(*) \; \textstyle\sum(\alpha) = \sum(\beta) \leftrightarrow \alpha \sim \beta$$

where α and β range over items of some sort, where $\sim$ is an equivalence relation on such items, and where $\sum$ an operator that maps such items to objects. The neo-Fregeans are particularly fond of *Hume's Principle*, which says that the number of Fs (symbolized as $\#F$) is identical to the number of G just in case the F and the Gs can be one-to-one correlated (symbolized as $F \approx G$):

$$(\text{HP}) \; \#F = \#G \leftrightarrow F \approx G$$

This principle has the amazing mathematical property that, when added to second-order logic along with some definitions, we are able to derive all of ordinary (second-order Peano-Dedekind) arithmetic. Abstraction principles are available for many other kinds of abstract object as well, for instance directions, geometrical shapes, and linguistic types.

If true, an abstraction principle will provide unproblematic epistemic and semantic access to the objects invoked on the left-hand side of an abstraction principle: we simply proceed via its unproblematic right-hand side. However, what reason do nominalists have to accept Hume's Principle and other abstraction principles as true? The neo-Fregean response to this challenge turns on regarding the objects invoked on the left-hand side as thin.

This response can be developed in the form of a view of what is required for a singular term t to refer (Hale & Wright 2009a). At the very least the term must have sense. But more is presumably required. What is this further requirement? The question can be put in terms of the following equation:

(E) t has sense $+ X \Leftrightarrow t$ has reference

where '$\Leftrightarrow$' means something like mutual conceptual entailment. That is, what requirement X do we have to add to the claim that t has sense to get something that is conceptually equivalent to the claim that t has reference?

When t is an *abstraction term* – that is, a term of the form '$\Sigma(\alpha)$' – then Hale and Wright claim that the further requirement X that is needed to advance from sense to reference is just that the item α associated with t be equivalent to itself: $\alpha \sim \alpha$. That is, they propose the following abstractionist solution to the equation (E):

(A) '$\Sigma(\alpha)$' has sense $+ (\alpha \sim \alpha) \Leftrightarrow$ '$\Sigma(\alpha)$' has reference

According to this view, the left-hand side of (A) conceptually entails the right-hand side and its claim that the abstraction term '$\Sigma(\alpha)$' refers. The notions of reference and objecthood have been "scaled" so as to ensure that (A) comes out right (Hale & Wright 2009b). This abstractionist approach to thin objects will serve as the starting point for my own approach to be outlined below.

Although the idea of thin objects holds great promise, it also faces a number of problems which any successful version of minimalism must be capable of addressing.

> **The problem of existence**. Why should we believe that there are such things as thin objects in the first place? Why should certain innocent facts suffice for the existence of certain controversial objects? What prevents someone from accepting the innocent facts while denying that this suffices for the existence of the objects?
>
> **The problem of overgeneration**. Assume that the problem of existence can be solved. Then the question arises just how thin various kinds of object actually are. Few people would want to claim that elementary particles are thin. But once we open the door to thin objects, what right do we have to deny that other objects, such as elementary particles, are thin as well?
>
> **The problem of lack of uniformity**. Assume that the problem of overgeneration can be solved. Then we still face the question how much thin and thick objects have in common. Do these kinds of item belong under the same rubric at all? Perhaps the words 'existence' and 'object' are being used ambiguously.
>
> **The problem of consistency**. The last and potentially most fatal problem is the threat of inconsistency. The acceptable abstraction principles turn out to be surrounded by unacceptable ones, which are incoherent or downright inconsistent, or which conflict with one another. This is known as *the bad company problem*.[4]

In what follows I develop a version of minimalism which I believe will allow us to answer all of these problems. This version is inspired by the abstractionist approach described above. My argument proceeds in three steps. The first step glosses the notion of object as a possible referent of a singular term. The second step glosses the notion of a referent of a singular term in terms of the notion of a semantic value. The third step offers a minimalist account of what it takes for a singular term to possess a seman-

---

[4] See Linnebo (2009) for an introduction and further references.

tic value. Taken together, the three steps provide a minimalist account of what is required for the existence of an object.

5 OBJECTS AS REFERENTS OF SINGULAR TERMS

Let's begin with the first step. One may wonder how an inquiry into the concept of an object can even be possible. For as Frege observes, this concept is "too simple to admit of logical analysis" (Frege (1891), p.140). Although Frege is no doubt right that a "proper definition" of the concept of an object is out of the question, I believe it is both possible and reasonable to ask for some further explication of the concept. Even if the concept cannot be *defined* in more basic terms, it can still be glossed or characterized, for instance by relating it to other concepts and by explaining the role that it plays in our thought and reasoning. Compare the notion of conjunction. Although this notion too is a primitive which cannot be defined in more basic terms, a lot can be said to gloss or characterize it. We can for instance describe its inferential properties and its possession conditions.

So let's examine the role that objects play in our semantic theories. There appear to be two different but related roles: objects serve as referents of singular terms and as values of bound first-order variables. Frege's explication of the notion of object focusses on the former role of objects as the referents of singular terms. He takes objects to be the kinds of item that singular terms refer to. Quine, on the other hand, focuses on the latter role of objects as values of bound variables, as encapsulated in his famous slogan that "to be is to be the value of a bound variable". Since the referent of any singular term can also serve as the value of a bound variable, it follows that everything that is an object in Frege's sense is also an object in Quine's sense. I will return to the question of whether the converse holds.

Which explication is better? My own preference is for Frege's explication over Quine's. For I take singular terms and their reference to be more fundamental than quantifiers and their ranges. Quantification is explained in terms of its relation to its instances, which involve singular terms. I therefore propose the following Fregean alternative to Quine's slogan: To be is to be a possible referent of a singular term.

The second step of my argument relates the notion of a referent of a singular term to that of a semantic value. In semantics and the philosophy of language it is widely assumed that each component of a complex expression makes some definite contribution to the meaning of the complex expression. This contribution is known as its *semantic value*. I will write [[**E**]] for the semantic value of an expression **E**. For instance, Frege held that the semantic value of a sentence is its truth-value and that the semantic values of other expressions are their contributions to the truth-values of sentences in which they occur. In particular, the semantic values of singular terms are just their referents.

It is also widely assumed that the meaning of a complex expression is functionally determined by the semantic values of its components and their syntactic mode of combination. This assumption is known as *compositionality*. For instance, according to Frege the semantic value of a simple sentence such as 'John runs' is determined by the equation:

$$(1)\ [[\text{John runs}]] = [[\text{runs}]]\,([[\text{John}]])$$

That is, the semantic value of the sentence 'John runs' is the result of applying the function which is the semantic value of the predicate 'runs' to the argument which is the semantic value of the subject 'John'. More generally, let C be some syntactic operation applicable to syntactic expressions $E_1,\ldots,E_n$. Then there is some semantic operation C^* corresponding to C such that the semantic value of the result of applying the syntactic operation C to the expressions $E_1,\ldots,E_n$ is identical to the result of applying the semantic operation C^* to the expressions' semantic values:

$$(2)\ [[C(E_1,\ldots,E_n)]] = C^*([[E_1]],\ldots,[[E_n]]).$$

Why should the ordinary notion of reference be explicated in terms of the technical notion of semantic value? My main reason for doing so is that the notion of semantic value carries with it much less intuitive baggage than that of a referent. The ordinary notion of a referent is naturally understood in a thick way. A referent is naturally taken to be something that one can somehow encounter, that plays an ineliminable role in the truth of predications, and that is completely independent of us and our representational devices. The technical notion of a semantic value carries no such baggage.

234

However, provided that these thick connotations are set aside, I have no objection to continued talk about the semantic values of singular terms as their referents.

7 WHEN DOES A SINGULAR TERM HAVE A SEMANTIC VALUE?

The third step consists of a sufficient condition for a singular term to have a semantic value. This is the most important and distinctive step of the argument.

Let $SV(t, a)$ be the relation that holds between a singular term t and its semantic value a. What makes it the case that t has a as its semantic value? Since the relation can hardly be a primitive one, there must be something that is responsible for its obtaining. Compare the relation of ownership, which also isn't a primitive one. So when I bear the ownership relation to my bicycle, there must be something responsible for the obtaining of this relation. The study of what it is in virtue of which expressions have semantic values is sometimes called *meta-semantics*.

The sufficient condition for possession of semantic value that I wish to defend is inspired by the abstractionist approach outlined above. I will thus be concerned with languages whose singular terms are associated with an item α and a relation $\sim$ defined on such items. For instance, in the language of directions, each singular term is associated with a line l and the equivalence relation of parallelism. The item associated with a singular term must not be confused with the term's referent. The role of these items is rather to present the referents. For instance, a line serves to present the direction that it has. Let's refer to the items that play this role of presenting the proper referents as *presentations*. The role of the relation $\sim$ is to specify when two presentations determine the same referent. Let's refer to relations that play this role as *unity relations*.

Recall that the abstractionist view claims that it suffices for an abstraction term to refer that it has sense and that its presentation stands in the relevant unity relation to itself. Since a singular term is guaranteed to have sense already by the fact that it is associated with a presentation and a unity relation, the abstractionist view is simply that it suffices for a term to refer that it has been assigned a presentation and a unity relation.

I will illustrate this view by means of the example of directions. Let D be a domain of lines and other directed items. Assume $\mathcal{L}$ is a first-order language with identity such that:

(i) the variables of L range over D,
(ii) each singular term of L has been assigned an element of D,
(iii) each atomic predicate of L is defined on each element of D,
(iv) for any two singular terms t_1 and t_2 that have been assigned l_1 and l_2 we have: $\ulcorner t_1 = t_2 \urcorner$ is true iff $l_1 \parallel l_2$.

When these assumptions are met, I say that L has a *pre-interpretation*. A pre-interpretation is much like a proper interpretation except that it is based on a domain of presentations (in this case lines) instead of proper referents (in this case directions). A consequence of this is that the identity predicate is interpreted non-standardly: the identity predicate can be true of two non-identical lines provided they are parallel. Note that the standard laws of identity require that every predicate P of L be a congruence with respect to parallelism, in the sense that the following holds:

Assume P is n-adic and that $l_i \parallel l_i'$ for each i from 1 to n. Then P holds of $l_1,..., l_n$ iff P holds of $l_1',..., l_n'$.

My sufficient condition says roughly that a pre-interpretation suffices for a proper interpretation. But let's be more precise. Assume L has a pre-interpretation and that t_i are singular terms of L which have been assigned lines l_i respectively. Then the sufficient condition says that expressions from L can be assigned semantic values such that:

(a) singular terms have the same semantic value iff the lines they have been assigned lines are parallel, that is: $[[t_1]] = [[t_2]] \leftrightarrow l_1 \parallel l_2$

(b) the principle of compositionality holds for simple predications, that is: $[[P(t_1,..., t_n)]] = [[P]]([[t_1]],..., [[t_n]])$

(c) the semantic values are *sui generis*.

Some explanations are in order. The first claim, (a), says that the semantic value assigned to a singular term t_i depends only on the assigned line l_i up to parallelism. There is thus a function d such that the semantic values of the terms t_i are given as

$$[[t_i]] = d(l_i)$$

and such that

236

$$d(l_i) = d(l_j) \leftrightarrow l_i \parallel l_j.$$

Note that this latter formula is just an abstraction principle. So we now have an explanation of why such principles are so important: they play an important role in the meta-semantic account of reference.

To understand the second claim, (b), let's consider an example. Assume L contains a two-place predicate **P** which is true of t_i and t_j iff l_i and l_j are orthogonal. Then (b) says that **P** has a semantic value **P** which is true of the directions $d(l_i)$ and $d(l_j)$ iff the lines l_i and l_j are orthogonal. This means that **P** is an orthogonality predicate on directions. We are here relying on the fact that two directions are orthogonal iff any two lines whose directions they are, are orthogonal.

Claims (a) and (b) are highly plausible. To see this, recall what semantic values are supposed to do. The semantic value of an expression was explained as the contribution that the expression makes to the truth-value of sentences in which it occurs. Assume that L has a pre-interpretation and that the singular term t has been assigned a line l as its presentation. What is the semantic contribution that t makes to the truth-values of sentences in which it occurs? Clearly t makes *some* contribution: for all sentences involving the term have truth-values which typically depend on the presentation l. But the contribution cannot be anything as specific as the line l. For we know that any parallel line l' would make precisely the same contribution. Rather, the semantic contribution of t must be something which is shared by all lines l' that are parallel with l. But this is exactly the sort of contribution that claim (a) ascribes to t. An analogous motivation can be provided for (b). Clearly the atomic predicates make some semantic contribution. But this contribution does not discriminate between singular terms with the same semantic value, as asserted by (b).

In pure mathematics it would be natural to represent the semantic contribution of the singular term t as the equivalence class of l under the equivalence relation of parallelism, that is, as the set of all lines l' that are parallel to l. This too would ensure that claim (a) holds. Moreover, we could let the semantic value of the predicate for orthogonality be the function that maps two such equivalence classes to the true iff any two lines from each of the two classes are orthogonal, and to the false otherwise. This is easily seen to ensure that claim (b) holds. So this provides a useful model of the desired assignment of semantic values.

However, a model of an assignment is not the same as the intended assignment itself. Although the semantic values of the language of directions can be *represented by* equivalence classes of lines, they should not be *identified with* such equivalence classes. Doing so would ascribe to the semantic values properties that go beyond the contribution that the relevant terms make to the truth-values of sentences in which they occur. For instance, equivalence classes have set theoretic elements, which is a notion that is completely foreign to the geometrical language in question. Accordingly the third claim of the sufficient condition, (c), says that it is permissible to assign to the expressions in question semantic values that are primitive and *sui generis* and not just set theoretic constructs. These semantic values are nothing more than the contributions made by the relevant singular terms. This provides a good beginning of a response to what I called the problem of existence. In other work I argue that this version of minimalism allows for good responses to the other three problems as well.

REFERENCES

Benacerraf, Paul: "Mathematical Truth", in *Journal of Philosophy* 70, 1973, pp.661–679.
Field, Hartry: *Realism, Mathematics, and Modality*, Oxford: Blackwell, 1989.
Hale, Bob & Wright, Crispin: *Reason's Proper Study*, Oxford: Clarendon, 2001.
Hale, Bob & Wright, Crispin: "The *Metaontology* of Abstraction", in David Chalmers et al. (eds.): *Metametaphysics: New Essays on the Foundations of Ontology*, Oxford: Oxford University Press, 2009. (Hale & Wright 2009a)
Hale, Bob & Wright, Crispin: "Focus Restored: Comments on John MacFarlane", in *Synthese*, 2009, forthcoming. (Hale & Wright 2009b)
Linnebo, Øystein: "Epistemological Challenges to Mathematical Platonism", in *Philosophical Studies* 129, 2006, pp.545–574.
Linnebo, Øystein: "Introduction", in *Synthese*, 2009, forthcoming (DOI 10.1007/s11229-007-9267-5).
Wright, Crispin: *Frege's Conception of Numbers as Objects*, Aberdeen: Aberdeen University Press, 1983.

RUSSELL'S MANY POINTS

THOMAS MORMANN

University of the Basque Country, Donostia-San Sebastián

Abstract

Bertrand Russell was one of the protagonists of the programme of reducing "disagreeable" concepts to philosophically more respectable ones. Throughout his life he was engaged in eliminating or paraphrasing away a copious variety of allegedly dubious concepts: propositions, definite descriptions, knowing subjects, and points, among others. The critical aim of this paper is to show that Russell's construction of points, which has been considered as a paradigm of a logical construction *überhaupt*, fails for principal mathematical reasons. The constructive aim of this paper is to show that one can save Russell's programme by using the conceptual resources of modern pointless topology.

1 POINTS IN RUSSELL'S PHILOSOPHY

Bertrand Russell was one of the protagonists of the programme of reducing "disagreeable" objects to philosophically more respectable ones. Throughout his life he was engaged in eliminating or paraphrasing away a copious variety of suspicious objects: propositions, definite descriptions, knowing subjects, and many others.

For Russell, the method of scientific philosophy was logical analysis. The aim of logical analysis was the elimination of suspicious or otherwise undesired entities from the discourse of scientific philosophy. In *Our Knowledge of the External World as a Field for Scientific Method in Philosophy* (Russell 1914) Russell attempted to show

> "by means of examples, the nature, capacity, and limitations of the logical-analytic method in philosophy. ... The central problem by which I have sought to illustrate method is the problem of the relation between the crude data of sense and the space, time and matter of mathematical physics." (Russell 1914, p.10)

More precisely, Russell attempted to show that the basic mathematical structures of physical spacetime – conceived as structured sets of spatial points and temporal points – could be reconstructed from "crude sense data", later to be characterized as "events". He credited Whitehead with the basic ideas of this approach characterizing his own version as a "rough preliminary account":

> "I owe to Dr. Whitehead the definition of points, the suggestion for the treatment of instants and "things", and the whole conception of the world of physics as a *construction* rather than an *inference*. What is said on these topics here is, in fact, a rough preliminary account of the more precise results which he is giving in the fourth volume of our *Principia Mathematica.*" (ibidem, pp.10, 11)

Actually, points had played a role in Russell's thinking already before he had started his collaboration with Whitehead on *Principia Mathematica*. From his youthful *Essay on the Foundations of Geometry* (Russell 1897)[1] up to *My Philosophical Development* (1959) "points" were a recurrent theme in many of his writings. The most detailed account of spatial points can be found in *The Analysis of Matter* (Russell 1929), the last original work on matters of points (more precisely on temporal points) was the paper *On Order in Time* (Russell 1936), but still in the retrospective *My Philosophical Development* (Russell 1959) he ascribed to the issue of points an important place in his philosophical development:

> "As regards points, instants, and particles, I was awakened from my "dogmatic slumber by Whitehead. Whitehead invented a method of constructing points, instants, and particles as sets of events, each of finite extent. This made it possible to use Occam's razor in physics in the same sort of way in which we had used it in arithmetic. I was delighted with this fresh application of the methods of mathematical logic." Russell (1959, p.77).

Taking into account Russell's assertion that "the question of the construction of point-instants ... was already very much in my mind in 1911" (Russell 1959, 121) one may say that Russell considered the topic of the logical construction of spatial and temporal points as an important philosophical topic for almost 50 years. Nevertheless, he never got it right, although he was quite clear about the general idea of how the construction of points from less queer entities such as regions or events should be carried out. In *The Analysis of Matter* (Russell 1927) he compared his reductionist pro-

---

[1] In the *Essay on the Foundations of Geometry*, still under the spell of Bradley's idealism, Russell conceived points cryptically as "contradictory" objects that evidenced the "dialectical structure" of science according to which the most basic science (= geometry) was not an independent science but pointed to some "higher" science, i.e. physics: "The antinomy of the Point proves the relativity of space, and shows that Geometry must have some reference to matter ..." Russell (1897, pp.196–199).

gram with the standard approach of point set topology and differential geometry:

> "In *analysis situs* (= topology, T.M.) both points and neighborhoods are given. We, on the other hand, wish to define our points in terms of "events", where *"events" will have a one-one correspondence with certain neighborhoods. ... We have to assign to our events such properties as will enable us to define the points of a topological space as classes of events, and the neighborhoods of the points as classes of points.* (Emphasis mine, T.M.) But we have to remember that we do not want to construct merely a topological space: what we want to construct is the four-dimensional space-time of the general theory of relativity." (Russell 1927, p.298)

It should be noted that this constructional programme has a circular structure: we start with a certain set E of events that are assumed to have certain (relational) properties. Then we construct points as certain classes of events and the neighborhoods of these points (classes of events) as certain classes of points (classes of classes of events). There is no reason to stop here: we may consider the newly constructed neighborhoods of constructed points as events in their own right and consider them as building blocks for the construction of new "second order" points. For these second order points we may construct neighborhoods again, i.e., second order events, and so on. Continuing in this way, things tend to be complicated, or so it seems. Therefore it seems advisable to confine this undesired profusion of higher order points and events. The simplest one is the assumption that iterating the construction of points and events from already constructed points and events does not yield anything new. That is to say, the classes of points and events of higher order are required to be isomorphic to the classes of points and events of first order. This is a reasonable assumption, since the constructions of points of modern pointless topology do satisfy it. Thus, from now on, this requirement of "stability" is considered as a condition that every good construction programme has to satisfy. One of the main negative results of this paper is that Russell's original construction is *not* stable, rather, it produces a diverging profusion of points and events of ever higher order.

Notwithstanding this flaw I think it is remarkable fact that already in 1927 Russell quite explicitly formulated here the programme of what later was to become "pointless topology", namely, "to assign to events such properties as will enable us to define the points of topological spaces as classes of events, ..." (ibidem). Although Russell identified the task of that future discipline with admirable clarity, he did not much to accomplish it.

He never offered any elaborated proposal of what the "properties of events" might be that would "enable us to define points in terms of events". Rather, he was content to conceive the class E of events as a similarity structure $(E, \sim)$, i.e. as a set E endowed with a binary relation $\sim$ to be interpreted as non-trivial overlapping.

Consequently, his programme never really got off the ground. Russell never gave a correct definition of points in terms of events, to say nothing about the envisaged construction of the topological and differential structures of the space-time manifolds. In the following we leave aside the projected higher layers of this construction and concentrate on its most basic level – the construction of points and their topological neighborhoods.

Cast in terms of some appropriate set theory (instead of the framework of *Principia Mathematica* as Russell did), his plan for the construction of points (spatial, temporal, and spatio-temporal points) may be outlined as follows: One starts with a set E of events, whereby the concept of "event" is assumed to be a primitive term, i.e. there is no explicit definition of what an event is to be, rather, only some intuitive and informal hints are given. The reader may think of events as more or less well-formed regions of the Euclidean plane, or in the special case of purely temporal events, of intervals of the real line $\mathbf{R}$ endowed with its usual order structure. For the moment, he may take those regions as certain point sets, but it is important to keep in mind that finally events are not to be thought as point sets – rather, points have to be constructed from events in such a way that events and their relations are faithfully *represented* by appropriate point sets and set-theoretical relations.

Let $pt(E) := \{p; p$ is a point of $E\}$ denote the set of points to be constructed from E. For the moment, the only thing we know about points is that they are to be sets of events, i.e., the set $pt(E)$ of points is a subset of PE, PE being the power set of E. In the next sections we are going to determine more precisely, what kind of subsets are points to be. The basic idea of constructing points as sets of events is intuitively appealing and simply. This is not to say, that the constructions to be carried out are simple. Actually they are not, and for reasons of space it is not possible to present all the concepts and arguments in full detail. The underlying mathematical facts may be succinctly described as follows. The general mathematical framework is provided by topology and lattice theory, more precisely the theory of Heyting algebras. From a modern point of view, Russell's programme of defining points in terms of events is located in a conceptual space that is determined by the following facts:

FACT 1: Let H be a regular continuous Heyting algebra. The elements of H are to be intuitively conceived as "events" in the sense of Russell. Up to isomorphism there is a unique topological space $(pt(H), O(pt(H)))$ such that the Heyting algebra $O(pt(H))$ of its open sets and H are isomorphic. Hence, without loss of generality one can assume that H can be thought of as a set-theoretical Heyting algebra, i.e. the elements of H are isomorphic to subsets of $pt(H)$, and the lattice-theoretical operations of H are just the familiar set-theoretical operations of union and intersection.

FACT 2: Russell's construction of ersatz points as maximal co-punctual subsets of H yields a profusion of undesired ersatz points of which only a small minority corresponds to real points, i.e. to elements of $pt(H)$. In order to show this, we will not rely on Russell's original construction but on a slightly improved variant, but even this improved construction is doomed to fail.

FACT 3. Russell's programme of defining "points in terms of events" can be saved by using some more sophisticated concepts of modern pointless topology. The most important device is the notion of an "interior parthood" relation $\ll$. This relation is used to define maximal *round* filters as ersatz points for which a 1-1-correspondence with the real points of H, i.e. the elements of pt(H), can be established.

Before we go on some explanatory remarks on FACTS may be in order:

Remark 1: It is the definition of a regular continuous Heyting algebra, which encapsulates the "appropriate properties of our events" that allow us to "define points in terms of events". The explicit definition of this structure from scratch is rather complicated and would need more several pages. Thus some hints to the literature must suffice. Davey and Priestley (1990) provide a useful introduction to general lattice theory. The basics of the theory of complete Heyting algebras may be found in chapter II of Johnstone (1982), for a rather exhaustive treatment of continuous Heyting algebras the reader may consult the authoritative treatise of Gierz et al. (2003).

Important examples of regular continuous Heyting algebras, which will be treated in some detail in the following sections, are the Heyting algebras OX of open sets of "nice" topological spaces (X, OX). Again, the exact definition of "niceness" used here is somewhat involved. Be it sufficient to state that Euclidean spaces belong to the class of nice spaces whose Heyting algebras of open sets are regular continuous Heyting algebras (cf. Gierz el al. 2003). On the other hand, the rational numbers $\mathbf{Q}$ endowed with their standard order do *not* form a continuous Heyting algebra.

Remark 2. In section 3 we give an elementary example that shows that Russell's construction yields too many ersatz points, i.e., at least some of the constructed points do not correspond to real points. This and other examples were known to mathematicians and logicians such as Hausdorff and Tarski, probably already to Cantor. Thus, Russell could have known that his method was doomed to fail if he had paid attention to the then contemporary mathematics.

Remark 3: The "new methods" alluded to in FACT 3 belong to the realm of mathematics sometimes called "pointless topology". As a forerunner of this discipline one may consider Stone's work on the representation of Boolean algebras B by topologically defined subsets of their Stone spaces $St(B)$ (cf. Stone (1936, 1938)). For a brief but complete account of Stone's representation theorem see Davey and Priestley (1990); for some remarks on the history of pointless topology see Johnstone (1982) and Gierz et al. (2003).

The outline of this paper is as follows: in the next section we discuss the basic properties of Russell's construction of points. For intuitive reasons, this construction may be dubbed the "onion construction"; mathematically, it is characterized as the construction of maximal filters for appropriate structures. Applying the axiom of choice to an appropriately structured set of events allows us to define ersatz points in the sense of Russell's programme. In section 3 we consider a very simple set-theoretical model of space and show that it has too many ersatz points. This may be taken as evidence that Russell's programme is doomed to fail for principal reasons. In section 4 concepts of pointless topology are used to overcome the difficulties of Russell's original approach. In particular it is shown that the replacement of ordinary filters by "round" filters suffices to eliminate the profusion of ersatz points Russell's original construction was plagued with.[2] We conclude with a general assessment of Russell reconstructional programme in section 5.

---

[2] For reasons of space the special case of temporal points, i.e. instants, cannot be dealt with in this paper. For temporal points *mutatis mutandis* the same arguments apply as to spatial points. Russell treated the case of instants in *On Order in Time* (Russell 1936).

2 The Onion Construction

Let us take the Euclidean plane P as a typical example of a well-behaved topological space and take as the set E $(= E(P))$ of events an appropriate set of well-formed regions of P. For the moment we need no worry about what precisely is meant by "well-formed region". The reader may think of parts of the plane with "nice" boundaries and without interior crackles and holes, for instances circles, ellipsoides, and similar figures. Intuitively, these figures may be arranged in such a manner that they form an "onion" or a nested system of neighborhoods such that the elements of this system "approximate" a point x of E that lies in the interior of all of them.

The system $N(x)$ of nested neighborhoods of can be taken as a representative of the point x, since at least for nice spaces such as Euclidean ones two different points x and y give rise to two different "onions" $N(x)$ and $N(y)$, respectively, since we may always find a neighborhood of x that does not contain y, and vice versa.

If we could characterize systems like $N(x)$ independently from and without reference to the points x of which they are neighborhood systems we would have met Russell's challenge of "defining points in terms of events". In modern terms, Russell's proposal for achieving this task amounts to something like this. The class of events E is considered as a not just a set with some kind of a mereological or lattice-theoretical structure: given two events a and b, they may overlap, i.e. there may be a region $(a \wedge b)$ such that $(a \wedge b)$ is a part of the regions a and b, and every region c that is part of a and b has $(a \wedge b)$ as part. The concept of overlapping should be structurally well behaved. For instance, the overlapping $(a \wedge b)$ of a and b should be the same as the overlapping $(b \wedge a)$ of b and a etc. In sum, the class of events should be conceived (at least) as a (semi)lattice $E = (E, \wedge, 0)$, 0 being the bottom element of E (cf. Davey and Priestley 1990, Chapter 3, p.58). Then we can as usual define "overlapping" in terms of the lattice-theoretical operation by defining that a and b overlap if and only if $(a \wedge b) \neq 0$.[3]

After these conceptual preparations we are ready to approach Russell's proposals of defining ersatz points solely in terms of events:

---

[3] Russell did not traffick with these technicalities but took them for granted.

(2.1) Definition (Russell (1928, p.299)) Let E be the class of events. A set $F \subseteq E$ is called *co-punctual* if and only if every five regions $a_1, \ldots, a_5$ of F overlap:

$$a_1 \wedge \ldots \wedge a_5 \neq 0.$$

A *Russell point* is a *maximal* co-punctual subset F of E, i.e. a subset that cannot be enlarged without ceasing to be co-punctual. ♦

This definition is the very core of Russell's programme of reducing spatio-temporal points to some more respectable entities such as events or regions. Thus, some explanatory remarks may be in order.

The first question that probably comes to mind is whether there is any deeper meaning why co-punctional F are defined via the non-trivial overlapping of *five* regions – why not two, three, or seventeen? Obviously one can define "co-punctuality" with respect to every n, $n \geq 1$. The answer is that Russell wanted to reconstruct the points for the four-dimensional space-time manifold of relativity theory. For some not very clear reasons he believed that for the construction of an n-dimensional space one needed co-punctuality with respect to $(n+1)$ regions. Indeed, he explicitly asserted that for ordinary three-dimensional space one needed co-punctuality with respect to four regions, and for the reconstruction of temporal points (instants) of the one-dimensional time manifold he required co-punctuality with respect to two events (intervals), see Russell (1936).

Secondly, an interesting problem arises with respect to maximal co-punctual subsets of E, i.e. Russell points. How do we know that they exist? Can we construct them in some explicit sense? Russell was well aware that for the construction of maximal co-punctual subsets F of E the axiom of choice or a similar principle was necessary. Points are not for free, rather, one has to rely on a logical (or set-theoretical) principle that is far from trivial. Even the modern constructions of points have to use such a principle.

The details are as follows. Let S be any well behaved space, e.g. Euclidean space. Assume that S has points in the usual sense, i.e., S is as a point set endowed with some further geometrical or topological structure. Defining the set of regions of S as a set of well behaved subsets of S we may then attempt to apply Russell's recipe of (re)constructing the points of S as sets of maximal co-punctual regions. The result turns out to be a failure since there are many more Russell points than real points, i.e., elements of S. Describing the outcome as "many more ersatz points than real points" is to put it mildly. Actually, the cardinality of ersatz points is the cardinality of the power set of the power set of real points! Thus, Russell's construction is quite off the mark as it is much too prolific in generating ersatz points. The first step to prove this is the following definition:

(2.2) Definition Let E be a lattice. A *Stone point* of E is a subset F of E satisfying the following conditions:
(1) $0 \notin F \neq \varnothing$.
(2)   If $a, b \in F$, then $a \wedge b \in F$.
(3)   If $a \in F$ and $a \leq b$, then $b \in F$.
(4) F is maximal with respect to (1)–(3), i.e. if $x \notin F$, there is an $a \in F$ such that $a \wedge x = 0.$ ◆

Defining as usual $a \leq b := a$ one may succinctly characterize a Stone point as a maximal upper subset of E closed under finite intersections. Usually a "Stone point" of E is called *maximal filter* or *ultrafilter* of E.[4]

Filters are quite common mathematical objects considered in many realms of logic, lattice theory, topology and elsewhere. The following elementary lemma shows that for our purposes we may replace the Russell points by the more manageable Stone points:

(2.3) Lemma Let E be a lattice. Then every Stone point of E is a Russell point of E.

Proof: Let F be a Stone point of E. Let $a_1,\ldots, a_5$ be five regions of F. By the very definition of a Stone point $(a_1 \wedge a_2)$ is a region that belongs to F. Hence $((a_1 \wedge a_2) \wedge a_3)$ is an element of F. Iterating this argument, one obtains that the regions $a_1,\ldots, a_5$ are co-punctual in the sense of Russell. In order to show that F is a maximal set of copunctual elements we proceed by reductio. Assume that F is not a maximal co-punctual subset of E. Then there is a maximal co-punctual set G that properly contains F. Moreover, there is a region x in G that is not a region of F. Since F is a maximal Stone point, there is a y in F such that $x \wedge y = 0$. Hence $x \wedge y \wedge y \wedge y \wedge y = 0$. Hence G is not a maximal co-punctual set in the sense of Russell. This is a

---

[4] I'd propose to call maximal filters "Stone points" because in the special case of E being a Boolean algebra, the maximal filters of E are just the points of a topological space $St(E)$ which is usually called the Stone space or the Boolean space of E (cf. Davey and Priestley 1990, Chapter 10, p.197).

contradiction. Thus already F is a maximal co-punctual set, i.e. a Russell point. ◆

In the next sections we will prove that a space X has more Stone points than real points (cf. Proposition (3.3)). In other words, the set $St(X)$ of Stone points of X, to be called the Stone space of X, is not isomorphic to X. Roughly, the basic flaw of Russell's constructional programme may be diagnosed as the error of confounding the Stone space $St(X)$ with X. Thus we obtain from (2.3) and (3.3):

> **(2.4). Corollary** If X is a space, then X has Russell points that do not correspond to real points of X. In other words, Russell's recipe for constructing ersatz points fails. ◆

In the next few sections we will forget about Russell points and concentrate on the mathematically better behaved Stone points. Before we deal with the technicalities it may be helpful to point out that the neighborhood systems of points of "nice" spaces define Stone points in a natural way. In some more detail, this may be spelt out as follows.[5] Let (X, OX) be a topological space, i.e. a set X endowed with a topological structure $OX \subseteq PX$. The elements of OX are called the open sets of X. $A \in OX$ with $x \in A$ is called an open neighborhood of x. The system $N(x)$ of all open neighborhoods of x is a filter, i.e. $N(x)$ satisfies the following conditions:

(1) $\emptyset \notin N(x) \neq \emptyset$.
(2) $A \in N(x) \,\&\, A \subseteq B \Rightarrow B \in N(x)$.
(3) $A, B \in N(x) \Rightarrow A \cap B \in N(x)$.

Invoking the axiom of choice it is easily proved that there exists a maximal filter $F(x)$ containing $N(x)$.[6] For nice topological spaces two different points x and y have neighborhood filters $N(x)$ and $N(y)$ that contain neighborhood $A(x)$ and $A(y)$ of x and y, respectively, such that the intersection $A(x) \cap A(y)$ is empty. Then one can easily prove that x and y define different Stone points $F(x)$ and $F(y)$, i.e. maximal filters that contain $N(x)$ and

---

[5] For a succinct presentation of the basic topological concepts used in this paper, the reader may consult the Appendix of Davey and Priestley (1990) or any textbook of topology.
[6] There is no reason to expect that $F(x)$ is unique. As it seems, Russell was not aware of the analogous fact for sets of co-punctual events.

$N(y)$, respectively, are different. "Nice" spaces in this sense are Euclidean spaces, and more generally, Hausdorff spaces.

In the following section we show that nice spaces X have more Stone points than real points, i.e. $X \neq St(X)$. More precisely, we will show that for a space X every real point x defines a Stone point $F(x)$, but there is a wealth of Stone points that do not correspond to any real points. Actually, Stone points related to real points turn out to be an exception. Since all Stone points are Russell points, this implies that Russell's original constructional programme is flawed.

3 A MINIMALIST MODEL OF SPACE

In this section we consider a simple set-theoretical model of space and show that it has too many Stone points, and a fortiori, too many Russell points. In later sections it will be shown that this simple model does indeed reflect the essential features due to which every construction based on Stone or Russell points *must* fail. Moreover, we show how to modify the construction of points such that the profusion of ersatz points is cut down in such a way that there can be established a 1-1 correspondence between modified Stone points and real points.

Let X be a set, and let us regard X as a topological space (X, OX) by endowing it with the discrete topology $OX = PX$. (X, PX) is called a discrete topological space. With respect to this special topological structure just any $Y \subseteq X$ with $x \in Y$ is an open neighborhood of x. Moreover, the system $N(x)$ of all open neighborhoods of x is the set of all subsets of X containing x. This implies that in this case the system $N(x)$ has the following properties:

(1) $\emptyset \notin N(x) \neq \emptyset$.
(2) $A \in N(x) \,\&\, A \subseteq B \Rightarrow B \in N(x)$.
(3) $A, B \in N(x) \Rightarrow A \cap B \in N(x)$.
(4) $C \notin N(x) \Rightarrow A \cap C = \emptyset$ for some $A \in N(x)$.

Since $\{x\} \in N(x)$ one has $C \in N(x) \Leftrightarrow x \in C$. In other words, for every real point $x \in A$ the neighborhood system $N(x)$ is a Stone point. Moreover two real points x and y are equal iff the neighborhood systems $N(x)$ and $N(y)$ are equal. Hence for (X, PX) the neighborhood systems $N(x)$ are faithful representatives for real points $x \in X$. Since neighborhood systems are maximal filters on PX, and maximal filters on PX can be characterized without explicit reference to points by (2.2) we seem to have made great progress on our way of defining points as systems of events – at least in the special case of X being a discrete topological space (X, PX). There is missing only one piece: Although we know that every "real" point $x \in X$ defines a unique Stone point $N(x)$, it might be that there are still other maximal filters that do *not* correspond to any real point x. Russell assumed without argument that this is not the case. As it seems, he took it for granted that all maximal filters on a set X arise as the neighborhood system $N(x)$ of some point x of X. Actually, this assumption is true only for X with finitely many elements. For infinite sets X it is false. For them there are many more abstract neighborhood systems N than real points.

It would take us too long to prove this result in full generality, instead, let us prove that an infinite set X has at least one Stone point that does not correspond to any real point x of X.

(3.1) Proposition (The Finite/Infinite Filter) Let X be a set with infinitely many elements, and define F to be the set of subsets Y of X whose complements consist of finitely many elements:

$$F := \{Y;\ Y \subseteq X \text{ and } \mathbf{C}F \text{ finite}\}$$

The there is a Stone point $N(F)$ that contains F but there is no element $x \in X$ such that $N(F) = N(x)$.

Proof. Clearly F is non-empty since $X \in F$ and $\emptyset \notin F$ since X is infinite. Since the finite union of finite sets is finite, F is closed with respect to finite intersections. Moreover F is upward closed. In other words, F is a filter. Invoking the axiom of choice or a similar principle one infers that there is a maximal filter $N(F)$ containing F. But $N(F)$ cannot come from some principal filter $N(x)$. If this were the case, x would be an element of all elements of $N(F)$, a fortiori it would be an element of all elements of F. But clearly $X–\{x\}$ is an element of F that does not contain x. Hence there is at least one abstract neighborhood system that does not correspond to a real point $x \in X$. ◆

One might hope that the maximal filter $N(F)$ is somehow an exception and that "usually" a Stone point of X comes from some real point of X. This hope is shattered by the following classical result due to Hausdorff and Tarski:

(3.2) Proposition Let X be an infinite set with cardinality $\langle X \rangle$. Then the set of Stone points $St(X)$ of X has the cardinality of the power set of the power set of X, i.e. $\langle St(X) \rangle = \langle PPX \rangle$. In other words, there are many more Stone points than real points.

Proof. Bell and Slomson (2006, p.108, Theorem 1.5). ◆

Remark. The proof of (3.2) is somewhat complicated but elementary in the sense that it can be carried out using only the concepts that are already available to us. Its essential ingredient is, of course, the axiom of choice. Without it, or some similar principle, one cannot show the existence of even one maximal filter. This was known already to Russell (cf. Russell (1936)).

One may object that (3.2) can hardly count as a refutation of a Russellian programme of constructing points from events since the topological structure PX of X is just too meager as to capture the relevant features of the topological relations between "points" and "neighborhoods" that Russell wanted to put to use. Prima facie, this suspicion is not unreasonable; nevertheless it turns out to be wrong. More precisely it can be shown that for every reasonable space X (in particular for the Euclidean space E) and every reasonable set of events of X an analogous theorem to (3.2) holds according to which the cardinality of Stone points is much larger than the cardinality of real points of X:

(3.3) Proposition (Theorem of Balcar-Franêk) Let B be an infinite complete Boolean algebra. Then the cardinality of the set of maximal filters on B is the cardinality of the power set PB of B.

Proof. Koppelberg (1989, Theorem 13.6, p.197). ◆

Every maximal filter on O^*X gives rise to at least one maximal filter on OX, since the inclusion $O^*X \text{-----} i \text{-----} \!\!> OX$ is a monomorphism that preserves overlapping, i.e. $i(x \wedge y) = i(x) \wedge i(y)$. This implies that there are at least as many maximal filters on OX as there are maximal filters on O^*X. For X a nice space, the cardinality of O^*X is at least the cardinality of X. Hence, Russell's construction yields too many points not just for the discrete topological structure (X, PX) but for every nice topological space (X, OX). In other words, the trivial topological structure of minimalist set theoretical model of space cannot be blamed for the failure of Russell's programme. Rather, as will be shown in the next section, the culprit for the profusion of undesired ersatz points is the too primitive "non-topological" notion of a filter employed.

4 TOPOLOGY TO THE RESCUE

Let us take stock what we have achieved so far, and what remains to be done. Given a topological space (X, OX) with a system of regions OX we did the first step to realize Russell's programme, namely, improving upon Russell's own account of ersatz points as maximal copunctual sets of regions, we defined ersatz points as maximal filters of X. In a sense, this works quite well – for every real point $x \in X$ we can construct an ersatz point. In the case of $OX = PX$ this ersatz point is even unique. The only flaw in this construction is that it yields too many ersatz points.

In this situation it is natural to attempt to restrict somehow the profusion of ersatz points by singling out a small class of particularly "nice" ersatz points. This is indeed possible, if we put to use the topological structure of the space X. It is here, where we encounter something new that has no counterpart in Russell's original attempt to "define points in terms of events".

In order to use the topological structure of a space as a tool for cutting down the profusion of ersatz points we have to delve somewhat deeper into the details of topology. Recall that given a topological space (X, OX) the closed subsets of X are defined as the set-theoretical complements of the open sets. Every subset Y of X there is the smallest closed subset $cl(Y)$ containing Y, where $cl(Y)$ is defined as the intersection of all closed subsets containing Y. This defines an operator $PX\text{-}\text{-}\text{-}\text{-}>PX$ mapping each subset Y to its closed hull $cl(Y)$. Complementarily the open kernel $int(Y)$ of a set Y is defined by $int(Y) := Ccl(CY)$, C being the set-theoretical complement of Y in X. A set Z is called regular open if and only if $Z = int(cl(Z))$. If Y is any subset of X, an open covering of Y is a family U_i of open subsets of X such that $Y \subseteq \cup U_i$. The covering is finite if and only if it consists of finitely many elements U_i. A subset Y is compact if and only if every open covering contains a finite subcovering. Now we are ready to define the crucial concept of interior parthood:

(4.1) Definition Let a, b open sets of the topological (X, OX). The region a is an *interior part* of the region b, $a \ll b$, if and only if the closure $\mathrm{cl}(a)$ of a is contained in b, and $\mathrm{cl}(a)$ is compact:

$$a \ll b := \mathrm{cl}(a) \subseteq b \text{ and } \mathrm{cl}(a) \text{ is compact.} \blacklozenge$$

Intuitively, the relation $a \ll b$ is to convey the meaning that the region a plus its boundary $\mathrm{bd}(a)$ is fully contained in b, and moreover, that a is somehow "small". Compactness may indeed be interpreted as a topological version of "smallness" or even "finiteness" as the following topological analogue of the finite/infinite filter (see Proposition (3.1)) shows:

(4.2) Example (A topological version of the Finite/Infinite Filter)
Let (X, OX) be a nice non-compact space, for instance the real line **R** or an Euclidean space. Define the filter F as a maximal filter that contains all sets of the form $X–K$, K compact. Then it is easily seen that F does not contain the open neighborhood filter $N(x)$ of any $x \in X$: if x and y are two different points of X, since x has an open neighborhood $U(x)$ such that $\mathrm{cl}(U(x))$ is compact and does not contain y. This proves that there is a Stone point of (X, OX) that does not correspond to any real point $x \in X$. In other words, Russell's construction yields too many points. $\blacklozenge$

The concept of interior parthood can be used to single out a special class of filters as follows:

(4.3) Definition Let (X, OX) be a topological space with interior parthood relation $\ll$.

(a) A subset $F \subseteq OX$ is a *round* filter (with respect to $\ll$) if and only if F is a filter and satisfies the further condition that for all $b \in F$ there is an $a \in F$ with $a \ll b$.[7]

(b) A maximal round filter F is called a (round) ersatz point. $\blacklozenge$

As is easily shown by the axiom of choice, round ersatz points exist. Moreover, under some mild conditions on the topology of X the filters $N(x)$ of open neighborhoods of real points x are round filters. Indeed, the class of

---

[7] For a detailed discussion of "round filters" see Gierz and Keimel (1981) and Gierz et al. (2003).

maximal round filters is the class of ersatz points we were looking for. Let us first deal with the special case (X, PX):

> **(4.4) Proposition** Let (X, PX) be a discrete topological space. Then the real points of X are in a 1-1-correspondence with the maximal round filters of X.

Proof. First let us prove that for (X, PX) $a \ll b$ if and only if a is a finite subset of b. Assume that $a \ll b$. By definition this means that $cl(a)$ is a compact subset of b. But $cl(a) = a$, since the topology of X is trivial; using this fact once again, we observe that every singleton $\{x\}$ is open. Hence, a set is compact if and only if it has only finitely many elements. By definition a round maximal filter F must contain a finite set. But then it is easily seen that in order to be maximal F must even contain a singleton $\{x\}$. Hence it is the principal filter $F(x)$ generated by x. The other direction is trivial. ♦

In other words, in the case of a discrete topological space (X, PX) the topologically defined round maximal filters correspond in a 1-1-fashion to the real points of X.

This result not only holds for discrete topological spaces (X, PX), but for a large class of "nice" topological space (X, OX). The task of defining exactly what is meant by "nice", would lead us to far away.[8] Be it sufficient to state that the class of nice spaces comprises the class of metrical spaces, in particular the Euclidean spaces:

> **(4.5) Proposition** Let (X, OX) be a nice topological space with interior parthood relation $\ll$. Then there is a 1-1-correspondence between the real points $x \in X$ and the round ersatz points of X, i.e., the maximal $\ll$-round filters on OX.

Proof (Sketch). The proof of this proposition naturally falls into two parts. First, one has to show that each real point gives rise to a uniquely defined maximal round filter, secondly one has to show that each maximal round filter comes from a uniquely defined real point. Let x be a real point of X. Then we can consider the filter $R(x)$ of regular open neighborhoods of x. Due to niceness, $R(x)$ is easily shown to be a round filter with respect to the interior parthood relation $\ll$. By the axiom of choice there is a maximal

---

[8] For the cognoscenti: locally compact regular Hausdorff spaces will do as "nice" spaces. Russell seems to have overlooked this completely.

round filter $N(x)$ containing x. Again by niceness (Hausdorff property) for two different points x and y maximal round filters $N(x)$ and $N(y)$ must be different. Hence, if X is nice, every real point gives rise to (at least) one ersatz point such that the ersatz points are different for different points.

It remains to show that every maximal round filter corresponds exactly to one real point. Assume that N is a maximal round filter. Consider the intersection $\cap \mathrm{cl}(Y_i)$ of the closed hulls $\mathrm{cl}(Y_i)$ of all elements of N. Since N is round, we may assume that X is compact without loss of generality. The set $\cap \mathrm{cl}(Y_i)$ is not empty, since otherwise there would be a finite family of sets $\mathrm{cl}(Y_i)$ with empty intersection. This is impossible, since N is a filter. Choose a point $x \in \cap \mathrm{cl}(Y_i)$. Since for every Y there is a Y' with $\mathrm{cl}(Y') \subseteq Y$ we obtain $x \in Y$ for every element of N, i.e. x is an element of every element of the filter N. In other words, N is contained in the neighborhood filter of x. In other words, the neighborhood filter $N(x)$ of x is the only maximal round filter containing x. This establishes a 1-1-correspondence between real points and maximal round filters as ersatz points. ◆

This is an important step on the path of realizing Russell's programme of defining "points by events". In should be noted, however, that we yet we have not accomplished our final goal. Up to now, we have assumed that the events we employ for the construction of ersatz points are point sets, namely, the open sets of a topological structure OX defined on the set X. In other words, in the definition of ersatz points as maximal round filters the real points of X still play an essential role, or so it seems. Actually this is not the case. But it needs some extra effort to show this.

Roughly, it works like this: one starts from a topological space (X, OX) endowed with an interior parthood relation $\ll$ and constructed the ersatz points as maximal round filters. To get rid of the underlying point structure, one forgets about the point set X and retaining only the topological structure OX, conceived of not as a set of open sets, but as an abstract lattice. As is well known, the lattice OX is a complete Heyting algebra. For topologically nice spaces the lattice OX is even a regular continuous Heyting algebra (cf. Johnstone (1982), Gierz et al. (2003)). The point is that these structures can be defined without reference to points, i.e. the elements of such algebras need not be conceived of as point sets. Moreover, every regular continuous Heyting algebra H comes along with a binary relation $\ll$ (the way below relation) that may be interpreted as an interior parthood relation. Then one can define the set $pt(H)$ of maximal round filters of H as ersatz points of H. Next one shows that the set $pt(H)$ can be endowed with a topology $O(pt(H))$ such that $(pt(H), O(pt(H)))$ is a topologi-

255

cal space. Finally it is proved that $O(pt(H))$ and H are naturally isomorphic as Heyting algebras. Thus one has obtained a *stable* (see section 1) method of defining points in terms of events: starting with the algebra H of events, one constructs the topological space $(pt(H), O(pt(H))$, taking $O(pt(H))$ as a system of events in its own right one constructs a set $pt(O(pt(H)))$ of points of second order, for which one can construct neighborhoods $O(pt(O(pt(H)))$ etc. Fortunately these iterations yield nothing new, due to the isomorphism between H and $O(pt(H))$ (see FACT 1).

Conceiving H as the class of events this construction may be considered as a mathematically rigorous reconstruction of Russell's programme of "defining points in terms of events" that he envisaged some 80 years ago in *The Analysis of Matter* (Russell 1927) or even earlier in *Our Knowledge of the External World* (Russell 1914). Conceptually, this construction is not too difficult to understand – it amounts to an enhanced onion construction discussed in section 2, but technically it is somewhat involved. Hence, the details cannot be given here, see Gierz et al. (2002), Johnstone (1982), Mormann (1997).

Russell never imagined the technical complexity of this endeavor, since he never cared about the details of the relational structure of the set E of events. He simply assumed that the class E of events was endowed with some binary relation of overlapping whose structural properties he never specified. In contrast, the definition of a continuous Heyting algebra, which provides the true basis for a rigorous construction of points, is a non-trivial task.

Finally, it should be noted that our reconstruction only accomplishes a part of Russell's programme: we only defined the topological structure "in terms of events" while Russell planned to reconstruct not only that structure but also the geometrical and differential structure of the space-time manifold as well.

5 CONCLUSION

We are left with a mixed assessment of Russell's programme of defining points in terms of regions. On the one hand, it is clear that Russell did not have the technical skills to realize this programme in a mathematically satisfying and rigorous manner. With respect to higher dimensional spaces he never got beyond some informal sketches that might be intuitively appealing but that did not hit upon the conceptual essence of the matter. His attempted construction of instants, i.e. temporal points, scores somewhat better, but this is a special case that depends on the linear order of time, and therefore cannot be applied to the case of general topological spaces. On the other hand, Russell had a surprisingly clear vision of the general task of what today is called "pointless topology".

It was the American mathematician M.H. Stone, who laid the foundations for this discipline in the thirties. Stone's famous representation theorem of Boolean algebras may be considered as the first successful example of constructing points for something (Boolean algebras) that at first view exhibited no spatial features at all (cf. Stone (1936, 1938)). According to the experts Stone's theorem is one of the most important theorems of 20th century mathematics that has influenced an ever-growing variety of mathematical disciplines (cf. Johnstone 1982). For an informal account of Stone's mathematical achievements, see Piazza (1995). Unfortunately, the spaces that Stone constructed as representations for Boolean algebras are quite remote from any intuitive interpretation. In particular, Stone's spaces were quite different from Euclidean and other familiar spaces. Hence, his work, although highly appreciated by mathematicians and logicians (for instance Tarski), remained virtually unknown to philosophers during the following decades.[9] In particular, Russell never took notice of Stone's work, although this would have helped him a lot in the task of coming to terms with the task of "defining points in terms of events". In philosophy, Russell's topological sketches were received with respect. But there were not many attempts to develop it further. Consequently, up to how, topology – to say nothing of pointless topology – can hardly be said to belong to a philosopher's toolkit even when he is accustomed to use formal methods. If Russell's reconstructional programme, in particular his attempt of developing pointless topology, had been taken up more seriously by his fellow philosophers, topology might have played a major role – to the benefit of philosophical disciplines such as metaphysics, epistemology and ontology. In sum, then, I'd contend that Russell has had a point with his early programme of pointless topology – despite its mathematical flaws.

---

[9] The collection *Topology for Philosophers* (Smith and Zelaniec (eds.) 1996) still provides ample evidence for this claim: Stone and his work is not mentioned even once.

REFERENCES

Bell, J.L., Slomson, A.B., 2006 (1969), Models and Ultraproducts, New York, Dover.

Gierz, G., Keimel, K., 1981, Continuous Ideal Completions and Compactifications, in Lecture Notes in Mathematics 871, Berlin and Heidelberg, Springer, pp.97–124.

Gierz, G., Hofmann, K.H., Keimel, K., Lawson, J.D., Mislove, M., Scott, D.S., 2003, Continuous Lattices and Domains, Cambridge, Cambridge University Press.

Hausdorff, F., 1936, Über zwei Sätze von G. Fichtenholz und L. Kantorovitch, Studia Mathematica 6, pp.18–19.

Johnstone, P.T., 1982, Stone Space, Cambridge, Cambridge University Press.

Koppelberg, S., 1989, Handbook of Boolean Algebras, Volume 1, edited by J.D. Monk with the cooperation of R. Bonnet, Amsterdam and New York, North-Holland.

Mormann, T., 1998, Continuous Lattices and Whiteheadian Theory of Space, Logic and Logical Philosophy 6, pp.35–54.

Mormann, T., 2005, Description, Construction, and Representation: From Russell and Carnap to Stone, in G. Imaguire and B. Linsky (eds.), On Denoting 1905–2005, München, Philosophia Verlag, pp.333–360.

Piazza, M., 1995, "One Must Always Topologize": Il teorema di Stone, la 'topologia influente' e l'epistemologia matematica, Rivista di storia della scienza (ser. II) 4, pp.1–24.

Russell, B, 1896 (1996), An Essay on the Foundations of Geometry, London, Routledge.

Russell, B., 1914 (1995), Our Knowledge of the External World as Field for Scientific Method in Philosophy, London, Routledge.

Russell, B., 1927 (2001), The Analysis of Matter, London, Routledge.

Russell, B., 1936 (1994), On Order in Time, in B. Russell, Logic and Knowledge, London, Routledge, pp.347–363.

Russell, B., 1959, My Philosophical Development, London, Routledge.

Smith, B., Zelaniec, W., 1996, Topology of Philosophers (eds.), The Monist 79(1), LaSalle Illinois, The Hegeler Institute.

Stone, M.H., 1936, The Theory of Representations for Boolean Algebras, Transactions of the American Mathematical Society 40, pp.47–111.

Stone, M.H., 1938, The Representation of Boolean Algebras, Bulletin of the American Mathematical Society 44, pp.807–816.

FROM DESCRIPTIVE FUNCTIONS TO SETS OF ORDERED PAIRS[1]

BERNARD LINSKY
University of Alberta

In this paper I respond to one of the familiar objections to the project in *Principia Mathematica* of reducing mathematics to logic. In particular, I want to refute the notion that *PM* is inferior to a non-logical axiomatic theory such as Zermelo-Fraenkel set theory as a foundation for mathematics because it relies an the obscure notion of "propositional function" in contrast with set theory which provides a simple account of functions as sets of ordered pairs, themselves reduced to certain other sets. Below I will present the theory of "descriptive" functions presented in *PM* and suggest that it was Russell's view that the account of descriptive functions provides a logicist account which is superior to both the Frege's account of functions, and the notion of functions as sets of sets. There was a deliberate choice made in *PM* not to found the theory of functions in set theory, and not to identify functions with sets of ordered pairs. In tracing the history of this topic, I will show that current treatments of functions in logic are more sensitive to these issues than one might at first think. Below I will first review the account of "descriptive functions" in *PM*, and then compare this with Frege's analysis of functions, then show how functions are treated in contemporary logic. Next, I will describe Norbert Wiener's reduction of relations to sets and then review the evidence that Russell proposed his own account deliberately as an improvement over Frege's, and finally conclude with some discussion of what this reveals about propositional functions.

---

[1] An earlier version of this paper was presented at the 31st International Ludwig Wittgenstein Symposium. Thanks to Allen Hazen, James Levine, Paul Oppenheimer and Ed Zalta for discussion of this topic and George Bealer for comments at the conference. A companion to this paper, "Russell and Frege on the Logic of Functions" was presented at the 4th International Symposium for Cognition, Logic and Communication: 200 Years of Analytic Philosophy, at the University of Latvia in Riga, August 29, 2008, and will appear in the 4th issue of the *Baltic International Yearbook for Cognition, Logic and Communication*.

The notion of "descriptive function" in *PM* makes essential use of the theory of definite descriptions and, indeed, that use seems to be the sole technical function of the theory of descriptions in the work. The theory of descriptions in *12 is based on a pair of contextual definitions, which allow the elimination of expressions for definite descriptions from the contexts in which they occur. The primary definition is:

$$*14\cdot01. \ [(\imath x)\phi x] \ . \ \psi(\imath x)(\phi x) \ . = : (\exists b) : \phi x \ . \equiv_x . \ x = b : \psi b \quad \text{Df}$$

This can be paraphrased as saying that 'the ϕ is ψ' means the same as 'There is a b such that anything x is ϕ if and only if that x is identical with b, and that b is ψ'. Here 'ψ' is the context from which the description '$(\imath x)(\phi x)$' is to be eliminated. That this is the scope of the description is indicated by the prefixed occurrence of the description in square brackets: '$[(\imath x)(\phi x)]$'. This definition allows the replacement of formulas in which definite descriptions appear in subject position. A further contextual definition is provided for the occurrence of descriptions as, '$E!(\imath x)(\phi x)$', which expresses the assertion that a description is *proper*, that is, that there is exactly one ϕ.

Just as the definitions of *14 allow for the elimination of definite descriptions from different contexts, so the theory of classes in *20 is based on a series of contextual definitions. Occurrences of class expressions '$\hat{z}\psi z$' read as 'the class of z which are ψ', can be eliminated from contexts 'f' via the primary definition:

$$*20\cdot01. \ f\{\hat{z}(\psi z)\} \ . = : (\exists\phi) : \phi!x \ . \equiv_x . \ \psi x : f\{\phi!\hat{z}\} \quad \text{Df}$$

To say that the class $\hat{z}(\psi z)$ is f is to say that there is some (predicative) function ϕ which is coextensive with ψ and that ϕ is f. There is no explicit mention of scope, but in all regards this definition closely copies that of definite descriptions. The definition of class expressions is completed by a series of other definitions, including those which use variables that range over classes, the "Greek letters" such as 'α', which are used both as bound (apparent) and free (real) variables for classes. Together, the definitions of *20 provide a reduction of the theory of classes to the theory of propositional functions. One immediate consequence of this definition is that a solution for Russell's paradox is provided by the restrictions of the theory of types. The "class of all classes that are not members of themselves", upon analysis, requires a function to apply to another function of the same type, which is prohibited by the theory of types.[2] While this "no-classes" theory of classes succeeds in resolving the paradoxes via the elimination of talk of classes in favor of talk about propositional functions, it is precisely at this point that we part ways with the now standard, alternative, project of founding mathematics on axiomatic set theory.

The next section of *Principia Mathematica*, "∗20 General Theory of Relations" presents the extension of the "no-classes" theory to the corresponding notion for binary relations, the theory of so-called "relations in extension". By analogy with the way the no-classes theory of ∗20 which defines a class expression '$\hat{z}(\psi z)$' using a contextual definition, in ∗20 we are given contextual definitions for eliminating expressions of the form '$\hat{x}\hat{y}\,\psi(x,y)$', which represents the "relation in extension" which holds between x and y when $\psi(x,y)$ obtains:

$$∗21{\cdot}01.\, f\{\hat{x}\hat{y}\,\psi(x,y)\}\, . = : (\exists\phi) : \phi!\,(x,y)\, . \equiv_{x,y} . \,\psi(x,y) : f\{\phi!\,(\hat{u},\hat{v})\} \quad \text{Df}$$

The relation of x bearing ψ to y has the property f just in case some predicative function ϕ, which is coextensive with ψ has the property f. From ∗21 onwards, "Capital Latin Letters", i.e. 'R', 'S', 'T', etc., are reserved for these relations in extension. They are variables, replaced by such expressions as '$\hat{x}\hat{y}\,\psi!(x,y)$', as Whitehead and Russell say, "just as we used Greek letters for variable expressions of the form $\hat{z}\phi!z$." ([PM] 201). These new symbols for relations in extension are written between variables, as in 'xRy' or 'uSv'. A propositional function would precede the variables, as in '$\phi(x,y)$'. (It is not clear how this notation for relations in extension would be extended to three or four place relations. Indeed in general below, as in discussion of the analysis of relations in terms of sets of ordered pairs, the discussion will always be restricted to binary relations.) It should be noted, as Quine has observed, that the intensional propositional functions represented by 'ϕ' and 'ψ', etc., drop out here from the development of *Principia Mathematica*, and that from this point on we only encounter relations in extension, symbolized by 'R', 'S', 'T', etc.[3]

Definite descriptions, though of course very important to the later development of the philosophy of language, do not appear in the later sections of *PM* where the work of reducing mathematics to logic is really carried out. In fact after ∗30·01 descriptions disappear from the symbolism,

---

[2] See my Linsky [2002].
[3] See Quine ([1963], p.251).

having performed their most important function. We are now ready for the notion of "descriptive functions." This takes the form of yet another definition, in this case of the expression 'R‘y', read as "the R of y":

$$*30{\cdot}01. \quad R‘y = (\imath x)\,(xRy) \quad \text{Df}$$

The expression 'R‘y' is defined by the definite description '$(\imath x)(xRy)$'. If 'xRy' means 'x is father of y' then 'R‘y' is 'the x such that x is father of y', or 'the father of y'. As Whitehead and Russell point out, this definition is not a contextual definition that shows how expression 'R‘y' is to be eliminated from a context, such as '$f\{R‘y\}$', but rather is simply an explicit instruction about to replace the symbols 'R‘', wherever they occur.

The notion of "descriptive function" provides an analysis of the ubiquitous "mathematical functions" of arithmetic and analysis that are reduced to logical notions in later numbers of *Principia Mathematica*. Whitehead and Russell say:

> The functions hitherto considered, with the exception of a few particular functions such as $\alpha \cap \beta$ have been propositional, *i.e.* have had propositions for their values. But the ordinary functions of mathematics, such as x^2, sin x, log x, are not propositional. Functions of this kind always mean "the term having such and such a relation to x." For this reason they may be called *descriptive* functions, because they *describe* a certain term by means of its relation to their argument. ([*PM*], p.231)

Descriptive functions provide *Principia Mathematica's* analysis of mathematical functions. It is a logicist analysis of mathematical functions in terms of the logical notions of relation in extension and definite descriptions. It has been said that Frege "mathematicized" logic in preparation for his analysis of arithmetic.[4] That mathematization involved not only the invention of symbolic logic, but also relied on the mathematical notion of function as a primitive notion in his logic. Concepts are functions from objects to truth values. Frege's notion of the extension of a concept is its course of values, which is a notion that applies to all functions. The notion of course of values is centrally implicated in Russell's paradox, and so is seen, like Whitehead and Russell's theory, as one of the unsuccessful logicist attempts to avoid postulating sets as primitive, mathematical, entities. The account of descriptive functions in *30 thus brings out clearly, some might think, the primary objections to Whitehead and Russell's version of

---

[4] By Burton Dreben for one, according to Peter Hylton, ([1993], n.28).

logicism. It relies on notions much better understood within the mathematical theory of sets. A function, on this account, is simply as set of ordered pairs, ordered pairs themselves being sets of a certain sort, and a propositional function would be a function from arguments to propositions. As propositions are not needed for the extensional, first order, logic in which axiomatic set theory is formulated, *30 thus epitomizes the wrong path taken by Whitehead and Russell's version of logicism.

I would like to suggest that an examination of the development of the idea of function in logic from Frege and Russell on into the early part of the twentieth century will defend the notion of descriptive function as a successful way of reducing the mathematical notion of function to logical notions alone.

While it is correct to say that Frege relies on the notion of mathematical function as a primitive, that is not to say that he did not provide a famously original and ground breaking logical analysis of function expressions and variables. Frege's 1891 paper "Function and Concept" and most explicitly his 1904 paper "What is a Function?" talk about the mathematical notion of function, of which concepts are a special case. Frege explains the nature of variables as linguistic entities which may be assigned different values and not as signs of "variable quantities" as many had confusedly described them to be. Frege's further notion of concepts as "unsaturated entities" which are completed by objects and yield truth-values is well known. A function expression in general, and those for mathematical functions among them, will also refer to unsaturated entities which yield objects as values. A function expression, then, such as 'sin x', 'x^2', and 'log x' will have as its *Bedeutung*, or reference an unsaturated entity which, when applied to a number as argument, yields a number as value. The logical status of expressions for functions is that they are "incomplete" names for numbers. Just as Frege had problems in even naming concepts such as "the concept horse", similarly there is a difficulty with naming functions. In fact the sine function ought to be expressed somehow as 'sin( )' with a blank or hole to indicate its unsaturated nature. The expression 'sin x', on the other hand, expresses a given number, the value of the function, for each assignment of a number to the variable 'x'. It is clear from the discussion of the problem of naming concepts that Frege would have rejected Church's lambda notation as a way of naming functions, for example, with '$\lambda x \sin x$' as naming the sine function.

In his *Introduction to Mathematical Logic*, Alonzo Church manages to turn Frege's view into the current standard current view on the logical syntax of function expressions and terms. Church avoids Frege's talk of function expressions having as a reference (*Bedeutung*) some unsaturated (and unnameable) entity, which, when saturated by an argument, gives a value. Instead we find:

> If we suppose the language fixed, every singulary form (function expression) has corresponding to it a function f (which we will call the *associated function* of the form) by the rule that the value of f for an argument x is the same as the value of the form for the value x of the free variable of the form ... (Church [1956], p.19)

This account avoids the expressions "denoted" or "designates", instead using the neutral "corresponding to" and "associated with." Church wishes to explain the semantics of function expressions without running afoul of Frege's "concept horse" problem by saying that functional expressions *name* functions.[5] But this is Frege's account of the semantics. Church, and those after him for some time, took the difference in kind between functions and objects as a difference of logical type. It was only in the late 1930s that, following Quine, it became standard to view logic as first order logic, and relations and functions, via their reduction to sets of ordered pairs, as themselves just objects.[6]

In contemporary logic texts one finds this tentative reformulation of Frege's view fully transformed into the now standard account of the role of functions in logic. In the definition of the syntax of formal languages there is a notion of a *term*, and the semantics, based on the notion of the satisfaction of a formula by a sequence, there is a clause for terms. The following, then, is typical. First we specify an set A of variables and logical symbols, and a set S of non-logical relation symbols, function symbols and constants, and the notion of the set of strings of elements of that alphabet, $(A \cup S)^*$.[7]

> Definition. *Terms* are those strings in $(A \cup S)^*$ obtained by finitely many applications of the following rules:
> (1) Every variable is a term.
> (2) Every constant is a term.

---

[5] Frege introduces this problem in "Function and Concept"([1891], p.196).

[6] See Mancuso ([2005], pp.335–339).

[7] Following Ebbinghaus *et.al.* ([1993], p.15), but Enderton [2001] and others are almost identical. This is a standard account.

(3) If $t_1, t_2, \ldots, t_n$ are terms and f is an n-ary function symbol, then $f t_1, t_2, \ldots, t_n$ is a term.

The semantics is based on the notion of a *structure* A for the language, which includes a set D as its domain, and individual c^A in D for each constant c and an n-ary function f^A for each n-ary function symbol f. An *assignment* β in a structure A is a function which maps the variables into the domain D of the structure A. An *interpretation* I is a pair $\langle A, \beta \rangle$ consisting of a structure A and an assignment β in A. The notion of the interpretation of a term, $I(t)$ is defined as follows:

(a) For a variable x, let $I(x) = \beta(x)$
(b) For a constant c, let $I(c) = c^A$
(c) For a function symbol f, let $I(f) = f^A$
(d) For any n-ary function symbol f and terms $t_1, t_2, \ldots, t_n$,
$I(f t_1, t_2, \ldots, t_n) = f^A(I(t_1), I(t_1), \ldots, I(t_n))$

The notion $I \models \varphi$ of truth of a formula φ on an interpretation I is then defined in the familiar way, and given that sentences are formulas without free variables, the notion $A \models \varphi$ of the truth of φ in the structure A is defined as truth of φ on all interpretations in A.

The notion that functions and relations are sets of ordered pairs is often included in logic texts, but it is either in a separate first chapter on set theoretic "preliminaries" or in a later chapter on set theory as an example of a first order theory, formulable with only one non-logical constant, the relation symbol '$\in$'.[8] As mentioned above, this change came late in the development of logic, and was only finally settled on by Tarski and Quine around 1940. The resulting separation of this theory of functions and relations in set theory from the treatment of functions in logic is universal. One simply won't find an account by which the value of '$f(t)$' is the "second member of the ordered pair that has the interpretation of t as its first element, from the set of ordered pairs that is the interpretation of f."

The notion that relations are sets of ordered pairs and of the ordered pair $\langle x, y \rangle$ in turn as a certain cleverly selected set containing sets contain-

---

[8] Enderton [2001] has a "Chapter 0: Useful Facts about Sets" and in it we find: "A *function* is a relation F with the property of being *single-valued*: for each x in dom F there is only one y such that $\langle x, y \rangle \in F$. As usual, this unique y is said to be the value $F(x)$ that F assumes at x." (Enderton [2001], p.5). Suppes ([1957], pp.229ff.) includes this material in "Part II: Elementary intuitive Set Theory".

ing x and y was introduced as an improvement to *Principia Mathematica* by Norbert Wiener [1914]. In the introductory material in ([1967] 224-226), van Heijenoort credits the origin of the idea to Hausdorff and Kuratowski, and Wiener himself says that "... what we have done is practically to revert to Schröder's treatment of a relation as a class of ordered couples."

In *PM*, however the ordered pair of x and y, $x{\downarrow}y$, is defined using the relation between elements of α and elements of β in extension, and $\alpha{\uparrow}\beta$ which is already defined by:

*35·04. $\alpha{\uparrow}\beta = \hat{x}\,\hat{y}\,(x \in \alpha \,.\, y \in \beta)$ Df

The $\downarrow$ relation is then defined by:

*55·01. $x{\downarrow}y = \iota\text{'}x \uparrow \iota\text{'}y$ Df

In other words, $x{\downarrow}y$ holds if x stands in the relation in extension to y that holds just in case $x \in \{x\}$ and $y \in \{y\}$.[9] This definition should be contrasted with that which Norbert Wiener [1914] proposed, by which the pair is defined as:

$\iota\text{'}(\iota\text{'}\iota\text{'}x \cup \iota\text{'}\Lambda) \cup \iota\text{'}\iota\text{'}\iota\text{'}y$

In modern notation this is $\{\{x\}, \Lambda\},\{\{y\}\}\}$. The definition from Kuratowski [1921] is used more commonly now to define ordered pairs as $\{\{x, y\}, x\}$.[10]

In his autobiography, *Ex-Prodigy*, Wiener describes this paper as arising out of his reading course on mathematical logic with Russell, and constituted his introduction to writing:

---

[9] The $\iota\text{'}$ descriptive function, which maps a class α onto the class with α as its unique member, the "unit class" of α, began in Peano's notation as the converse of an operation which mapped a unit class onto its unique member. That converse operation was indicated with the rotated, or "inverted" iota which later symbolized the definite description operator.

[10] It is interesting to note that our now current account of functions as sets of ordered pairs, no two of which have the same *second* member, is in fact a reversal of the order in Russell. Thus "the R of y" is defined as "the x such that xRy", and thus the first member of the relation in extension in the value. One will find a page long discussion (p.24) in Quine [1963], in which he defends this older practice, which he attributes to Peano and Russell, against the later development.

266

Nevertheless, in connection with the course I did one little piece of work which I later published; and although it excited neither any particular approval on the part of Russell nor any great interest at the time, the paper which I wrote on the reduction of the theory of relations to the theory of classes has come to occupy a certain modest permanent position in mathematical logic. (Wiener [1953] p.191)

While remarking that Russell did not react to the paper, Wiener describes this as a now standard part of mathematical logic. If what we have seen above is correct, of course Russell would find the analysis of relations in terms of classes of ordered pairs, and ordered pairs themselves as further constructions from classes, as getting things front to back. Russell's analysis of functions in terms of relations in extension, and those in terms of propositional functions, is in the opposite direction. Wiener is here claiming credit for the alternative set theory approach to these aspects of the foundations of mathematics, which was eventually to prevail over Whitehead and Russell's logicist account. It is no wonder that Russell did not particularly "approve" of this as an important contribution to mathematical logic.

Given this discussion of mathematical functions, it is possible to shed light on a major issue for the interpretation of Russell's logic, the nature of propositional functions. It is standard to approach the topic of propositional functions by explaining how they differ from the mathematical functions with which we are now familiar, these arbitrary sets of ordered pairs, no two of which have the same second member. How do they differ from mathematical functions?

Peter Hylton [1993] has tried to understand Bertrand Russell's notion of propositional functions by first distinguishing them from the more familiar mathematical functions on which Frege's work are thus based. Hylton's interest is in contrasting Frege's notion of "three-stage" semantics, with its names, *Sinn*, or sense, and *Bedeutung*, or reference, with Russell's more direct "two-stage semantics" of names and referents. Hylton points out that propositional functions "yield propositions as values" which propositions contain their arguments as constituents. A mathematical function simply yields an object as value, in which there is no trace of the argument. The number 4 does not contain any trace of its being the value of the squaring function applied to 2. Instead, if anything, it is the sense of a function expression that embodies the mapping of argument onto value, and preserves the sense of the name of the argument in the sense of the expression for the value. Thus the sense of '2^2', will record that is the value of the function for a particular argument, even though the reference of the expression is simply the number 4.

Hylton is right to point out this important aspect of propositional functions. Propositional functions, for Russell, are certainly not mathematical functions from objects to propositions that need not include the argument as a constituent. In fact it was Ramsey, in his 1925 paper, "Mathematical Logic" (Ramsey [1931]), who was the first to propose that propositional functions should be treated as such arbitrary mathematical functions from objects to propositions. Russell reviewed Ramsey's papers twice (Russell [1931] and [1932]). In the review in *Mind* of 1931 he credits Ramsey with three main objections to *Principia*; "supposing that all classes and relations in extension are definable by finite propositional functions", then the criticism for which Ramsey is best known, "a failure to distinguish two kinds among the contradictions, of which only one requires the theory of types, which can accordingly be much simplified" and the third, "the treatment of identity." The second review describes Ramsey's notion of extensional functions, but expresses some qualms:

> If a valid objection exists – as to which I feel uncertain – it must be derived from inquiry into the meaning of "correlation." A correlation, interpreted in a purely extensional manner, means a collection of ordered pairs. Now such a collection exists if somebody collects it, or if something logical or empirical brings it about. But, if not, in what sense is there such a collection? (Russell [1931], p.117)

Russell seems not to accept the idea of an arbitrary function in extension, which is not determined by some relation, at least for the special case of functions from objects to propositions. On the other hand, Russell clearly understood the consequences of Cantor's theorem about the cardinality of the set of subsets of a given set, for, as he says later in *My Philosophical Development*, it was Cantor's theorem, applied to the "class" of everything, that led him to the paradox in the first place.[11] So, Russell would certainly have held that there are more classes than expressions for them, and so more functions than there are definable relations.[12] But the further step is to accept that there are more classes than relations, that is, more sets than

---

[11] See Russell, ([MPD], p.58).

[12] It is interesting to note that Hintikka and Sandu [1992] have charged that Frege also did not have the idea of an arbitrary function from objects to truth values, and so did not have the notion of arbitrary set needed to have a "standard" second order logic. Burgess [1995] suggests that the evidence is not so clear.

there are extensions of propositional functions or relations. When Russell speaks of "something logical" which "brings about" a collection, this need not be anything that can be grasped by the human mind, or expressed in a language, as propositional functions, which are part of logic, may go beyond anything definable in language.

Beyond having values that record the identity of their arguments, propositional functions differ even further from the mathematical functions with arguments and values that Frege used throughout his logical theory. The most appropriate semantic theory for a system with propositional functions may not interpret their semantic values as functions at all. This point can be put precisely, as it has by Paul Oppenheimer and Ed Zalta [ms], with their distinction between "relational type theory" and "functional type theory". They show how in a theory with relations (and propositions) such as Zalta's "Object Theory", it is possible to interpret propositional functions as relations, but not as functions. Their point can be illustrated by looking at Alonzo Church's [1976] notation for the types of propositional functions. His notation does not require a type for propositions. Instead there is a type for individuals, ι and monadic propositional functions with individuals as arguments (ι), but there is no type for propositions. Some type theories, including that of Church himself for other purposes, represent types with symbols for arguments and values. Thus one might use o as a type for propositions, and $\iota \rightarrow o$ as the type for functions from individuals to propositions. But Church's notation uses the formulation of an empty pair of parentheses ( ) to indicate the type of propositions. This notation indicates the arguments that a propositional function takes, but does not require a semantics of functions from arguments to values as its interpretation. Instead one might simply give truth conditions for the result of "applying" a propositional function $\phi \hat{x}$ to an argument, rather than assigning it a proposition as value in the semantics. Indeed this fits well with Russell's official abandonment of propositions in the Introduction to *PM*, following the problematic "multiple relation theory of judgment." Officially, at least, there are no propositions in the type theory of *PM*, even though the logic is a system of propositional functions. Oppenheimer and Zalta show that in a particular formal type theory, that of Zalta's "Object Theory" there are relational expressions, the counterpart of propositional functions, which simply cannot be treated as denoting functions. Instead they will denote relations, where those are intensional entities, built up with operations on primitive relations using the analogues of operators from algebraic semantics. So, while Ramsey explicitly proposed that propositional functions be treated as mathematical functions from objects to propositions, and discussions of propositional functions use the language of functional application, there is still no need to interpret propositional functions as a species of mathematical functions.

George Bealer has been pointed out that the notion of mathematical function does at least provide an account of predication.[13] If the meaning of a predicate F is a function, then the meaning of the result of the application of the predicate F to a subject term t can be seen as the result of the application of the function that interprets F, that is $\| F \|$, to the object that interprets a, that is, $\| t \|$. But a propositional function $F\hat{x}$ is not supposed to be a mathematical function. How then do we explain what happens when F is predicated of t? We get a proposition Ft, of which $\| t \|$ is a constituent. The propositional function $F\hat{x}$ is not a constituent, so then what relates the function to the proposition which is its value?[14] I prefer to think that Russell saw this as a primitive notion, best not explained in terms of the derivative notion of mathematical function.

Russell's views about the relation between mathematical functions and propositional functions, or relations, are not primarily driven by a reaction to Frege. They seem to be independently motivated. Consider the following from "On Meaning and Denotation" [1903]:

> If we take denoting to be fundamental, the natural way to assert a many-one relation will not be xRy but $y = \phi x$. This, of course, is the usual mathematical way; and there is much to be said for it. All the ordinary functions, such as x^2, $\sin x$, $\log x$, etc., seem to occur more naturally in this form than as $_7\hat{R}|x$. Again, in ordinary language, "y is the father of x" clearly states an identity, not a relation: it is "y = the father of x". ([CP4], p.340)

> But if we take *propositional* functions to be fundamental – as I have always done, first consciously and then unconsciously – we must proceed through relations to get to ordinary functions. For then we start with ordinary functions such as "x is a man"; these are originally the only functions of one variable. To get at functions of another sort, we have to pass through xRy; but then, with 7, we get all the problems of denoting. And, as we have seen, a form of denoting more difficult than 7 is involved in the use of variables to start with. Thus denoting seems impossible to escape from. ([CP4], p.340)

---

[13] At the conference from which this paper derives.

[14] At ([PM] 38) we find: "Thus for example, the proposition "Socrates is human" can be perfectly apprehended without regarding it as a value of the function "x is human." But, famously, Russell held that we must be acquainted with the constituents of a proposition in order to understand, or apprehend it. This requires that functions are not constituents of propositions.

270

So, Russell does see propositional functions, or rather, relations, as more fundamental than mathematical functions. However, he sees the move to them as problematic, infected with the problems of denoting. Although Russell may have found propositional functions to be more basic than mathematical functions, until he solved the problem of denoting in "On Denoting" [1905] he was not justified in thinking that he had explained the less obvious in terms of the more basic, instead the reduction of mathematical functions led directly to his big problem that concerned him in those days, the problem of denoting.

With a proper theory of denoting, in particular, the theory of descriptions of *12 of *Principia Mathematica*, in hand, Whitehead and Russell are then ready to complete the logicist analysis of mathematical functions as "descriptive functions" in *30. This, one might conclude, is probably the most important role for the theory of definite descriptions in the logicist project of *PM*.

REFERENCES

Burgess, John P., 1995. "Frege and Arbitrary Functions", in *Frege's Philosophy of Mathematics*, William Demopoulos, ed., Cambridge: Harvard University Press, pp.89–107.

Church, Alonzo, 1956. *Introduction to Mathematical Logic*, Princeton, New Jersey: Princeton University Press.

Church, Alonzo, 1976. "Comparison of Russell's Resolution of the Semantical Antinomies with that of Tarski", *Journal of Symbolic Logic*, 41: pp.747–760.

Ebbinghaus, H.-D., Flum, J., Thomas, W., 1993. *Mathematical Logic*, 2nd ed., New York: Springer.

Enderton, Herbert B., 2001. *A Mathematical Introduction to Logic*, San Diego: Harcourt.

Frege, Gottlob, 1891. "Funktion und Begriff", translated as "Function and Concept" in *Collected Papers* [1984], pp.137–156.

Frege, Gottlob, 1904. "Was ist eine Funktion?", translated as "What is a Function?" in *Collected Papers* [1984], pp.285–292.

Frege, Gottlob, 1984. *Collected Papers on Mathematics, Logic and Philosophy*, Brian McGuiness, et. al., eds., Oxford: Basil Blackwell.

Hintikka, Jaakko and Sandu, Gabriel, 1992. "The Skeleton in Frege's Cupboard: The Standard versus Nonstandard Distinction." *The Journal of Philosophy* 6, June, pp.290–315.

Hylton, Peter, 1993. "Functions and Propositional Functions in *Principia Mathematica*", in A.D. Irvine and G.A. Wedeking, eds., *Russell and Analytic Philosophy*, Toronto: University of Toronto Press, pp.342–360.

Kuratowski, K., 1921. "Sur la notion de l'ordre dans la théorie des ensembles," *Fundamenta Mathematica*, 2, pp.161–171.

Linsky, Bernard, 2002. "The Resolution of Russell's Paradox in *Principia Mathematica*", in *Philosophical Perspectives*, 16, *Language and Mind*, James E. Tomberlin, ed. Boston and Oxford: Blackwell, pp.395–417.

Mancosu, Paolo, 2005. "Harvard 1940-1941: Tarski, Carnap and Quine on a Finitistic Language of Mathematics for Science", *History and Philosophy of Logic*, 26, pp.327–357.

Oppenheimer, Paul and Zalta, Edward N., ms. "Relations versus Functions at the Foundations of Logic: Type-Theoretic Considerations", manuscript.

Quine, Willard Van Orman, 1963. *Set Theory and Its Logic*, Cambridge, Mass: Harvard University Press.

Ramsey, F.P., 1931. *Foundations of Mathematics and Other Logical Essays*, R.B. Braithwaite, ed., London: Kegan Paul.

Russell, Bertrand, 1903. "On Meaning and Denotation", manuscript. [CP4], pp.315–358.

Russell, Bertrand, [PoM] *Principles of Mathematics*. Cambridge: Cambridge University Press, 1903.

Russell, Bertrand, 1905. "On Denoting", *Mind*, 14 (Oct. 1905): pp.479–493. [CP4], pp.415–427.

Russell, Bertrand, 1931, 1932. Review of Ramsey [1931], *Mind*, 40 (Oct 1931): pp.476–482 and *Philosophy*, 7 (Jan 1932): pp.84–86. Reprinted in [CP10], pp.107–114, 114–117.

Russell, Bertrand, [MPD] *My Philosophical Development*, London: Unwin, 1959.

Russell, Bertrand, [CP4] *Foundations of Logic 1903–1905*. Alasdair Urquhart, ed. (*The Collected Papers of Bertrand Russell: Vol.4*). London and New York: Routledge, 1994.

Russell, Bertrand, [CP10] *A Fresh Look at Empiricism 1927–42*. John G. Slater, ed. (*The Collected Papers of Bertrand Russell: Vol.10*). London and New York: Routledge, 1996.

Suppes, Patrick, 1957. *Introduction to Logic*, New York: Van Nostrand.

van Heijenoort, Jean, 1967. *From Frege to Gödel: A Source Book in Mathematical Logic, 1879–1931*, Cambridge Mass: Harvard University Press.

Whitehead, A.N., and Russell, B.A., [PM] *Principia Mathematica*, Cambridge: Cambridge University Press, 3 vols., 1910–13, 2nd ed, 1925–27.

Wiener, Norbert, 1914. "A Simplification of the Logic of Relations", *Proceedings of the Cambridge Philosophical Society* 17, pp.387–390. Reprinted with a preface in van Heijenoort [1967], pp.224–227.

Wiener, Norbert, 1953. *Ex-Prodigy: My Childhood and Youth*, New York: Simon and Schuster Inc. Reprinted MIT Press, 1964.

DIAGONALIZATION, THE LIAR PARADOX, AND THE INCONSISTENCY OF THE FORMAL SYSTEM PRESENTED IN THE APPENDIX TO FREGE'S *GRUNDGESETZE*: *VOLUME II*

ROY T COOK
University of Minnesota & University of St Andrews

Abstract
The *Liar Paradox* is constructed within Frege's *Grundgesetze* using a variant of Gödel's diagonalization lemma. The particular instance of Basic Law V that triggers the *Liar paradox* is identified, and it is observed that this is exactly the principle that Frege himself identified as the root of *Russell's paradox* in the appendix to Volume II of the *Grundgesetze*. Unfortunately, the amended version of Basic Law V which Frege suggests as a patch to his system blocks neither the derivation of the diagonalization theorem nor the construction of the Liar paradox.

1 DIAGONALIZATION IN THE GRUNDGESETZE

The standard description of the formal system presented in Gottlob Frege's *Grundgesetze* is typically described as follows: Frege's system amounts to nothing more than (or, more carefully, is equivalent to) higher-order logic plus the inconsistent *Basic Law V*:

$$\text{BLV}: (\forall X)(\forall Y)[(\S(X) = \S(Y)) = (\forall z)(Xz = Yz)]^1$$

Such a description is incorrect, however: There are a number of aspects of Frege's logic that differentiate it from standard higher-order systems such

---

[1] Here, and below, I use modern symbolism instead of Frege's two-dimensional notation, primarily for typographical convenience. All proofs, etc., can be straightforwardly translated into Frege's original formalism. Particular attention should be paid to the use of identity, since in Frege's system identity holding between two statements (i.e. names of truth values) is roughly equivalent to our biconditional.

as those studied in Shapiro [1991]. An exploration of these differences, and how they affect the proof-theoretic strength of Frege's system and various natural modifications of it, promises to shed light both on Frege's logical thought, and on the roots of a number of central paradoxes

The first difference between the system of Frege's *Grundgesetze* and modern formal systems is that Frege treats statements (or, more carefully, what *we* would think of as statements) as names of truth values. Thus, the connectives represent, quite literally, truth-functions, and quantification into sentential position is allowed. (These are first-order quantifiers, distinguishing Frege's approach from higher-order logics which allow for second-order quantification into sentential position, interpreting such quantifiers as ranging over 'concepts' of zero arity). For example, the *Grundgesetze* analogue of:

$$(\exists x)(\sim x)$$

is both well-formed and a theorem in Frege's *Grundgesetze*.

Once we realize that the quantifiers of the *Grundgesetze* range over not just value ranges and other mathematical (and perhaps non-mathematical) objects, but also over truth values, the second aspect of Frege's system which will be of interest becomes apparent. Frege's language contains a falsity predicate:

$$x = \sim(\forall y)(y = y)$$

In other words, an object is the false if and only if it is identical with the truth value denoted by:

$$\sim(\forall y)(y = y)$$

Note, however, that the falsity predicate (and the corresponding truth predicate) constructed within the *Grundgesetze* operates a bit differently from the manner in which falsity predicates (and corresponding truth predicates) operate within formal systems today: The intended extension of a truth predicate is normally understood today to be the class of all true statements (or, if working within arithmetic and using Gödel coding, the class of all natural numbers that code true statements). In Frege's system, however, the falsity predicate is the predicate that holds of the false – that is, of the unique object that is the referent of all false statements.

274

Thus, within the *Grundgesetze*, we can quantify over statements and we can construct a falsity predicate. The natural next question to ask is whether the *Liar Paradox* can be constructed within Frege's system. The answer is "Yes". To do so, we first define a diagonalization relation as follows:

$$\text{Diag}(x, y) = (\exists Z)(y = §Z \wedge x = Z(y))$$

"Diag" holds between x and y if and only if y is the value-range of some concept Z and x is the truth value obtained by applying Z to y – that is, by applying Z to the value-range of Z. We can now prove the following version of diagonalization:

Theorem 1: In the *Grundgesetze*, for any predicate $\Phi(x)$, there is a sentence G such that:

$$\Phi(G) = G$$

is a theorem.

Proof: Given $\Phi(x)$, let:

$$F(y) = (\exists x)(\text{Diag}(x, y) \wedge \Phi(x))$$
$$G = F(§F)$$

The following are provably equivalent in the *Grundgesetze*:

(1) $\Phi(G)$
(2) $\Phi(F(§F))$
(3) $(\forall x)(F(x) = F(x)) \wedge F(§F) = F(§F) \wedge \Phi(F(§F))$
(4) $(\exists Z)((\forall x)(F(x) = Z(x)) \wedge Z(§F) = Z(§F) \wedge \Phi(Z(§F)))$
(5) $(\exists Z)(§F = §Z \wedge Z(§F) = Z(§F) \wedge \Phi(Z(§F)))$
(6) $(\exists x)(\exists Z)(§F = §Z \wedge x = Z(§F) \wedge \Phi(x))$
(7) $F(§F)$
(8) G

[(1) and (2) are equivalent by the definition of G, (2) and (3) by logic, (3) and (4) by logic, (4) and (5) by BLV, (5) and (6) by logic, (6) and (7) by the definition of F, and (7) and (8) by the definition of G.]

The basic idea underlying this proof is that we can 'fake' the standard proof of diagonalization (see e.g., Boolos, Burgess & Jeffrey [2007], Chapter 17, pp.220–231) by using the value ranges of concepts as 'names' of those concepts, and quantification over truth values in lieu of quantification over (Gödel numbers of) statements, thereby sidestepping the need for Gödel numbers or analogous coding devices.

Given the diagonalization result above, we can immediately generate the *Liar paradox*. Applying Theorem 1 to our falsity predicate results in a sentence Λ such that:

$$\Lambda = (\Lambda = {\sim}(\forall y)(y = y))$$

is a theorem. But this straightforwardly entails:

$${\sim}(\forall y)(y = y)$$

a patent contradiction.

Thus, we can prove an analogue of Gödel's diagonalization lemma within the *Grundgesetze* and use it to construct the *Liar paradox*. The reader might wonder why we have made so much of these results, however. After all, we already knew that the *Grundgesetze* (including BLV) was inconsistent, so the news that one can construct the *Liar paradox* as well as *Russell's paradox* within Frege's system is not exactly earth-shattering news (although the 'naturalness' of the construction of the *Liar paradox* in the *Grundgesetze* is somewhat surprising, at least to the author).

The interest of these results lies in their connection to Frege's attempted fix of the *Grundgesetze* in the appendix to Volume II, to which we now turn.

2 DIAGONALIZATION AND THE APPENDIX TO GRUNDGESETZE

A quick examination of Theorem 1 reveals that the full strength of BLV is not required in order to prove the full, biconditional form of diagonalization. Instead, we merely need the resources to infer line (2):

$$\Phi(F(\S F))$$

from line (5):

$$(\exists Z)(\S F = \S Z \land Z(\S F) = Z(\S F) \land \Phi(Z(\S F)))$$

In order to get from (5) to (2), we do not need it to be the case that concepts with the same value range are *always* co-extensive. Instead, we merely need concepts which have the same value range to agree on their shared value-range. Thus, we can recapture Theorem 1 by replacing BLV with the (prima facie weaker) Fixed-Point Principle for value-ranges:

FPP: $(\forall X)(\forall Y)(\S(X) = \S(Y) \to (X(\S X) = Y(\S X)))$

If FPP holds, then we can move from:

$$\S F = \S Z$$

to:

$$F(\S F) = Z(\S F)$$

and thus from:

$$\Phi(Z(\S F))$$

to:

$$\Phi(F(\S F))$$

The moral is simply this: Any principle meant to replace BLV and provide identity conditions for value ranges cannot, on pain of *Liar*-induced contradiction, imply FPP. Surprisingly, Frege was aware of this moral: In response to the detection of *Russell's paradox*, and without any (apparent) knowledge that the *Liar paradox* could also be derived within the *Grundgesetze*, Frege isolated FPP as exactly the problematic consequence of BLV.

In the appendix of Volume II of the *Grundgesetze*, Frege begins his discussion of *Russell's paradox* by distinguishing between the two 'directions' of BLV:

BLVa: $(\forall X)(\forall Y)((\forall z)(X(z) = Y(z)) \to \S X = \S Y)$
BLVb: $(\forall X)(\forall Y)(\S X = \S Y \to (\forall z)(X(z) = Y(z)))$

He notes that, if we are to individuate concepts extensionally (an assumption he is unwilling to give up), then BLVa cannot be the problem – after all, *any* function f from concepts to objects will satisfy:

$$(\forall X)(\forall Y)((\forall z)(X(z) = Y(z)) \rightarrow fX = fY)$$

So BLVb must be where the problem lies, and Frege sets out to discover exactly what goes wrong with this principle. He outlines his strategy as follows:

> We shall now try to complete our inquiry by reaching the falsity of (Vb) as the final result of a deduction, instead of starting from (Vb) and thus running into a contradiction. ([1893], p.288 in the Frege Reader)

Frege thought that the best strategy for gaining an understanding of exactly what it is about BLVb that causes the problem is to begin by finding a simple, direct proof of its negation – relying on a *reductio* of BLVb via Russell's construction might be enough to show us that the principle is problematic, but it does little to show us *why* it is problematic.[2]

In other words, Frege requires a direct proof of:

$$(\exists X)(\exists Y)(\S X = \S Y \wedge (\exists z)(X(z) \wedge \neg Y(z)))$$

In searching for such a proof, Frege discovers that he can obtain a stronger result, which I have come to call:

Frege's Little Theorem: For any function f from concepts to objects one can prove:

$$(\exists X)(\exists Y)(f(X) = f(Y) \wedge X(f(X)) \wedge \neg Y(f(X)))$$

Informally, this is just the claim that, given any function from concepts to objects, there exist two concepts such that the function maps both concepts to the same object, yet the concepts differ on that very object.

Here is the rub: The instance of *Frege's Little Theorem* obtained by substituting the value range operator "$\S$" for "f" is the negation of FPP! In other words, the principle that Frege identifies as the root of *Russell's*

---

[2] Frege's proto-constructivist rejection of *reductio* proofs as uninformative, at least in this particular case, deserves an essay all its own!

paradox is exactly the principle that is needed to prove the version of the diagonalization lemma given above.

The proof of *Frege's Little Theorem* is as follows (see Frege [1893], pp.285–288 in the *Frege Reader*, for Frege's original proof):

Proof: Given a function f from concepts to objects, let:

$$R(x) = (\exists Y)(x = f(Y) \wedge \neg Y(x))$$

Then:

(1)	$\neg R(f(R))$	Assump
(2)	$\neg(\exists Y)(f(R) = f(Y) \wedge \neg Y(f(R)))$	(1), Df. of R
(3)	$(\forall Y)(f(R) = f(Y) \rightarrow Y(f(R)))$	(2)
(4)	$R(f(R))$	(3)
(5)	$R(f(R))$	(1)–(4), *Reductio*
(6)	$(\exists Y)(f(R) = f(Y) \wedge \neg Y(f(R)))$	(5), Df. of R
(7)	$(\exists Y)(f(R) = f(Y) \wedge R(f(R)) \wedge \neg Y(f(R)))$	(5), (6)
(8)	$(\exists X)(\exists Y)(f(X) = f(Y) \wedge X(f(X)) \wedge \neg Y(f(X)))$	(7), Logic

Frege concludes that such 'fixed points' are the root of Russell's paradox:

> We can see that the exceptional case is constituted by the extension itself, in that it falls under only one of the two concepts whose extension it is; and we see that the occurrence of this exception in no way can be avoided. Accordingly the following suggests itself as the criterion for equality in extension: The extension of one concept coincides with that of another when every object that falls under the first concept, except the extension of the first concept, falls under the extension of the second concept likewise, and when every object that falls under the second concept, except the extension of the second concept, falls under the first concept likewise. ([1893], p.288 in *The Frege Reader*)

As a result, Frege suggests a modification of BLV:

$$\text{BLV* } (\forall X)(\forall Y)((\S X = \S Y) = \\ (\forall z)((z \neq \S X \wedge z \neq \S Y) \rightarrow (X(z) = Y(z))))$$

According to the amended principle two concepts receive the same value range if and only if they hold of exactly the same objects other than their value ranges.

The inadequacy of Frege's BLV* is well-known, although the reasons commonly given for its failure are mistaken. The well-known works addressing the technical aspects of BLV*, Frege's so-called 'way out', such as Quine [1955] and Geach [1956], report that Frege's amended principle is consistent, but inadequate for his purposes (or any substantial purpose, really), since it implies that at most one object exists. What they fail to appreciate, however, is that since Frege's *Grundgesetze* allows for quantification into sentential position, one can (without any version of BLV, amended or not) prove the existence of at least two objects (the true and the false).[3] In other words:

$$(\exists x)(\exists y)(x \neq y)^4$$

is a theorem of the *Grundgesetze*. As a result, from the perspective of Frege's *Grundgesetze*, BLV* is just as inconsistent as was BLV.

Proving that BLV* implies the existence of no more than one object (along the lines of Quine [1955] or Geach [1956], perhaps) and then noting the existence, within the *Grundgesetze*, of at least two truth values is certainly enough to show that BLV* is inconsistent. Such a demonstration does not, however, provide much insight into the particular reasons underlying this inconsistency, or into the roots of paradox more generally. Fortunately, it turns out that we can do better – we can derive a version of the diagonalization lemma directly using BLV* (although the proof turns out to be much more difficult than it was in the case of BLV!) and thus reconstruct the *Liar paradox* in the amended system. The remainder of this essay is devoted to doing just that, and hopefully arriving at some insight into the nature of paradoxes (both semantic and set-theoretic) along the way. Before providing the main proof, however, a number of lemmata are required, and we now turn to this task.

---

[3] Landini [2006] comes closest to this result,, since he proves that BLV* is inconsistent if the truth values are their own singletons, as Frege intended, and also proves that BLV* is inconsistent if the truth values are not value-ranges at all.

[4] This theorem can be simply obtained from two applications of existential introduction to any instance of: $\Phi \neq \sim \Phi$.

3 LEMMATA[5]

In this section we shall prove some preliminary results that will be needed in what follows. First, for convenience we shall introduce an abbreviation for the analogue of set-theoretic singletons within Frege's *Grundgesetze*:

$$\{b\} =_{df} \S(x = b)$$

In other words, the Fregean singleton of an object b is the extension of the concept that holds of exactly the objects that are identical to b – that is, the concept that holds of b and b alone. With this notation in place, we can prove our three required lemmata:

Lemma 1: $BLV^* \Rightarrow (\forall x)(\forall y)((x = \{x\} \wedge y = \{y\}) \rightarrow x = y)$

Proof:

(1)	$a = \{a\} \wedge b = \{b\}$	Assump.
(2)	$(\forall z)((z \neq \{a\} \wedge z \neq \{b\}) \rightarrow ((z = \{a\}) = (z = \{b\})))$	Tautology
(3)	$(\forall z)((z \neq \{a\} \wedge z \neq \{b\}) \rightarrow ((z = a) = (z = b)))$	(1), (2)
(4)	$\{a\} = \{b\}$	(3), BLV*
(5)	$a = b$	(1), (4)
(6)	$(a = \{a\} \wedge b = \{b\}) \rightarrow a = b$	(1)–(5), CP
(7)	$(\forall x)(\forall y)((x = \{x\} \wedge y = \{y\}) \rightarrow x = y)$	(6)

Thus, for any two objects, if they are both identical to their own singletons, then they are identical to each other. We shall call this result L1 in what follows.

Lemma 2: $BLV^* \Rightarrow (\forall x)(\forall y)(\{x\} = \{y\} \rightarrow x = y)$

Proof:

(1)	$\{a\} = \{b\}$	Assump.
(2)	$(\forall z)((z \neq \{a\} \wedge z \neq \{b\}) \rightarrow ((z = a) = (z = b)))$	(1), BLV*
(3)	$(a \neq \{a\} \wedge a \neq \{b\}) \rightarrow ((a = a) = (a = b))$	(2)
(4)	$(a \neq \{a\} \rightarrow a = b)$	(1), (3)

[5] This section is deeply indepted to the excellent discussion of these issues in Burgess [1998] and [2005].

$$(5) \quad (b \neq \{a\} \land b \neq \{b\}) \rightarrow ((b = a) = (b = b)) \qquad (2)$$
$$(6) \quad (b \neq \{b\} \rightarrow a = b) \qquad (1), (5)$$
$$(7) \quad a \neq b \qquad \text{Assump.}$$
$$(8) \quad a = \{a\} \land b = \{b\} \qquad (4), (6), (7)$$
$$(9) \quad a = b \qquad (8), \text{L1}$$
$$(10) \; a \neq b \rightarrow a = b \qquad (7)\text{–}(9), \text{CP}$$
$$(11) \; a = b \qquad (10)$$
$$(12) \; \{a\} = \{b\} \rightarrow a = b \qquad (1)\text{–}(11), \text{CP}$$
$$(13) \; (\forall x)(\forall y)(\{x\} = \{y\} \rightarrow x = y) \qquad (12)$$

Thus, for any two objects, if the singletons of those objects are identical, then the objects are themselves identical. We shall call this L2 in what follows.

Lemma 3: BLV* $\Rightarrow (\forall x)(x = \{\{x\}\} \rightarrow x = \{x\})$

Proof:

$$(1) \quad a = \{\{a\}\} \qquad \qquad \text{Assumpt}$$
$$(2) \quad (\forall z)((z \neq \{a\} \land z \neq \{\{a\}\}) \rightarrow ((z = \{\{a\}\}) = (z = \{a\}))) \; \text{Tautology}$$
$$(3) \quad (\forall z)((z \neq \{a\} \land z \neq \{\{a\}\}) \rightarrow ((z = a) = (z = \{a\}))) \qquad (1), (2)$$
$$(4) \quad \{a\} = \{\{a\}\} \qquad (3), \text{BLV*}$$
$$(5) \quad a = \{a\} \qquad (4), \text{L2}$$
$$(6) \quad a = \{\{a\}\} \rightarrow a = \{a\} \qquad (1)\text{–}(5), \text{CP}$$
$$(7) \quad (\forall x)(x = \{\{x\}\} \rightarrow x = \{x\}) \qquad (6)$$

Thus, any object that is identical to the singleton of its singleton is also identical to its singleton. We shall call this L3 in what follows.

The basic idea underlying these three results is that the singletons provided by BLV* are extremely well-behaved[6], and, in addition, for the most part they behave much as one would expect (e.g. Lemma 2 is a straightforward consequence of the extensionality axiom found in most standard set theories). We will make extensive use of this 'good' behavior in our revised proof of the diagonalization lemma.

---

[6] Lemmas 1 and 3 are both theorems of the non-well-founded set theories AFA and FAFA, but neither is a theorem of the non-well-founded set theory known as BAFA (see Aczel [1988] for details).

4 BLV* AND THE DIAGONALIZATION LEMMA

Before proving the diagonalization lemma, we need a new diagonalization relation:

$$\text{Diag*}(x, y) = (\exists Z)(y = \{\S Z\} \wedge x = Z(y))$$

"Diag*" holds between x and y if and only if y is the singleton of the value-range of some concept Z and x is the truth value obtained by applying Z to y – that is, of applying Z to the singleton of the value-range of Z. We can now prove our new version of diagonalization:

Theorem 2: In the *Grundgesetz–BLV+BLV**, for any predicate $\Phi(x)$, there is a sentence G such that:

$$\Phi(G) = G$$

is a theorem.

Proof: Given $\Phi(x)$, let:

$$F(y) = (\exists x)(\text{Diag*}(x, y) \wedge \Phi(x))$$
$$G = F(\{\S F\})$$

$(\rightarrow)$

(1)	$\Phi(G)$	Assump.
(2)	$\Phi(F(\{\S F\}))$	Df. of G
(3)	$(\forall x)(F(x) = F(x)) \wedge F(\{\S F\}) = F(\{\S F\}) \wedge \Phi(F(\{\S F\}))$	(2)
(4)	$(\exists Z)((\forall x)(F(x) = Z(x)) \wedge Z(\{\S F\}) = Z(\{\S F\}) \wedge \Phi(Z(\S F)))$	(3)
(5)	$(\exists Z)(\S F = \S Z \wedge Z(\{\S F\}) = Z(\{\S F\}) \wedge \Phi(Z(\{\S F\})))$	(4), BLV*
(6)	$(\exists Z)(\{\S F\} = \{\S Z\} \wedge Z(\{\S F\}) = Z(\{\S F\}) \wedge \Phi(Z(\{\S F\})))$	(5), BLV*
(7)	$(\exists x)(\exists Z)(\{\S F\} = \{\S Z\} \wedge x = Z(\{\S F\}) \wedge \Phi(x))$	(6)
(8)	$F(\{\S F\})$	(7), Df.of F
(9)	G	(8), Df.of G

$(\leftarrow)$

(1)	G	Assump.
(2)	$F(\{\S F\})$	(2), Df. of G
(3)	$(\exists x)(\exists Z)(\{\S F\} = \{\S Z\} \wedge x = Z(\{\S F\}) \wedge \Phi(x))$	(3), Df. of F
(4)	$(\exists Z)(\{\S F\} = \{\S Z\} \wedge Z(\{\S F\}) = Z(\{\S F\}) \wedge \Phi(Z(\{\S F\})))$	(4)
(5)	$\{\S F\} = \{\S R\} \wedge R(\{\S F\}) = R(\{\S F\}) \wedge \Phi(R(\{\S F\}))$	Assump.
(6)	$\{\S F\} = \{\S R\} \wedge \Phi(R(\{\S F\}))$	(5)
(7)	$\S F = \S R \wedge \Phi(R(\{\S F\}))$	(6), L2
(8)	$\sim\Phi(F(\{\S F\}))$	Assump.
(9)	$F(\{\S F\}) \neq R(\{\S F\})$	(7), (8)
(10)	$\{\S F\} = \S F$	(7), (9), BLV*
(11)	$(\forall z)((z \neq \{\S F\} \wedge z \neq \S F) \rightarrow ((z = \S F) = F(z)))$	(10), BLV*
(12)	$(\forall z)(z \neq \S F \rightarrow \sim F(z)))$	(11)
(13)	$a \neq \S F$	Assump.
(14)	$\{\{a\}\} \neq \S F$	(10), (13), L2
(15)	$\sim F(\{\{a\}\})$	(12), (14)
(16)	$\sim(\exists x)(\exists Z)(\{\{a\}\} = \{\S Z\} \wedge x = Z(\{\{a\}\}) \wedge \Phi(x))$	(15), Df. of F
(17)	$(\forall x)(\forall Z)((\{\{a\}\} = \{\S Z\} \wedge x = Z(\{\{a\}\})) \rightarrow \sim\Phi(x))$	(16)
(18)	$(\forall Z)(\{\{a\}\} = \{\S Z\} \rightarrow \sim\Phi(Z(\{\{a\}\})))$	(17)
(19)	$\{\{a\}\} = \{\{a\}\} \rightarrow \sim\Phi(a = \{\{a\}\})$	(18)
(20)	$\sim\Phi(a = \{\{a\}\})$	(19)
(21)	$a = \{\{a\}\}$	(2), (7), (8), (9)[7]
(22)	$a = \{a\}$	(21), L3
(23)	$a = \S F$	(22), L1
(24)	$a \neq \S F \rightarrow a = \S F$	(13)–(23), CP
(25)	$a = \S F$	(24)
(26)	$(\forall x)(x = \S F)$	(25)
(27)	$F(\{\S F\}) = \S F$	(26)
(28)	$R(\{\S F\}) = \S F$	(26)
(29)	$F(\{\S F\}) = R(\{\S F\})$	(27), (28)
(30)	$\Phi(F(\{\S F\}))$	(7), (29)

---

[7] A note on the passage from line (20) to line (21) is probably appropriate, since at first glance it might look like a non-sequitur. The reasoning, in more detail, is as follows: The expression "$F(\{\S F\})$" names the true (line (2)), and the truth values named by "$F(\{\S F\})$" and "$R(\{\S F\})$" are distinct (line (9)), so (since "$R(\{\S F\})$" must name a truth value) "$R(\{\S F\})$" names the false. So, Φ holds of the false (line (7)), but not the true (line 8). So, since "$a = \{\{a\}\}$" must name a truth value, and Φ fails to hold of it, it must name the true. Although tedious, this line of reasoning could of course be explicitly reconstructed within the *Grundgesetze* itself.

(31) $(\sim\Phi(F(\{\S F\}))) \rightarrow \Phi(F(\{\S F\}))$ (8)–(30), CP

(32) $\Phi(F(\{\S F\}))$ (31)

(33) $\Phi(F(\{\S F\}))$ (5)–(32), EE

(34) $\Phi(G)$ (33), Df. of G

We can now apply this new version of the diagonalization result to the falsity predicate defined in 1 above to obtain a contradiction, much as before. Thus, contrary to the well-established folk-wisdom, Frege's amended version of the *Grundgesetze*, as presented in the appendix to the second volume of this work, is no more consistent than the *Russell* and *Liar paradox* prone system presented in the first volume.

4 WHAT HAS GONE WRONG?

Thus, Frege's amended version of the *Grundgesetze* obtained by replacing BLV with BLV* is inconsistent. But we might fairly ask what went wrong. After all, doesn't *Frege's Little Theorem* provide a deep insight into the working of abstraction principles – one that suggests that BLV* was on the right track?

The correct answer to this question is that *Frege's Little Theorem* provides some insight into the roots of these paradoxes, but not enough.. As a result, the restriction on extensions suggested by *Frege's Little Theorem* – that is, the replacement of BLV with BLV* – does not go far enough. In order to see this we need merely note that a much stronger version of *Frege's Little Theorem* can be proven:

Generalized Frege's Little Theorem: A function f is extension-injective on @ iff:

$$(\forall X)(\forall Y)(f(@X) = f(@Y) \rightarrow @X = @Y)$$

Given any extension-injective function f and any abstraction operator @:

$$(\exists X)(\exists Y)(@X = @Y \wedge X(f(@X)) \wedge \neg Y(f(@X)))$$

In order to prove this result, we need a generalization of the Russell predicate (i.e. a unique Russellesque predicate for each function f):

f-Russell Predicate: $R_f(x) =_{df} (\exists Y)(x = f(@Y) \land \neg Y(x))$

Proof:

(1)	$\neg R_f(f(@R_f))$	Assump.
(2)	$\neg(\exists Y)(f(@R_f) = f(@Y) \land \neg Y(f(@R_f)))$	(1), df. of R_f
(3)	$(\forall Y)(f(@R_f) = f(@Y) \rightarrow Y(f(@R_f)))$	(2)
(4)	$f(@R_f) = f(@R_f) \rightarrow R_f(f(@R_f))$	(3)
(5)	$R_f(f(@R_f))$	(4)
(6)	$\neg R_f(f(@R_f)) \rightarrow R_f(f(@R_f))$	(1)–(5), CP
(7)	$R_f(f(@R_f))$	(6)
(8)	$(\exists Y)(f(@R_f) = f(@Y) \land \neg Y(f(@R_f)))$	(7), df. of R_f
(9)	$f(@R_f) = f(@P) \land \neg P(f(@R_f))$	Assump.
(10)	$@R_f = @P \land \neg P(f(@R_f))$	(9)
(11)	$@R_f = @P \land R_f(f(@R_f)) \land \neg P(f(@R_f))$	(7), (10)
(12)	$(\exists X)(\exists Y)(@X = @Y \land X(f(@X)) \land \neg Y(f(@X)))$	(11)
(13)	$(\exists X)(\exists Y)(@X = @Y \land X(f(@X)) \land \neg Y(f(@X)))$	(8)–(12), EE

We can now see what went wrong in Frege's attempted 'fix' of the *Grund-gesetze*: If we assume BLV*, then it follows that the singleton operator is an extension-injective function (since it is injective in general, according to Lemma 2 above). Given that the singleton operator is extension-injective, however, *Generalized Frege's Little Theorem* tells us that there must be two concepts that have the same extension yet which disagree on the *singleton* of that extension. It is this fact that is not accounted for by BLV*, which only allows for concepts which have the same extension but which disagree on that extension (not its singleton), and it is for this reason that BLV* fares no better than its predecessor.[8]

---

[8] A careful examination of the proof of diagonalization above will convince the reader that *Generalized Frege's Little Theorem* is exactly what is at issue. In effect, what the proof of diagonalization does is to find two concepts that have the same extension, but which might differ on the singleton of that extension. If they do, however, then the singleton of this extension must be identical to the extension itself, and as a result our three lemmata can be utilized to obtain the desired result.

5 LESSONS LEARNED

The ultimate failure of Frege's attempt to salvage his life's work does not imply that the it contains nothing of value. I will conclude by identifying two lessons that can, and should, be drawn from all of this.

The first is that we should take care in attributing the inadequacies of BLV* to some sort of panicked, half-hearted attempt by Frege to amend his formal system. Quine describes this common attitude to the appendix of *Grundgesetze Volume II*:

> It is scarcely to Frege's discredit that the explicitly speculative appendix now under discussion, written against time in a crisis, should turn out to possess less scientific value than biographical interest. Over the past half century the piece has perhaps had dozens of sympathetic readers who, after a certain amount of tinkering, have dismissed it as the wrong guess of a man in a hurry. (1955, p.152)

While the 'fix' might have been written in a hurry, and BLV* is inconsistent, the discussion leading up to it has much to teach us about the mathematics of abstraction principles in general and the roots of *Russell's Paradox* (unsurprisingly) and the *Liar Paradox* (surprisingly) in particular. In this respect, *Frege's Little Theorem*, and the amended version of BLV based on this result, are not the incorrect guesses of a man in a hurry, but on the contrary represent a deep insight into the puzzling nature of abstraction and the paradoxes that can arise from its unfettered application. Unfortunately, this insight was not enough to save the amended system from similar paradoxes, but this does not mean that Frege's Little Theorem was not an insight nonetheless.

This brings us to the second lesson. Connections are often drawn between the *Liar paradox* and *Russell's paradox* (and between the semantic and set-theoretic paradoxes more generally), but these connections tend to be quite loose, relying on the intuition that circularity of some vicious sort is at the root of both phenomena[9] (for a project that draws the connections much more tightly, however, the reader is urged to consult Cook [2007]!). The construction of the *Liar paradox* within Frege's system, and his identification of the exact principle that is the root of both this paradox and the one communicated to him by Russell, suggests that further study of Frege's system (or modern variants that retain object-level quantification into sen-

---

[9] For a careful examination of the arguments for and against such a connection, see Terzian [2008].

tential position, such as that provided in Landini [2006]) hold promise for a deeper understanding of these paradoxes individually and of the links that might or might not bind them together.[10]

REFERENCES

Aczel, P. [1988], *Non-Well-Founded Sets*, Stanford: CSLI.

Beall, J. (ed.) [2007], *Revenge of the Liar*, Oxford: Oxford University Press.

Boolos, G. J. Burgess, & R. Jeffrey, [1989] *Computability & Logic*, 5th Ed., Cambridge: Cambridge University Press.

Burgess, J. [1998], "On a Consistent Subsystem of Frege's *Grundgesetze*", *Notre Dame Journal of Formal Logic 39*: pp.274–278.

Burgess, J. [2005], *Fixing Frege*, Princeton: Princeton University Press.

Cook, R. [2007] "Embracing Revenge: On the Indefinite Extensibility of Language", in Beall [2007]: pp.31–52.

Frege, G. [1893], 1903 *Grundgezetze der Arithmetik I & II*, Hildesheim: Olms.

Frege, G. [1997] *The Frege Reader*, M. Beaney (ed.), Oxford: Blackwell.

Geach, P. [1956] "On Frege's Way Out", *Mind 65*, pp.408–409.

Gödel, K. [1992], New York: Dover.

Hieke, A. & H. Leitgeb (eds.) [2008], *Reduction and Elimination in Philosophy and the Sciences: Preproceedings of the 31st International Wittgenstein Symposium*, Kirchberg am Wechsel, Austrian Ludwig Wittgenstein Society.

Landini, G. [2006] "The Ins and Outs of Frege's Way Out", *Philosophia Mathematica 14*, pp.1–25.

Quine, W.V.O. [1955] "On Frege's Way Out", *Mind 64*, pp.145–159.

Shapiro, S. [1991], *Foundations Without Foundationalism: The Case for Second-Order Logic*, Oxford: Oxford University Press.

Terzian, G. [2008], "Structure of the Paradoxes, Structure of the Theories: A Logical Comparison of Set Theory and Semantics", in Hieke & Leitgeb [2008]: pp.347–349.

---

[10] Thanks go to Philip Ebert, Marcus Rossberg, Greg Taylor, and Giulia Terzian, for helpful discussion of earlier versions of this paper and suggestions for improvement. In addition, the present paper has benefited greatly from feedback received at *Arché: The Philosophical Research Centre for Logic, Language, Metaphysics, and Epistemology at the University of St Andrews* and to the *31st International Wittgenstein Symposium*, where earlier versions of this paper were presented.

288

A PROBLEM AND A SOLUTION FOR NEO-FREGEANISM*

MICHAEL GABBAY
Kings College London

Abstract

I argue that Benacerraf's famous objection to mathematical realism in his paper *"What Numbers Could Not Be"* can be adapted to present severe difficulties for the Neo-Fregean programme. I formulate an alternative abstraction principle and argue that there is no reason for the natural numbers to generated by one abstraction principle rather than the other.

Independently of this conclusion, the formal comparison of the two abstraction principles involves a result of interest to Neo-Fregeans: I offer a solution to the *bad company* objection.

1 BENACERRAF ON WHAT NUMBERS COULD NOT BE

In his celebrated paper, *"What numbers could not be"*, Benacerraf presents a challenge to theories identifying numbers with set theoretic constructs. He asks why the numbers should be identified with sequence (1), the Von Neumann ordinals, rather than sequence (2), the Zermelo ordinals.

$$\varnothing, \{\varnothing\}, \{\varnothing, \{\varnothing\}\}, \{\varnothing, \{\varnothing\}, \{\varnothing, \{\varnothing\}\}\} \tag{1}$$
$$\varnothing, \{\varnothing\}, \{\{\varnothing\}\}, \{\{\{\varnothing\}\}\} \tag{2}$$

Benacerraf concludes that there is no reason why the number 3 should be identified with an element from one construction rather than another. 3 cannot be identified with both as the constructs have incompatible properties. For example in (1) the fourth element has three members, but in (2) the fourth element has only one member. Since the number 3 cannot be both $\{\varnothing, \{\varnothing\}, \{\varnothing, \{\varnothing\}\}\}$ and $\{\{\{\varnothing\}\}\}$ and there is no fact of the matter whether it is one or the other, it is neither. Thus the attempted identification of numbers with sets has been refuted.

---

* I gratefully acknowledge the support of the British Academy under grant PDF/2006/ 509.

... if the number 3 is really one set rather than another, it must be possible to give some cogent reason for thinking so. But there seems to be little to choose among the accounts *for the accounts differ at places where there is no connection whatever between features of the accounts and our uses of the words in question.* [Benacerraf 1965]

It is not hard to see that this objection generalises to any theory of numbers that has an ontology containing different sequences of objects that could serve as references of our number language. Realists may escape Benacerraf's argument either by finding a suitably miserly ontology of abstract objects (the ontology of sets is too vast), or simply refusing to get involved in the metaphysics of abstract objects.

I shall argue that Neo-Fregean ontology suffers from Benacerraf's objection in much the same way as the ontology of sets. I conclude, analogously to Benacerraf's original argument, that Neo-Fregean ontology is necessarily too rich and therefore does not provide a satisfactory foundation for arithmetic.

First I shall sketch the Neo-Fregean account of arithmetic, I shall assume that the reader is largely familiar with the formal concepts behind it (in particular, I assume the reader has some knowledge of the workings of *Frege's Theorem* [Wright 2000]).

2   NEO-FREGEANSIM ON WHAT NUMBERS COULD BE

2.1 Hume's principle

The aim of the Neo-Fregean programme is to provide a metaphysics of abstract objects together with an informative account of our epistemic link to them. According to Neo-Fregeanism, reference to the abstract objects that are *the numbers* derives from logic and definitions alone. Logic then entails arithmetic truths and, in this sense, arithmetic is *analytic*.

Neo-Fregeanism promises to provide a realist theory of number that can respond to Benacerraf's argument. According to Neo-Fregeanism, certain abstract objects exist, and we can know and refer to them via *abstraction principles*. The natural numbers are among those abstract objects we can know about via a particular abstraction principle, *Hume's Principle*:

The number of F = the number of G iff
the F and the G are in one-one correspondence $\qquad$ (3)

For each predicate F, Hume's principle identifies or allows reference to, an object that is the number of F. This formalisation should be familiar to the reader:

$$\forall F \forall G[nx.Fx = nx.Gx \leftrightarrow F1{\sim}1G] \qquad (4)$$

Hume's principle is to be taken as a *definition*, in terms of one-one correspondence, of the binding term-former $nx.(...)$. Furthermore, the Neo-Fregeans argue that one-one correspondence is a fundamental application and concept of cardinal numbers. So the abstract entities, reference to which is generated by Hume's principle, really are the cardinal numbers (they are the only abstract entities tied appropriately to the application of counting).

Since I intend to dispute that the binding operator $nx.(...)$ really does refer to the numbers it would beg the question against my arguments to continue reading it as a shorthand for 'the number of ...'. It is therefore more convenient to regard Hume's principle as follows:

The Hume-abstract of F = the Hume-abstract of G iff
the F and the G are in one-one correspondence $\qquad$ (5)

which is formalised as

$$\forall F \forall G[hx.Fx = hx.Gx \leftrightarrow F1{\sim}1G] \qquad (6)$$

I now take Neo-Fregeanism to be a view that make the following two claims:

- Hume's principle implicitly defines a binding operator $hx.(...)$ that refers to certain abstract entities, Hume-abstracts.
- The Hume-abstracts (or at least some of them) are the cardinal numbers

2.2 Frege's theorem

I now sketch how Neo-Fregeans use Hume's principle to provide a realist foundation for arithmetic.

Following Frege, the strategy is to define suitable properties and relations that satisfy the second order Peano axioms of arithmetic. To distinguish the defined terms of this section with the defined terms of Section 3.2, I subscript them with H for 'Hume'.

First a successor/predecessor relation is defined:

$$Pre_H(t, t') \quad \text{means} \quad \exists F \exists z[t' = hx.Fx \land Fz \land t = hx.(Fx \land x \neq z)] \quad (7)$$

So t is the predecessor of t' when t' is the number of some property F and t is the number of the Fs that are not z, for some z that is F.

Zero is defined to be the number of any inconsistent property, e.g. $0_H = nx.(x \neq x)$, it does not matter which as all empty properties are in one-one correspondence.

A natural number is then defined as being any number in the transitive closure of the predecessor relation from 0_H. More formally, the transitive closure of any binary relation R may be defined as:

$$R^*(t, t') \quad \text{means} \quad \forall F [(Ft \land \forall x \forall y(Fx \land R(x, y) \rightarrow Fy)) \rightarrow Ft'] \quad (8)$$

And now we may define the natural numbers as all those objects in the transitive closure of the predecessor relation from 0_H:

$$Nat_H(t) \quad \text{means} \quad Pre_H^*(0_H, t') \quad (9)$$

So a natural number is any referent of an abstraction $nx.Fx$ that can be 'reached' from 0_H by following the relation Pre_H. As did Frege, Neo-Fregeans go on to define individual number terms:

$$
\begin{array}{lll}
0_H & \text{means} & hx.(x \neq x) \\
1_H & \text{means} & hx.(x = 0_H) \\
2_H & \text{means} & hx.(x = 0_H \lor x = 1_H) \dots
\end{array}
\quad (10)
$$

From these definitions we can derive all of Second order Peano Arithmetic, which completely characterises a natural number structure.

3 AN ALTERNATIVE ABSTRACTION PRINCIPLE

3.1 Benacerraf's principle

Now I turn to the argument that the Neo-Fregean ontology contains too many abstract objects. I do this by presenting an abstraction principle that is similar to Hume's principle. This alternative abstraction principle can do the same work as Hume's principle and in a similar way. But, as with the (1) and (2) above, the two abstraction principles yield two distinct sequences of abstract objects. As was argued in the case of sets, I shall argue that there is nothing to decide which abstraction principle yields the 'true' natural numbers.

The new principle is simpler than Hume's principle, call it Benacerraf's Principle:

> the Benacerraf-abstract of F = the Benacerraf-abstract of G iff
> neither F nor G are singletons, or
> F and G have the same extension $\qquad\qquad$ (11)

Say that F is *unitary* if it has exactly one element in its extension. Then Benacerraf's principle identifies, for each predicate F, an object that is the *Benacerraf-abstract of F*. We can write 'the Benacerraf-abstract of F' as $bx.Fx$, and then Benacerraf's principle is:

$$\forall F \forall G[bx.Fx = bx.Gx \leftrightarrow ((\neg \exists!xFx \wedge \neg \exists!xGx) \vee \forall x(Fx \leftrightarrow Gx))] \quad (12)$$

Benacerraf's principle is to be taken as a *definition*, in terms of being unitary, of the binding operator $bx.(\ldots)$. The intuition for Benacerraf-abstracts is that one can abstract out of a unitary property its 'unitariness', or the way in which it is unitary. Any non-unitary properties are unitary in the same way: they are not. The way unitary properties are differentiated, in the spirit of Frege's Basic Law V (see (14)) is through their extension.

Benacerraf-abstracts can be seen as abstractions over the unit. If F is a unit property then its Benacerraf-abstract is unique to it. If any two properties are not units then they have the same Benacerraf-abstract which represents their non-unity. So for each unit property there is a distinct abstract unit, its Benacerraf-abstract, associated with it (compare this with Frege's discussion of Jevons and Schröder in [Frege 1953, §29–§44]).

The concept of a unit is at least as fundamental to our concept of number as one-one correspondences. After all, a one-one correspondence is a correspondence between unit objects; when we count, we count unit individuals; variables of first order quantifiers range over unit entities; the symbols of the language necessary to express even basic propositions are discrete, discernable units. To develop the notion of one-one correspondence we need to be able to conceive of the world as not being completely amorphous but as being made up of individuals, units.

Without the concept of a unit, a discrete thing, a single entity, we cannot even begin a logical enquiry let alone ground arithmetic in one-one correspondences.

In particular notice that Hume's principle (5) cannot be formulated without a formalisation of one-one correspondence which itself requires some formalisation of what it is for a property to be unitary. Thus, Benacerraf's principle uses no formal concepts or technical details *that are not required to understand Hume's principle*. In this sense Benacerraf's principle *is more elementary* than Hume's principle.

Hume's principle abstracts objects out of a formalisation of a relation of *being both in one-one correspondence*, Neo-Fregeans then argue that Hume-abstracts are numbers. Benacerraf's principle abstracts objects out of a formalisation of the relation of *being both unitary*, and as we shall see, we can develop an analogous theory of arithmetic if we take the Benacerraf-abstracts to include the natural numbers.

Frege himself discusses and rejects the possibility of developing a theory of arithmetic based on units. But his compelling refutations are aimed at theories of numbers as agglomerations or sums of (distinct) units [Frege 1953, §29–§44]. Frege objects that such accounts either make no sense, or fail to generate arithmetic. He did not consider the possibility that the unit, thought of as a property of properties, and derived by a similar abstraction method to Frege's own, could do the same work as his favoured theory of number.

3.2 An analogue of Frege's theorem

I now sketch how Benacerraf's principle can be used to define the numbers along Neo-Fregean lines. To distinguish the defined terms of this section with those of Section 2.2 I subscript them with B for 'Benacerraf'. We begin with zero:

$$0_B \quad \text{means} \quad bx.(x \neq x)$$
$$1_B \quad \text{means} \quad bx.(x = 0_B)$$
$$2_B \quad \text{means} \quad bx.(x = 1_B) \ldots \tag{13}$$

It is not hard to show that the i_B are derivably distinct. For example suppose that $0_B = 1_B$, then $bx.(x \neq x) = bx.(x = 0_B)$. So by Benacerraf's principle either $\neg \exists! x(x \neq x) \wedge \neg \exists! x(x \neq 1_B)$ or $\forall x(x = 0_B \leftrightarrow x \neq x)$. Each of these is derivably false in even first order logic.

We can go on to define the predecessor relation as follows:

$$Pre_B(t, t') \quad \text{means} \quad \exists F[t = bx.Fx \wedge t' = bx.(x = t)] \tag{14}$$

A version of Frege's theorem now arises out of adopting Benacerraf's principle rather than Hume's principle. We use (6) to define the natural numbers to be exactly the entities in the transitive closure of Pre_B. This yields the second order Peano axioms.

$$Nat_B(t) \quad \text{means} \quad Pre_B^*(0_B, t') \tag{15}$$

I omit the remaining details here as they are almost identical to those of the proof of Frege's theorem in [Wright 1983].

3.3 The attack on Neo-Fregeanism

Let $0_H, 1_H, 2_H, \ldots$ denote the entities abstracted and defined using Hume's Principle, call them the *Hume-numbers*. Let $0_B, 1_B, 2_B, \ldots$ be the entities abstracted and defined using Benacerraf's principle call them the *Benacerraf-numbers*. It should be clear that an analogue of Benacerraf's original challenge arises. Benacerraf's original argument now applies, both the Hume-numbers and the Benacerraf-numbers serve as characterisations of the natural numbers. Furthermore there is no reason for the natural numbers to be identified with the Hume-numbers rather than the Benacerraf-numbers. Therefore Neo-Fregeanism is to be rejected alongside set theoretic reductionism by a variant of Benacerraf's original argument.

The penultimate claim, that there is no choosing between the Benacerraf and the Hume numbers, is in need of justification. I sketch a justification of it in Section 4 by comparing the systems obtained from the two abstraction principles and showing that there is little that can be done with Hume's principle that cannot also be done with Benacerraf's principle.

The reader should note that I am not arguing for Benacerraf's principle over Hume's principle. Neither am I arguing just that there is a mere burden of proof for Neo-Fregeans to justify their position further. My argument, like Benacerraf's, is that there is nothing in our arithmetic practices or concepts that determines which abstraction principle (out of many possible abstraction principles) really generates reference to numbers. I conclude that neither of them do and that numbers are therefore not founded in Hume's principle as the Neo-Fregeans argue.

4   A COMPARISON OF TWO ABSTRACTION PRINCIPLES

4.1 The concept of number

Perhaps an analysis of our concept of number will differentiate between the two principles. After all, it is Frege's discussion of the concept of number that initiated the whole debate.

There is a strong sense in which one-one correspondence is fundamental to our number concepts. This being the case we might argue in favour Hume's principle, over Benacerraf's principle, as follows.

- There is a conceptual connection between one-one correspondence and sameness of cardinal number.
- Hume's principle abstracts the referring expression 'the Hume-abstract of ...' over sameness of number and Benacerraf's principle abstracts over something other than sameness of number.
- Therefore Hume's principle is the correct abstraction principle for reference to numbers and the Hume-abstracts really are the numbers.

The case for the first premise of this argument appears strong. There seems to be little, if anything, more to sameness of number than one-one correspondence. Furthermore it seems that someone who fails to use one-one correspondence in making judgements about cardinality has failed to understand the concept. The conclusion then looks inevitable that Benacerraf's principle offers the wrong conceptual analysis of cardinal number and so can be discounted.

A first response to this argument is that it conflates a necessary equivalence with a conceptual reduction. It is hard to deny that if F and G are

296

in one-one correspondence then that *entails* that their number is the same. But it is a separate matter entirely whether one-one correspondence is conceptually tied of sameness of number. Why could it not be that the concept of number is obtained from elsewhere in such a way that sameness of number and one-one correspondence are merely necessary equivalents? I think the Neo-Fregeans can meet this response reiterating the point that one makes a conceptual mistake if one thinks that two properties have the same number but are not in one-one correspondence.

The Neo-Fregean appears on strong ground in his case against Benacerraf's principle. For it seems correct that the only way of obtaining a simple referring term such as 'the number of ...' that is appropriately conceptually linked to one-one correspondence is via Hume's principle.

But the considerations contain a hidden assumption that tends to be disguised by the usual formulation of Hume's principle as it is in (4) and (5). The assumption is that the sense of the expression 'the number of ...', is a simple one has a simple logical form that is correctly analysed by a single term former such as $nx.(...)$ or $hx.(...)$. An alternative position is that 'the number of F' actually has a more complex logical form which describes an assignment of abstract objects (obtained from elsewhere) to concepts via one-one correspondence. Applied to Benacerraf's principle, the more complex logical form of 'the number of F' would be:

The Benacerraf number the predecessors of which
are in one-one correspondence with F (16)

so that a sentence like 'there are n apples' is analysed as

The Benacerraf number the predecessors of which
are in one-one correspondence with the apples, is n_B (17)

(where 'the predecessors of which' is formalised in terms of Pre_B^* the transitive-reflexive closure of the predecessor relation on Benacerraf numbers).

With this analysis there is not only a necessary connection between sameness of number and one-one correspondence, but also a conceptual one. The conceptual connection between sameness of number and one-one correspondence is to be found, not in the means of abstracting numbers, but in the complex logical form of the natural language expression 'the number of ...'.

So we have two theses that seem to account equally well for the conceptual connection between one-one correspondence and sameness of number.

I. 'the number of ...' has a simple sense implicitly tied to one-one correspondence by Hume's principle.
II. 'the number of ...' has a complex sense that ties explicitly one-one correspondence and Benacerraf's numbers.

The first thesis is the Neo-Fregean position, the second is the Benacerraf-number alternative. Both theses have cardinal number assertions conceptually tied to one-one correspondence. According to both theses a central, fundamental and standard use of numbers is to be assigned to concepts or properties according to how many things fall under them. The difference is that in Thesis I the assignment is implicit in the logical form of the number assertion, but in Thesis II it is explicit in the meaning of the phrase 'the number of ...'.

The difference between I and II is sufficiently slight that an example is in order here. Consider a grocery stall at which different fruit are on sale. The manager of the stall has assigned numbers to each type of fruit for the purposes of carrying out an inventory. Now, there are at least two readings of the manager's assertion when he says:

$$\text{The apples are 30} \tag{18}$$

On one reading the manager is describing how many apples there are, on another reading he is describing what number they are assigned in his inventory. According to I the two readings have different logical forms, one standard, the other nonstandard. For example, according to Thesis I the standard reading has the form of a simple identity:

$$nx.Apple(x) = 30 \tag{19}$$

Whereas the nonstandard reading has a more complex form like:

$$\text{The number assigned by relation } R \text{ to } Apple(x) \text{ is 30} \tag{20}$$

According to II however, both readings have the same more complex form, perhaps like (17), but where the relation R is standard in the first (one-one correspondence) and nonstandard in the second (an inventory assignment).

This example should highlight the difference between I and II, it should also indicate that this difference is subtle and that intuitions in favour of one might as well favour the other. I doubt that any psycho-linguistic test indicate conclusively whether our standard assertions of cardinality really are straightforward identities like (16), or slightly more complex predications like (17). So I claim that both positions, I and II, are equally tenable and there is nothing to choose between them. Therefore I maintain that the attack on Neo-Fregeanism of Section 3.3 stands. There is nothing in our practices that fixes whether we obtain our number concepts and language using Hume's principle following Thesis I, rather than using Benacerraf's principle following Thesis II. So I conclude that, in fact, we do neither.

4.2 How to avoid bad company

Formally, Hume's and Benacerraf's principles are acceptable abstraction principles. I argue for this here by presenting a condition on good abstraction principles (i.e. I offer a solution to the bad company problem) and show that both abstraction principles satisfy it.

A famous worry for the Neo-Fregean project, called the 'bad company' problem, relates to the fact that not all abstraction principles are consistent. A famously inconsistent abstraction principle is Frege's notorious Basic Law V:

$$\forall F \forall G \, [\varepsilon x.Fx = \varepsilon x.Gx \leftrightarrow \forall x(Fx \leftrightarrow Gx)] \tag{21}$$

We can use (21) to derive Russell's paradox. An argument of Heck [Heck 1992] shows that there are many undesirable abstraction principles. For example, there are many Φ for which the abstraction principle:

$$\forall F \forall G \, [\varepsilon x.Fx = \varepsilon x.Gx \leftrightarrow \Phi \vee \forall x(Fx \leftrightarrow Gx)] \tag{22}$$

entails that Φ. It is not hard to find plenty of second order formulae Φ (some of which contain F and G) that are entailed by an abstraction principle like (19) which we would certainly think ought not to be true. Furthermore, different abstraction principles can be incompatible with each other, although individually consistent; this is strange, as abstraction principles are supposed to be analytic and so ought to be true, and hence compatible, in any context. There is then a question whether some principle can be given to discern the acceptable abstraction principles from the unacceptable ones (see [Weir 2003] for many examples of unacceptable abstraction principles). I now present such a principle.

Let λ be any infinite cardinal, then the *consistency constraint* for λ is the condition that any abstraction principle should have the form:

$$\forall F \forall G \, [\varepsilon x.Fx = \varepsilon x.Gx \leftrightarrow \Psi_\lambda(F, G)] \tag{23}$$

Where

    i. $\Psi_\lambda(F, G)$ is a second order sentence containing no free variables other than F and G, and also does contain the 'new' abstraction operator εx.

    ii. Ψ_λ is a reflexive, transitive and symmetric relation on *unary* predicates. That is:
        $- \Psi_\lambda(F, F)$
        $- \Psi_\lambda(F, G)$ implies $\Psi_\lambda(G, F)$
        $- \Psi_\lambda(F, G)$ and $\Psi_\lambda(G, H)$ implies $\Psi_\lambda(F, H)$

    iii.   For any model M of cardinality λ, there are at most λ many valuations σ such that $\sigma(\Psi_\lambda(F, G)) = \bot.$[1]

Note that the familiar examples of 'bad' abstraction principles (e.g. in [Weir 2003]) violate this condition. For example in Frege's Basic Law V has the form

$$\forall F \forall G \, [\varepsilon x.Fx = \varepsilon x.Gx \leftrightarrow \forall x(Fx \leftrightarrow Gx)]$$

which clearly violates this condition for any λ. Note also that Benacerraf's principle and Hume's principle satisfy the consistency constraint for any infinite λ. Now we can show that any abstraction principle satisfying the consistency constraint for λ can be interpreted in *any* second order model

---

   [1] This says that the (second order) property represented by Ψ_λ groups the properties of the domain into at most λ many different equivalence classes. In other words, Ψ_λ is only allowed to distinguish up to extensionality, all properties (i.e. subsets of $|M|$) of cardinality $< \lambda$. Ψ_λ must be unable to distinguish all but λ of the 2^λ properties of cardinality λ.

of cardinality λ. Let M_λ be a model (that can interpret the language of Ψ) with domain $|M_\lambda|$ of cardinality λ. Let R be a relation on properties (i.e. a relation on subsets of $|M_\lambda|$) such that

$$R(P, Q) \text{ iff } \sigma(\Psi_\lambda(F, G)) = \text{T}$$

for any valuation σ such that $\sigma(F) = P$ and $\sigma(G) = Q$.[2] In other words, R is the interpretation of Ψ_λ in the model M_λ. Since $\Psi_\lambda(F, G)$ contains no free first or second order variables other than F and G, R does not depend on σ.

If $P \subseteq |M_\lambda|$ then let $P_R = \{Q : R(P, Q)\}$. Clearly, P_R is an equivalence class. Now consider the set A = $\{P_R : P \subseteq |M_\lambda|\}$ and let μ be its cardinality. If $\mu > \lambda$, then there would be more than λ many valuations σ that falsify $\Psi_\lambda(F, G)$ (at least one for each of the μ-many pairs of different equivalence classes in A). This would violate condition (iii) of the consistency constraint for λ. So $\mu \leq \lambda$, i.e. the cardinality of A is less than or equal to the cardinality of $|M_\lambda|$. It follows then, that there is an injection f from $\{P_R : P \subseteq |M_\lambda|\}$ into $|M_\lambda|$.

We may use f to identify elements $e_P \in |M_\lambda|$:

$$e_P = f(P_R) \tag{24}$$

It is now a straightforward matter to check that

$$e_P = e_Q \quad \text{iff} \quad R(P, Q)$$

It follows that we can extend any second order model M_λ of cardinality λ, with an abstraction principle satisfying the consistency constraint for λ: we define the e_P as in (24) and then extend the language of M_λ to include the abstraction operator $\varepsilon x.(\ldots)$; then we extend the inductive defition of how valuations σ assign elements to terms using (25):

$$\sigma(\varepsilon x.\Phi) = e_{\{m:\ m \in |M_\lambda| \text{ and } \sigma_{[x/m]}(\Phi) = \text{T}\}} \tag{25}$$

(where Φ is any second order formula).

_____

[2] σ assigns elements of M_λ to first order variables and subsets of M_λ to second order variables; $\sigma_{[x/m]}$ is a valuation that agrees with σ on all variables except that it maps the variable x to m; σ also assigns, by means of an inductive definition, elements of M_λ to complex terms and truth values for formulae.

Let me describe this interpretation in English: Ψ_λ forms equivalence classes of properties; the conditions on Ψ_λ guarantee that there is a one-one function f from these equivalence classes into the domain $|M_\lambda|$ of M_λ; we interpret the referent of $\varepsilon x.Fx$ under valuation σ as the element e which the function f assigns to the equivalence class of properties that Ψ_λ forms from the extension of F.

We now have in (20) a general criterion for the legitimacy of abstraction principles. This criterion legitimates Benacerraf's principle *as well as* Hume's principle. The only difference between them being that extending a model to validate Benacerraf's principle is slightly more straightforward than Hume's principle. Say that an abstraction principle is *almost analytic* if it satisfies the consistency constraint for any infinite λ. It is now a matter of dispute whether the fact that λ has to be infinite detracts from the analyticity of Hume's principle and Benacerraf's principle. A point in favour of the Neo-Fregean programme is that we can give an independently motivated formal reasons for treating Hume's principle as analytic and rule out principles like Basic Law V. However, a point against the Neo-Fregean programme is that Benacerraf's principle also comes out as analytic, and the argument of Section 3.3 stands.

4.3 Distinguishing the abstracts

Perhaps Neo-Fregeans should not try to rule out the Benacerraf-numbers as legitimate references of our number language, but embrace them. There is nothing to stop a Neo-Fregean accepting that in the abstract realm there are at least two number-like sequences of abstract objects. A good line for a Neo-Fregean to take might be that the Hume-numbers are the referents of our numbers-as-cardinals language, whereas the Benacerraf-numbers are the referents of our numbers-as-ordinals language. A Neo-Fregean could then argue that there are two main uses of number language, perhaps even two concepts of number (cardinal and ordinal) and so see no reason to be worried if there are two collections of abstract entities associated with them. Indeed, such a result could be regarded as a success of the Neo-Fregean programme.

The problem is that the Benacerraf-numbers are *not* ordinals: Benacerraf's principle involves no characterisation of ordering or any criterion of position correspondence. To understand Benacerraf's principle we need nothing that is not needed to understand Hume's principle. There is nothing about Hume-numbers that rules them out as being ordinals, and there

302

is nothing about Benacerraf-numbers that rules them out as being cardinals. The concept of a unit is no less important to that of cardinality than the concept of one-one correspondence. Benacerraf's principle and Hume's principle each could be taken as allowing reference to the natural numbers *as cardinals*. But then Neo-Fregeanism must account for why our arithmetic language refers to the Hume-numbers rather than the Benacerraf-numbers (or vice versa). I have been arguing that that we stand in no significant relation to Hume's principle that we do not also stand in to Benacerraf's principle. So if the Neo-Fregean accepts that the two abstraction principles allow reference to different abstract entities, then he has made no progress overcoming the objection of Section 3.3.

5 CONCLUSION

I have argued that there is no particular abstraction principle that we can associate with the natural numbers. At least two similar, but formally distinct, abstraction principles are capable of lying at the heart of the Neo-Fregean programme. The principles are distinct enough that there is no natural way of equating the abstract objects they give reference to. The principles are however sufficiently similar that there is no principled criterion that identifies one over the other as 'the correct' abstraction principle for elementary arithmetic. I conclude that numbers are not the abstract objects referred to by either abstraction principle, or of any other abstraction principle. The point to emphasise here is that neither the Hume-numbers nor the Benacerraf-numbers are really *the natural numbers*. The whole Neo-Fregean framework of abstraction principles is just another way of generating sequences that *encode* the natural numbers. This conclusion is independent of questions regarding the metaphysics of abstraction and whether abstraction principles really refer to any abstract objects at all.

REFERENCES

Benacerraf, Paul 1965 "What Numbers Could Not Be", *The Philosophical Review*, 74(1).

Frege, Gottlob 1953 *The Foundations of Arithmetic*, tr. by J.L. Austin, Blackwell, Oxford.

Heck, Richard 1992 "On the Consistency of Second-order Contextual Definitions", *Noûs*, 26.

Weir, Alan 2003 "Neo-Fregeanism: An Embarrassment of Riches", *Notre Dame Journal of Formal Logic*, 44(1).

Wright, Crispin 1983 *Frege's Conception of Numbers as Objects*. Aberdeen University Press.

Wright, Crispin 2000 "Neo-Fregean Foundations for Real Analysis: Some Reflections on Frege's Constraint", *Notre Dame Journal of Formal Logic*, 41.

ED ZALTA'S VERSION OF NEO-LOGICISM – A FRIENDLY LETTER OF COMPLAINT

Philip A. Ebert
Department of Philosophy
University of Stirling
Stirling, FK9 4AL
Scotland, UK

Marcus Rossberg
Department of Philosophy
344 Mansfield Road
University of Connecticut
Storrs, CT 06269-2054
USA

Subject: Ed Zalta's version of Neo-Logicism – a friendly letter of complaint

Dear Ed,

It was great to meet you again, especially in such a beautiful setting as Kirchberg, Austria. We had a great time at the conference and in particular at the neo-logicism workshop, and we thoroughly enjoyed our many very stimulating and engaging discussions on just this topic. We are grateful for the patience you showed in explaining and clarifying your views. We are, however, not yet (or rather still not) convinced of your version of neo-logicism, and we would like to take this opportunity to outline our main points of disagreement regarding the philosophical foundations of mathematics.

Rather than indulging in smaller details our aim here is to outline three rather general areas of concern. First, we will discuss broader epistemological issues and your explanation of mathematical knowledge. Second, we will draw attention to some "unusual" consequences of your theory. Last, but not least, we will take issue with your claim that your account of mathematics follows in the footsteps of Frege's logicism and is thus deservedly called a 'neo-logicist' or even a 'logicist' account of mathematics.

In a recent paper, co-written with Bernard Linsky, you write: "Our version of neologicism constitutes an epistemic foundation, in the sense that it shows how we can have knowledge of mathematical claims."[1] The solution that you offer, is not one that explains how we can have knowledge of *some specific* mathematical theory, such as Peano arithmetic (PA) or even Zermelo-Fraenkel set theory (ZF), rather you offer a very liberal account of which mathematical theory we can properly know. It is so liberal that it accounts for all written and even all yet to be written mathematical theories; including mathematical theories that seem to be mutually exclusive. You write: "This allows us to have knowledge of all the axioms and theorems of mathematical theories, including for example the truths of ZF and those of alternatives to ZF such as Aczel's non-wellfounded set theory. The fact that these latter two theories are inconsistent with one another doesn't mean that we can't have knowledge of their claims." (Linsky and Zalta 2006, p.41). You advertise the fact that this account is all-encompassing to this extent as a unique "feature" rather than a flaw.

Yet, it comes at a price – a price that we are not willing to pay. We fail to see how your conception can account for *genuine* categorical mathematical knowledge. Your epistemic foundation of any mathematical theory is based on a two-step approach. First your show how we can re-interpret any mathematical theory within your theory – third-order Object Theory. Then, in a second step, you show how we can have knowledge of just those re-interpreted statements. That is, your epistemic account only applies to the imported statements of Object Theory. Our claim is that knowledge of these re-interpreted statements is not categorical. To see this more clearly, let us first outline how it is so much as possible to have knowledge of "inconsistent" theories and then explain how you can account for our knowledge of *any* mathematical theory. This will help to see why the resulting knowledge is non-categorical.

The reason why we can have knowledge of "inconsistent" theories is that theories imported in the manner you envisage concern different types of objects and so have their own theory-dependent domain. Hence, they are strictly speaking *not* inconsistent since they concern a different subject matter.

---

[1] See p.61 of Linsky, B., and Zalta, E.N. "What is Neologicism", *The Bulletin of Symbolic Logic* 12/1 (2006): pp.60–99.

The reason why we can have knowledge of any mathematical theory is because each axiom, imported in the appropriate way, will be true since it is reformulated into what we call a *hedged* statement that is *trivially* true. So, for example, Peano's axiom that zero is a number will result, once imported into third-order Object Theory, in a hedged statement of the form: 'In Peano Arithmetic, $N_{PA}0_{PA}$'.[2] In the same way, any other theory (including merely possible or yet to be written theories) can be, in principle, reinterpreted and given a *true* reading in your theory. Since the account is truly liberal we can even explain our knowledge of some inconsistent theory in this way.

Our claim is that this is only possible by regarding our mathematical knowledge as hypothetical. Hedged statements, statements that are prefaced by the 'in theory T'-operator are clearly not categorical statements and so our resulting mathematical knowledge is non-categorical. Now, even if you can drop the *explicit* occurrence of the 'in theory T'-operator, the content of the imported statements is still hedged, albeit now in a clandestine way. The imported statement is about properties and objects that are always theory-bound – and in this sense our knowledge of these statements is non-categorical.[3]

Note also that our mathematical knowledge is easy to come by; and we think: a little too easy. On your account there is, as we have seen, no epistemically relevant difference between mathematical knowledge of a consistent theory and "mathematical knowledge" of an inconsistent theory. Also, if we follow you, the mark of mathematical knowledge, in contrast to, say, fictional knowledge, is not a matter of substance. Knowledge is mathematical if the underlying theory (story) is generally regarded mathematical, it is fictional, if, the underlying theory (story) is generally regarded to be that of a fiction.[4]

All this, of course, is not to say that your explanation of our knowledge of mathematics is internally flawed, but rather that the resulting conception of non-categorical mathematical knowledge is not the right type of explanation, at least to our taste.

---

[2] Where 'N_{PA}' and '0_{PA}' are the obvious arithmetical constants, indexed to the theory in question.

[3] This point is further developed and discussed in Ebert, P.A. & Rossberg, M. "What Neo-Logicism Could Not Be" (forthcoming).

[4] See p.260 of Zalta, E.N. "Neo-Logicism? An Ontological Reduction of Mathematics to Metaphysics", *Erkenntnis*, 53/1–2 (2000): pp.219–265. Our criticism is further developed in Ebert, P.A. and Rossberg, M. "What is the Purpose of Neo-Logicism?" *Traveaux de Logique* 18 (2007): pp.33–61.

Leaving aside these epistemic issues, let us briefly note what we regard as unhappy metaphysical consequences of your neo-logicist account of mathematics. We noted earlier that ZF, re-interpreted in Object Theory, has its private domain of sets, while Aczel's non-wellfounded set theory also has its own distinct domain of sets. The same applies to other theories of sets. As a result, none of the candidate set theories is, or can be, *the* theory of all set-like objects, but there are many distinct domains of sets. From this it follows for example that there are many, presumably infinitely many, *empty sets*. One for each mathematical theory that states the existence of an empty set. This sounds very unappealing to us.

A further interesting consequence for your conception is that there are strictly speaking no genuine disputes about the truth of a mathematical theory. Since every axiom is, once re-interpreted in Object Theory, (trivially) a logical consequence of its respective theory, there can only be mathematical disagreement whether a certain statement does in fact follow from a set of axioms, and thus merely the question who of the disagreeing parties made a mistake in their proof. There is simply no point in arguing about the possible falsity or the truth of a given theory of some mathematical subject matter. Yet, classical mathematicians and constructivists do not simply talk past each other, it seems to us; neither are disputes about the existence of large cardinals merely verbal. Well, some (at least one person) might consider this result a welcome *feature*, while some others (at least two others) regard it as a *flaw*.

Lastly, in your presentation in Kirchberg you labeled your conception as a true version of logicism and not just neo-logicism. We thought we just note here briefly our reservation about calling your view a neo-logicist, or even logicist, conception. First to note is that your very liberal view of acceptable mathematical theories is surely not one that Frege, the founder of logicism, would have welcomed. Yet, more importantly, Frege's aims in reducing mathematics to logic were at least twofold: first, his mathematical motive was to prove theorems within logic and so reduce the enterprise of mathematics to logic. This is not, however, what happens in your theory since you take what mathematicians have proved and only then import it into Object Theory. Second, Frege also had an epistemological motive. Namely, by reducing mathematics to logic he hoped to establish the philosophical status of arithmetical knowledge, showing, ultimately, how it flows from pure logic. Again, we don't think you offer an explanation of our mathematical knowledge as based upon our logical knowledge. Hence we are hesitant in regarding your view a logicist conception of mathematics if, by this, you mean to follow in the footsteps of Frege's logicist project.

Yours truly,

Philip Ebert   Marcus Rossberg

REPLY TO P. EBERT AND M. ROSSBERG'S FRIENDLY LETTER OF COMPLAINT

EDWARD N. ZALTA
Center for the Study of Language and Information
Stanford University
Stanford, CA 94305
USA

Subject: Reply to P. Ebert and M. Rossberg's friendly letter of complaint

Dear Philip and Marcus,

Thanks very much for your interesting letter. I, too, enjoyed the time we spent doing philosophy at the Kirchberg meetings. I think we furthered our understanding of each other's views, especially during the workshop on neologicism and during the extended dinner conversations in the evenings.

Let me reply to your criticisms of my neologicist views, many of which I've developed with co-author Bernard Linsky. I've consulted with Bernie about your letter. From my reading of it, I found 9 critical conclusions. But let me preface my replies to specific criticisms with some context.

When I first developed the theory of abstract objects and modeled mathematical objects in the theory, I assumed abstract objects exist independently of us in some special domain and that we get knowledge of them via some kind (or faculty) of intuition. I assumed that the best we could do as philosophers would be to use mathematical rigor to systematize this domain by way of a group of axioms that included a single existence principle that comprehended the domain. But I've subsequently come to believe that epistemological considerations require a more refined view of the mind-independent existence and objectivity of abstract objects, and of the axiom that comprehends them. Linsky and I (1995) argued that one cannot apply the usual model of the mind-independence and objectivity of concrete objects to explain knowledge of abstract objects.[1] A different model is called for, and we described it at some length in our paper.

I suspect you have a different understanding of the mind-independence and objectivity of abstract objects, and it is not clear to me that it matches up with the objectives of the neologicist project, whether yours or ours. You don't provide, for example, a conception of abstract objects in general, but rather insist that they are the kind of thing that we can come to know on the basis of certain Fregean biconditionals and the existence of the equivalence relations on which they are based. I think this is in tension with your view that neologicism implies a single theory of extensions. Linsky and I argued that abstract objects are defined by our conceptions of them and that a plenitude principle, like the comprehension principle I've developed (which yields a different abstract object for each different conception) is what is needed to put logicism and Platonism on a sound (epistemological) basis. And a plenitude principle that encodes the properties connected with each distinct conception into a distinct abstract object yields not only an understanding of the nature of abstract objects, but explains why mathematicians and story-tellers have wide latitude and a great deal of conceptual freedom when they bring their imaginative powers into play as they develop mathematical theories and tell stories (modulo certain crucial differences of course, to be described below). From this point of view, one will be less likely to suppose that there is a single, true theory of sets, for example.

I therefore think it is a mistake to suppose that mathematicians are in the business of determining, for each pair of competing theories, whether one is true and the other false. Instead, one should think of mathematicians as interested in (a) systematizing conceptions of mathematical objects and relations in the most powerful and interesting way, and (b) finding proofs of claims that follow from those conceptions once the governing principles are clear. When Gauss, Lobachevsky, Bolyai, and Riemann became interested in geometries in which the sum of the three angles of a triangle is less (or more) than 180° (or more generally, in which Euclid's fifth postulate is replaced with one of its denials), the truth or falsity of those alternative theories wasn't at stake; rather what was at stake was the interest, power, and applicability of the theorems implied by the different conceptions of point, line, triangle, etc. that could be used to develop spherical and hyperbolic geometries. Similarly, though it may be that Weierstrass thought that

---

[1] See 'Platonized Naturalism versus Naturalized Platonism', *Journal of Philosophy*, XCII/10 (October 1995): pp.525–555.

analysis formulated with infinitesimals was 'false', what he *did* was to systemize a conception of analysis that eliminated infinitesimals and on which the relevant concepts and theorems of analysis become defined and derived from the definition of a limit. That didn't *falsify* analysis based on infinitesimals, given Robinson's work, but rather founded analysis on a different, more rigorous, conception than the one available at the time.

As to set theory, I don't think that the issue before Cantor, Zermelo, Fraenkel and the other early set theorists was to *refute* one or another set theory; the problem was to show that one could systematize conceptions of 'set' and 'membership' in ways that avoided the paradoxes, and show that the resulting theory was a more powerful systematization of those notions. To put it bluntly, I think it would be philosophically naive for a set theorist like Woodin to claim that Aczel's nonwellfounded set theory is just 'false'. Such a claim is not philosophically justified, and indeed, just misses the point. If set theorists do use the language of truth and falsity (if not in connection with Aczel, then in connection with extensions of ZFC employing definable determinacy or large cardinals) to describe competing theories, philosophers would be better served to characterize the debate as a disagreement about the way to develop the most powerful conception of 'set' and 'membership'. Each set theory embodying a different conception of these notions should be seen as characterizing a distinctive domain. And so on for other mathematical theories, applied or unapplied.

With this in mind, I can reply briefly to your critical conclusions.

1. The analysis of mathematical statements Zalta defends turns the categorical statements of mathematics into non-categorical 'hedged' statements.
2. Even if he were to drop the 'theory operator' from the analysis of each mathematical claim, the resulting statement still wouldn't be categorical because the terms are indexed to their respective theories.

I am not sure I understand the definition of 'categorical' you are using. To take an example, consider the language of ZF and the claim that "the null set has no members", expressed in that language. I've analyzed this claim, in the first instance, as the following truth about ZF:

$$\text{ZF} \models [\lambda y \, \neg \exists z (z \in_{ZF} y)] \, \varnothing_{ZF}$$

which asserts that, in the theory ZF, the null set of ZF exemplifies the property of having no members (where the membership relation is the one characterized by the theorems of ZF).[2] This is a categorical claim about the theory ZF. Moreover, given the ambiguity I postulate in natural language predication, I also provide two readings of the unadorned claim "the null set has no members", one true and one false, as follows:

$$\emptyset_{ZF}[\lambda y \, \neg\exists z(z \in_{ZF} y)] \quad \text{(true)}$$
$$[\lambda y \, \neg\exists z(z \in_{ZF} y)]\emptyset_{ZF} \quad \text{(false)}$$

The first asserts that the null set of ZF *encodes* the property of having no members, while the latter asserts that the null set *exemplifies* the property of having no members. Both readings are categorical (they are both atomic formulas with a complex predicate), and the former one preserves the intuition that mathematicians have asserted something true with this claim. The fact that they talk about the particular object "the null set of ZF" and the particular relation "the membership relation of ZF" doesn't undermine the categoricity of the claims. Are these claims 'hedged' in some illegitimate way? Well, only if you suppose that there is a single, true theory of sets and the membership relation. That is something I deny, for the reasons mentioned above.

3. The view Zalta defends doesn't entail an epistemically relevant difference between mathematical knowledge of a consistent theory and 'knowledge' of an inconsistent theory.

To answer this criticism, consider an example. Although we can detect the inconsistency in Frege's system syntactically, nevertheless, when you pick up a copy of Frege's *Grundgesetze* you come to understand its language because the terms of his language have a semantic significance and the sentences in the *Grundgesetze* are meaningful. I further believe that the way we come to know the significance of the terms, and meaningfulness of the sentences, deployed in Frege's theory is just like the way we come to know the significance of the terms, and meaningfulness of the sentences, deployed in other mathematical theories. So, in fact, in some deep sense, there is no epistemically relevant difference in the way we come to understand, and have knowledge of, consistent and inconsistent theories.

---

[2] The statement 'ZF $\models p$' is defined in object theory to be: ZF$[\lambda y \, p]$, i.e., ZF encodes the property *being such that p*.

314

But object theory does imply there is a difference between the two kinds of theories. In the former, the terms denote objects that are typically incomplete with respect to their encoded properties, i.e., objects x which are such that, relative to the properties F expressible in the language of the theory, x neither encodes F nor encodes the negation of F. But the terms of inconsistent theories denote objects that encode every property expressible in the language of the theory. The objects denoted are *uninteresting* by comparison. For example, the empty extension of Frege's *Grundgesetze* encodes every property F expressible in the language of *Grundgesetze*, since it is defined as the object that encodes exactly the properties F such that, in the theory of the *Grundgesetze*, the empty extension exemplifies F. Given the inconsistency in *Grundgesetze*, the empty extension of that theory encodes every property. Note that this does not trivialize the meaning of the expressions in Frege's language as long as you distinguish the sense and reference of those expressions. Though the denotations of the terms (predicates) in Frege's system become analyzed, on the above scheme, as abstract objects (relations) that encode every property expressible in the system, the *senses* of these expressions should not be so analyzed. The senses are abstracta that encode just the properties that strike our cognitive understanding as we come to understand Frege's system, and given that Frege himself didn't recognize that there was an inconsistency when he proposed his axioms, we might suppose that the senses of the terms are consistent (i.e., encode properties that are jointly consistent). So, when we discover that a theory is inconsistent, we learn that the objects denoted by the terms of the theory have (in the encoding sense) every property expressible in the language of the theory.

4. The view Zalta defends doesn't entail that the difference between mathematical knowledge and knowledge of fictions is substantive.

I'm not sure what 'substantive' means in this context. Clearly, we do have knowledge of fictional entities. We know the ancient Greeks worshiped Zeus, that Holmes is more famous than Pinkerton, etc. Does the fact that a theory treats fictions and mathematical objects both as abstract objects (and identified relative to their background conceptions) mean that there is no substantive difference in our knowledge of these entities? I don't think so. For one thing, stories are objects that are closed under relevant entailment, not logical entailment, whereas mathematical theories are closed under logical entailment, not relevant entailment. That seems like a substantive difference in the way we conceive of these objects, and thus a substantive difference in the way we come to know them. But more importantly, theoretical mathematical objects encode only abstract relations (relations which are themselves subject to the analysis of higher-order object theory), whereas fictional objects typically encode ordinary relations.[3] The exceptions to this are stories involving fictional relations (e.g., the property of *being a hobbit* in *The Lord of the Rings*). Fictional relations are analyzed in object theory as abstract relations that encode properties of relations. Note that the properties of relations encoded by *being a hobbit*, such as being a species in which the individuals are human in form, with legs, arms, hairy feet, etc., involve ordinary properties. By contrast, the object-theoretic identifications of abstract mathematical relations, like *less than, membership, group addition*, etc., involve properties of relations that never reference ordinary properties. This strikes me as a substantive difference between fictional relations and mathematical relations.

5.   Logicism implies that there is a single theory of sets and thus, by extensionality, a unique empty set, whereas the analysis Zalta offers implies that there is a different empty set for each distinct mathematical theory of sets.

Although I replied to this criticism in the preface, let me say that I'm not sure that it is true that logicism implies that there is a single empty set. Russell and Whitehead were logicists, but their theory implies there is an empty set at each type. And should we also believe that logicism implies that there is a single theory of numbers? That seems clearly false: Frege held that the natural numbers were different from the real numbers; he used different symbols for them: $\emptyset, 1, \ldots$ for the naturals and $0, 1, \ldots$ for the reals. If logicism were to imply all these things, I think it would be false, since there is no single, true theory of sets and no single, true theory of numbers. There are as many different theories of sets and numbers as there are con-

---

[3] I distinguish here 'theoretical' mathematical objects, like the null set of ZF, from 'natural' mathematical objects, like the number of planets, the class of humans, the direction of line *a*, etc. See my 'Essence and Modality', *Mind*, 115/459 (July 2006): pp.659–693. Natural mathematical objects are not identified relative to a background story or theory, but can be defined in object theory using logical notions and distinguished equivalence relations. These natural mathematical objects may indeed encode ordinary properties: the number of planets, for example, encodes the property of being a planet.

ceptions of 'set' and 'number'. Fortunately, I don't think logicism does imply there are single, true theories of sets and numbers.

6. The view Zalta defends entails that there are no genuine disputes about the truth of a mathematical theory.

7. Since my view of what counts as acceptable mathematical theories is liberal and would not appeal to Frege's logicist way of thinking, it can't be counted as neologicist (or logicist).

I've already responded to (6) in the preface to my replies. As to (7), I think the practice of mathematics establishes that we must be liberal as to what counts as a mathematical theory. The range of mathematical theories and the freedom mathematicians have to innovate is clear by inspection. The suggestion that one can reduce, by way of relative interpretability, all mathematical theories to logic strikes me as false, and if the early logicists believed in such a reduction, then they had the wrong notion of reducibility. If relative interpretability is the standard of reduction, then logic must already include the power of mathematics if arbitrary mathematical theories can be reduced to it. But there is no conception of logic I know of on which it does have this power.

8. The view Zalta defends is not neologicist (or logicist) because it doesn't achieve Frege's aim to prove theorems within logic to reduce the enterprise of mathematics to logic.

I think we are now returning to the core of our differences. For the reasons just mentioned, I believe Frege and the early logicists were using the wrong notion of reduction. I see no hope for a successful logicist or even neologicist reduction of mathematics to logic if relative interpretability is the standard of reduction. (Kit Fine has given us a good idea of what the limits of abstraction are for neologicism.) While it is true that Frege aimed to prove theorems within logic to reduce mathematics to logic, it is important to recognize that his aim was motivated by a larger strategy, namely, that of explaining how we grasp or apprehend mathematical objects without appealing to (some faculty of) intuition. I think we can achieve the goal of Frege's larger strategy by reducing mathematics to logic using a different standard of reduction, i.e., in terms of ontological reducibility instead of relative interpretability.[4] Third-order object theory gives us the means to analyze both the individual terms and predicates of arbitrary mathematical theories in terms of canonical descriptions of abstract individuals and abstract relations. And object theory gives us the means to produce categorical, and indeed provably true, readings of the theorems of mathematical theories. These readings, and the descriptions used to express them, all derive from a single abstraction principle, which has a legitimate claim to being called 'analytic'. That addresses Frege's larger goal of eliminating appeals to (a faculty of) intuition when apprehending mathematical objects, and it does so in a way that Frege might endorse, namely, in terms of a single analytic principle added to logic.

9. The view Zalta defends is not neologicist (or logicist) because he hasn't offered an epistemology that shows how mathematical knowledge is based on logical knowledge.

Bernard Linsky and I offered an answer in our 2006 paper[5] and I developed it further in my talk at the Wittgenstein Symposium. Let me illustrate the answer with an example. Consider the ZF statement "the null set has no members," which (we saw above) has a true reading: $\varnothing_{ZF}[\lambda y \neg \exists z(z \in_{ZF} y)]$. This true reading turns out to be a theorem of object theory and its derivation rests on:

- Third-order logic with a relational λ-calculus
- (Second-order) Abstraction for abstract individuals
  $\iota x(A!x \ \& \ \forall F(xF \equiv \phi))G \equiv \phi^{G,F}$
- (Third-order) Abstraction for abstract relations
  $\iota R(A!R \ \& \ \forall F(RF \equiv \phi))S \equiv \phi^{S,R}$
- The analytic truth "According to ZF, the null set has no members," which is imported into object theory receiving the analysis described above.

I think the axioms of third-order logic are analytically true, since logically true. Using second-order logic under extremely small, general models (in which λ-conversion, i.e., the β-reduction principle of the λ-calculus, is log-

---

[4] The notion of ontological reduction was illustrated in my paper 'Neologicism? An Ontological Reduction of Mathematics to Metaphysics', *Erkenntnis*, 53/1–2 (2000): pp.219–265.
[5] See 'What is Neologicism?', *Bulletin of Symbolic Logic*, 12/1 (2006): pp.60–99.

ically true) as an analogy, I argued that the abstraction principles for abstract individuals and abstract relations (which are themselves true in extremely small models) are similarly analytically true, since logically true. Finally, I argued that the claim "According to ZF, the null set has no members" is analytically true. We need no special faculty of intuition to know these four classes of analytic truths. And since the theorems derived from analytic truths are also analytic, I conclude that the claim "the null set has no members", under its true encoding reading, is also analytic and thereby knowable.[6]

This ends my replies. I've enjoyed our exchange and look forward to our future discussions about these issues.

Respectfully yours,

Edward N. Zalta
Senior Research Scholar
zalta@stanford.edu

---

[6] This complements what Linsky and I argued in 1995 (*op. cit.*), namely, that knowledge of mathematical objects and mathematical relations is by description, since each mathematical object and relation is identified in object theory using a canonical description. Indeed, we argued that knowledge by acquaintance and knowledge by description collapse in the case of abstract objects.

III.
Analysis

ON THE BENEFITS OF A REDUCTION OF MODAL PREDICATES TO MODAL OPERATORS

VOLKER HALBACH
University of Oxford

For many modal notions English contains a predicate along with an adverb: *is necessary* is a predicate expression; 'necessarily' is an adverb.[1] In formal languages this distinction is mirrored by the contrast between modal operators and modal predicates. A modal operator has to be combined with a formula to obtain a new formula; a predicate has to be combined with a singular term. The symbol □ of modal logic is a modal operator; from the syntactical point of view, □ behaves like the negation symbol: written in front of a formula it yields a new formula. The symbol □ is often used to symbolise necessity. Similar remarks apply to many modal notions other than necessity such as analyticity, being known, being believed, being a priori, being true in the future.

In some cases one can easily dispense with the predicate for necessity. The sentence

The proposition that water is H_2O is necessary.

may be taken to be equivalent to

Necessarily, water is H_2O.

There may be some qualms about the correctness of this paraphrase: The original version seems to be about a certain proposition while the second does not refer to propositions at all; but here I'm not concerned with these

---

[1] Here I am dealing exclusively with adverbial phrases that can be understood as modificators of entire sentences not of parts of sentences. Some of what I am saying applies also to modificators of verbs (or, more generally, of predicates), but here I do not want to go into the intricacies of such cases. Consequently, I focus on *de dicto*-modalities only.

qualms, as there are far more problematic cases where one does not even have an obvious candidate of the above kind for a paraphrase.

Sentences involving a predicate of necessity and quantification over the objects that may be necessary cannot be easily reformulated without the predicate:

(i) All laws of physics are necessary.
(ii) Some necessary propositions are not a priori.
(iii) All mathematical truths are necessary.

Therefore, disallowing a predicate of necessity and keeping the adverb or the modal operator only, seems to result in a restriction of the expressive power of the language.

If necessity is formalised as the modal operator $\Box$, the above sentence (i)–(iii) cannot be formalised without further tricks. The sentence $\forall x(\text{Law}(x) \rightarrow \Box(x))$ not well formed. If necessity is treated as a predicate, these sentences can be formalised in a straightforward way.

Despite the problems with quantified sentences and against Quine's advice, philosophical logicians and other philosophers have continued to treat necessity as a modal operator and not as a predicate of certain objects. There might be a socio-historical explanation for this adherence to the operator conception: the paradoxes arising on the predicate account (Montague 1963) and the rise of possible-worlds semantics for modal logic surely contributed to the success of the operator account as elegant technical frameworks for the operator conception became available. Here in this paper I will argue that there are also strong *philosophical* motives for eliminating predicates of necessity in favour of the corresponding adverbs or operators.

1 FIRST BENEFIT: MODAL LOGIC

If the predicate conception of necessity is adopted, then modal logic is no longer adequate for formal treatments of necessity, and modal logic would have to be rejected as a general framework for studying modal notions. Together with modal logic, presumably also its possible-worlds semantics, at least in its usual form, would have to go. As large parts of philosophy are based on possible worlds as a basic tool (or even more), philosophers should have a strong interest in trying to retain the operator conception of necessity as the only conception and not to admit along with the operator conception also the predicate account of necessity. If the operator approach is rejected, then many uses of intensional logics are called into doubt and with it large parts of philosophical logic from deontic over epistemic to temporal logic.

Of course, the existence of a large body of philosophical work based on the adequacy of modal logic and possible-worlds semantics does not show that the operator approach must be sound. But many philosophers would be reluctant to to relinquish all this work.

The existence of possible-worlds semantics for necessity and other modal notions, as developed by Halbach et al. (2003), may be seen as an attempt to salvage some insights gained from modal logic and possible-worlds semantics if one opts for the predicate approach. But as Halbach et al. (2003) demonstrated, the predicate conception is subject to severe constraints because of the paradoxes from diagonalisation, and thus also the possible-worlds semantics for modal predicate deviates in many important aspects from the usual possible-worlds semantics for operators.

2 SECOND BENEFIT: PARADOXES FROM SELF-REFERENCE

Montague (1963) used a strengthening of the liar paradox to question predicate approaches to the analysis of necessity. Here is a variation of Montague's paradox with the epistemic-modal predicate 'is known (by someone)'.

(M) The proposition expressed by sentence M is not known.

If the proposition expressed by sentence labelled (M) is known, then, by the *ab necesse ad esse*-principle or factivity of knowledge, the proposition expressed by sentence M is not known, because this is was the sentence says. Hence the proposition expressed by sentence M is not known, that is, sentence M is established, and therefore it *is* known, which is a contradiction.

For the paradox it is not required that 'is known' is conceived as a predicate of *propositions*. One could equally well use sentences in the place of propositions if one is worried about the ontology of propositions and if one thinks that sentences rather than propositions are the objects that can be known.

Montague's paradox is a variation or strengthening of the liar paradox (for an analysis and comparison see Halbach et al. 2003), but it applies to many further notions. There are also more sophisticated paradoxes such as Curry's paradox. One important ingredient for these paradoxes is *diagonalisation* or self-reference. The predicate 'is known' cannot be eliminated and be replaced with a construction that works like an adverb, for instance with the phrase 'as is known'.

Possible-worlds semantics shows that the operator is not threatened by paradox in the same way as the predicate account of modal notions.

3 THIRD BENEFIT: PARADOXES FROM THE INTERACTION OF MODAL PREDICATES

Even once the paradoxes from self-reference concerning the different modal notions are resolved in the one or the other way, other paradoxes may well remain that arise from the interaction of two or more modal predicates. Examples of such paradoxes were given by Horsten and Leitgeb (2001), Niebergall (2006), Halbach (2006), Halbach (2008, and Petzolt (2009). Here I provide a simple example. In the example the paradox arises from the interaction of predicates for necessity and aprioricity.

The following axioms and rules are inconsistent with a basic theory of syntax:

A1   If 'A' is a priori, then A (where A does not contain 'a priori')

A2   rule of inference: If 'A' has been proved, one may infer ' "A" is a priori.' (where A does not contain 'a priori')

A3   If 'A' is necessary, then A (where A does not contain 'necessary')

A4   rule of inference: If 'A' has been proved, one may infer ' "A" is necessary.' (where A does not contain 'necessary')

If the other axioms and rules don't allow one to prove contingent or a posteriori truths, then A1–A4 ought to be intuitively correct.

Since in the axioms in A1 the predicate of being a priori applies only to sentences without this predicate, it should also be plausible that Montague's paradox does not go through for this theory of a prioricity. In fact, under weak assumptions the consistency of A1 and A2 plus a base theory can easily be established; the same holds for A3 and A4. Basically, in this theory Montague's paradox is avoided by invoking Tarski's solution to the liar paradox where the truth predicate does not provably apply to any sentence containing the very same truth predicate.

Using Gödel's diagonalisation technique one can obtain a sentence D with the following property:[2]

D if and only if 'the sentence "D" is necessary' is not a priori.

The sentence can be chosen in such a way that it does not contain the predicate 'is necessary', not even within quotation marks. Mentioned occurrences of expressions, that is, occurrences within quotation marks, can be replaced be using structurally descriptive names (or other names) for expressions in the sense of Tarski 1935 or by using Gödel codes. In order to keep the following discussion more perspicuous I assume that in A1, for instance, A must contain no used occurrence of 'is apriori'; mentioned occurrences can be avoided by using the mentioned techniques. Analogous remarks apply to the other type restrictions in A2–A4 as well.

Thus, if the sentence 'the sentence "D" is necessary' is a priori, then not-D. But also if the sentence 'the sentence "D" is necessary' is a priori, then the sentence "D" is necessary by A, and therefore, by A, also D. It follows that the sentence 'the sentence "D" is necessary' is not a priori, because the assumption that it is a priori implies both, not-D and D.

Therefore D follows, as D is equivalent to the claim that 'the sentence "D" is necessary' is not a priori. Applying A4 to D yields that D is necessary. Using A2 I conclude that 'the sentence "D" is necessary' *is* a priori. This is a contradiction.

In this derivation the predicate of aprioricity has been applied only to sentences not containing this predicate, and the predicate of necessity has been applied only to sentences not containing the predicate expressing necessity (except for merely eliminable mentioned occurrences). Of course D is 'somehow' about a sentence containing the aprioricity predicate, but this is allowed in solutions of the paradoxes relying on a distinction between an object and metalanguage. Ruling out such indirect occurrences of predicate

---

[2] For obtaining self-reference I cannot invoke the informal trick of labelling a sentence labelled with a number that refers to that very same number. Because then the derivations would depend on the contingent fact that the sentence has been labelled in this particular way. As I am dealing with necessity here I could not then apply the rule of necessitation.

would be very difficult: it is a complicated (non-recursive) task to decide if a sentence refers to such a predicate predicate.

It is usually assumed that the semantic paradoxes can be blocked by applying predicates such as 'is true', 'is necessary', or 'is a priori' only to sentences that do not contain the respective predicate. This is not to say that this solution is generally accepted; it is only thought to be *safe* even though it might be rejected by many as too restrictive. The above inconsistency, however, shows that the solution falters if it is applied to two predicates simultaneously. Thus even the highly restrictive language-level method is insufficient for blocking inconsistencies arising from the interaction of two modal predicates.

One could now impose more restrictions on the axioms and rules A1–A4: one could allow only instances of A1 where the instantiating sentences contains neither an occurrence of 'is a priori' *nor* an occurrence of 'is necessary'. Curtailing the axioms and rules A1–A4 in this way would block the derivation of the contradiction; but this solution comes at a high price: predicates such as 'is necessary' would no longer be applicable to sentences containing predicates like 'is priori', 'is true', 'is known', and so on. Basically one would prohibit any interaction between modal and semantic predicates and thereby declare many philosophical accounts concerning the relation between these notions as ill conceived because they do not conform with the syntactic restrictions on the axioms for these notions.

Moreover, it seems very hard to predict which axioms for different modal notions might interact in a detrimental way. It no longer seems sensible to develop theories of various modal notions separately. In order to avoid inconsistencies, when developing the theory of a modal notion, one would also have to keep an eye on *all* other modal notions. Basically one would have to develop the theory of all these notions with one fierce sweep, which seems next to impossible as the list of modal notions is fairly long, diverse, and perhaps even open ended.

At any rate, the problems arising from the interaction of these predicates can be resolved by eliminating modal *predicates*. If necessity, aprioricity, and so on are conceived as modal operators only, then diagonalisation is not possible and the interaction of the various concepts can be studied in intensional logics featuring modal operators for the different notions.

4 Fourth Benefit: Ontology

On the standard semantics, predicates apply to objects. Hence, if 'is necessary' and so on are predicates, they need to apply to objects. Philosophers have attributed necessity to propositions conceived as language independent objects, to sentence types or tokens of an ideal language or a language of thought, or to sentence types or tokens of a natural language. Even if one settles for propositions, there are disparate views on how propositions are individuated.

I am not generally worried about accepting objects and, in particular, abstract objects of which necessity can be predicated. I am worried about the requirement for a unified account: usually analyticity is conceived as a predicate of *sentences*, while necessity is conceived as a property of propositions and being known is presumably also a property of propositions but of more finely grained propositions than those propositions of which necessity is predicated. One might be tempted to say that logically equivalent sentences of a language express the same proposition as far as necessity is concerned but not as far as being known is concerned as the proposition expressed by a sentence can be known while the proposition expressed by a logically equivalent sentences is not known. Of course there is an extensive literature on the ontology of beliefs and of propositions in general, and I cannot go into the details here, but if, for instance, as it is usually done, necessity is predicated of (language independent) propositions and analyticity of predicates, then nothing that is analytic can be necessary and vice versa, simply because sentences are not propositions and vice versa.

On the operator account one needs a unified account of propositions (or sentences) that can be used for all modal and semantic predicates: analyticity must be applicable, in some way, to propositions; or necessity must be applicable to sentences. Alternatively, one could understand a claim like

There are necessary beliefs that are not analytic

(where beliefs are neutral between sentences and propositions) as shorthand for a more complicated claim of the following kind:

There are necessary propositions that are expressed by (some?) (only by?) sentences that are not analytic.

On such an approach relations connecting the objects to which modal predicates are attributed are needed. Besides the relation used above that obtains between sentences and the propositions they express, one would presumably also invoke a relation that allows to go from finer grained propositions to coarse grained propositions and vice versa. At any rate a sizable ontological apparatus is needed to accommodate various modal predicates into a common framework.

Developing such an apparatus would have to be prior to an analysis of modal notions. However, if there is hope to reduce modal predicates to modal operators, then there is also hope to bypass the need for an intricate and comprehensive ontological theory. On the operator account, no objects to which modal predicates can be attributed are needed.

Thus not only the paradoxes arising from the interaction of modal predicates but also ontological problems impede the development of a unified framework in which various modal and semantic notions can be studied simultaneously.

5 REDUCTIONS

I have argued in this paper that there are good reasons for trying to eliminate modal predicates and to retain only modal operators. In the present section I'll sketch some attempts to perform this elimination. It is to be expected that the elimination comes at a certain price if quantified statements involving modal notions still are to be expressible. Here I'll not reach a conclusion, but I'll indicate some aspects that will have to be taken into account.

Above I have shown how one might go about eliminating the modal predicate from sentences like the following by using modal operators:

The proposition that water is H_2O is necessary.

Only when one turns to quantified statements as (i)–(iii) above, the elimination of modal predicates cannot be carried in a straightforward way. Various proposals have been made for formalising such sentences using an operator rather than a predicate.

Universally quantified statements are often formalised as *schemata*. The sentence saying that all laws of physics are necessary would be expressed by the schema $L\varphi \rightarrow \Box \varphi$, where L is an operator expressing 'it's a law of physics that' and φ ranges over all sentences of the language. One obvious problem is that now one is forced to reexpress predicates like 'is a law of physics' as operators, which might add additional problems as one might want to treat it as a predicate in 'There are no laws of physics.'

Even if this problem can be solved, this approach will work only for simple universally quantified sentences; but if the quantification is embedded into other connectives and quantifiers then they would also have to be pushed into the metalanguage, so that the formalisation of many sentences would end in an unhappy mix of expressions in the object- and the metalanguage. Thus I cannot see this strategy succeed.

In order to express this quantified statements within the objectlanguage one could invoke special quantifiers. The sentence saying that all laws of physics could then be formalised as $\forall \varphi (\text{Law}(\varphi) \rightarrow \Box(\varphi))$ using a predicate 'Law(x)', a modal operator $\Box$ for necessity and the special quantifier with the variable φ that stands in object and sentence places. Of course one would need a semantics for this new kind of quantifier that does not reintroduce the ontological problems of the predicate account through the backdoor: in particular, if $\forall \varphi$ is taken as a quantifier ranging over sentences, propositions or the like, it is not unlikely that one will be confronted with the same problems that were to be solved in virtue of the elimination of the modal operators. A substitutional reading of this quantifier seems to overcome these problems.

Kripke (1976) investigated this kind of substitutional quantification in close connection with his work on truth (1975). In fact one can show that languages with this kind of quantification and languages with a truth predicate are intertranslatable.

To me it seems that the use of a truth predicate is much closer to natural language (and in the end conceptually leaner than the use of special quantifiers). In order to express quantification involving modal notions we often use an adverb plus the truth predicate as in 'Some a priori beliefs aren't necessarily true' instead of 'Some a priori beliefs aren't necessary.'

The use of a truth predicate comes at a price, however. The use of the truth predicate seems to reintroduce the problems I tried to block by eliminating modal notions: truth needs to apply to objects, so there will be ontological problems; and truth is prone to paradox. But I think that there are some important gains in a reduction of modal notions to modal operators and a truth predicate, which I will highlight in the following.

First, logicians and philosophers can continue to use modal logic for analysing modal notions such as necessity. The quantification problem is solved via the truth predicate and no predicate of necessity is needed. Thus one will need a theory of truth, but one can retain intensional logics and possible-worlds semantics as a general framework for analysing modal notions.

Second, only the paradoxes of truth need to be solved. Paradoxes arising from self-reference do not arise for modal notions anymore as they are treated as operators that cannot be used in diagonalisations. At least all the problems about paradoxes are concentrated on truth. Montague's and similar paradoxes can be regained in the framework proposed: but they become truth-theoretic paradoxes and they do not threaten the theory of necessity and other modal notions different from truth.

Third, there cannot be paradoxes arising from the interaction of modal predicates, simply because there is only one such predicate left: truth.

Fourth, also the ontological problem of a unique category of objects to that all modal notions can be applied disappears as there are not any modal predicates left that need to apply to objects. Of course, truth still needs to apply to objects but one does not need any longer objects to which predicates of necessity, analyticity, and belief can be applied in the same way. One does not need anymore a common category of objects that can be necessary, be known, and so on.

In (2009) Philip Welch and I have tried to provide the formal framework for carrying out the proposed reduction of modal notions to modal operators plus a truth predicate. There are some formal obstacles to the proposed elimination of modal predicates, but they can be overcome under certain assumptions, which are far from being uncontroversial. For instance, in this paper we rely on Kripke's (1975) solution of the truth-theoretic paradoxes. Here I do not go on to discuss further aspects of this discussion as my main topic has been only the motivation for carrying out this reduction.

In the proposed reduction the truth predicate is used for expressing generalisations. Thus, according to many philosophers, we have made use of a merely deflationist truth predicate. However, the availability of a deflationist truth predicate might allow one to eliminate modal predicates and therefore enjoy the above benefits of this reduction. Thus a mere device of generalisation might impinge on issues in ontology, the paradoxes and other central areas of philosophy. Deflationist truth might be only a tool, but, if used in the right way, it might turn out to be a sharp razor.

REFERENCES

Halbach, Volker (2006), 'How Not to State the T-sentences', *Analysis* 66, pp.276–280. Correction of printing error in vol.67, p.268.

Halbach, Volker (2008), 'On a Side Effect of Solving Fitch's Paradox by Typing Knowledge', *Analysis* 68, pp.114–120.

Halbach, Volker, Hannes Leitgeb and Philip Welch (2003), 'Possible Worlds Semantics for Modal Notions Conceived as Predicates', *Journal of Philosophical Logic* 32, pp.179–223.

Halbach, Volker and Philip Welch (2009), 'Necessities and Necessary Truths: A Prolegomenon to the Metaphysics of Modality', *Mind*. to appear.

Horsten, Leon and Hannes Leitgeb (2001), 'No Future', *Journal of Philosophical Logic* 30, pp.259–265.

Kripke, Saul (1975), 'Outline of a Theory of Truth', *Journal of Philosophy* 72, pp.690–712. reprinted in Martin (1984).

Kripke, Saul (1976), 'Is There a Problem about Substitutional Quantification?', in G.Evans and J.McDowell, eds, *Truth and Meaning: Essays in Semantics*, Clarendon Press, Oxford, pp.325–419.

Martin, Robert L., ed. (1984), *Recent Essays on Truth and the Liar Paradox*, Clarendon Press and Oxford University Press, Oxford and New York.

Montague, Richard (1963), 'Syntactical Treatments of Modality, with Corollaries on Reflexion Principles and Finite Axiomatizability', *Acta Philosophica Fennica* 16, pp.153–167. Reprinted in (Montague 1974, pp.286–302).

Montague, Richard (1974), *Formal Philosophy: Selected Papers of Richard Montague*, Yale University Press, New Haven and London. Edited and with an introduction by Richmond H. Thomason.

Niebergall, Karl-Georg (1991), *Simultane objektsprachliche Axiomatisierung von Notwendigkeits- und Beweisbarkeitsprädikaten*, Master's thesis, Ludwigs-Maximilians-Universität München.

Petzolt, Sebastian (2009), 'A Paradox Remains', *Logique et Analyse*. to appear.

CALCULI OF INDIVIDUALS AND SOME EXTENSIONS: AN OVERVIEW[*]

KARL-GEORG NIEBERGALL
Humboldt University Berlin

1 INTRODUCTION

Calculi of individuals are usually regarded as paradigmatic examples of nominalistic theories.[1] This view is fine with me.[2] Nonetheless, it may be asked: what do or should we understand by "calculus of individuals" and "nominalistic theory"? Now, although there are clear cases of theories which are accepted as nominalistic or calculi of individuals – or fail to be so – I admit that we have no general convincing explications of these predicates at our disposal. In the case of "nominalistic theories", I guess this is something we have to live with; but that may be nothing to worry about (see Niebergall 2005 and 2007 for more on this topic, and also footnote 5). When it comes to calculi of individuals, however, the situation is different, and it may be better. As a starting point, let me repeat an explication of "calculus of individuals" from Niebergall 2007.

Let $L^1[o]$ be the 1st order language with the 2-place predicate "o" – read "overlaps" – as its sole non-logical primitive expression. Consider the theory CI in $L^1[o]$ axiomatized as follows:[3]

O	$\forall xy(\exists z(z\Pi x \wedge z\Pi y) \leftrightarrow x \text{ o } y)$,
SUM	$\forall xy \exists z \forall u(z \text{ o } u \leftrightarrow x \text{ o } u \vee y \text{ o } u)$,
NEG	$\forall x(\exists y \forall u(u\Pi y \leftrightarrow \neg u \text{ o } x) \leftrightarrow \neg \forall w \, w \text{ o } x)$.

[*] This paper was presented under the title "Mereologische Theorien" at the 31st International Wittgenstein Symposium 2008. I would like to thank the scientific directors, Alexander Hieke and Hannes Leitgeb, and the Österreichische Ludwig Wittgenstein Gesellschaft for the invitation, and the participants of the talk for comments.
[1] For Goodman (1951), *the* calculus of individuals was a specific theory in $L^1[o]$; it is called "CI + FUS^1" below. In the meantime, "calculus of individuals" has become a predicate which is now ascribed to many theories.
[2] Let me add, however, that even if the first statement of this paper is beyond dispute for 1st order languages and theories, it might be worthwhile to rethink it for 2nd order ones.
[3] "y is part of x" is defined as follows: $y\Pi x :\leftrightarrow \forall u(u \text{ o } y \rightarrow u \text{ o } x)$.

Let's then define:

(D1) T is a calculus of individuals $:\Leftrightarrow T$ is formulated in $L^1[o] \wedge CI \subseteq T$

Being formulated in $L^1[o]$ is certainly not sufficient for a theory T to be called a "calculus of individuals": "o" might be axiomatized in a way which does not conform to its preferred paraphrase "overlaps". The addiion of "$CI \subseteq T$" is supposed to exclude such unintended readings (cf. Niebergall 2007). Are there proper extensions T of CI formulated in $L^1[o]$ which should not be regarded as calculi of individuals (see section 2.1 for some of them)? This is difficult to say. For on the one side, I doubt that there are such T which have about the same degree of plausibility as CI, given the intended readings "overlaps" and "part of" of "o" and "Π": only CI is well motivated. Yet, if no sentence independent of CI can be determined as being correct (under the intended reading), none can be pinned down as incorrect. But on the other side, whatever the intended reading of $L^1[o]$ is, if φis a sentence of $L^1[o]$, either it or its negation must be true under that reading. Nonetheless, our linguistic intuitions on their own are just not determined enough for us to answer which one.

Actually, whereas we may want to determine a unique correct theory with a unique model (up to isomorphism) when doing number theory (which sadly does no work nicely), calculi of individuals are used with a different aim: they should be applicable in many situations, that is, for many quite diverse relational systems which only have some structural similarities. In that situation, I think that the appropriate *general methodic approach* is to attempt to obtain results about *all* the theories from $L^1[o]$ which extend CI. For with this method, we get those results also for the "real" calculi of individuals (in $L^1[o]$), whatever they may be.

Coming back to (D1), we have to deal with a further possibility: *There could be theories T formulated in extensions L+ of $L^1[o]$ that deserve to be called "calculi of individuals".*

I would certainly not regard all such T as calculi of individuals. As an example, take an L+ which results from $L^1[o]$ by the addition of the 2-place predicate "$\in$", and let T be CI + ZF (where the ZF-component is stated only in that part of L+ which is built over "$\in$").

But then, consider these types of extensions L+ of $L^1[o]$:

– L+ is 1st order, but contains additional predicates or functions signs, such as: "is with", "has the same size as", "matches", "is a quale" (see Goodman 1951, Breitkopf 1978); "is connected with", "lies in the interior of" (i.e., topological vocabulary); "lies between", "is congruent with" (i.e., geometrical vocabulary); "is next to" (see Lewis 1970); "contains fewer points than" (Field 1980), "is longer than", "has more bits than"; "is finite".

– L+ is a 2nd order language which results from $L^1[o]$ by the addition of monadic 2nd order variables (see Field 1980, Lewis 1991).[4]

And take theories T in these languages which fix the use of the new expressions in a way appropriate to the readings just given (thus, they are supposed to extend CI).

It has been suggested repeatedly that these L+ and T are nominalistically admissible (see, e.g., Lewis 1970, Field 1980; for 2nd order languages in particular, see Leonard/Goodman 1940, Field 1980, Lewis 1991); and the T have also been classified as calculi of individuals (see Clarke 1981, 1985; for both claims, see Goodman 1951, Breitkopf 1978). Moreover, for 1st order theories this has usually been done without much further ado. A reason for the latter assessments could be that in these cases, the relata of the newly introduced relations are most naturally viewed as concrete objects, or individuals, or particulars.[5] Of course, all of this is far from providing a *general explicans* or criterion for "T is a calculus of individuals". Since, however, it seems that serious doubts have not been raised as to the rightfulness of the above classifications, I accept them here[6] and call those T just mentioned "L+ calculi of individuals".

In this text, I will, adhering to the general methodic approach just sketched, first present a sort of a classification theorem and some further relevant metalogical results for almost all extensions of CI which are for-

---

[4] One may also think about the addition of "unusual" quantifiers (i.e., quantifiers which are not 1st order definable) to 1st order languages. In the context of a nominalistic program, this has been suggested by Field 1980.

[5] Lewis (1970) is an exception, citing Goodman 1951 and 1958. But the definitions of „nominalistic system" Goodman puts forward there is not precise; moreover, it may be interpreted as implying that CI + ZF is nominalistic (see Niebergall 2005 for more on this).

[6] As far as I know, "calculus of individuals" is in distinction to, e.g., "nominalism" and "individual", a term of art. Therefore, it is hard to find criteria for its proper use which are independent from what the philosophers and logicians working on calculi of individuals have stipulated.

mulated in $L^1[o]$. When it comes to L+ calculi of individuals, however, the domain of admissible languages and theories (even for a specific choice of L+) is much too wide and open for similar metatheorems to hold. Here, I merely state a general dilemma for such theories and give two examples for it: one is taken from mereotopology, the other is concerned with infinity. In the final section, 2nd order variants of calculi of individuals are addressed. For reasons of space, much will be carried out only *sketchily*. In particular, theorems will be stated without proofs.

2 CALCULI OF INDIVIDUALS IN $L^1[o]$

Let's start with identity. I prefer to treat "=" as a "logical sign" which is axiomatized *via* "$x = y \leftrightarrow \forall u\,(u\text{ o }y \leftrightarrow u\text{ o }x)$", reflexivity and substitutivity (a schema that is stated for $L^1[o]$ first, but which I assume to be extended to whatever language L+ is taken into account).[7]

2.1 Optional axioms and theories for "o"

Then we also have several options for axioms which are specific for "o". First some abbreviations:

$At(y) :\leftrightarrow \forall z\,(z\Pi x \rightarrow z = x)$ ("y is an atom")
$y\Pi^- x :\leftrightarrow y\Pi x \wedge \neg(x\Pi y)$ ("y is a proper part of x")
$\exists_{>n}x At(x) :\leftrightarrow \exists x_0...x_n(At(x_0) \wedge ... \wedge At(x_n) \wedge x_0 \neq x_1 \wedge ... \wedge x_{n-1} \neq x_n)$
    ("there are more than n atoms")
$\exists_{n+1}x At(x) :\leftrightarrow \exists_{>n}x At(x) \wedge \neg\exists_{>(n+1)}x At(x)$ ("there are $n+1$ atoms")

Now the axioms:

AT	$\forall x \exists y(y\Pi x \wedge At(y))$
AF	$\forall x \exists y\, y\Pi^- x$
HYPEXT	$\forall xy[\forall z(At(z) \wedge z\Pi y \leftrightarrow At(z) \wedge z\Pi x) \rightarrow x = y]$
DE	$\forall xy(y\Pi^- x \rightarrow \exists z(y\Pi^- z \wedge z\Pi^- x))$
PROD	$\forall xy(x\text{ o }y \rightarrow \exists z \forall u(u\Pi z \leftrightarrow u\Pi x \wedge u\Pi y))$

---

[7] "=" could also be *defined* in $L^1[o]$: $x = y :\leftrightarrow \forall u(u\text{ o }y \leftrightarrow u\text{ o }x)$. But here, too, the adjustment has to be taken care of.

There are also two axiom-schemata: the *fusion schema* FUS^1 (with variants; see, e.g., Eberle 1970) and the *nucleus schema* (see Goodman 1951, Breitkopf 1978). Since the latter follows from CI + FUS^1, I only deal with FUS^1. Thus, let $\varphi(x)$ be a formula of $L^1[o]$ (possibly containing further free variables). Then set

$$\text{FUS}^1_{\varphi} := \ulcorner \exists x\varphi(x) \rightarrow \exists z \forall y (z \text{ o } y \leftrightarrow \exists x(\varphi(x) \wedge x \text{ o } y)) \urcorner;$$

and let FUS^1 be the set of all the formulas FUS^1_{φ} (with φ in $L^1[o]$).

The intended reading of these sentences is obvious: AT asserts that each object has an atomic part, AF that each object has a proper part. HYPEXT says that objects are determined by their atomic parts (see Goodman 1958, Yoes 1967), DE expresses density (and possibly also infinity), PROD that meets of overlapping objects exist (note that we do not have a null object). Finally, FUS^1 is an infinitary version of SUM.

Are there further natural axioms in $L^1[o]$ which are in harmony with CI? There could well be: it depends on the reader's imagination to find them. But in a specific sense, the answer is (almost): No; see section 2.4. Moreover, some of the above axioms are superfluous.

Lemma 1: CI $\vdash$ AT $\leftrightarrow$ HYPEXT, $\neg$AF $\leftrightarrow$ $\exists x$At(x), AF $\rightarrow$ DE, $\exists y \forall x \, x\Pi y$, PROD.

Given the above implications between the optional additional axioms, the following are the theories in $L^1[o]$ which suggest themselves as extensions of CI.

First there are the extensions of CI by AT, AF and their negations:

ACI := CI + AT (for "atomic calculus of individuals"),
FCI := CI + AF (for "atomfree calculus of individuals"),
MCI := CI + $\neg$AT + $\neg$AF (for "mixed calculus of individuals").

Second there are extensions of those in which the number of the atoms is addressed:

$\text{ACI}_{>n}$:= ACI + $\{\exists_{>n}x\text{At}(x)\}$,
ACI_{n+1} := ACI + $\{\exists_{n+1}x\text{At}(x)\}$,
ACI_{ω} := ACI + $\{\exists_{>n}x\text{At}(x) \mid n \in \omega\}$,
$\text{MCI}_{>n}$:= MCI + $\{\exists_{>n}x\text{At}(x)\}$,

$$MCI_{n+1} := MCI + \exists_{n+1}xAt(x),$$
$$MCI_\omega := MCI + \{\exists_{>n}xAt(x) \mid n \in \omega\}.$$

Of course, in each case instances of FUS^1 could be added as further axioms.[8]

2.2 The general methodic approach and metalogical considerations

Given the general methodic approach from section 1, the best one could hope for here would be a complete grasp of all the consistent extensions T of CI in $L^1[o]$. For a start, this includes the investigation of what may be called „absolute properties" of such T. Thus, we should ask

(F1) Which T are consistent, maximal consistent, decidable, κ-categorical etc.

But we should also be interested in „relational properties" of these T, i.e., in intertheoretic relations between them, and in relations between them and established other theories. I believe that for these aims, one should address:

(F2) Which arithmetic and set theories are relatively interpretable in extensions of CI?[9]

(F3) What is the relation between the extensions of CI with respect to relative interpretability?

Whereas almost nothing has been published on (F2) and (F3), some partial results concerning (F1) can be found in the relevant literature:

(i)   ACI is decidable.

(ii)   Each ACI_{n+1} is categorical, maximal consistent and decidable.

---

[8] ACI, the ACI_{n+1}'s and ACI_ω are the theories treated in Hodges/Lewis 1968. The theory presented in Goodman 1951 amounts to CI + FUS^1 (see also Breitkopf 1978, Ridder 2002). For the other theories, see Hendry 1982.

[9] A relative interpretation from theory S in theory T is a map from the set of formulas of $L[S]$ to the set of formulas of $L[T]$ which preserves quantificational structure (apart from relativizing quantifiers) and maps S into T; see Tarski et.al. 1953 and Feferman 1960. For a defense of the claim that relative interpretability provides a good *explicans* for "reducibility", see Niebergall 2000 and 2005.

(iii) ACI_ω is maximal consistent and decidable (of course, it cannot be categorical).

(iv) ACI_ω is not $\aleph_0$-categorical.

(v) $FCI + FUS^1$ is $\aleph_0$-categorical, maximal consistent and decidable.

(vi)   Each $MCI_{n+1} + FUS^1$ is $\aleph_0$-categorical, maximal consistent and decidable.

(vii)   The maximal consistent extensions of ACI are exactly the ACI_{n+1} and ACI_ω.

For (i), (ii), (iii) and (vii) see Hodges/Lewis 1968 (they established (ii) *via* a normal form theorem; but a model-theoretic proof is easier and obvious). For (iv) see Hellman 1969. For (v) and (vi), see Hendry 1982.

Section 2.4 contains a report about strengthenings of these metatheorems. In particular, I present a comprehensive list of the maximal consistent extensions of $CI + FUS^1_{AT}$. Here, FUS^1_{AT} abbreviates "$\exists x At(x) \rightarrow \exists z \forall y (z \ o \ y \leftrightarrow \exists x(At(x) \wedge x \ o \ y))$". Furthermore, in section 2.5 there are results concerning (F2) and (F3). But let's start with Boolean algebras, which turn out to be very useful.

2.3 Mereological and Boolean Algebras

For structures in which $L^1[o]$ can be evaluated, I usually write $\langle M, o^M \rangle$ $(=: \mathscr{M};$ with $M \neq \emptyset$ and $o^M \subseteq M^2)$. Those of them which satisfy CI I call "mereological algebras". A *Boolean algebra* $\mathscr{B}$, which is a structure of the form $\langle B, \sqcap^B, \sqcup^B, -^B, 0^B, 1^B \rangle$, may also be viewed as a model of a theory BA which is stated in the corresponding equational 1st order language L[BA] (see Halmos 1963).

Despite their different signatures, it is quite easy to turn a Boolean algebras into a mereological algebra and *vice versa* (and it is well known how to do it). For my purposes, it suffices to explain how to obtain a mereological algebra $\mathscr{B}^-$ from a Boolean algebra $\mathscr{B}$.

$$\mathscr{B}^- = \langle B^-, o^{B^-} \rangle, \text{ with } B^- := B\backslash\{0^B\} \text{ and for } a, b \text{ in } B^-, a \ o^{B^-} b :\Leftrightarrow a \sqcap^B b \neq 0^B.$$

This correspondence induces a relative interpretation $\mathscr{I}$ from CI in BA which is *faithful* (i.e., nontheorems of CI are mapped to nontheorems of BA). $\mathscr{I}$ being a recursive function, we therefore get at once the first main result from the decidability of BA (for a detailed sketch of the proof, see Niebergall 2007):

Theorem 1: CI is decidable.

Boolean algebras also provide for models of the theories from section 2.1:

Set $\mathcal{B}_{n+1} = \langle \wp(\{0,\ldots,n\}), \cap, \cup, \setminus, \emptyset, \{0,\ldots,n\}\rangle$;
then $\mathcal{B}_{n+1}^- \models \mathrm{ACI}_{n+1} + \mathrm{FUS}^1$.
Set $\mathcal{B}_\omega = \langle \wp(I\!N), \cap, \cup, \setminus, \emptyset, I\!N\rangle$; then $\mathcal{B}_\omega^- \models \mathrm{ACI}_\omega + \mathrm{FUS}^1$.
Let RO($I\!R$) be the set of regular open sets of $I\!R$ (given the usual topology on $I\!R$) and set $\mathcal{B}_R = \langle \mathrm{RO}(I\!R), \cap, \cup, \setminus, \emptyset, I\!R\rangle$;
then $\mathrm{B}_R^- \models \mathrm{FCI} + \mathrm{FUS}^1$.
Consider $\mathcal{B}_{n+1} \times \mathcal{B}_R$ (the product of $\mathcal{B}_{n+1}$ with $\mathcal{B}_R$, explained in the natural way);
then $(\mathcal{B}_{n+1} \times \mathcal{B}_R)^- \models \mathrm{MCI}_{n+1} + \mathrm{FUS}^1$.
Consider $\mathcal{B}_\omega \times \mathcal{B}_R$; then $(\mathcal{B}_\omega \times \mathcal{B}_R)^- \models \mathrm{MCI}_\omega + \mathrm{FUS}^1$.

2.4 Absolute metalogical results: (F1)

First, we have some slight amendments of the results mentioned in section 2.2:

(v)+ FCI is $\aleph_0$-categorical, maximal consistent and decidable.
(vi)+ Each MCI_{n+1} is $\aleph_0$-categorical, whence maximal consistent and decidable.

Then there is the second main new result:

Theorem 2: $\mathrm{MCI}_\omega + \mathrm{FUS}^1_{\mathrm{AT}}$ is maximal consistent and decidable, but not $\aleph_0$-categorical.

As a roundup, there is what I have called a *classification theorem*:

Theorem 3: The maximal consistent extensions of $\mathrm{CI} + \mathrm{FUS}^1_{\mathrm{AT}}$ in $\mathrm{L}^1[\mathrm{o}]$ are exactly the ACI_{n+1} and MCI_{n+1}, ACI_ω, FCI and $\mathrm{MCI}_\omega + \mathrm{FUS}^1_{\mathrm{AT}}$.

This has surprising and nice consequences, such as:

Corollary 1:
(i) $ACI \vdash FUS^1$, and $CI + FUS^1_{AT} \vdash FUS^1$.
(ii) $ACI = Th$(the class of finite mereological algebras) (which is decidable).[10]

2.5 Relative interpretability: (F2) and (F3)

Calculi of individuals should be widely applicable; but they are not supposed to contain only logical truths. In fact, it has been repeatedly suggested that they can play the role of set theories while at the same time avoiding the unpleasant ontological commitments of the latter. This lends a particular importance to (F2). Now, Theorem 1 quite directly yields a strong answer to that question:

Theorem 4: No consistent extension of CI (in $L^1[o]$) interprets Q.[11]

The consequences of this metatheorem for a nominalistic reduction program should be taken seriously; but I think there are not disastrous. There are other theories which come to the nominalist's rescue (see Niebergall 2005 for a suggestion).

Let me finally come to (F3). Here is a list of the central (non-) interpretability results I am aware of. In what follows, "$S \preccurlyeq T$" is supposed to stand for "S is relatively interpretable in T".

Theorem 5: For arbitrary $k, n \in IN$,
(i) $\neg(ACI_{n+1} \preccurlyeq ACI_{k+1})$, if $n \neq k$,
$\neg(ACI_\omega \preccurlyeq ACI_{n+1})$, $\neg(ACI_{n+1} \preccurlyeq ACI_\omega)$,
$\neg(FCI \preccurlyeq ACI_{n+1})$,
$\neg(FCI \preccurlyeq ACI_\omega)$, $\neg(ACI_\omega \preccurlyeq FCI)$,
(ii) $ACI \preccurlyeq MCI + FUS^1_{AT}$, $ACI_{n+1} \preccurlyeq MCI_{n+1}$,
$ACI_\omega \preccurlyeq MCI_\omega + FUS^1_{AT}$,

---

[10] Proofs can be found in the unpublished manuscript Niebergall 2009b; see also Niebergall 2007. The proofs of (vi)+ and Theorem 2 use a specific back-and-forth-construction, plus results mentioned in section 2.5.

[11] Q, i.e., Robinson-Arithmetic, is a weak subtheory of PA; cf. Tarski et.al. 1953. For a transfer of Theorem 4 to the domain of set theories and further refinements, see Niebergall 2007.

(iii) $\neg(MCI \leqslant ACI_{n+1})$, $\neg(MCI \leqslant ACI_\omega)$, $\neg(ACI_\omega \leqslant MCI_{n+1})$,
(iv) $FCI \leqslant MCI + FUS^1_{AT}$.

Some of these claims follow by applying general metatheorems about relative interpretability. (ii) and (iv) rest on specifically chosen translations $\mathscr{T}_A$ and $\mathscr{T}_F$. In both cases, "$x \circ y$" is mapped to itself. Moreover (employing quasi-quotation),

$$\mathscr{T}_A(\ulcorner \forall x\varphi \urcorner) = \ulcorner \forall x\, (\delta_A(x) \to \mathscr{T}_A(\varphi)) \urcorner \text{ and}$$
$$\mathscr{T}_F(\ulcorner \forall x\varphi \urcorner) = \ulcorner \forall x\, (\delta_F(x) \to \mathscr{T}_F(\varphi)) \urcorner,$$

where $\delta_A(x) = \ulcorner \forall y(y\Pi x \to \exists z(z\Pi y \wedge At(z))) \urcorner$ and $\delta_F(x) = \ulcorner \forall y(y\Pi x \to \neg At(y)) \urcorner$.

3 CALCULI OF INDIVIDUALS IN EXTENDED 1ST ORDER LANGUAGES

3.1 The WS-dilemma

Why have 1st order extensions L+ of $L^1[o]$ and L+ calculi of individuals T been introduced in the first place? I presume that from a systematic point of view, the answer is: to have languages that enrich $L^1[o]$ and theories that strengthen the calculi of individuals as defined by (D1), yet nevertheless preserve the salient features of the latter. Now, I think that those salient features include above all freedom from ontological commitment to abstract objects or universals. Actually, I find it somewhat difficult to understand how calculi of individuals could be interesting when they are not viewed as contributions to a nominalistic reduction program. To this, one may answer with recourse to the idea of *resource boundedness:* Calculi of individuals are proof theoretically weak, but just strong enough for what they are supposed to deliver. But why could not also, e.g., weak set theories be suitable for this role?

Be this as it may – I think that these considerations point to what may be a dilemma for L+ calculi of individuals: the WS-dilemma (for "wide-strong-dilemma"), as I will call it.

On the one side, as I understand the above mentioned "to have languages that enrich $L^1[o]$ and theories that strengthen the calculi of individuals as defined by (D1)", it should imply at least that if T is a calculus of individuals in $L^1[o]$, an extension S of T in L+ should not merely be a *definitional extension* of T. With the abbreviation

$S \mid L^1[o] := \{\varphi \mid \varphi \text{ is a } L^1[o]\text{-sentence} \wedge S \vdash \varphi\},$

this can be stated as follows (for "possible definition", see Tarski et.al. 1953):

> (S) Not: for each consistent L+ calculus of individuals S, there are possible definitions D in $L^1[o]$ for the new vocabulary from L+ such that S is a subtheory of $S \mid L^1[o]$ extended by D.[12]

On the other side, just as for calculi of individuals in $L^1[o]$, there is no unique intended L+ calculus of individuals – at least if L+ is one of the extensions of $L^1[o]$ mentioned in the introduction. That is, if one wants to add only evident or at least rather plausible new axioms formulated in L+ to a calculus of individuals T in $L^1[o]$, one will most probably obtain rather weak extensions of T. And since for such a T, only CI is a choice which is beyond dispute, we get in particular:

> (W) If S is a consistent L+ calculus of individuals, $S \mid L^1[o]$ is not maximal consistent (in $L^1[o]$).

(S) and (W) certainly do not contradict each other. But it may be that, in practice, they are not easily realized simultaneously. Let me present examples for that claim in the following two subsections.

3.2 Mereotopology

Topology is a mathematical discipline dealing with topological spaces and (structure preserving) mappings between them. In that approach, "x is a topological space" is defined purely set theoretically: no topological axioms are given. Now Kuratowski has found a *definiens* for "topological space" which does not use "$\in$", but only "$\subseteq$" in an essential way. This can therefore easily be turned into axioms. Thus, let's extend $L^1[o]$ by a function sign "C" (read: "closure of") to $L^1[o,C]$ and consider the new axioms:

(AxC) $\forall x\, x \Pi Cx,\ \forall xy(x\Pi y \rightarrow Cx\Pi Cy),\ \forall x\, Cx = CCx$

---

[12] This way of making the basic intuition precise is just a first suggestion. It may be weakened, e.g., by mentioning relative interpretations instead of definitions, but also strengthened. Actually, the latter takes place in Lemmata 2 and 4.

Here we have a version of mereotopology. It can be found in Grze-gorczyk 1951 (in principle), but surprisingly has not been very successful: for alternative mereotopological vocabularies see Clarke 1981, 1985 (adding "is connected to"), Kleinknecht 1992 and Smith 1996 (adding "is an interior part of") and perhaps Lewis 1970 (adding "is next to"). In consequence, mereotopological theories differ widely. But *modulo* definition or translation, certain basic principles are common to most of them. As an example, consider this list of axioms which are accepted both by Kleinknecht (1992) and Smith (1996); it is formulated in $L^1[o, \lhd]$, where "$\lhd$" is a 2-place predicate read as "is an interior part of":[13]

(AxTop)
$\forall xy(x \lhd y \to x\Pi y)$,
$\forall xy(x \lhd y \wedge y\Pi z \to x \lhd z)$, $\forall xy(x\Pi y \wedge y \lhd z \to x \lhd z)$,
$\forall x \exists y\, x \lhd y$,
$\forall xyz(x \lhd y \wedge x \lhd z \to x \lhd y \otimes z)$,
$\forall xy(x \lhd y \to x \lhd \sigma z(z \lhd y))$,
$\forall x[\exists y\varphi(y) \wedge \forall y(\varphi(y) \to y \lhd x) \to \sigma y\varphi(y) \lhd x]$,
    for each formula $\varphi(y)$ in $L^1[o, \lhd]$.[14]

But now, we have the first horn of the WS-dilemma. Let's define

(D2) $x \lhd y :\leftrightarrow x\Pi y$.

Lemma 2:
(i) $CI + FUS^1 (+ (D2)) \vdash (AxTop)$.
(ii)   If T is a consistent extension of $CI + FUS^1$ in $L^1[o]$, then $T +$ (AxTop) is a subtheory of a definitional extension of T.

Similar metatheorems can be shown for Clarkes theory and also for (AxC). Thus mereotopological axioms should be added. But which ones? On the one hand, Grzegorczyk (1951) has found a list of sentences in $L^1[o, C]$ for which he claims that they relatively interpret Q. That's an impressive result. But these sentences can hardly be claimed to be plausible as new mereotopological axioms. Kleinknecht (1992) and Smith (1996), on the other hand, have tried to find such principles: their common idea is to

---

[13] I follow the presentation in Ridder 2002.
[14] I write „$y \otimes z$" for the common part of y and z (when these overlap) and $\sigma y\varphi(y)$ for the fusion of the φ's.

give boundaries an important status. Kleinknecht defines "xGy" (for "x is part of a boundary of y") as "$\forall u\,(u \lhd y \vee u \lhd \text{-}y \rightarrow \neg u \text{ o } x) \wedge y \neq 1$" (Smith's *definiens* is equivalent for $y \neq 1$).[15] And both accept

$$\forall y(y \neq 1 \rightarrow \exists z\, zGy)$$

as a theorem of their axiom systems. When it comes to the further axioms, however, a remarkable branching can be found. Whereas

$$\forall x \exists y\, y \lhd x,$$

is a theorem of Kleinknecht's system Kl,

$$\forall x(\text{At}(x) \rightarrow \neg \exists y\, y \lhd x)$$

can be proved in Smith's theory Sm. That is, Kl is inconsistent with Sm if the existence of atoms is assumed. Now, who of those two is right intuitively? I must say that I have no strong naive preferences here. But from the point of view of the WS-dilemma, it seems clear to me that Kl is unacceptable: for Kl proves that there is exactly one object.

Lemma 3: Kl $\vdash \forall x(x = 1)$.

This is incompatible with the 2nd horn of the dilemma (if Kl is a $L^1[\text{o}, \lhd]$ calculus of individuals).

3.3 Infinity

It is sometimes held that our universe W (say, at a specific time), the sum of all concrete things, is finite, or that we should not assume that it is infinite, or that we simply do no know. I think that all these assessments presuppose that "W is (in-) finite" is understood. That may be the case; but it is quite another thing to actually lay down a definition for that phrase. As far as I know, "x is infinite" has only been defined set-or type-theoretically. And *prima facie*, W is no set or higher-order object: W is as concrete as its parts.

---

[15] I write "$\text{-}y$" for the complement of y (when it exists) and "1" for that object which has all objects as parts.

Now, to start with, what could a definition of "x is finite" be when we have only $L^1[o]$ at our disposal? That is, I am searching for a formula $\alpha(x)$ from $L^1[o]$ which expresses that x is finite.[16] I certainly do not ask whether there is sentence φ in $L^1[o]$ such that for all models $\mathscr{M}$ of T (when T is consistent), $\mathscr{M} \models \varphi \Leftrightarrow M$ is finite. For by general model-theoretic reasons (i.e., compactness), there can be none. But this type of result holds for, e.g., ZF, too. And that fact doesn't keep us from believing that there *is* a set-theoretic formula $\alpha(x)$ which does express that x is finite: for example, "$\exists y(y \in \omega \wedge x$ has the same cardinality as $y)$" may be chosen for $\alpha(x)$.

I think that when one attempts to determine if there is a similar α in $L^1[o]$, one first has to lay down axioms for finiteness. In our case, they have to be stated in $L^1[o, F]$, i.e., $L^1[o]$ extended by a new 1-place predicate F for "x is finite". Here is my suggestion for them:

$(\text{AxFin}(F))$
$\forall x(\text{At}(x) \to Fx),$
$\forall xy(Fx \wedge Fy \to F(x \oplus y)),$
$\forall x(\text{At}(x) \to \psi(x)) \wedge \forall xy(\psi(x) \wedge \psi(y) \to \psi(x \oplus y)) \to$
$\qquad \forall x(Fx \to \psi(x))$, for each formula ψ from $L^1[o,F]$,
$\forall x(\neg Fx \to \exists_{>n} y \, (y \Pi x))$, for each $n \in I\!N$.[17]

It is unpleasant that the WS-dilemma shows up again; but here it is surprising: "x is finite", as it axiomatized through $(\text{AxFin}(F))$, is definable in $L^1[o]$. More precisely, define

(D3) $F(x) :\leftrightarrow \forall y(\forall z(\text{At}(z) \to z \Pi y) \to x \Pi y).$

Lemma 4:
(i) $CI + FUS^1_{AT} (+ (D3)) \vdash (\text{AxFin}(F))$
(ii)   If T is a consistent extension of $CI + FUS^1_{AT}$ in $L^1[o]$, then
$\qquad T + (\text{AxFin}(F))$ is a subtheory of a definitional extension of T.

---

[16] The topic of what it generally means for a formula $\alpha(x)$ to express: x is so-and-so, is a large one. For the special case that $\alpha(x)$ is a set theoretical formula that should express that x is (in-) finite, I have presented a suggestion in Niebergall 2009a. I take this to by typical; but that view is not defended in Niebergall 2009a.

[17] I write "$y \oplus z$" for the fusion of y and z and "$\exists_{>n} y(y \Pi x)$" for "x has more than n parts" (cf. section 2.2).

I am nevertheless reluctant to accept that "$F(x)$" expresses that x is finite. Here is a reason: it can be shown that $ACI_\omega \vdash \forall x F(x)$. Now in each model of ACI_ω, this would mean that its 1 were finite; in fact, however, each has infinitely many parts (naively understood). The most interesting way out of this quandary seems to be to find a better axiomatization: but what could that be?

4 VARIANTS OF CALCULI OF INDIVIDUALS IN 2ND ORDER LANGUAGES

4.1 The general framework

The simplest way to extend $L^1[o]$ to a 2nd order language $L^2[o]$ is to add 1-place 2nd order variables ("X",...) to it and define the set of second order terms and formulas by employing these new expressions. Given that, let's look for analogues of the extensions of CI in $L^1[o]$. I will call these theories, whether they deserve it or not, "2nd order calculi of individuals". To start with, the 1st order sentences from section 2.1 are a good choice for specific axioms. As regards FUS^1, one should change it to a 2nd order version. Two amendments are particularly natural:

FUS^2, the full 2nd order fusion schema, is the set of all formulas FUS^2_φ, with
$$FUS^2_\varphi := \lceil \exists x \varphi(x) \to \exists z \forall y (z \circ y \leftrightarrow \exists x (\varphi(x) \wedge x \circ y)) \rceil,$$
where $\varphi(x)$ is a formula of $L^2[o]$ (possibly containing further free variables);

FUS-Ax, the 2nd order fusion axiom:
$$\forall X (\exists x Xx \to \exists z \forall y (z \circ y \leftrightarrow \exists x (Xx \wedge x \circ y))).$$

Further plausible 2nd order principles for "o" are not that easy to find. But there are other 2nd order sentences which usually are taken to be beyond dispute, to be even logical truths. One is a Leibniz principle for identity:

(Leib) $\forall yz (\forall X (Xy \leftrightarrow Xz) \to y = z)$.

It will be a consequence of other accepted axioms, however. More interesting and problematic are *comprehension schemata*. Again, two versions are worthy of special attention:

Comp^2, the full 2nd order comprehension schema, is the set of all formulas Comp$_\varphi$, with

$$\text{Comp}_\varphi := \ulcorner \exists X \forall x (Xx \leftrightarrow \varphi(x)) \urcorner,$$

where $\varphi(x)$ is a formula of L^2[o] (possibly containing further free variables);

Comp^1, the restricted 2nd order comprehension schema, is the set of all formulas Comp$_\varphi$, where φ is a formula of L^2[o] containing no bound 2nd order variables.

On first sight, we therefore have four 2nd order variants of one 1st order calculus of individuals T: $T \cup \{\text{FUS-Ax}\} \cup \text{Comp}^1$, $T \cup \{\text{FUS-Ax}\} \cup \text{Comp}^2$, $T \cup \text{FUS}^2 \cup \text{Comp}^1$, $T \cup \text{FUS}^2 \cup \text{Comp}^2$. Normally, we are not interested in sets of axioms, however, but in the theories induced by them. And this is the place where one has to be careful when dealing with 2nd order languages instead of 1st order ones. For there are many non-equivalent ways to define logical consequence for 2nd order languages. Two types of them are employed in practice. Thus, we usually have two serious candidates for the theory T given by *one* set of 2nd order sentences Σ.

Let me recall the two definitions of "φ follows from Σ", where Σ is a set of sentences from L^2[o] and φ is a sentence from L^2[o].

The structures which are appropriate for evaluating expressions from L^2[o] are now taken to be of the form $\langle M, \Omega, o^M \rangle$, in short $\mathcal{M}^2$. If Ω is a nonempty subset of $\wp(M)$, $\mathcal{M}^2$ is called a *generalized 2nd order structure* (in short: g2-structure). In the special case that $\Omega = \wp(M)$, it is called a *standard 2nd order structure* (in short: s2-structure).

Let $\mathcal{M}^2$ be a g2-structure. A variable assignment β (relative to $\mathcal{M}^2$) is a function defined on the set of 1st and 2nd order variables which maps the 1st order variables to elements of M and the 2nd order variable to elements of Ω. Given all that, *evaluation in a structure* is defined as it is known from the 1st order case, with one interesting clause added (for a formula φ of L^2[o]; $\beta(X:C)$ is the variant of β which differs from β at most in mapping X to C):

350

$$\mathscr{M}^2, \beta \models \forall X\varphi \Leftrightarrow \forall C(C \in \Omega \Rightarrow .\mathscr{M}^2, \beta(X{:}C) \models \varphi).^{[18]}$$

Now the common metalogical vocabulary, such as "satisfiability", "logical truth" and "logical consequence", can be defined as usual, *via* g2-structures. But there is also the alternative of taking only s2-structures into account. Thus, let's consider *logical consequence* (if Σ is a set of sentences from $L^2[o]$ and φ is a sentence from $L^2[o]$):

$$\Sigma \models^{g2} \varphi :\Leftrightarrow \forall M\Omega o^M (\langle M, \Omega, o^M\rangle \text{ is a g2-structure} \Rightarrow \\ (\langle M, \Omega, o^M\rangle \models \Sigma \Rightarrow \langle M, \Omega, o^M\rangle \models \varphi)),$$

$$\Sigma \models^{s2} \varphi :\Leftrightarrow \forall M\Omega o^M (\langle M, \Omega, o^M\rangle \text{ is a s2-structure} \Rightarrow \\ (\langle M, \Omega, o^M\rangle \models \Sigma \Rightarrow \langle M, \Omega, o^M\rangle \models \varphi)).$$

Since each s2-structure is a g2-structure, we immediately get: $\Sigma \models^{g2} \varphi \Rightarrow \Sigma \models^{s2} \varphi$. But for 2nd order languages in general, the converse is far from true. In addition, the notorious incompleteness and categoricity metatheorems which are so often attributed to 2nd order "logic" and to certain 2nd order theories are only true under the presupposition that the 2nd order languages for which they are stated are interpreted employing only s2-structures. If all of the g2-structures are admitted as models instead, these "metatheorems" are false: in this case, we have a completeness and compactness theorem for 2nd order consequence and versions of the Löwenheim-Skolem theorems (see Leivant 1994 for more on this).

4.2 Some metatheorems

With the distinctions just sketched as a background, let me introduce some abbreviations. In what follows, let Σ be a set of $L^2[o]$-sentences.

$$\Sigma^{g2+} := \{\varphi \mid \varphi \text{ is a } L^2[o]\text{-sentence} \wedge \Sigma \cup CI \cup FUS^2 \cup Comp^2 \models^{g2} \varphi\},$$
$$\Sigma^{g2-} := \{\varphi \mid \varphi \text{ is a } L^2[o]\text{-sentence} \wedge \Sigma \cup CI \cup \{FUS\text{-}Ax\} \cup Comp^1 \models^{g2} \varphi\},$$
$$\Sigma^{g2} := \{\varphi \mid \varphi \text{ is a } L^2[o]\text{-sentence} \wedge \Sigma \cup CI \cup FUS^2 \cup Comp^1 \models^{g2} \varphi\},$$
$$\Sigma^{s2} := \{\varphi \mid \varphi \text{ is a } L^2[o]\text{-sentence} \wedge \Sigma \cup CI \cup FUS^2 \cup Comp^2 \models^{s2} \varphi\}.$$

---

[18] s2-structures in particular may alternatively be construed as being the same objects as 1st order structures, i.e., ordered pairs $\langle M, o^M\rangle$. Satisfaction in such structures is for 2nd order quantifiers explained as follows:

$$\langle M, o^M\rangle, \beta \models \forall X\varphi \Leftrightarrow \forall C\,(C \subseteq M \Rightarrow \langle M, o^M\rangle, \beta(X{:}C) \models \varphi).$$

Lemma 5:
(i) $\Sigma^{g2-} \subseteq \Sigma^{g2} \subseteq \Sigma^{g2+} \subseteq \Sigma^{s2}$.
(ii) If Σ is a set of $L^1[o]$-sentences, then $\Sigma + CI + FUS^1 \subseteq \Sigma^{g2-}$.
(iii) If $\mathcal{M}$ is a s2-structure, then $\mathcal{M} \models Comp^2$.
(iv) $\Sigma^{s2} = \{\varphi \mid \varphi$ is a $L^2[o]$-sentence $\wedge \Sigma \cup CI \cup \{FUS\text{-}Ax\} \models^{s2} \varphi\}$.

The correspondence between mereological and Boolean algebras and the translation from $L^1[o]$ to $L^1[BA]$ can be extended to the 2nd order counterparts of the structures and of the languages. Let me mention merely some of the consequences of this approach:

Lemma 6: If $\langle B, \sqcap^B, \sqcup^B, -^B, 0^B, 1^B \rangle$ is a complete Boolean algebra, then $\langle B^-, \wp(B^-), o^{B^-} \rangle \models FUS\text{-}Ax$.

Now the Boolean algebras from section 2.3 are complete (i.e. have suprema for each nonempty subset of their domain). Therefore, they induce s2-structures which are models of the $(ACI_{n+1})^{s2}$ and $(MCI_{n+1})^{s2}$, or of $(ACI_\omega)^{s2}$, $(FCI)^{s2}$ or $(MCI_\omega)^{s2}$, respectively.
We also have sort of a converse to Lemma 6:

Lemma 7: For each $\mathcal{M}$ $(= \langle M, \wp(M), o^M \rangle)$ which is a s2-structure satisfying CI, FUS-Ax, there is a complete Boolean algebra $\mathcal{B}$ such that $\mathcal{B} = \langle M, o^M \rangle$.

In the 1st order case, there is a similar, if weaker, metatheorem:

Lemma 8: For each mereological algebra $\mathcal{M}$ which satisfies FUS^1_{AT}, there is a complete Boolean algebra $\mathcal{B}$ such that $\mathcal{B} \equiv \mathcal{M}$.

Lemma 8 can nonetheless be employed to obtain a rather strong conservativity result:

Theorem 6:
(i)   If Σ is a set of $L^1[o]$-sentences, then $\Sigma + CI + FUS^1 \mid L^1[o] = \Sigma^{s2} \mid L^1[o]$.
(ii) If Σ is a set of $L^1[o]$-sentences, then Σ^{g2-}, Σ^{g2}, Σ^{g2+} and Σ^{s2} contain the same sentences from $L^1[o]$.

By the above observations, all of the 2nd order variants of the 1st order theories ACI_{n+1} and MCI_{n+1}, ACI_ω, FCI and $MCI_\omega + FUS^1_{AT}$ are consistent and not distinguishable by their 1st order consequences. But are they maximal consistent? And what is their relation as to arbitrary sentences from $L^2[o]$? A lot of research has still to be done here. Let me close this paper with the nontrivial example of 2nd order extensions of ACI_ω.

Lemma 9:

(i) $(ACI_\omega)^{s2}$ is not maximal consistent.

(ii) All s2-structures of cardinality $2^{\aleph_0}$ which are models of $(ACI_\omega)^{s2}$ are isomorphic with each other.

(iii) There is a sentence "CounAt"[19] from $L^2[o]$ such that for all s2-structures $\langle M, \wp(M), o^M \rangle$ which are models of $(ACI_\omega)^{s2}$, $\langle M, \wp(M), o^M \rangle \models$ CountAt $\Leftrightarrow \{a \mid a$ is an atom$^M\}$ is countably infinite.

Theorem 7:

(i) All s2-structures which are models of $(ACI_\omega + CounAt)^{s2}$ are isomorphic with each other.

(ii) $(ACI_\omega + CounAt)^{s2}$ is maximal consistent.

In distinction, $(ACI_\omega + CounAt)^{g2+}$ is a proper subtheory of $(ACI_\omega + CounAt)^{s2}$ and therefore fails to be maximal consistent.

REFERENCES

BREITKOPF 1978: A. Breitkopf, Axiomatisierung einiger Begriffe aus Nelson Goodmans *The Structure of Appearance*, in: Erkenntnis 12 (1978), pp.229–247.

CLARKE 1981: B. Clarke, A Calculus of Individuals Based on 'Connection', in: *Notre Dame Journal of Formal Logic* 22 (1981), pp.204–218.

CLARKE 1985: B. Clarke, Individuals and points, in: *Notre Dame Journal of Formal Logic* 26 (1985), pp.61–75.

EBERLE 1970: R. Eberle, *Nominalistic Systems*, Dordrecht: Reidel.

FEFERMAN 1960: S. Feferman, Arithmetization of Metamathematics in a General Setting, in: *Fundamenta Mathematicae* 49 (1960), pp.35–92.

FIELD 1980: H. Field, *Science without Numbers: A Defence of Nominalism*, Oxford: Blackwell.

GOODMAN 1951: N. Goodman, *The Structure of Appearance*, Dordrecht: Reidel.

---

[19] This sentence is taken from Lewis 1991.

GOODMAN 1958: N. Goodman, On Relations that Generate, in: *Philosophical Studies* 9 (1958), pp.65–66; reprinted in N. Goodman, *Problems and Projects*, Indianapolis: Bobbs-Merril. pp.171–172.

GRZEGORCZYK 1951: A. Grzegorczyk, Undecidability of some topological theories, in: *Fundamenta Mathematicae* 38 (1951), pp.137–152.

HALMOS 1963: P. Halmos, *Lectures on Boolean Algebras*. Princeton, NJ: Van Nostrand.

HELLMAN 1969: G. Hellman, Finitude, infinitude, and isomorphism of interpretations in some nominalistic calculi, in: *Noûs* 3 (1969), pp.413–425.

HENDRY 1982: H.E. Hendry, Complete Extensions of the Calculus of Individuals, in: *Noûs* 16, pp.453–460.

HODGES/LEWIS 1968: W. Hodges/D. Lewis, Finitude and infinitude in the atomic calculus of individuals, in: *Noûs* 2 (1968), pp.405–410.

KLEINKNECHT 1992: R. Kleinknecht, Mereologische Strukturen der Welt, in: *Wissenschaftliche Zeitschrift der Humboldt-Universität zu Berlin, Reihe Geistes- und Sozialwissenschaften* 41 (1992), pp.40–53.

LEIVANT 1994: D. Leivant, Higher Order Logic, in D. Gabbay, C.J. Hogger, J.A. Robinson (ed.): *Handbook of Logic in Artificial Intelligence and Logic Programming*, Volume 2, Clarendon Press, pp.229–321.

LEONARD/GOODMAN 1940: H. Leonard/N. Goodman, The Calculus of Individuals and its Uses, in: *The Journal of Symbolic Logic* 5 (1940), pp.45–55.

LEWIS 1970: D. Lewis, Nominalistic Set Theory, in: *Noûs* 4 (1970), pp.225–240.

LEWIS 1991: D. Lewis, Parts of Classes, Oxford: Blackwell.

NIEBERGALL 2000: K.G. Niebergall, On the Logic of Reducibility: Axioms and Examples, in: *Erkenntnis* 53 (2000), pp.27–61.

NIEBERGALL 2005: K.G. Niebergall, Zur nominalistischen Behandlung der Mathematik, in J. Steinbrenner, O. Scholz und G. Ernst (Hrsg.): *Symbole, Systeme, Welten: Studien zur Philosophie Nelson Goodmans*, Heidelberg: Synchron Wissenschaftsverlag der Autoren, pp.235–260.

NIEBERGALL 2007: K.G. Niebergall, Zur logischen Stärke von Individuenkalkülen, in: H. Bohse und S. Walter (Hgg.); *Ausgewählte Sektionsbeiträge der GAP.6, Sechster Internationaler Kongress der Gesellschaft für Analytische Philosophie, Berlin, 11.–14. September 2006.* (CD-ROM) Paderborn: mentis.

NIEBERGALL 2009A: K.G. Niebergall, Unendlichkeit ausdrücken und Unendlichkeitsannahmen machen, to appear in: *Deutsches Jahrbuch Philosophie* 3.

NIEBERGALL 2009B: K.G. Niebergall, *Zur Metatheorie mereologischer Theorien*, manuscript, Berlin 2009.

RIDDER 2002: L. Ridder, *Mereologie. Ein Beitrag zur Ontologie und Erkenntnistheorie*. Frankfurt a.M.: Klostermann.

SMITH 1996: B. Smith, Mereotopology: a theory of parts and boundaries, in *Data and Knowledge Engineering* 20 (1996), pp.287–303.

TARSKI/MOSTOWSKI/ROBINSON 1953: A. Tarski/A. Mostowski/R.M. Robinson, *Undecidable theories*, Amsterdam: North-Holland.

YOES 1967: M.G. Yoes, Jr., Nominalism and non-atomic systems, in: *Noûs* 1 (1967), pp.193–200.

DEFINITE DESCRIPTIONS: LANGUAGE, LOGIC, AND ELIMINATION

NORBERT GRATZL
University of Salzburg

Abstract

Definite descriptions are in the focus of philosophical discussion at least since Russell's famous paper "On Denoting". In this paper, we present a logic with descriptions in Russell's spirit. The formulation, however, is closely related to Schütte's development of predicate logic, i.e. the formulation of the calculus uses positive- and negative-parts. With respect to this slightly more sophisticated formulation it is possible to formalize Russell's convention which is originally stated in the meta-language of his theory of descriptions within our calculus. In this paper we prove an elimination theorem for this calculus.

1 INTRODUCTION

Russell's theory of definite descriptions is an intellectual offspring of finding (adequate) solutions to puzzling philosophical oddities, e.g. for Meinong's ontological jungle. In this article we focus on a calculus with descriptions that is very much in the spirit of Bertrand Russell's treatment of descriptions in the *Principia Mathematica* *14 (*P.M.**14). However, it is not the same. This is due to several reasons:

(a) Russell's theory of descriptions is not focussed on the whole class of descriptions but just on descriptions of a very simple kind.

(b) Russell does not develop his theory in a purely formal way. Essential parts of it are found in the context that explains some important facts, e.g. the use of the scope-operator.

(c) The language and logic (developed below) is void of intensional functors.

According to Russell a description has the following form:

the so-and-so

where 'the' is in the singular and 'so-and-so' is a (possibly) complex expression. (Definite) descriptions occur in two contexts – as Russell says, e.g.

- The present King of France is wise.
- The present King of France exists.

Following Russell, the above statements can be formally represented as follows:

(*14.01) $[\iota x A(x)]B(\iota x A(x)) \leftrightarrow \exists x \forall y((A(y) \leftrightarrow x = y) \wedge B(x))$
(*14.02) $E!\iota x A(x) \leftrightarrow \exists x \forall y(A(y) \leftrightarrow x = y)$

Kurt Gödel remarks (1944, p.126) in his contribution to the Schilpp-volume that honours Russell:

> It is to be regretted that this first comprehensive and thorough going representation of a mathematical logic and the derivation of Mathematics from it is so greatly lacking in formal precision in the foundations (contained in *1–*21 of *Principia*), that it represents in this respect a considerable step backward as compared with Frege. What is missing, above all, is a precise statement of the syntax of the formalism. Syntactical considerations are omitted even in cases where they are necessary for the cogency of the proofs, in particular in connection with "incomplete symbols".[1]

Russell licenses the inference from (*14.01) to

(*14.101) $B(\iota x A(x)) \leftrightarrow \exists x \forall y((A(y) \leftrightarrow x = y) \wedge B(x))$

with the following convention:

> It will be found that, in most cases in which descriptions occur, their scope is, in practice, the smallest proposition enclosed in dots or brackets in which they are contained. [...] For this reason it is convenient that, when the scope of an occurrence of $(\iota x)(\phi x)$ is the smallest proposition enclosed in dots or other

---

[1] Interestingly, B. Russell did not respond to Gödel in the Schilpp-volume.

brackets, in which the occurrence in question is contained, the scope need not be indicated by "$[(\iota x)(\phi x)]$." [...] This convention enables us in the vast majority of cases that actually occur, to dispense with the explicit indication of the scope of a descriptive symbol; [...]

In the light of the quite critical remarks of Gödel, we develop in this paper a *thorough going* treatment of descriptions.

At several occasions Russell points out that definite descriptions have *no meaning in isolation* and that definite descriptions are *incomplete symbols*. In our view the phrase "no meaning in isolation" is a semantical thesis and is treated elsewhere (e.g. Gratzl (submitted)). In this paper I shall focus on the phrase "incomplete symbol", that means – according to our understanding – that there is to each formula A containing a definite description a formula B without any definite descriptions and the formulas A and B are provable equivalent relative to a certain translation. The details of this formal interpretation of "incomplete symbols" will be stated below – in section 4.

2 LANGUAGE

The alphabet of L consists of a denumerable set of free individual variables, a denumerable set of bound individual variables, a denumerable set of n-ary predicates variables, the logical symbols: $\wedge$, $\vee$, $\neg$, $\forall$, $\exists$, ι, [...], $=$, $E!$ and the auxiliary signs (and). We use as syntactical variables a, b, c for free individual variables; x, y, z for bound variables; u, v for any term and P^n, Q^n, R^n, S^n for any n-ary predicate variable.

2.1 Definition (Formulas and Terms of L)

1. Free individual variables are terms.
2. If $a_1,\ldots, a_n$ are terms and P^n is an n-ary predicate variable, then $P^n(a_1,\ldots, a_n)$ is a formula.
3. If a, b are terms, then $(a = b)$ is a formula.
4. If A is a formula, then $\neg A$ is a formula.
5. If A, B are formulas, then $(A \wedge B)$, $(A \vee B)$ are formulas.
6. If $A(a)$ is a formula, such that the bound individual variable x does not occur in it, then $\forall x A(x)$ and $\exists x A(x)$ are formulas.
7. If $A(a)$ and $B(b)$ (a and b are not necessarily distinct) are formulas such that the bound individual variable x does not occur

in them, then $\iota xA(x)$ is a term and $[\iota xA(x)]B(\iota xA(x))$ and $B(\iota xA(x))$ are formulas.

8.   If $\iota xA(x)$ is a term, then $E!\iota xA(x)$ is a formula.
9.   If $[\iota xA(x)]B(\iota xA(x))$ and $[\iota xC(x)]D(\iota xC(x))$ are formulas, then:
      $[\iota xA(x), \iota xC(x)](B(\iota xA(x)) \wedge D(\iota xC(x)))$ and
      $[\iota xA(x), \iota xC(x)](B(\iota xA(x)) \vee D(\iota xC(x)))$ are formulas.[2]
10.   If $\iota xA(x, a)$ is a term and $B(a)$ is a formula, then
      $\forall y([\iota xA(x, y]B(\iota xA(x, y)))$ and $\exists y([\iota xA(x, y]B(\iota xA(x, y)))$ are
      formulas.
11.   Nothing else is a formula or a term.

The remaining connectives are defined as usual.

2.2 A brief note on E!

Russell writes in the *PM* on p.174 (Russell/Whitehead 1970):

> When in ordinary language or in philosophy, something is said to "exist," it is always something *described, i.e.* it is not something immediately presented, like a taste or a patch of colour, but something like "matter" or "mind" or "Homer (meaning "the author of the Homeric poems"), which is known by description as "the so-and-so," and is thus of the form $(\iota x)(\phi x)$. Thus in all such cases, the existence of the (grammatical) subject $(\iota x)(\phi x)$ can be analytically inferred from any true proposition having this grammatical subject. It would seem that the word "existence" cannot be significantly applied to subjects immediately given; *i.e.* not only does our definition give no meaning to "E!x," but there is no reason, in philosophy, to suppose that a meaning of existence could be found which would be applicable to immediately given subjects.

Without entering the epistemological distinction between *knowledge by acquaintance* and *knowledge by description* we take it from this quote for granted, that for Russell the E!-predicate can only sensibly be applied to ι-terms. This is reflected in the definition of terms and formulas – condition 8.

---

[2] This clause simply allows multiple occurrences of ι–terms in the scope. Although we shall not deal explicitly with such formulas in this article.

2.3 Examples

The following two examples should indicate that even quite simple examples taken from natural language show that the logical structure might already have a certain complexity, e.g. ι-terms can *overlap* in such a way that the bound variable of a ι-term occurs in the basis of another one. The first example is:

- The first born child of its father inherits the farm.

I use the following symbols:

$P(x, y)$ stands for: y is father of x
$Q(x, y)$ stands for: x is a firstborn child of z
$R(x)$ stands for: x inherits the farm

So the the sentence ist formalized as:

$R(\iota x Q(x, \iota y P(x, y)))$

The second example is:

- • The first born child of its father inherits the fatherly farm.

This quite easily understandable sentence will be expressed in the language developed above, by using the following symbols:

$P(x, y)$ stands for: y is father of x
$Q(x, z)$ stands for x is a firstborn child of z
$R(x, z)$ stands for: x inherits z
$S(z, y)$ stands for: z is farm of y

'The first born child of its father inherits the fatherly farm.' then is formalized as:

$R(\iota x Q(x, \iota y P(x, y)), \iota z S(z, \iota y P(z, y)))$

2.4 Definition (Positive and negative parts of formulas)

In section 3 we shall state an extended form of a Schütte-style calculus for predicate logic including rules dealing with definite descriptions. Schütte's formulation of the predicate calculus makes use of positive and negative parts; those should be thought of generalized notions of antecendent (i.e. negative parts) and and consequent (i.e. positive parts) of Gentzen's sequents.

The following definition of positive and negative parts of formulas is due to Schütte (1960, p.11).

1. F is a positive part of F.
2. If $\neg A$ is a positive part of F, then A is a negative part of F.
3. If $\neg A$ is a negative part of F, then A is a positive part of F.
4. If $(A \lor B)$ is a positive part of F, then both A and B are positive parts of F.
5. If $(A \land B)$ is a negative part of F, then both A and B are negative parts of F.

In the following presentation of (ιC) we make use of subscript plus und subscript minus: these are devices to mark positve- and negative-parts within formulas.

3 ι-CALCULUS (ιC)

Axioms

$(\iota 1)\ F[A_+, A_-]$
$(\iota 2)\ F[(a = a)_+]$
$(\iota 3)\ F[(a = b)_-, A(a)_-, A(b)_+]$

Rules of inference

$(\iota R1)\ F[A_+],\ F[B_+] \Rightarrow F[(A \land B)_+]$
$(\iota R2)\ F[A_-],\ F[B_-] \Rightarrow F[(A \lor B)_-]$
$(\iota R3)\ F[A(a)_+] \Rightarrow F[(\forall x A(x)_+]$

(ιR4) $F[A(a)\_] \Rightarrow F[(\exists xA(x)\_]^3$
(ιR5) $F[(\forall xA(x))\_] \vee \neg A(a) \Rightarrow F[(\forall xA(x))\_]$
(ιR6) $F[(\exists xA(x))_+] \vee A(a) \Rightarrow F[(\exists xA(x))_+]$
(ιR7) $F[(a = b)_+], G[(a = b)\_] \Rightarrow F[\ldots] \vee G[\ldots]$
(ιR8) $F[([ιxA(x)]B(ιxA(x)))_+] \Rightarrow F[(B(ιxA(x)))_+]$
(ιR9) $F[(B(ιxA(x)))_+] \Rightarrow F[(\exists x\forall y((A(y) \leftrightarrow x = y) \wedge B(x)))_+]$
(ιR10) $F[(B(ιxA(x)))\_] \Rightarrow F[([ιxA(x)]B(ιxA(x)))\_]$
(ιR11) $F[([ιxA(x)]B(ιxA(x)))\_] \Rightarrow F[(\exists x\forall y((A(y) \leftrightarrow x = y) \wedge B(x)))\_]$
(ιR12) $F[(E!ιxA(x))_+] \Rightarrow F[(\exists x\forall y(A(y) \leftrightarrow x = y))_+]$
(ιR13) $F[(E!ιxA(x))\_] \Rightarrow F[(\exists x\forall y(A(y) \leftrightarrow x = y))\_]$

(ι1)–(ι3) and (ιR1)–(ιR8) are the usual axioms and rules of inference of predicate logic with equality. The rules (ιR8)–(ιR13) deal with definite descriptions and are formulated in such a way that Russell's "contextual definitions" are provable.

Provability is defined as follows: (i) Every axiom is provable, and (ii) if the premises of a rule of inference are provable, then the conclusion of this rule of inference is provable. It is easily seen that Russell's so-called *contextual definitions* are provable in $(ιC)$,. i.e. (*14.01, *14.02, and *14.101).

4 ELIMINATION OF ι-TERMS

4.1 Definition (ι-rank, rank)

The number of occurrences of the ι-symbol in a given formula is called the ι-rank ($ιrk$) of this formula. The number of logical signs in a formula is the rank (rk) of this formula.

4.2 Inductive definition of F* relative to F

(i) If $ιrk(F) = 0$, then F^* is F.
(ii) If $ιrk(F) > 0$, then:
  (a) If F is $B(ιxA(x))$ where $ιxA(x)$ is the leftmost ι-term, and B is not of the form $\neg C$, $[ιxA(x)]C$, $[ιxA(x)]\neg C$, then F^* is $(\exists x\forall y((A^*(y) \leftrightarrow x = y) \wedge B^*(x)))$.

---

[3] Both (ιR3) and (ιR4) are subject to the condition on variables, i.e. the free individual variable *a* must not occur in the conclusion.

(b)   If F is $E!\iota x A(x)$, then F^* is $\exists x \forall y (A(y) \leftrightarrow x = y)$.
(c)   If F is $\neg B(\iota x A(x))$, where $\iota x A(x))$ is the leftmost ι-term, then F^* is $\exists x \forall y ((A^*(y) \leftrightarrow x = y) \wedge \neg B^*(x))$.
(d)   If F is $\neg [\iota x A(x)] B(\iota x A(x))$, where $\iota x A(x)$ is the leftmost ι-term, then F^* is $\neg (\exists x \forall y ((A^*(y) \leftrightarrow x = y) \wedge B^*(x)))$.
(e)   If F is $[\iota x A(x)] \neg B(\iota x A(x))$, where $\iota x A(x)$ is the leftmost ι-term, then F^* is $\exists x \forall y ((A^*(y) \leftrightarrow x = y) \wedge \neg B^*(x))$
(f)   If F is $[\iota x A(x)] B(\iota x A(x))$, where $\iota x A(x)$ is the leftmost ι-term, then F^* is $\exists x \forall y ((A^*(y) \leftrightarrow x = y) \wedge B^*(x))$

4.3 Elimination Theorem

If $(\iota C) \vdash F$ with $\upsilon rk(F) \geq 0$, then there is a formula F^* relative (to the inductive definition stated above), such that $(\iota C) \vdash F \leftrightarrow F^*$.

In effect this theorem expresses that everything that can be said with the aid of ι-terms can be stated in predicate logic with equality (lets call it (C) without any loss, i.e. (ιC) is a conversartive extension of (C). However, the *reduced* formula, i.e. the formula obtained by elimination of ι-terms, may be quite cumbersome to read.

Proof sketch: The proof is an induction on the number of ι-terms, i.e. ι-rank, of a formula F. If $\upsilon rk(F) = 0$, then there is nothing to prove. If $\upsilon rk(F) > 0$, then several cases (according to the translation *) have to be considered. This proof-step – although every step is quite easy to prove – will be illustrated with an example:

$(\iota C) \vdash [\iota x A(x)] B(\iota x A(x) \leftrightarrow \exists x \forall y ((A(y) \leftrightarrow x = y) \wedge B(x))$ such that $\iota x A(x)$ is the left-most ι-term.

1. $[\iota x A(x)] B(\iota x A(x) \rightarrow [\iota x A(x)] B(\iota x A(x)$ $(\iota 1)$
2. $[\iota x A(x)] B(\iota x A(x) \rightarrow B(\iota x A(x)$ $(1., (\iota R8))$
3. $[\iota x A(x)] B(\iota x A(x) \rightarrow \exists x \forall y ((A(y) \leftrightarrow x = y) \wedge B(x))$ $(2., (\iota R9))$
4. $[\iota x A(x)] B(\iota x A(x) \rightarrow [\iota x A(x)] B(\iota x A(x)$ $(\iota 1)$
5. $\exists x \forall y ((A(y) \leftrightarrow x = y) \wedge B(x)) \rightarrow [\iota x A(x)] B(\iota x A(x)$ $(4., (\iota R11))$
6. $[\iota x A(x)] B(\iota x A(x) \leftrightarrow \exists x \forall y ((A(y) \leftrightarrow x = y) \wedge B(x))$ $(3., 5., \text{Def.} \leftrightarrow)$

By eliminating each ι-term from the left to the right in a given formula F the procedure eventually terminates.

5 CONCLUDING REMARKS

The elimination theorem for the ι-Calculus (ιC) is intended to state a formal interpretation of the phrase that definite descriptions are "incomplete symbols" – as Russell put it. Despite the constructive features of (ιC) it still needs proving – as Kripke (2005, p.1033) notes:

"In these cases, however, I recall proving – though it really takes proving! – that there are no real hydras. Every path eventually terminates, and all are equivalent."

REFERENCES

Gödel, K. (1944): "Russell's Mathematical Logic", in: Schilpp, P. (1951, ed.) *The Philosophy of Bertrand Russell*, New York, pp.123–153.
Gratzl, N. (submitted): "Second thoughts on Principia Mathematica *14".
Kripke, S. (2005): "Russell's Notion of Scope", in: *Mind*, Vol.456, pp.1005–1037.
Russell, B., Whitehead, A.N. (1970): *Principia Mathematica to *56*, Cambrigde.
Schütte, K., 1960: *Beweistheorie*, Berlin-New York.

FROM LANGUAGE GAMES TO SOCIAL SOFTWARE

ROHIT PARIKH
CUNY

> *"But is this counting only a use then?*
> *Isn't there also some truth corresponding to this sequence?"*
> The *truth* is that counting has proved to pay.
> Ludwig Wittgenstein

Abstract

It is well known that Ludwig Wittgenstein was not a fan of formalization. It was likely, in his view, that formal results might engender the illusion that some *philosophical* progress had been made, when in fact no such progress was possible. Nonetheless, in the process of attacking the theory of language formulated in the *Tractatus*, in the first 45 sections of the *Philosophical Investigations*, Wittgenstein does put down a road map which would allow us to construct a (partial) theory of meaning. Indeed, once one asks what that theory of meaning might be, the answer is obvious and fits remarkably well with Wittgenstein's remarks.

One could say, roughly speaking, that the *Tractatus* described *one* language whose role was to *describe* the world, and which had therefore to be *outside the world*. The *Philosophical Investigations, PI*, by contrast sees language as being *in the world* and as consisting of a large variety of language games, each of which plays some role in our lives. Our purpose in this paper is to point to at least *some* similarity among the language games of *PI* and to propose an account of the role of language which is larger than that contemplated in the *Tractatus*.

1 INTRODUCTION

Fairly early in the *Philosophical Investigations (PI)*, Wittgenstein says, (§2) "It is interesting to compare the multiplicity of the tools in language ... with what logicians have said about the structure of language."

"But," one might say, "aren't they all *tools* ?" And note that the tools in a toolbox (§11) have little in common with the various items, lipstick, mirror, etc, to be found in a woman's purse. It is unlikely (albeit possible) that lipstick will be found in an ordinary toolbox, or that a spirit level will be found in a woman's purse. Thus it may well be that the tools in a toolbox have more in common with each other than Wittgenstein allows, and noticing this fact may allow us to build a partial theory of language. Partial, to be sure, but covering a much larger area than that considered by the author of the *Tractatus*.

The theory I shall propose will allow us not only to think about the 'meaning', or 'use' of words like "beam", "slab" but also of words like "this", "that", "five" and "red". In particular we will not understand "red" as a unary predicate.

Wittgenstein himself gives us a hint in §7. "I shall call the whole, consisting of a language and the actions into which it is woven, the 'language game'." It is this *weaving* which much contemporary philosophy of language (albeit not pragmatics) has ignored.[1]

The first suggestion I now make says that a communication situation consists of a parametrized family of procedures and that the way in which a word is used decides which *particular* member of this family is supposed to be performed by the addressee. This is only a first suggestion and we will need to clarify and expand it as we go along.

Thus consider the command, "Bring x to me" where x is the parameter in question. The four actions which the addressee might perform, i.e., the four members of our family, are, *bringing a slab*; *bringing a pillar*; *bringing a beam*; and *bringing a block*. If pronouncing the word "slab" results in the bringing of a slab, and the builder is happy with this action, then we can say that "slab" means slab in this context.[2]

Of course there are 24 ways of correlating the four words with the four actions, and if the convention had been that the command "Slab!" resulted in the bringing of a pillar, *and the builder was happy with this*, then

---

[1] A little boy who had learned a little arithmetic at home, went to his first day of formal schooling and was asked by his mother how his day went. "Everything was fine but the teacher doesn't know anything!", exclaimed the boy. "Why so?" asked the mother. "Well, she actually asked me what two plus three was. Of course I said, five, but shouldn't she have known herself?" said the boy. The boy was used to the game in which A asks B a question to which A does not know the answer. He was not used to the game where A, who already knows, asks B a question to see if B knows the answer. Cf. the last two paragraphs of §6 (in *PI*).

[2] It is crucial that the builder be happy with the assistant's action, a matter addressed later by both Grice and Lewis [3, 5].

we would say that the word 'slab' meant a pillar at least in that variant game.[3]

Note now that the same four words (with the normal usage) could be used in a different language game. Imagine that there is a large wooden box at some distance from the builder, and a lot of stones of various shapes lying at the builder's feet. Now in this new game, when the builder says "Slab!", the assistant takes a slab from near the builder's feet and puts it into the wooden box.

Let us call our original language game G, and the new game G'. Does the word "slab" have the *same* meaning in both games? "Of course", one might say, "for it means a slab in both games." Or one could say, "Of course not, for the assistant does different things in the two games." In game G, the word "slab" causes a slab to be brought *to* the builder whereas in G', the same word causes the slab to be taken *away* from the builder. But in both games, it is the slab which is moved. I want to say, as I suspect Wittgenstein would say, "It is as you please." After all, there is nothing sacred about the word "same".

But clearly the two games cannot be played *together* because there would be confusion.

However, we can invent a third, larger game, $G+G'$ in which the builder utters sentences of the form, "x, X" where x is one of the four words, "slab, beam, pillar, block", and X is one of the two words "here", "there". And now "slab here" will result in a slab being brought *to* the builder, and "pillar there" will result in a pillar being put into the wooden box.

And now we see the 'difference' between the command "Slab!" in game G, and the command "slab, here" in game $G+G'$. Both these commands result in a slab being brought to the builder. But nonetheless, there is a difference. Clearly the discussion in §19–20 fits with our analysis. It is not necessary to say more than "Slab!" if one is playing either *one* of the two games G, G'. But in the bigger game $G+G'$, the words "here" and "there" are necessary and make a crucial difference to whether the object in question is to be brought or taken away. Ordinary language of course is a gigantic game, and it is hard for us to think that "Slab!" is not just an abbreviation for "Bring me a slab!"

But there is no point in saying that "Bring me a slab!" is complete either, for suppose that the builder has two assistants Beth and Carl. If the

---

[3] See, for instance [5] on the importance of speaker and listener agreeing on an interpretation.

builder says, "Bring me a slab", Beth might well respond, "Do you want me or Carl to bring the slab?" The context is always crucial.

But roughly speaking, the same procedure as a member of a larger family of procedures requires more parameters than it does as a member of a smaller family. If the builder and assistant are playing a game in which it is *always* the case that the assistant brings something to the builder, then it is fine to use the shorter expression, and just say "Slab!" rather than the longer, "Slab, here!".

We have already seen how words like "here" and "there" are used. But now suppose that in a game still larger than $G+G'$, say G'', the builder also uses the word "box" to indicate the location to which an object should be taken. Now "slab, there" and "slab, box" will result in the same action. Does that mean that "there" means "box"?

Well, if this is the *only* game played, then the answer could be "yes". But let us suppose that in the game G'', the builder has been standing near a chair. Then "slab, here" results in a slab being brought near the chair and "slab, there", like "slab, box" results in the slab being taken to the box. Suppose now, however, that the builder moves so that he is standing near the box. In that case, "slab, box" will still result in the slab being put in the box, but "slab, there" will now result in the slab being put near the chair. Thus the application of "here" and "there" is sensitive to the builder's position whereas that of "box" is not. It would no longer work to say, "there" means "box". Again, if there were several boxes, then "slab, box" may no longer be sufficiently clear.

Let us now consider a word like "five". Suppose, for simplicity that five is the highest number used in the game.[4] The five procedures which the grocer is to choose among are, *put one red apple in the bag; put two red apples in the bag; put three red apples in the bag; put four red apples in the bag* and *put five red apples in the bag.* Now the order "five red apples", chooses the last of the five procedures to be performed by the grocer, whereas "two red apples" would choose the second one. Again there is nothing sacred about the fact that the word "five" results in choosing the last of the five procedures. There are 120 correlations between the five words, "one, two,..., five" and the five procedures. Any of these correlations could be used by the community. But for the customer to be happy with the grocer's actions, it is important that they use the same correlation.

In the example which Wittgenstein uses in §1, the grocer counts out the five apples one by one. Would it make a difference if the grocer was

---

[4] This restriction is not necessary and is only being made for convenience.

able to take in five apples at a glance, and pick them up as a single group?[5] Again, it is as we please. The difference between two ways of picking out five apples might be germane, or it might not. But it is hardly likely that one might complain to the grocer, "I wanted you to *count out* the apples!" But sometimes the process itself does matter. If the first prize in some competition is awarded to the best player without a single match being played, then we will not be happy, even though we might admit that he would have won anyway.

In the game just described, it is always apples which are ordered, and always red. So the single word "five" would have sufficed. But if apples of different colors, and fruits other than apples might also be ordered on some occasion, then the words "red" and "apple" are not superfluous.

We have now given the 'semantics' for various words of rather different kinds, and which is no longer confined to the sort of things, i.e., objects, which St. Augustine was speaking about. In the case of words like "slab" or "beam" which do fit Augustine's theory better, the missing part in the procedure could indeed be filled by pointing to the object in question. If the assistant were to say, "And what do you want me to bring when you say 'Slab!'?" the answer could be given by pointing to the slab.[6] In the case of the number five, pointing to an object, say some group of five objects would likely misfire, (as Wittgenstein notices) although it is not hard to imagine that in some possible world, there might be five pebbles kept in a sealed box in Paris whose function was to be consulted in case there was ever any doubt as to which number five was (or more precisely, how the word "five" was to be used).

Anyhow, each semantics sits within the context of a language game, and the larger the game, the longer the command needs to be which spells out a particular procedure from the multitude.

"But how does the grocer, or the assistant know which game is being played?" Or, in our terms, which is the family of possible actions from which one is to be chosen? One could say, "Explanations come to an end somewhere." But in fact more *can* be said on this.

It is by living in society that we learn, within a given context, which game is being played, and what the various alternatives are. It is presumed,

---

[5] This might well be possible if the apples were small.

[6] Although here too, confusion could arise if the assistant thought the word to mean "This particular slab", rather than "any object which looks like this." If the assistant thought that the word meant this particular slab, then he could not fulfill the order "Slab!" a second time.

when you are taking part in a language game, that you already know most of the game, and only *some* of the parameters are missing. These missing parameters can then be supplied by one of the speakers, but there is no way to explain the *entire game* in words. At some point, *training* has to precede explanation, and it is by being members of the same species that we are *trainable* in particular ways.[7]

The case of Alex, the Pepperberg parrot, is instructive. Suppose a parrot is repeatedly shown a spoon, and each time, someone says the word "spoon", then an association between the word and the object will be established in the parrot's mind.[8] But as yet he does not know *what to do* with this association. In other words, the parrot does not know how this association is *woven into* the language game he has to play.

In order to teach this crucial aspect to the parrot, Irene Pepperberg [11] employed the following procedure. She would employ a subject other than the parrot, and then, with the parrot watching, show the subject the spoon and say, "What is this?" If the subject said, "spoon", then he would get the spoon. If he said something else, Pepperberg would frown and take the spoon away from the subject. Sometimes the subject and Pepperberg herself would interchange roles. After a while the parrot learned to say, "spoon" if he was shown a spoon accompanied by the question "What is this?"

I would like to say, that although he had already associated the word "spoon" with the object spoon, he did not know at first the *family of actions* in which the word "spoon" would fit as a parameter. After the work with the other subject had taught the parrot the family of possible actions from which one was to be chosen, he knew what to do when a spoon was shown along with the question "What is this?"

In most of these situations the parrot played subgames of the *examination game*, where we are tested on our knowledge of something, but we do not actually 'make use of' our knowledge. However, when a bored and tired Alex said, "Wanna go back", he was indeed asking to go back to his

---

[7] A friend of mine, Sally Gross, who had taught her grandson to play chess found that he was not playing as she expected. When she complained, he said, "But I am following the rules!" "But you are supposed to try to win," she responded. "Why?" said he, and she had no answer. Is it one of the rules of chess that one has to try to win, and if so, how is this rule enforced? Surely not merely by losing, because one can try to win and still lose, and less likely but possible, one can win even if not trying to win. So there can be no rule that one must try to win, and yet surely it is part of the spirit of the game – a sort of unwritten rule.

[8] I apologize for the anthropomorphic word 'mind'. Feel free to substitute 'brain'.

cage, and be finished with his "exam." These words, "Wanna go back" were then being used for real. It does seem that parrots do not like exams any more than humans do.

2 ASSERTIONS

We have been ignoring the part of language which has played the dominant role in the philosophy of language since Frege (if not earlier). So what about assertions?

Here we will heed a suggestion made by Leonard Savage ([12] p.160), and which is of course important also for Austin [1].

> *Whatever an assertion may be, it is an* act *and deciding what to assert is an instance of deciding how to act.*

An important category is definitions of the form '*a* means *A*'. Then someone who is already used to *A* as a parameter in some family of games may then be able also to use *a* also as a parameter. Thus suppose Sylvia is given the command "Feed the hungry" and asks, "Who is hungry?" On being told, "Jack and Jill are hungry. Bill and Carol are not hungry – they have had their dinner" she will then interpret the command "Feed the hungry," as "Feed Jack and Jill."

In [9] the following model of an agent's belief space is used. The belief space B consists of belief states which cause an agent to act and to make choices. Belief states reveal themselves through these choices, which include choices not only of what to do, but also of what to say and what to assent or disagree with. A belief state may be altered by *observation* of an event, by *hearing* a sentence, and by a *deduction* where an agent makes explicit some fact already implicit in his other beliefs.

As in Savage, [12], choices are affected not only by an agent's belief state, but also by the agent's preferences. An agent who would assent to, "It is raining", and who *prefers not to get wet*, will then take an umbrella when going out.

Since sentences heard change an agent's belief state, the function of an utterance to one agent A by another agent B will then consist of B wanting to influence A's belief state in order to affect A's actions.[9]

---

[9] Sometimes more than an assertion might be needed as Al Capone noted: "You can get much further with a kind word and a gun than with a kind word alone."

If we assume the co-operative stance presumed by Grice [3], then the sole purpose of B speaking to A would be to improve A's decision making abilities. Conventionally, we would regard *being truthful* to A as B's way of fulfilling this obligation. However, as Grice points out, being truthful to A might not be sufficient.

Suppose for instance that A says, "My car is out of gas", and B responds, "There is a gas station around the corner," then B has implicated, but not said, that as far as B knows, the gas station is open. Thus A is entitled to conclude more than B has actually said, *assuming* that A and B are involved in a co-operative situation. Thus if B were to say, "There is a gas station around the corner," knowing full well that it wasn't open, he would be truthful, but he would not be playing the game properly.

Now in the gas station example, at least the semantics of "There is a gas station around the corner," and "There is a gas station around the corner and it is open," are clear enough.

However, in [7] an example is given of a sentence which is indeed helpful but where there is no agreed upon semantics. In this example, Ann and Bob are both professors at a small college, Ann has gone to school but forgotten her topology book which she needs for class. She says to Bob:

Bob, can you bring my topology book when you come in?
Bob: *What does it look like?*
Ann: *It is blue.*
Bob: *OK.*

However, Bob and Ann assign different extensions to the word "blue".[10]

In particular, among Ann's 1,000 books, there are 250 to which Ann would assign the color blue, and of these 250, Bob would also assign the color blue to 225. However, Bob also considers blue another 75 books which Ann would not call blue. On hearing Ann say, "It is blue," Bob will look among the 300 books that *he* considers blue, following up, if needed, with a search through other books that are, from his point of view, *arguably blue*.

Thus there is no *proposition* which Ann is conveying to Bob when she says that her book is blue. The sentence uttered by Ann is interpreted differently by Ann and Bob. Nonetheless, given a book that Ann calls blue, there is a fairly high chance that Bob would also call it blue.

---

[10] This is not a qualia issue, but simply a function of the fact that there are of necessity slight or even substantial differences in individual usages of color words.

It is shown in [7] that Ann's statement "It is blue" reduces Bob's time in looking for the topology book by (at least[11]) 60%. Thus Ann has helped Bob (and herself) even though strictly speaking, no 'information' has been received by Bob.

Despite valiant attempts, there has been no fully successful theory of vague predicates, and therefore of the meaning of the sentence "It is blue." But if we ask, "What *use* is an utterance of 'It is blue? '", then the answer is ready at hand.

3 DECEPTION

The assumption made by Grice is to the effect that when two people are communicating, there is co-operation between them, and the presumption of the co-operation allows for more to be conveyed than is literally said. However, the presumption of co-operation cannot always be taken for granted. There are occasions when A's interests and B's interests do not coincide perfectly, or when B has more at stake than simply benefitting A.

A mathematical analysis of such a phenomenon (in the context of conventional utility theory) was carried out by Crawford and Sobel [2] in 1982.[12] They show that in their framework, the amount of information which B can transmit to A is limited by the extent to which A and B have common interests. In particular, if the interests are completely opposed, as happens in a zero sum game, *no* information can reliably be conveyed. Clearly B, in attempting to influence A's actions, is attempting to benefit himself, and in a zero sum game, any benefit to B is a loss to A. A, knowing this, will take all of B's statements with a grain of salt. Moreover, B cannot take for granted that A will take all of B's statements to be lies, since A knows perfectly well that if B could rely on A taking B's statements to be lies, B could take advantage of this knowledge.

In brief, there is no *Nash equilibrium* of information transmission in a zero sum game.

However, it may well be that the interests of the two parties are sufficiently aligned that some communication is possible. For instance, during the cold war, the US and the USSR were opponents. But avoiding all out war was something that both sides wanted. Thus their interests were par-

---

[11] Had Bob had the same denotation for 'blue' as Ann did, the time would have been reduced by 75%.

[12] See also [14].

tially aligned. Having a *hot line*, for instance, was a way of acknowledging the commonality of interests, and the possibility of partial communication.

Crawford and Sobel show that in the situation where the interests of the two sides are partially aligned, some limited communication is possible. While neither party can wholly trust the other, *partially* believing the other party can be to one's advantage.

4 CONCLUSION

We have suggested in this paper that the usage of words can often be understood in terms of a particular word picking out a particular action (or perhaps procedure) from a family of such possible actions. And there is also a presumption that the particular action which is picked out is the one which is 'wanted' in some sense. if we accept Wittgenstein's tacit suggestion that language games are played because there is some benefit to society, then we can see him as having anticipated, at least in spirit, some of the more recent developments in game theory, and especially in game theoretic pragmatics, see, for instance, [6].

Moreover, the question, "What use is this assertion?" may allow us to understand communication better than the question, "What does this sentence *mean* ?"

ACKNOWLEDGEMENT

This work was partially supported by a grant from the PSC-CUNY faculty research assistance program.

REFERENCES

[1] J.L. Austin. *How To Do Things With Words*, Harvard University Press, Cambridge, second edition, 1975. ed. J. O. Urmson and Marina Sbisa.
[2] V. Crawford, and J. Sobel (1982) "Strategic Information Transmission", *Econometrica* 50, pp.1431–1451.
[3] Paul Grice, *Studies in the Way of Words*, Harvard U. Press, 1989.
[4] Jeffrey Helzner, "Expected content", *The Review of Symbolic Logic*, 1:4, December 2008, pp.424–432
[5] David Lewis, *Convention: a Philosophical Study*, Havard U. Press, 1969.

[6] Prashant Parikh. "Communication and Strategic Inference", *Linguistics and Philosophy*, 14, pp.473–514, 1991.

[7] R. Parikh, "Vagueness and Utility: the Semantics of Common Nouns", *Linguistics and Philosophy*, 17 (1994), pp.521–535.

[8] R. Parikh, "Social Software", *Synthese*, 132, Sep 2002, pp.187–211.

[9] R. Parikh, "Sentences, Belief and Logical Omniscience, or What does Deduction Tell Us?" *Review of Symbolic Logic* 1:4 (2008), pp.459–476.

[10] R. Parikh, and R. Ramanujam, "A Knowledge based Semantics of Messages", in *J. Logic, Language and Information*, 12, (2003), pp.453–467.

[11] Irene Pepperberg, "Talking with Alex: Logic and Speech in Parrots; Exploring Intelligence," *Scientific American Mind*, August 2004.

[12] L. J. Savage, *The Foundations of Statistics*, Wiley 1954.

[13] R. Stalnaker, *Context and Content*, Oxford University Press, 1999.

[14] R. Stalnaker, "Saying and Meaning, Cheap Talk and Credibility", In Anton Benz, Gerhard Jäger, and Robert van Rooij, editors, *Game Theory and Pragmatics*, pp.83–100. Palgrave Macmillan, New York, 2006.

[15] Ludwig Wittgenstein, *Philosophical Investigations*, MacMillan, 1958.

[16] Ludwig Wittgenstein, *Remarks on the Foundations of Mathematics*, revised edition, MIT press, 1978.

[17] Ludwig Wittgenstein, *Tractatus Logico-philosophicus*, London, Routledge & Paul; New York, Humanities Press, 1961.

ON THE RELATION BETWEEN GAMES IN EXTENSIVE FORM AND GAMES IN STRATEGIC FORM

SIMON M. HUTTEGGER
University of California, Irvine

Abstract
Von Neumann and Morgenstern (1944) claimed that a game in extensive form can always be reduced to a game in strategic form without loss of essential information about the structure of the game. We will evaluate this claim from the point of view of evolutionary game theory. The bottomline is that due to certain generic equilibrium structures of extensive form games they have other dynamical properties than games in strategic form.

1 INTRODUCTION

John von Neumann and Oskar Morgenstern started their *Theory of Games and Economic Behavior* by developing so-called games in extensive form. A game in extensive form is an interactive decision problem which is described by a sequence of moves on a game tree. The game starts at a root, where a player or Nature chooses an action (Nature being an additional player used for introducing chance moves). Each action leads to a node where another player chooses. It can also lead to a terminal node where the game ends. At a terminal node, each player receives a payoff which is expressed in terms of a von-Neumann-Morgenstern utility function.

This description of games in extensive form can be formalized in a number of different ways.[1] There are two concepts which are of particular interest. An *information set* is a subset of the set of nodes of the game tree where the same player chooses; the nodes in this set cannot be distinguished by the player. This means that the player does not know at which decision node in the information set she is. The second concept is called *perfect recall*. It means that a player never forgets something that she already knew. Perfect recall is a standard assumption for games in extensive form.

---

[1] There are many excellent introductions to game theory. The interested reader should e.g. consult Binmore (2007) or Fudenberg and Tirole (1991).

An example of a game in extensive form is depicted in Fig.1. It will serve as our main example for this paper. It is Selten's famous Chain Store paradox (Selten, 1978), which is also called the Entry Deterrence game. Player 1 chooses whether to enter a market dominated by a chain store (Player 2). She can either enter (E) or not enter (N). If she enters, then Player 2 can either fight (F) or yield (Y). If Player 1 does not enter, then the status quo gets enshrined. If Player 2 chooses to fight after Player 1 has entered, then both suffer losses, but Player 1 more heavily. If Player 2 chooses to yield, then the players share the market. Notice that each information set is a singleton.

Games in extensive form model the sequence of moves of the players. In strategic form games, a set of strategies is associated with each player. The payoffs to a player then result from strategy combinations. Each player chooses one strategy from her strategy set. The players choose simultaneously. A player's utility function depends on her strategy and the other players' strategies.

Consider Fig. 2. There are two players, each one having two strategies. Their payoff can be given in a payoff table. Each strategy combination results in a payoff for each player.[2]

Von Neumann and Morgenstern (1944) described a way of how games in extensive form can be represented as games in strategic form (see Section 2 below). They also claimed that this can be done without loosing important mathematical information about the game's structure. This claim was rejected by Selten (1965, 1975, 1978) on grounds of the players' rationality (see also Harsanyi and Selten, 1988).

We will reject the claim on grounds of evolutionary and dynamical considerations. Thus, extensive form games cannot be genuinely reduced to games in strategic form in the sense that the strategic form representation retains all relevant mathematical properties of the extensive form. In this paper I shall develop this argument in more detail. It is based on the topology of Nash equilibria (Section 2) and its dynamical implications (Sections 3 and 4).

---

[2] A more detailed account of games in strategic form can as well be found in standard textbooks.

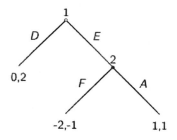

Fig. 1: The Entry-Deterrence game

	L	R
U	a_{11}, b_{11}	a_{12}, b_{12}
D	a_{21}, b_{21}	a_{22}, b_{22}

Fig. 2: A two-player two-strategy game in strategic form. The entries of the table give the payoffs to the row player and to the column player, respectively.

2 THE TOPOLOGY OF NASH EQUILIBRIA

Suppose we are given a game in extensive form. Consider all information sets of a player. A pure strategy is a choice of action at each of those information sets. A players' set of (pure) strategies is given by all the different ways she can choose at each of her information sets. We can rephrase this by saying that a pure strategy of a player prescribes the choice of a specific action at each of the players' information sets. It is as if the player commits to choosing at her information sets in a particular way before the game starts.

Defining the players' strategies in this way yields a strategic form of the extensive form game. Strategies are based on actions at information sets, and payoffs can also be calculated by using the extensive form payoffs.

This is the strategic form of an extensive form game as it was described by von Neumann and Morgenstern (1944). There are other, related, strategic forms as well. Sometimes, two different strategies can be regarded as equivalent if they describe the same probability distribution over terminal nodes. Behavior strategies are another way to represent extensive form games. A behavior strategy is given by a probability distribution over actions at an information set. This can, for instance, be interpreted as regarding each player as consisting of a number of agents – one for each of the player's information sets.

The Entry Deterrence game provides a convenient, though somewhat atypical example (due to the fact that there are only two moves and each information set is a singleton). In the standard strategic form of the entry deterrence game, each player has two strategies (see Fig. 3).

	F	A
D	0, 2	0, 2
E	−2, −1	1, 1

Fig. 3: The strategic form of the Entry Deterrence game.

In order to be able to point out certain differences between games in extensive form and games in strategic form we have to introduce the concept of Nash equilibria. A Nash equilibrium is a combination of strategies such that a player cannot gain by unilaterally deviating.[3]

Notice that the structure of Nash equilibria in the strategic form of the Entry Deterrence game is quite peculiar. There is one Nash equilibrium where Player 1 enters and Player 2 yields. This is also the subgame perfect Nash equilibrium of the game.[4] But there is also a set of Nash equilibria, which is given by Player 1 choosing not to enter and Player 2 choosing to fight with sufficiently high probability. This defines a line of Nash equilibria. Thus, the subgame perfect Nash equilibrium is isolated, while none of the other Nash equilibria is isolated.

Are non-isolated Nash equilibria typical for strategic form games? The answer to this question is no. Take the strategic form of Figure 2 as an example. Non-isolated Nash equilibria like the ones in the Chain-Store game are associated with a player receiving the same payoff for at least

---

[3] This means that a player attains her maximum payoff by choosing her part of a Nash equilibrium given that the other players choose their part of it. There may be other strategies that pay off equally well. If there are no such alternative strategies for any of the players, then the Nash equilibrium is strict.

[4] A Nash equilibrium is subgame perfect if it is a Nash equilibrium for each subgame of the extensive form of a game. For example, the part of the game tree of the Entry Deterrence game starting with the node where Player 2 chooses is a subgame. Subgame perfectness prescribes optimal choices even at information sets that are unreached in equilibrium.

two different choices of the other player. By perturbing the payoffs just slightly, the payoffs will be unequal. This argument can be developed precisely (Wu and Jiang, 1962). One way to put it is this: The payoff configurations which allow for non-isolated Nash equilibria are degenerate, i.e. they have measure zero in the space of all payoff configurations.

Thus, if we just look at games in strategic form we are led to think of Nash equilibria as being typcially isolated. Sets of Nash equilibria with other topological properties are naturally discarded as non-generic. This does not hold for games in extensive form, however. Take the Entry Deterrence game as an example. Perturbing the payoffs at the terminal nodes still results in one subgame perfect Nash equilibrium and a continuum of Nash equilibria where Player 1 does not enter the market and Player 2 fights with sufficiently high probability. The reason for this is that Player 2's decision node is not reached because Player 1 decides not to enter the market. This puts less constraints on Player 2's choice of action since in equilibrium she is never actually called to make a choice.

This is a feature of extensive form games in general (see Fudenberg and Tirole, 1991). By choosing particular actions, players forfeit parts of the game tree. This has profound consequences for the topology of the Nash equilibria of the corresponding strategic form games (the standard strategic form, the reduced strategic form and the representation in terms of behavior strategies as well). The payoff configurations will in general be confined to a subspace of the full space of payoff configurations of the strategic form. In the Entry Deterrence game, for instance, there are six payoff parameters, while the corresponding strategic form structure has eight payoff parameters. Payoffs of the extensive form are thus constrained to lie in a subspace of the corresponding strategic form payoff space. This fact allows for the genericity of Nash equilibria which are not isolated. Continua of Nash equilibria such as the one in the Entry Deterrence game are typical of games in extensive form, while they can be ignored for strategic form games.

But does this difference in the topology of Nash equilibrium sets have any important consequences? It does indeed when we move to evolutionary game theory.

3 STRUCTURAL STABILITY OF DYNAMICAL SYSTEMS

Let us introduce some important concepts from dynamical systems theory first. A dynamical system takes place in a state space X which is usually some subset of n-dimensional real space. (It can also be a Banach space, a metric space, or a n-dimensional manifold.) Furthermore, there is a deterministic rule for how states in X change their position over time; i.e. if x is in X then $T(x, t)$ yields the state x evolves to according to the function T after t units of time.

We shall mostly be concerned with dynamical systems as given by a system of (ordinary) differential equations:

$$dx/dt = f(x)$$

Here, the function f describes the rate of change relative to time for each state x in X. The corresponding deterministic rule $x(t)$ satisfies the condition $dx(t)/dt = f(x(t))$; i.e., the rate of change of the function agrees with the system of differential equations given by f. $x(t)$ is also called the solution orbit or simply the orbit of the system of differential equations.[5]

x is a rest point if $f(x) = 0$. Hence there is no change at a rest point x. If x is a rest point, then x is Liapunov stable if all nearby solutions stay nearby. If, in addition, nearby solutions converge to x, then x is called asymptotically stable. In general, a rest point x is an attractor if there exists a neighborhood U of x such that all orbits starting in U converge to x. Similar definitions exist for sets of points other than rest points, such as periodic orbits. For the purposes of this paper, considering rest points will be sufficient.

A well known example of a dynamical system for game theory is the replicator dynamics, which models interactions between strategy types as a selection process (Hofbauer and Sigmund, 1998). The replicator dynamics describes changes in the proportion of a strategy type over time. The rate of change in the frequency of strategy type i is given by i's current frequency and the difference between its payoff and the average payoff in the population. Thus, below-average types decrease in frequency while above-average types increase in frequency.

As an example we may consider the replicator dynamics of the Entry Deterrence game. Fig.4 shows a sketch of the solution orbits for a two-

---

[5] There are a number of comprehensive textbooks on dynamical systems and ordinary differential equations like, e.g., Hirsch and Smale (1974)

population replicator dynamics, where one population corresponds to Player 1 of the Entry Deterrence game and the second population corresponds to Player 2.

A basic proposition of evolutionary game theory states that each Nash equilibrium of the game is a rest point of the corresponding replicator dynamics. This can also be seen in Fig.4, where the Nash equilibria are a subset of the set of rest points. The property of being a Nash equilibrium alone does not determine the stability properties of the corresponding rest point. In the Entry Deterrence game, the subgame perfect Nash equilibrium (E, Y) is an asymptotically stable rest point of the corresponding replicator dynamics. Points on the line of Nash equilibria are Liapunov stable, except the point where $p = 1/3$. It is also important to notice that the line of Nash equilibria attracts an open set of initial conditions.

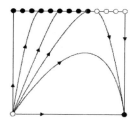

Fig. 4: Replicator dynamics of the Entry Deterrence game. Black dots indicate Nash equilibria. White dots indicate rest points which are not Nash equilibria.

Structural stability is a particularly important concept for dynamical systems. Informally, a dynamical system is structurally stable if all nearby dynamical systems are topologically equivalent. If we consider the dynamical system given by the function f, then g is nearby if the values $g(x)$ are sufficiently close to the values $f(x)$ and if the same holds for the partial (and perhaps higher order partial) derivatives of f and g. Two dynamical systems are topologically equivalent if there exists a homeomorphism (i.e. a continuous bijective function with continuous inverse) which maps the orbits of the system given by f on the orbits of the system given by g such that the direction of time is preserved (Kuznetsov, 2004). That is to say, two topologically equivalent systems have the same qualitative behavior; e.g., they have the same number of rest points or cycles of the same stability types.

It is important to know what would happen if we changed the specification of the dynamics just a little. After all, we may never be certain whether our specification of the dynamics is completely accurate. For a structurally stable system, sufficiently small perturbations will result in the same qualitative dynamical behavior. In this case, even if our specification is not completely accurate, the predictions of the dynamical model are the same up to topological equivalence. Perturbing a structurally unstable system will result in qualitative differences, however. This has important consequences for the relation between the extensive and the strategic form of a game.

4 STRUCTURAL STABILITY AND DYNAMIC GAMES

It is important to note that a continuum of rest points implies that the dynamical system under study is structurally unstable. To be somewhat more specific, the existence of a continuum of rest points implies the existence of zero eigenvalues of the Jacobian matrix of the system of differential equations evaluated at one of the rest points in the continuum. The rest point is non-hyperbolic. Zero eigenvalues indicate here that there is no change along the continuum of rest points. But zero eigenvalues will not persist under perturbations of the system. They will turn into positive or negative eigenvalues.

Let us consider the replicator dynamics of the Entry Deterrence game. The existence of a continuum of rest points M where Player 1 chooses not to enter and Player 2 mixes between fighting and yielding allows us to conclude that the replicator dynamics of this game is not structurally stable. Thus, small perturbations of the replicator equations will change the qualitative behavior of the dynamics close to M. In principle, a number of different changes are conceivable. M might collapse into a pair of rest points, one of them asymptotically stable and the other one unstable; or their might be no rest point close to M for the perturbation at all. (See Hofbauer and Huttegger, 2008; cf. Fig.5). Other scenarios are also possible. What happens under perturbations will depend on the properties of the perturbation terms.

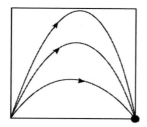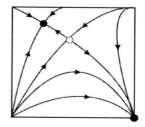

Fig. 5: Possible perturbations of the replicator dynamics for the
Entry Deterrence game.

Let us note this point concerning extensive form games and the replicator dynamics. Since continua of Nash equilibria are typical of games in extensive form (in the sense that they persist under payoff perturbations), and since Nash equilibria are rest points of the replicator dynamics, the replicator dynamics of extensive form games will typically be structurally unstable. Is the same true for games in strategic form?

I intend to give an answer to this question in terms of the muli-population replicator dynamics (i.e., one population for each player position). A Nash equilibrium is a solution to a system of inequalities: Each strategy in a Nash equilibrium has to be a best response to the other players' strategies. It can be shown that being a solution to this system of inequalities implies that the solution is also a zero of a system of equations which is the the multi-population replicator dynamics (Ritzberger, 2002, Section 6.5). This is just a restatement of the fact that Nash equilibria are rest points of the replicator equations. Given this fact, a Nash equilibrium s is defined to be regular if the Jacobian matrix J of the replicator equations evaluated at this point is non-singular. This is equivalent to saying that J has no eigenvalues with zero real part or that the rest point corresponding to s is hyperbolic. Hyperbolicity of a rest point implies that the replicator dynamics close to this rest point is structurally stable (Kuznetsov, 2004).

The subgame perfect equilibrium of the Entry-Deterrence game is an example of a regular Nash equilibrium. Nash equilibria in the continuum of Nash equilibria are not hyperbolic, however. But there is a sense in which regular Nash equilibria are typical for games in strategic form. It can be proven that for almost all games in strategic form all Nash equilibria are regular.[6] Again, this can be understood in terms of payoff perturbations. If we have a game in strategic form with a Nash equilibrium that is not regul-

---

[6] For proofs see Harsanyi (1973), Ritzberger (1994), or Wilson (1971).

ar, then an arbitrarily small perturbation of its payoffs yields a game with no such Nash equilibrium.

Thus we can note the following for games in strategic form. Typically, the replicator dynamics close to a Nash equilibrium is structurally stable. Small perturbations of the dynamics will not alter its qualitative behavior near Nash equilibria.

In this sense, the replicator dynamics and games in strategic form match each other in a way that is not the case for the replicator dynamics and games in extensive form. For the latter, the replicator dynamics will typically not be structurally stable close to Nash equilibria. This allows us to conclude that there is a significant mathematical difference between games in extensive form and games in strategic form from the viewpoint of evolutionary game theory.

5 CONCLUSION

The considerations above indicate that there is a significant difference between games in extensive form and games in strategic form when we consider the properties of the corresponding replicator dynamics. The replicator dynamics is arguably the central dynamical system of evolutionary game theory. It remains to be seen, however, to what extent this result carries over to other evolutionary dynamics. I suspect that there will be similar results for dynamics which respect the Nash equilibrium structure in the sense that Nash equilibria are rest points of the dynamics.

I would like to emphasize that the differences between the extensive form and the strategic form arises in the dynamic context for a similar reason as they arise in a rational choice context; in an extensive form game information sets may be unreached in equilibrium. This will result in mixed behavior strategies at these information sets and thus in structurally unstable dynamical systems.

REFERENCES

Binmore, K. (2007). *Playing for Real. A Text on Game Theory.* Oxford, Oxford University Press.
Fudenberg, D., and J. Tirole (1991). *Game Theory.* Cambridge, MA, MIT Press.
Harsanyi, J.C. (1973). Oddness of the Number of Equilibrium Points: a New Proof. *International Journal of Game Theory* 2: pp.235–250.

Harsanyi, J.C., and R. Selten (1988). *A General Theory of Equilibrium Selection in Games.* Cambridge, MA, MIT Press.

Hirsch, M., and S. Smale (1974). *Differential Equations, Dynamical Systems, and Linear Algebra.* Orlando, FL, Academic Press.

Hofbauer, J., and S.M. Huttegger (2008). Feasibility of communication in binary signaling games. *Journal of Theoretical Biology* 254: pp.843–849.

Hofbauer, J., and K. Sigmund (1998). *Evolutionary Games and Population Dynamics.* Cambridge, Cambridge University Press.

Kuznetsov, Y.A. (2004). *Elements of Applied Bifurcation Theory.* New York, Springer, 3rd edition.

von Neumann, J., and O. Morgenstern (1944). *Theory of Games and Economic Behavior.* Princeton, Princeton University Press.

Ritzberger, K. (1994). The Theory of Normal Form Games from the Differentiable Viewpoint. *International Journal of Game Theory* 23: pp.201–236.

Ritzberger, K. (2002). *Foundations of Non-Cooperative Game Theory.* Oxford, Oxford University Press.

Selten, R. (1965). Spieltheoretische Behandlung eines Oligopolmodells mit Nachfrageträgheit I und II. *Zeitschrift für die gesammte Staatswissenschaft* 121: pp.301–324, 667–689.

Selten, R. (1975). Re-examination of the Perfectness Concept for Equilibrium Points in Extensive Games. *International Journal of Game Theory* 4: pp.25–55.

Selten, R. (1978). The Chain Store Paradox. *Theory and Decision* 9: pp.127–159.

Wilson, R. (1971). Computing Equilibria of *n*-person Games. *Siam Journal of Applied Mathematics* 21: pp.80–87.

Wu, W.-T., and J.-H. Jiang (1962). Essential Equilibrium Points of *n*-person Noncooperative Games. *Scientia Sinica* 11: pp.1307–1322.

TWO ACCOUNTS OF SIMILARITY COMPARED

LIEVEN DECOCK and IGOR DOUVEN
VU University Amsterdam and University of Leuven

Abstract
Tversky's account of similarity could be said to reduce similarity to identity and thereby to reduce an allegedly philosophically problematic notion to an un-problematic one. In Gärdenfors's more recent account of similarity, similarity figures as a primitive, unreduced notion. We argue that this gives no reason for preferring Tversky's account to Gärdenfors's.

Both philosophical and psychological theorizing about similarity has long been dominated by what is sometimes called "the geometrical model of similarity" according to which similarity relations can be represented by means of a metric similarity space (see, e.g., Carnap [1928/1967], Coombs [1954], Shepard [1958], and Torgerson [1958], [1965]). A metric space is a pair (X, d) with X a set and d a metric (or distance function) on X, that is, d: $X \times X \rightarrow R$ with, for all a, b, and c in X:

Minimality:[1] $d(a, b) \geq 0$ and $d(a, b) = 0$ iff $a = b$
Symmetry: $d(a, b) = d(b, a)$
Triangle Inequality: $d(a, b) + d(b, c) \geq d(a, c)$

On this approach, a similarity relation is defined by reference to a fixed distance in the metric similarity space.[2] Specifically, objects a and b are said to be similar iff they are within some distance $\mathbf{t} \in R^+$:

$$\text{sim}(a, b) \Leftrightarrow d(a, b) \leq \mathbf{t}$$

---

[1] This condition is slightly stronger than the condition that Tversky [1977:328] calls "Minimality," which is this: $d(a, b) \geq d(a, a) = 0$. However, a function satisfying the latter condition together with Symmetry and Triangle Inequality is, contrary to what Tversky suggests, not guaranteed to be a metric, but only a pseudo-metric.

[2] Strictly speaking, the similarity function need not be the distance function; it may, for instance, also be an exponentially decaying function of the distance (see on this Shepard [1987], Nosofsky [1988], [1992], Hahn and Chater [1997]).

As plausible as the model might at first appear, in his influential "Features of similarity" ([1977]), the psychologist Amos Tversky shows that it fails dismally in accounting for certain empirical data. He therefore proposed to replace it by a set-theoretical approach to similarity that demonstrably does a much better job in explaining the relevant data. This approach has become hugely influential over the past two decades, and it is no exaggeration to say that at present it has the status of the received doctrine.

In the present paper, we contrast Tversky's popular account with a very recent proposal made by Peter Gärdenfors, which can be conceived as a refinement of the old geometrical model. While to date this refined model is not known to be empirically any less successful than Tversky's, the latter may seem to have the advantage that it reduces a notion that, following Nelson Goodman [1972], many philosophers have judged to be slippery – similarity – to one that is almost universally held to be "utterly simple and unproblematic" (Lewis [1986:192]), namely identity; by contrast, similarity figures as a primitive, unreduced – and for all we know irreducible – notion in Gärdenfors's account. We argue that, appearances to the contrary notwithstanding, this fails to give good reason for preferring Tversky's account to Gärdenfors's.

I

Tversky's main motive for dismissing the geometrical model of similarity is based on empirical evidence concerning the plausibility of the basic axioms of metric spaces when interpreted in terms of similarity. Minimality already poses a problem. For it entails reflexivity of similarity, that is, that S(a, a) is equal to S(b, b) for all objects a and b, whereas in psychological experiments the probability of judging two stimuli identical is not the same for all kinds of identical stimuli. Triangle Inequality is not corroborated by the data either; in some experiments in which objects were similar in entirely different respects, violation of Triangle Inequality occurred (Tversky and Gati [1982]). Nevertheless, in the first place, Tversky's critique concerns Symmetry. He demonstrated that people's similarity judgments are in many cases *not* symmetrical. For example, experiments reveal that North-Korea is typically judged to be more similar to China, than China to North-

Korea – which seems to provide a direct refutation of the geometrical model.

This led Tversky to develop a set-theoretical approach to similarity based on feature matching. In his ontology, objects in the domain $D = \{a, b, c,...\}$ are not characterized by points in a geometrical space, but by a set of features; for example, an orange may be represented by a set of features $A = \{$round, orange, medium-sized, juicy, ripe,...$\}$. Similarity is then defined in terms of certain set-theoretical relations obtaining (or otherwise) between sets of features representing different objects.

To be more exact, the similarity relation, on Tversky's proposal, must fulfil several conditions. The most important of these are the matching condition and the monotonicity condition. The first says that

$$S(a, b) = F(A \cap B, A\text{–}B, B\text{–}A),$$

for some real-valued ternary function F. In other words, the similarity of two objects a and b is strictly a function of the set of their shared features ($A \cap B$) and the two sets of their distinctive features ($A\text{–}B$, the set of features that belong to a but not to b, and $B\text{–}A$, the set of features that belong to b but not to a). According to the monotonicity condition,

> $S(a, b) \geq S(a, c)$ whenever (i) $A \cap C \subseteq A \cap B$; (ii) $A\text{–}B \subseteq A\text{–}C$; and (iii) $B\text{–}A \subseteq C\text{–}A$, with the inequality being strict iff at least one of the three inclusion relations is proper.

Less formally, an object b is more similar to an object a than another object c is if either the features a and b share are among the ones shared by a and c, or the features *not* shared by a and b are among the ones *not* shared by a and c, or both. Thus, similarity increases with addition of common features and/or deletion of distinctive features. In addition to these, there are also three more technical conditions: independence, solvability, and invariance; we refer the reader to Tversky [1977:351] for the definitions.

Tversky then proves a representation theorem to the effect that, if $S(. , .)$ fulfils the foregoing conditions, there is guaranteed to exist a similarity scale s and a nonnegative scale f such that for all a, b, c, d in the domain:

(i) $s(a, b) \geq s(c, d)$ iff $S(a, b) \geq S(c, d)$;
(ii) $s(a, b) = \theta f(A \cap B) - \alpha f(A-B) - \beta f(B-A)$, for some $\theta, \alpha, \beta \geq 0$;
(iii) f and s are interval scales.

This representation of the similarity relation has been named "the contrast model": similarity is expressed as a linear combination, or a contrast, of the measures of the common and the distinctive features.[3]

Based on this rough exposition, it should already be clear that the contrast model easily explains the experimentally established asymmetry in people's similarity judgments. For nothing in the model requires that $\alpha = \beta$ (the task presented to the participants in an experiment may be what Tversky calls "directional"), so that if the complement sets of features do not have the same measure (i.e., if $f(A-B) \neq f(B-A)$), we have the asymmetrical $S(a, b) \neq S(b, a)$. This simple fact has done much to propagate the popularity of Tversky's model.

II

It is also worth stressing that the representation theorem does not characterize a unique similarity scale s, but rather a family of such scales. For instance, if $\alpha = \beta = 0$, then we have a similarity relation that only depends on the shared features of two objects. If $\theta = 0$, we have a similarity relation that only depends on the distinctive features between the two objects. In addition to this, a function f must be fixed. This function is most naturally construed as a salience function. Certain sets of common or distinctive features contribute more to the similarity scale than others, and are thus more salient in the comparison of the objects.

This is a further virtue of Tversky's approach, for it helps in dealing with what had generally been recognized as another major obstacle – next to the asymmetry problem – for the geometrical model, to wit the context-dependence of similarity judgments. One of the first to emphasize this context-dependence, often approvingly cited in the literature (see, e.g., Medin et al. [1993:254] and Gärdenfors [2000:109]), was Goodman:

---

[3] Besides the contrast model, there are other models based on feature matching. An interesting alternative is the ratio model, according to which $S(a, b) = f(A \cap B)/[f(A \cap B) + \alpha f(A-B) + \beta f(B-A)]$; see Tversky [1977:333].

[C]omparative judgments of similarity often require not merely selection of relevant properties but a weighting of their relative importance, and variation in both relevance and importance can be rapid and enormous. Consider baggage at an airport checking station. The spectator may notice shape, size, color, material, and even make of luggage; the pilot is more concerned with weight, and the passenger with destination and ownership. Which pieces are more alike than others depends not only upon what properties they share, but upon who makes the comparison, and when. ... Circumstances alter similarities. (Goodman [1972:445])

For Goodman, the extreme context-dependence of the similarity relation was a reason to dismiss similarity as "a pretender, an impostor, a quack" ([1972:437]). Name calling aside, it is hard to see how the geometrical model could deal with this context-dependence, lacking, as it does, any parameter that might allow for contextual variation. By contrast, Tversky's model can be regarded as being an appropriate reply to Goodman's worries. Goodman argued that every use of the notion of similarity is in need of a frame of reference. Tversky's account can easily accommodate this kind of relativity precisely because, as intimated, the contrast model provides a *class* of similarity scales, and it is easily imaginable how, for instance, the salience of certain sets of features (the function f) may change from one context to another. Moreover, similarity, on the current proposal, is relative to a particular selection of features. The set of features that represents an object will in general be only a subset of the set of all the properties the object has. For the representation of the objects in the domain, only a limited set of features is considered relevant, and the selection of these features is relative to certain interests and purposes. For instance, in Goodman's example, the selected features of baggage are different for the bystander, the pilot, and the passenger. Needless to point out, these interests and purposes may vary per context. Further, the selection of the domain may be context-sensitive, which may have implications for the similarity judgments, as Tversky's extension effect illustrates (Tversky [1977:343]; see also Medin et al. [1993:361]). If all the objects under consideration share a feature, it becomes neutral in the comparison. However, if one adds an object not sharing it in a comparison task, the feature at once becomes salient. The activation of this feature may shift the similarity judgments between the former objects that do share the feature. In this way, adding a non-European country in a comparison task involving only European countries may have an impact on previous similarity judgments.

In fact, similarity judgments may be even more sensitive to context than Tversky anticipated. In his view, it is possible, at least in experimental set-ups, to prevent context shifts from occurring, and therefore also to select a priori a similarity scale appropriate for the context of the experiment relative to which the subjects' similarity judgments can be assessed. But, backed by experimental findings, Medin et al. [1993] doubt that this is correct. As they say:

> It is natural to assume that, to constrain similarity comparison appropriately, the representation of each of the constituent terms must be rigid [i.e., context-insensitive]. In contrast, our observations suggest that the effective representations of the constituents are determined in the context of the comparison, not prior to it. It is as if the two terms were dancers: Each dancer may have a repertoire of stylistic preferences, but the actual performance depends on an interaction between the two. For asymmetrical comparisons, the "base dancer" takes the lead and the "target dancer" follows. The result is appropriately constrained even though the constituents are quite flexible. (Medin et al. [1993:275])

In other words, the "respect" in which two objects are similar is, or at least may be, selected in the process of comparing the objects, and not (necessarily) a priori. Accordingly, Medin et al. put forward a double explanation of the asymmetry of certain similarity judgments. As in Tversky's account, the similarity scale s_C can be asymmetrical in context C. Furthermore, the order of presentation of the objects may determine which object "takes the lead." Reversing this order may result in the selection of a different context. Hence, in a particular situation, the similarity judgment $S(a, b)$ may be based on $s_C(a, b)$, while the similarity judgment $S(b, a)$ is based on $s_{C'}(b, a)$. This difference in context can either be a difference in the domain, a difference in selected features, a difference in salience of the selected features, a difference in the contrast parameters θ, α, β, or a combination of the foregoing.

Clearly, it is not difficult to adapt Tversky's contrast model so that it also accommodates this further kind of context-sensitivity: as the above already suggests, replacing the context-insensitive similarity scale $s(\,.\,,\,.\,)$ by a set of scales $\{s_C(\,.\,,\,.\,)\}$, containing one scale for each context C, should already do the job. Equally clearly, Medin et al.'s observation might seem to be the nail in the coffin of the geometrical model. Still, more context-dependence can only be more bad news for a model that, as we saw, appears unable to represent any context-dependence at all.

III

And yet some authors have recently tried to resuscitate the geometrical approach. Specifically, they have tried to modify the geometrical model in a way which enables it to account for both the asymmetry effect reported in Tversky's work and that pointed to by Medin et al. The result, we contend, is a serious rival of the contrast model.

Similarity *can* be thought of as having a geometrical structure, the said authors urged. But according to the original geometrical model, and in line with what some philosophers have claimed,[4] a single general metric similarity space underlies all similarity judgements. And that is a mistake, as is already amply testified by the manifest context-dependence of similarity judgments. To rectify the mistake, in recent psychological literature, most notably in Gärdenfors's *Conceptual Spaces* ([2000]), a *contextual* geometrical notion of similarity has been developed. The point of departure of these endeavors has been the plausible claim that general similarity judgments are not possible, and that, first, objects can only be similar in certain respects, and second, different respects can be salient in different contexts. They then argue that the relevant notion of respect can be cashed out by reference to conceptual spaces. For example, if one compares objects with respect to color, one invokes a color space. Another, perhaps even simpler, example of a conceptual space is a three-dimensional Euclidean space with a Euclidian metric serving to represent proximity in visual space.[5] Still further examples are the one-dimensional temporal space, the two-dimensional auditory space, olfactory and tactile spaces, and even shape spaces (see Gärdenfors [2000:94-98]). In short, one crucial idea is that, instead of a general similarity space, we have at our avail a multitude of conceptual spaces (or similarity spaces). The second crucial idea is that in each context typically only a subset of all these spaces is activated, to wit, those corresponding to the respects that are salient in the given context.

---

[4] In Carnap [1967], a complete reconstruction of our knowledge of the world is based on a single relation *Rs* (recollection of similarity). This relation is described as "the given." By means of *Rs*, one can easily define similarity itself. It is clear that a geometrical conception of similarity looms in the background. Though there is room for scholarly debate on the precise role of these geometrical notions in Carnap's *Aufbau*, the constitution system seems to imply the existence of a general geometrical notion of similarity.

[5] One often finds the term "phenomenal visual space" for this space (e.g., in Shepard [2001]). For a discussion of the metaphysical status of this space, see Decock [2006].

As a matter of fact, this is only one way in which the refined geometrical model is able to accommodate context-dependence. In addition to selecting, per context, different conceptual spaces, one can also rescale, per context, the distances within any single conceptual space, and thus obtain a related but different similarity relation. As a result, similarity judgments can also be relative to a particular distance function on the selected conceptual spaces.

Evidently, the foregoing furnishes adequate answers to the objections that Goodman and Medin et al. had levelled against the uncontextualized geometrical model. Just as importantly, it also answers Tversky's asymmetry objection, for nothing precludes that a comparison of China with North-Korea selects a different set of conceptual spaces than a comparison of North-Korea with China, or alternatively – or in addition – that the two tasks lead to different selections of distance functions on the same (or partly the same) conceptual spaces.

IV

It has now come to appear that the notion of similarity can be analyzed in at least two – very different – ways. Further, from a metaphysical viewpoint the two accounts are very different. Gärdenfors's account explains similarity by means of primitive conceptual or similarity spaces. For all he has shown, or we are aware of, contextualized geometrical similarity cannot be reduced to other notions. In Tversky's contrast model, on the other hand, similarity is a function of the sets of shared and distinct features. This effectively amounts to a reduction of the notion of similarity to basic set-theoretical concepts, the concept of context (or that of salience), and the concepts of sharedness and distinctness, where these last concepts can be further reduced to that of identity (that objects a and b share a feature means that there is a feature of a that is identical to a feature of b, and the set of distinct features consists of those that one of the objects has without the other having the identical feature). In brief, Tversky's account seems to have the distinctive virtue of reducing an allegedly problematic notion to an uncontested one (identity) and one that at least nowadays many analytic philosophers tend to regard as relatively unproblematic (the notion of context).

Therefore, even if the two accounts of similarity considered above are both empirically adequate – which they are, for all that is presently known[6] – then, purely on the basis of theoretical considerations, Tversky's account might still be said to be superior. However, this would be rash, for at least two reasons.

Firstly, even supposing the foregoing to be an advantage of Tversky's account, it may well be offset by advantages that Gärdenfors's account has in comparison with its rival. Without going into details, we point in this connection to the fact that conceptual spaces can at the same time partake in an explanation of categorization and concept formation. This is important, as in many cases there is an interdependence of categorization and similarity judgments (see, e.g., Gärdenfors [2000], Hahn and Ramscar [2001], and references therein). In Tversky [1977], this point is obfuscated by the fact that in all the experiments reported in that paper it was obvious which were the features relevant to the given comparison task, where moreover these features were always artificially precise (see for instance the highly stylized faces in Figure 2 on p. 331 of Tversky's paper). In real-life comparison tasks, by contrast, the relevant features are almost invariably of a more complex nature, and the selection of those features may not be straightforward at all.

Secondly, philosophical criticisms of the notion of similarity seem, at least in part, to have exploited the deficiencies of the traditional geometrical model, all of which seem to have been remedied in Gärdenfors's contextualized geometrical model. More generally, it seems to us that Gärdenfors has succeeded in establishing similarity as a scientifically kosher notion and thereby also – a lesson from naturalism that, we suppose, is broadly accepted nowadays – a philosophically respectable one.[7] At a minimum, Gärdenfors's important work should make the critics of similar-

---

[6] Our discussion is confined to accounts that aim to model similarity relations between single objects. As accounts of similarity relations between what in the literature are sometimes called "multipart scenes" (which typically involve multiple objects or figures), both Tversky's and Gärdenfors's account may fare less well; see Goldstone and Son [2005:22ff] and references given there.

[7] Note that this is not necessarily to deny Goodman's [1977] claim that similarity cannot do a lot of philosophically useful work. But, first, even if this claim is correct, that does not automatically make similarity philosophically suspect. For instance, if deflationists are right, then truth does not do a lot of philosophical work. Yet they do not claim that truth is philosophically suspect. Second, the remarks to be made in the final section of this paper, and more clearly the arguments given in Douven and Decock [2009], suggest that, pace Goodman, similarity does do important work for philosophers, if for no other reason then because it helps to dissolve the so-called paradoxes of identity.

ity want to reconsider their earlier harsh verdicts (recall Goodman's ear-lier-cited words: "Similarity ... is a pretender, an impostor, a quack"). In light of this, it is much less clear that it is advantageous for Tversky's ac-count that it reduces similarity to identity (and other ostensibly unproblem-atic notions).

One might respond here that even if similarity has been shown to be a philosophically respectable notion, we still prefer a metaphysics on which one of the notions of similarity and identity can be reduced to the other to a metaphysics that makes both come out as being fundamental. A proper assessment of this objection would require us to go much more deeply into the general topic of reductionism than we can do here. But even granting – what we doubt – that it is generally a good strategy to re-duce as many notions as possible to as few as possible, we would still be inclined to disagree that the fact that Tversky has managed to reduce simi-larity to identity gives grounds for favoring his account over Gärdenfors's. The reason is that even if the latter does not reduce similarity to identity, it may enable us to go in the other direction and reduce identity to similarity. We briefly explain this in the final section.

V

The paradoxes of identity – puzzle cases involving change over time and questions about constitution – exhibit that people's identity judgments have properties that cannot directly derive from the properties of the iden-tity predicate, as standardly conceived. For instance, they show that iden-tity judgments are context-sensitive, that they may fail to be transitive, that they can be vague or indeterminate, and that intuitions as to the correctness of a given identity judgment may vary greatly among people.

To give a well-worn example, few think that replacing one plank of a ship by a new plank yields a different ship. However, when more, possibly all, planks get replaced, people become more inclined to think that the re-sulting ship *is* different from the one that had all the original planks in place. More generally, we typically judge that small changes to an object preserve its identity, but a series of small changes may add up to a big change, and big changes are often not judged to preserve identity. This suggests that people's identity judgments may fail to respect the putative transitivity of the identity predicate.

Moreover, none of those who think that the final ship is no longer identical to the original ship will be able to specify an exact number n such that, for them, after the nth plank had been replaced, the new ship came into existence. Rather, they will say that, for some part of the transformation process, the ship was *more or less* identical to the original ship. It would thus seem that identity judgments can be vague to some extent.

In connection with this same example, Plutarch already remarked that identity judgments display a considerable interpersonal variability: he noted that, in discussing the example, philosophers reached different verdicts concerning the identity (or otherwise) of the ship with the original planks and the ship with the new planks. In fact, anyone who has ever taught an introductory metaphysics course will have first-hand knowledge of the point him- or herself.

The context-sensitivity of identity judgments is also illustrated nicely by some of the paradoxes of identity. One may think here of the various paradoxes of personal identity: in some contexts it may be perfectly all right to say that Harry at sixteen is not identical to Harry at sixty, whereas in other contexts that may seem wrong (see Douven and Decock [2009, Sect.I]). Or think of the famous puzzle concerning the statue and the lump of bronze that makes it up: in a context in which we are attending to the different modal and historical properties the statue and the lump of bronze may have, we are inclined to judge these to be different objects, but when the said properties are ignored, as often they are, then we may be as much inclined to judge them to be identical.

Patently, these features of our identity judgments cannot be directly explained, and even seem to put some pressure on, what one might call "the logical notion of identity". According to this, after all, the identity relation is context-invariant and transitive, and it holds categorically: its holding cannot be a matter of degree. The standard approach to explaining the said features has been to attribute misconceptions on our part of other metaphysical notions, like that of an object or that of a property. In Douven and Decock [2009], we have proposed a different approach. The basic idea is that the notion of identity at play in the identity judgments that appear to conflict in the paradoxes of identity is not the logical notion of identity but rather what we called "the folk notion of identity", according to which "identity" is to be interpreted as meaning "highly similar in all relevant respects," where both "highly" and "respect" are to thought of as context-dependent terms. We left open the possibility that this is the correct interpretation of the identity predicate *everywhere*, at least outside of mathematics. That this is so indeed, is still a conjecture, the case for which is yet to be made in full. But if the conjecture is correct – as we hope to show in future work – then Gärdenfors's account could be said to do as well as Tversky's also from a reductionist perspective.

We conclude that, at a minimum, the current orthodoxy concerning similarity has recently come to have a serious contender, and that reductionist considerations may not offer any help in deciding between the two.

REFERENCES

Carnap, R. [1928/1967]. *The Logical Structure of the World*, Berkeley: University of California Press.
Coombs, C.H. [1954]. "Method for the Study of Interstimulus Similarity", *Psychometrika*, 19, pp.183–194.
Decock, L. [2006]. "A Physicalist Interpretation of 'Phenomenal' Spaces", *Phenomenology and the Cognitive Sciences*, 5, pp.197–225.
Douven, I. & Decock, L. [2009]. "Identity and Similarity", *Philosophical Studies*, in press.
Gärdenfors, P. [2000]. *Conceptual Spaces*, Cambridge MA: Bradford.
Goldstone, R.L. & Son J.Y. [2005]. "Similarity", in: K.J. Holyoak & R.G. Morrison (eds.), *The Cambridge Handbook of Thinking and Reasoning*, Cambridge: Cambridge University Press, pp.13–36.
Goodman, N. [1972]. "Seven Strictures on Similarity", in: *Problem and Projects*, Indianapolis/New York: Bobbs-Merrill, pp.437–446.
Hahn, U. & Chater, N. [1997]. "Concepts and Similarity", in: K. Lambert & D. Shanks (eds.), *Knowledge, Concepts, and Categories*, East Sussex: Psychology Press, pp.43–92.
Hahn, U. & Ramscar, M. [2001]. *Similarity and Categorization*, Oxford: Oxford University Press.
Lewis, D. [1986]. *On the Plurality of Worlds*, Oxford: Blackwell.
Medin, D.L., Goldstone, R.L., & Gentner, D. [1993]. "Respects for Similarity", *Psychological Review*, 100, pp.254–278.
Nosofsky, R.M. [1988]. "Similarity, Frequency, and Category Representations", *Journal of Experimental Psychology: Learning, Memory, and Cognition*, 14, pp.54–65.
Nosofsky, R.M. [1992]. "Similarity Scaling and Cognitive Process Models", *Annual Review of Psychology*, 43, pp.25–53.
Shepard, R.N. [1958]. "Stimulus and Response Generalization: Tests of a Model Relating Generalization to Distance in Psychological Space", *Journal of Experimental Psychology*, 6, pp.509–523.
Shepard, R.N. [1987]. "Toward a Universal Law of Generalization for Psychological Science", *Science*, 237, pp.1317–1323.

Shepard, R.N. [2001]. "Perceptual-cognitive Universals as Reflections of the World", *Behavioral and Brain Sciences*, 24, pp.581–601.

Torgerson, W.S. [1958]. *Theory and Methods of Scaling*, New York: Wiley.

Torgerson, W.S. [1965]. "Multidimensional Scaling of Similarity", *Psychometrika*, 30, pp.379–393.

Tversky, A. [1977]. "Features of Similarity", *Psychological Review*, 84, pp.327–354.

Tversky, A. & Gati, I. [1982]. "Similarity, Separability, and the Triangle Inequality", *Psychological Review*, 89, pp.123–154.

CONTEXTUALISM, RELATIVISM, AND FACTIVITY. ANALYZING 'KNOWLEDGE' AFTER THE NEW LINGUISTIC TURN IN EPISTEMOLOGY

ELKE BRENDEL
University of Mainz

1 INTRODUCTION

Linguistic analysis provides a methodological instrument of utmost importance for theory-formation in contemporary epistemology. Peter Ludlow recently declared a "new linguistic turn in epistemology" that shares with the traditional "linguistic turn" the idea that linguistic analysis is important for assessing the correctness of epistemic positions, but is less ambitious than the traditional "linguistic turn" with regard to its goals: "We are not looking for quick solutions to (or dissolutions of) long-standing philosophical concerns about issues like scepticism, but rather we are looking at linguistic theory to help us probe specific components of more complex and subtle epistemological theories."[1] One example of this "new linguistic turn" in epistemology is the discussion about the plausibility of the *context-sensitivity of knowledge ascriptions*. In the following, I will assess the debate about contextualist accounts of knowledge with regard to their linguistic plausibility and logical correctness. I will show that contextualism is wrong in explaining the context-sensitivity of "know" in analogy to indexical terms such as gradable or scalar predicates. In analyzing the disanalogies between "know" and other indexical terms certain peculiarities of the context-sensitivity of "know" will become apparent that give rise to a new semantics of knowledge ascriptions. This new semantic approach of "informed contextualism" is superior to standard contextualism as well as to relativism. It can account for both, the variability of the semantic content of a knowledge ascription across contexts and for the phenomenon that we

---

[1] Ludlow (2005), p.12.

tend to retract earlier knowledge claims when standards rise. In contrast to a relativist assessment-sensitive semantics for "know", the proposed semantics can also account for the apparent asymmetry between the raising and the lowering of epistemic standards. Furthermore, it can resolve the factivity problem for knowledge.

2 CASE STUDIES IN FAVOUR OF CONTEXTUALISM

Contextualists appeal to both, *linguistic intuitions* concerning the truth-conditions of knowledge-attributing (and knowledge-denying) sentences and to *data of linguistic theories* concerning context-dependency of language, in order to attain a satisfying semantic theory of "know". They also claim that linguistic research into the semantics of knowledge attributions can provide a key to resolving some of the notorious problems with regard to knowledge, such as scepticism.

According to contextualists such as Stewart Cohen, Keith DeRose and David Lewis, the truth-conditions of sentences of the form "S knows that p" are determined in part by certain context-dependent standards of the speaker, i.e., the knowledge-ascriber.[2] In particular, the standards are determined by *error-possibilities* that are salient in the context of the speaker. The sentence "S knows that p" is true in a context c only if S meets the standards for knowledge in c, i.e., if S's epistemic situation allows her to rule out all error-possibilities to p that are salient in c. So, if S's epistemic situation does not allow S to rule out these error-possibilities, the sentence "S knows that p" is false *in this specific context c*, even if p turns out to be true. As a result, depending on the standards that are operant in the context of the knowledge-ascriber, the same sentence "S knows that p" can be true in one context and false in a different, more stringent context. This context-dependency of knowledge-attributing sentences seems to be strongly supported by our linguistic intuitions concerning many case studies that contextualists present.

Among the most prominent examples in favor of contextualist intuitions are certain variants on Fred Dretske's famous "zebra-example":[3] Let us assume that Christian and Markus are on a zoo visit. They stop at a paddock with black and white striped animals. Markus, after looking at one of

---

[2] See, for example, Cohen (1986, 1988, 1998, 2000, 2004), DeRose (1992, 1995, 1999, 2005), and Lewis (1979, 1996).

[3] See Dretske (1970), p.1016.

these animals, immediately identifies it as a zebra. Markus is looking at this animal under normal perceptual conditions and he has a good prior knowledge of what zebras look like. Let us further assume that the animal he is looking at is in fact a zebra. If Christian was asked whether Markus knows that this animal is a zebra, he would without hesitation say "yes". In the given context of a zoo visit, among the relevant error-possibilities that Markus has to rule out in order to know that the animal is a zebra are, for example, the possibilities that the animal is a donkey or a pony. Since Markus can reliably distinguish zebras from donkeys or ponies and since the animal he is looking at is in fact a zebra, Christian's claim that "Markus knows that the animal is a zebra" seems to be perfectly true *in this context*. But let us now modify Christian's context of knowledge-ascription. Christian has heard a rumour that in order to save money the zoo director adds some cleverly disguised mules that look exactly like zebras. By considering the possibility that the animal Markus is looking at is a disguised mule, the standards for knowledge have been raised compared to the standards operant in the context of the "normal" zoo visit. Since Markus cannot rule out this now salient error-possibility, Christian's claim "Markus does *not* know that the animal is a zebra" also seems to be perfectly true in *this higher standards context*.

Contextualists not only claim to provide an account of knowledge that is in accordance with our linguistic intuitions concerning the semantics of knowledge-attributing sentences, they also take the credit for having met the sceptical challenge. Since sceptical hypotheses, such as being a brain in a vat, are not salient in everyday contexts, a person need not rule out the possibility of being a (handless) brain in a vat in order to know that she has hands in such a context. So, in an everyday context, the sentence "Markus knows that he has hands" as well as "Markus knows that he is not a (handless) brain in a vat" can be true. Only if the knowledge-ascriber is contemplating sceptical hypotheses (and thereby raising the standards for knowledge extremely high) do her utterances of "Markus knows that he has hands" and "Markus knows that he is not a brain in a vat" come out false. Thus, one advantage of the contextualist's response to scepticism is that a contextualist can keep a certain contextualized version of *epistemic closure*: If "S knows that p" is true in context c and if "S knows that p implies q" is true in c, then "S knows that q" also turns out to be true in the same context c, even if q is the negation of a sceptical hypothesis. According to contextualism, contrary to the radical sceptic's general denial of the possibility of knowledge, most of our positive knowledge-attributing sentences can be true. The only concession to the sceptics a contextualist has to make is to admit that in sceptical high standards contexts our positive knowledge-ascriptions are indeed all false.

According to some contextualists, the standards for "know" are not only determined by salient error-possibilities that are operant in the speaker's context, but also by questions of interests and stakes given in the special situation of the knowledge-ascription. DeRose most prominently argues for such a "stake-induced" context determination of knowledge-ascribing sentences. Various case studies indicate[4] that, if a lot hinges on p being true or if we have a vital interest in the truth of p, we have the tendency to be more cautious and hesitant in claiming to know that p – compared to cases where not so much is at stake, if p turns out to be false.

The zebra example and other case studies support the general contextualist thesis that the truth-conditions of knowledge-attributing (or knowledge-denying) sentences are context-dependent. Stakes, interests, salient relevant error-possibilities etc. that are given in the context of the knowledge-ascription seem to determine in part the standards for truly or falsely ascribing knowledge to others or to ourselves. However, it is less clear and highly contested which linguistic data about context-sensitivity best explains this certain kind of context-dependency of knowledge-ascriptions.

3 THE INDEXICALITY OF "KNOW"

Contextualists usually treat "know" as a certain kind of an *indexical*. Cohen, in particular, stresses the point that the context-sensitivity of knowledge-ascriptions can be best explained by analogy with *gradable* or *scalar predicates*, such as "flat", "bald", "rich", "happy" etc.[5] As with knowledge ascriptions, the truth-conditions of sentences attributing gradable adjectives to objects can vary with the context of utterance. So for example, the sentence "Peter is tall" can be uttered truly by a speaker who uses the word "tall" in the context of "tall *for a first grader*". The same sentence can be falsely uttered by a speaker with more stringent standards of tallness (who, for example, uses "tall" in the sense of "tall *for a basketball player*").

But it has been argued quite convincingly, for example by Jason Stanley, that the analogy between "know" and gradable or scalar predicates, such as "tall", "flat" etc., breaks down on various points. There are

---

[4] See, for example, DeRose's "bank cases" in DeRose (1992), p.913.
[5] Cohen (2000), p.97.

important linguistic dissimilarities between "know" and gradable or scalar predicates. Unlike "tall" or "flat", "know" does not seem to allow for *degree modifiers*, such as "very", "really", "enough", or for *comparative constructions*.[6]

There is another crucial difference between gradable or scalar predicates, like "tall", and "know". Raising the standards of gradable predicates does normally not effect the truth-value of sentences in which the predicate is used in lower standards contexts. Even if Markus is in higher standards context in which "tall" means "tall for a NBA player", he could nevertheless truly utter the following sentence (1):

(1) Even if I am now using "tall" in the sense of "tall for a NBA player" (according to which I am not tall), I am still tall *for a Western European.*

But this does not seem to be true with regard to knowledge-ascriptions. If the fraudulent activities of the zoo director came to Markus's attention, he would surely *not* claim:

(2) According to ordinary standards contexts, I still know that the animal is a zebra, but in my present higher standards context I do not know that the animal is a zebra,

or

(2)' According to my present higher standards context, I know that I knew that the animal was a zebra when I was in lower standards context.

If a subject learns about relevant error-possibilities to p hitherto ignored, the new higher standards context now seems to be the decisive context that forms the background for self-ascriptions (or denials) of knowledge of p. The answer to the question whether her epistemic position allows ruling out all error-possibilities to p in the new *higher* standards context seems to be the crucial factor for an epistemic subject S in order to decide whether she now knows that p *and knew that p all along.* As long as S does not have good reasons to ignore the new error-possibilities in the high standards context or does not obtain some new evidence that renders these possibilities irrelevant, it does not seem right of her to claim ordinary stan-

---

[6] See Stanley (2004).

dards (or any other kind of lower standards) knowledge. This is why in the above example Markus will *withdraw* his earlier knowledge claim and will treat it as *false*. Rather than claiming (2) or even (2)', he will therefore assert something like the following:

> (3) My earlier knowledge claim (in ordinary standards context) "I know that the animal is a zebra" was false. I don't know that the animal is a zebra, and I didn't know it earlier.

4 THE FACTIVITY PROBLEM

The upshot of my above discussion concerning the semantics of knowledge-attributing (and denying) sentences is that there are crucial differences between "know" and gradable or scalar predicates, such as "tall", "flat" etc. In particular, the alleged analogies break down with regard to ascriptions of knowledge in some low standards context from the perspective of a higher standards context in which the subject no longer knows.

Appealing to *pragmatic explanations* or to a version of an *error theory* in order to account for the apparent tendency to retract former knowledge claims when standards rise but still treat sentences such as (2) or (2)' as *literally true*, does not seem to be an attractive manoeuvre for contextualists. It is not the case that these sentences only seem to be incorrect because of some pragmatic features or because speakers are simply mistaken about the correct semantics of knowledge ascriptions. The following *factivity problem for contextualism* shows that those sentences can even generate an *inconsistency* at the semantic level of contextualist knowledge ascriptions.

Let "M" refer to Markus, "p" to the proposition that the animal (Markus is looking at) is a zebra, "c_L" for the low or ordinary standards context of a "normal" zoo visit, "c_H" for the high standards context in which the cleverly disguised mule hypothesis has come to Markus's attention, and "$K(x, y, c_s)$" stands for the knowledge claim that subject x knows that y according to the standard of knowledge s associated with the context c.

We can now state the contextualist insight that Christian's utterance that Markus knows that p is true in low standards context, but not in high standards context by the conjunction of the following claims (a) and (b)[7]:

---

[7] For a similar version of the factivity problem for contextualism see Brendel (2003, 2005, 2007).

(a) $K(M, p, c_L) \land$ (b) $\neg K(M, p, c_H)$.

The claim that knowledge (in any context) is factive can be formulated by the following *contextualist factivity principle* ($\text{Fact}_{\text{context}}$):

($\text{Fact}_{\text{context}}$) $K(x, y, c_Z) \to y$
(for all subjects x, propositions y, and contexts c_Z).

As already mentioned, the contextualist embraces a *contextualised version of the principle of epistemic closure* ($\text{Clos}_{\text{context}}$) that can be formalized as follows:

($\text{Clos}_{\text{context}}$) $K(x, y_1, c_Z) \land K(x, (y_1 \to y_2), c_Z) \to K(x, y_2, c_Z)$
(for all subjects x, propositions y_1 and y_2, and contexts c_Z).

If contextualism is true and if "know" is like a gradable predicate, such as "tall", then Markus should know in high standards context that he knows in low standards context that the animal is a zebra, i.e, he should know in c_H that (a):

(i) $K(M, (a), c_H)$.

Furthermore, a competent speaker who possesses the concept of knowledge, should know that knowledge is factive, i.e., that a subject only knows that p, if p is true. It seems to me that a subject should know this conceptual truth of "know" even in very high standards contexts. Even in sceptical contexts in which brains in vats hypotheses are salient, subjects still know that knowledge implies the truth of the known proposition. So, it is fair to claim that Markus knows that knowledge is factive even in c_H. Thus, in particular, the following claim holds:

(ii) $K(M, (K(M, p, c_L) \to p), c_H)$.

But with (i), (ii), and ($\text{Clos}_{\text{context}}$), we get $K(M, p, c_H)$ – which contradicts the assumption (b).

5 ASSESSMENT SENSITIVITY OF KNOWLEDGE ATTRIBUTIONS AND MACFARLANE'S RELATIVISM

I have argued that the contextualist linguistic model of "know" is not fully adequate. There are crucial differences between "know" and gradable predicates. That "know" is indeed a very special notion can, in particular, be shown by the factivity problem. In a sense, unlike all the other terms with which "know" is linguistically compared, "know" seems to be a special *hybrid* concept. On the one hand, due to the factivity of "know", the concept of knowledge has an objective, non-epistemic, and context-insensitive part. That is why we strongly subscribe to the claim that we do not know that p, if p is not true. On the other hand, we have strong contextualist intuitions that indicate that the concept of knowledge also has an epistemic and context-sensitive part. That is why we strongly subscribe to the thesis that we do not know that p, if we are not able to meet certain standards that are operant in the context of the knowledge ascription. Relevant error-possibilities, stakes, and interests seem to determine to a great extent whether we attribute or deny knowledge to others and ourselves. Confronted with new and hitherto ignored error-possibilities to p that we render relevant and that we are not able to rule out, we are no longer inclined to claim to know that p in lower standards knowledge in which we were less scrupulous, i.e., as Hawthorne puts it, we tend to regard the higher standards context as the more "enlightened perspective", such that it is almost impossible to lower the standards again.[8] This is also the reason why we normally do not refer to different contexts or different uses of the verb "know" in order to meet challenges to our knowledge claims posed by someone confronting us with error-possibilities or stakes of which we were previously unaware. If Christian challenges Markus's claim that he knows that the animal is a zebra by confronting him with the facts about the corrupt zoo director, it seems to be extremely inappropriate if Markus tries to reconcile this conflict by clarifying that he was using "know" in lower standards knowledge. The only adequate reaction on Markus's side would be to give reasons why the painted mule hypothesis is not relevant, or simply too far-fetched, or extremely improbable in the present case, or to give in and claim that he doesn't know that the animal is a zebra. "[T]he fact that we have very few devices in ordinary life for implementing the clarification technique when it comes to 'knows'," is as Hawthorne claims,[9] a

---

[8] Hawthorne (2004), pp.164f.
[9] Hawthorne (2004), p.105.

good indication of a disanalogy between "know" and other context-sensitive terms.

But how are we to deal with the factivity problem and the other peculiarities of "know" while still adhering to our intuitions concerning the context-sensitivity of knowledge ascriptions?

John MacFarlane has argued for a *relativist* semantics for "know" according to which "know" is sensitive to the epistemic standards in play at the *context of assessment*.[10] MacFarlane's relativism has it that if we assess in a context $c2$ a knowledge claim made (by others or ourselves) at a different context $c1$, the epistemic standards relevant for fixing the truth-value of this knowledge claim are determined by $c2$. According to MacFarlane, the assessment sensitivity of knowledge claims can explain why we tend to withdraw knowledge attributions made at a lower standards context when assessing them in a higher standards context. Furthermore, assessment sensitivity is even supposed to explain why we claim in a higher standards context that we were *wrong* in claiming to know in a lower standards context: "We must be prepared to withdraw a knowledge attribution if standards change, even if the subject's epistemic position is just as we thought it was. Relatedly, when we challenge others for having made false knowledge claims, we may be assessing them in light of standards higher than the ones they recognized when they made them."[11]

MacFarlane's relativism seems to provide a resolution of the factivity problem: In the context of assessment c_H, Markus would *deny* (a). So, it wouldn't be true in c_H that he knows that (a). Since sentence (i) turns out to be false, no factivity problem would get off the ground.

It is nevertheless premature to conclude that assessment sensitivity provides the key to the correct semantics of knowledge attributions. To be sure, MacFarlane's relativism can account for both the apparent fact that the semantics for "know" depends on varying epistemic standards and for the phenomenon that we retract knowledge claims when assessing them in

---

[10] See MacFarlane (2005). Like contextualists, relativists treat knowledge ascriptions as context sensitive. But relativists disagree with contextualists on the indexicality of "know". Instead of claiming that a sentence of the form "S knows that p" can express different propositions in different contexts, relativists contend that such a sentence expresses a constant proposition but the truth-value of this proposition can vary with a certain circumstantial parameter. This paper is not concerned with the differences between the contextualist's and the relativist's accounts of proposition. Rather, it is the specification of the circumstantial parameter in MacFarlane's relativism, i.e., his assessment sensitivity account of knowledge, that I want to focus on.

[11] MacFarlane (2005), p.231.

a higher standards context in which hitherto ignored but relevant error-possibilities arise that our epistemic position does not allow to rule out. As a consequence, a relativist semantics can also deal with the factivity problem. But MacFarlane's relativism does not seem to be perfectly adequate with regard to situations in which the assessor is *less informed or more ignorant* than the epistemic subject whose knowledge claim is assessed. Let us assume that Markus – after having heard about the criminal activities of the zoo director – claims: "I do not know that this animal is a zebra". Christian, who does not possess this information, assesses Markus's knowledge claim by saying: "Markus was wrong in claiming not to know that the animal is a zebra." According to MacFarlane, Christian's withdrawal of Markus's knowledge claim should be *true* since the relevant standards that determine the truth-value of Christian's assessment are the standards operant in the context of assessment, i.e., the *lower* standards in Christian's context. But if the cleverly disguised mule hypothesis *is relevant* and if there is no counter-evidence to this hypothesis, Christian's withdrawal of Markus's knowledge claim does not seem to be correct. So contrary to MacFarlane's relativism, it seems that the relevant standards are not necessarily those in place at the context of assessment, but those standards operant in the *context of the best informed epistemic subject*.

MacFarlane's assessment-sensitive semantics for "know" is thus not sensitive enough to the apparent *asymmetry between the lowering and the raising of epistemic standards*. It seems to be much easier to raise standards by challenging knowledge claims than to lower them again. When standards rise, the truth of an earlier knowledge claim made by an epistemic subject S in a less stringent standards context is challenged. If S's epistemic situation does not allow S to react to the challenge by ruling out the new error-possibilities that are now salient in the higher standards context, the assessor can now withdraw S's earlier knowledge attribution and claim that S didn't know then. If S is identical to the assessor, then the assessor withdraws her own knowledge attribution made in a lower standards context. But once the standard is raised and the earlier knowledge attribution is retracted it does not seem to be appropriate to simply lower the standards again and put the earlier knowledge claim back into force. This is, as shown above, the crucial difference between "know" and gradable predicates. Whereas it is relatively easy to switch back and forth between different standards of "tall" or "flat" in different contexts of use, "easy knowledge manoeuvres" by lowering standards of knowledge are in many cases illegitimate. Since knowledge is factive, relevant error-possibilities to p

hitherto ignored will challenge the *truth of p* and as such challenge the truth of an earlier knowledge attribution "*S* knows that *p*" made in a lower standards context. Unlike MacFarlane who claims, that when standards fall again, speakers "go right back to their old ways, rather than becoming more cautious in attributing knowledge,"[12] I find it in many cases intellectually dishonest to lower standards by simply ignoring relevant error-possibilities. Lowering standards is, of course, legitimate if our evidential situation now allows ruling out the error-possibilities that were salient in the higher standards context (if, for example, the rumours about the corrupted zoo director have been proven false), or if we simply deal with a different situation that calls for a laxer epistemic evaluation (if, for example, Markus visits a *different* zoo where no rumours about a corrupted zoo director circulate and looks at an animal looking like a zebra …). But as long as there are no good reasons to lower the standards, attributing knowledge instead of refraining from knowledge does not seem to be correct. Similarly, if an assessor is simply ignorant and less informed than the speaker *S*, it is not the assessor's context that determines the truth or falsity of *S*'s knowledge attribution. Claiming from the ignorant assessor's perspective that *S* does (and did) know that *p* (although *S*'s epistemic situation does not allow to rule out relevant error-possibilities in *S*'s more "enlightened" context), is incorrect – and a semantics for "know" should account for this fact.

6 INFORMED CONTEXTUALISM

I have argued that many case studies that appeal to our linguistic intuitions show that, as a matter of fact, the concept of knowledge has a context-sensitive aspect. Relevant error-possibilities, stakes, interests etc. do seem to determine context-sensitive standards for "know". But I have also tried to show that the contextualist linguistic model for "know" is not completely adequate, since there are crucial differences between "know" and gradable or scalar predicates. These differences become manifest, in particular, in relations to higher knowledge ascriptions of lower knowledge. Treating "know" here on a par with other context-sensitive terms can even lead to a contradiction, as the problem of factivity shows. So, we are in need of a semantics for knowledge ascriptions that accounts for our contextualist intuitions, but still explains our tendency to retract knowledge when standards rise. Furthermore, the semantics for "know" should provide a solu-

---

[12] MacFarlane (2005), p.231.

tion to the factivity problem. MacFarlane's assessment-sensitive semantics for "know" seemed to be the right candidate for the correct semantics of knowledge ascriptions, but turned out to be inadequate with regard to contexts of assessment in which the assessor is in a less informed epistemic position than the speaker.

The semantics for "know" I would like to suggest regards "know" as sensitive to *the best informed standards context*. To have a label for this semantic account, I will call it *informed contextualism*. In the case where the context of use and the context of assessment of a knowledge ascription coincide, the truth-value assignments in informed contextualism are identical to those in standard contextualism. Consequently, informed contextualism can account for the variability of the semantic content of knowledge ascriptions across contexts. In the case where the context of use and the context of assessment fall apart and the assessor is in a *better* informed epistemic position than the speaker, the truth-value assignments in informed contextualism are identical to those in MacFarlane's relativism. Consequently, informed contextualism can account for the retraction of knowledge when standards rise. Furthermore, it can resolve the factivity problem since sentence (i) turns out to be false. In the case where the context of use and the context of assessment fall apart and the assessor is in a *less* informed epistemic position than the speaker, the decisive standards that determine the truth-value of the knowledge ascription are the standards operant in the *speaker*'s context. Consequently, informed contextualism can account for the fact that an unmotivated lowering of epistemic standards cannot turn a former knowledge-denying claim into a true knowledge assertion.

Of course, the proposed account of informed contextualism is in need of further elaboration. In order to develop a full-fledged semantic theory of knowledge attributions, much more has to be said about what counts as "the best informed standards context". If, for example, an epistemic subject *S* wants to successfully engage in ordinary life (or wants to conduct research into natural sciences), the extremely high standards of a sceptical context are not appropriate – unless there is evidence for the correctness of the sceptical hypothesis (as there was for the Matrix hero Neo). Here it seems correct of S to withdraw her former refusal to know when she was in a sceptical mood. So, the most sceptical standards context is not always the best informed standards context. The best informed epistemic standards context is the one that is the best warrant for the truth of the proposition that the speaker claims to know. Knowledge is factive after all. MacFarlane contends that "we think of knowledge attributions as temporary re-cord-keeping devices – tools for keeping track of a normative status keyed to ever-changing present circumstances – rather than straightforward state-ments of facts."[13] If informed contextualism is on the right track, knowl-edge attributions are closer to statements of facts than MacFarlane thinks.

REFERENCES

Brendel, Elke (2003): "Was Kontextualisten nicht wissen", *Deutsche Zeitschrift für Philosophie* 51, pp.1015–1032.

Brendel, Elke (2005): "Why Contextualists Cannot Know They Are Right: Self-Refut-ing Implications of Contextualism", *Acta Analytica* 20, pp.38–55.

Brendel, Elke (2007): "Kontextualismus oder Invariantismus? Zur Semantik epistemi-scher Aussagen", in: A. Rami/H. Wansing (eds.): *Referenz und Realität*, Pader-born: mentis, pp.11–37.

Cohen, Stewart (1986): "Knowledge and Context", *Journal of Philosophy* 83, pp.574–583.

Cohen, Stewart (1988): "How to be a Fallibilist", *Philosophical Perspectives* 2, pp.91–123.

Cohen, Stewart (1998): "Contextualist Solution to Epistemological Problems: Scepti-cism, Gettier, and the Lottery", *Australasian Journal of Philosophy* 76, pp.289–306.

Cohen, Stewart (2000): "Contextualism and Skepticism", *Philosophical Issues* 10, pp.94–107.

Cohen, Stewart (2004): "Knowledge, Assertion, and Practical Reasoning", *Philosophi-cal Issues* 14: *Epistemology*, pp.482–491.

DeRose, Keith (1992): "Contextualism and Knowledge Attributions", *Philosophy and Phenomenological Research* 52, pp.913–929.

DeRose, Keith (1995): "Solving the Sceptical Problem", *Philosophical Review* 104, pp.1–52.

DeRose, Keith (1999): "Contextualism: An Explanation and Defense", in: J. Greco/ E. Sosa (eds.): *Epistemology*, Oxford: Basil Blackwell, pp.187–205.

DeRose, Keith (2005): "The Ordinary Language Basis for Contextualism, and the New Invariantism", *The Philosophical Quarterly* 55, pp.172–198.

Dretske, Fred (1970): "Epistemic Operators", *The Journal of Philosophy* 67, pp.1007–1023.

Hawthorne, John (2004): *Knowledge and Lotteries*, Oxford: Clarendon Press.

Lewis, David (1979): "Scorekeeping in a Language Game", *Journal of Philosophical Logic* 8, pp.339–359.

Lewis, David (1996): "Elusive Knowledge", *Australasian Journal of Philosophy* 74, pp.549–567.

---

[13] MacFarlane (2005), p.213.

Ludlow, Peter (2005): "Contextualism and the New Linguistic Turn in Epistemology", in: G. Preyer/G. Peter (eds.): *Contextualism in Philosophy. Knowledge, Meaning, and Truth*, Oxford: Oxford University Press, pp.11–50.

MacFarlane, John (2005): "The Assessment Sensitivity of Knowledge Attributions", in: T.G. Gendler/J. Hawthorne (eds.): *Oxford Studies in Epistemology* 1, Oxford: Oxford University Press, pp.197–233.

Stanley, Jason (2004): "On the Linguistic Basis for Contextualism", *Philosophical Studies* 119, pp.119–146.

ontos
verlag

Publications of the
Austrian Ludwig Wittgenstein Society. New Series

Volume 1

TIME AND HISTORY

Friedrich Stadler and Michael Stöltzner (Eds)
Time and History
Proceedings of the 28. International Ludwig
Wittgenstein Symposium, 2005
ISBN 978-3-938793-17-6
621 pp., Hardcover € 79,00

Renowned scientists and scholars address the issue of time from a variety of disciplinary and cross-disciplinary perspectives in four sections: philosophy of time, time in the physical sciences, time in the social and cultural sciences, temporal logic, time in history/history of time, and Wittgenstein on time. Questions discussed include general relativity and cosmology, the physical basis of the arrow of time, the linguistics of temporal expressions, temporal logic, time in the social sciences, time in culture and the arts. Outside the natural sciences, time typically appears as history and in historiography in different forms, like a history of our conceptions of time. The first chapter of the book is dedicated to the major positions in contemporary philosophy of time. The importance of Wittgenstein for present-day philosophy notwithstanding, his ideas about time have hitherto received only little attention. The final chapter, for the first time, provides an extensive discussion of his respective views.

Volume 2

WITTGENSTEIN:
THE PHILOSOPHER
AND HIS WORKS

Alois Pichler, Simo Säätelä (Eds.)
Wittgenstein:
The Philosopher and his Works
ISBN 978-3-938793-28-2
461pp., Hardcover € 98,00

This wide-ranging collection of essays contains eighteen original articles by authors representing some of the most important recent work on Wittgenstein. It deals with questions pertaining to both the interpretation and application of Wittgenstein's thought and the editing of his works. Regarding the latter, it also addresses issues concerning scholarly electronic publishing. The collection is accompanied by a comprehensive introduction which lays out the content and arguments of each contribution.

Volume 3

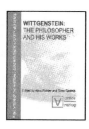

Cultures

Conflict - Analysis - Dialogue

Christian Kanzian, Edmund Runggaldier (Eds.)
Cultures. Conflict - Analysis - Dialogue
Proceedings of the 29th International
Ludwig Wittgenstein-Symposium 2006
ISBN 978-3-938793-66-4
431pp., Hardcover € 59,00

What can systematic philosophy contribute to come from conflict between cultures to a substantial dialogue? – This question was the general theme of the 29th international symposium of the Austrian Ludwig Wittgenstein Society in Kirchberg. Worldwide leading philosophers accepted the invitation to come to the conference, whose results are published in this volume, edited by Christian Kanzian & Edmund Runggaldier. The sections are dedicated to the philosophy of Wittgenstein, Logics and Philosophy of Language, Decision- and Action Theory, Ethical Aspects of the Intercultural Dialogue, Intercultural Dialogue, and last not least to Social Ontology.

ontos
verlag

Frankfurt • Paris • Lancaster • New Brunswick
P.O. Box 1541 • D-63133 Heusenstamm bei Frankfurt
www.ontosverlag.com • info@ontosverlag.com
Tel. ++49-6104-66 57 33 • Fax ++49-6104-66 57 34

ontos verlag

Publications of the
Austrian Ludwig Wittgenstein Society. New Series

Volume 3

Christian Kanzian, Edmund Runggaldier (Eds.)
Cultures. Conflict - Analysis - Dialogue
Proceedings of the 29th International Ludwig Wittgenstein-Symposium in
Kirchberg, Austria.
ISBN 978-3-938793-66-4
431pp., Hardcover, EUR 59,00

What can systematic philosophy contribute to come from conflict between cultures to a
substantial dialogue? – This question was the general theme of the 29th international
symposium of the Austrian Ludwig Wittgenstein Society in Kirchberg. Worldwide leading
philosophers accepted the invitation to come to the conference, whose results are published in
this volume, edited by Christian Kanzian & Edmund Runggaldier. The sections are dedicated
to the philosophy of Wittgenstein, Logics and Philosophy of Language, Decision- and Action
Theory, Ethical Aspects of the Intercultural Dialogue, Intercultural Dialogue, and last not least
to Social Ontology. Our edition include (among others) contributions authored by Peter
Hacker, Jennifer Hornsby, John Hyman, Michael Kober, Richard Rorty, Hans Rott, Gerhard
Schurz, Barry Smith, Pirmin Stekeler-Weithofer, Franz Wimmer, and Kwasi Wiredu.

Volume 4

Georg Gasser (Ed.)
How Successful is Naturalism?
ISBN 13: 978-938793-67-1
ca. 300pp., Hardcover, EUR 69,00

Naturalism is the reigning creed in analytic philosophy. Naturalists claim that natural science
provides a complete account of all forms of existence. According to the naturalistic credo
there are no aspects of human existence which transcend methods and explanations of
science. Our concepts of the self, the mind, subjectivity, human freedom or responsibility is
to be defined in terms of established sciences. The aim of the present volume is to draw the
balance of naturalism's success so far. Unlike other volumes it does not contain a collection
of papers which unanimously reject naturalism. Naturalists and anti-naturalists alike unfold
their positions discussing the success or failure of naturalistic approaches. "How successful
is naturalism?" shows where the lines of agreement and disagreement between naturalists
and their critics are to be located in contemporary philosophical discussion.

Volume 5

Christian Kanzian, Muhammad Legenhausen (Eds.)
Substance and Attribute
Western and Islamic Traditions in Dialogue
ISBN 13: 978-3-938793-68-8
ca. 250pp., Hardcover, EUR 69,00

The aim of this volume is to investigate the topic of *Substance and Attribute*. The way leading
to this aim is a dialogue between Islamic and Western Philosophy. Our project is motivated by
the observation that the historical roots of Islamic and of Western Philosophy are very similar.
Thus some of the articles in this volume are dedicated to the history of philosophy, in Islamic
thinking as well as in Western traditions. But the dialogue between Islamic and Western
Philosophy is not only an historical issue, it has also systematic relevance for actual
philosophical questions. The topic *Substance and Attribute* particularly has an important
history in both traditions; and it has systematic relevance for the actual ontological debate.
The volume includes contributions (among others) by Hans Burkhardt, Hans Kraml,
Muhammad Legenhausen, Michal Loux, Pedro Schmechtig, Muhammad Shomali, Erwin
Tegtmeier, and Daniel von Wachter.

ontos verlag

Frankfurt • Paris • Lancaster • New Brunswick
P.O. Box 1541 • D-63133 Heusenstamm bei Frankfurt
www.ontosverlag.com • info@ontosverlag.com
Tel. ++49-6104-66 57 33 • Fax ++49-6104-66 57 34

ontos
verlag

Publications of the
Austrian Ludwig Wittgenstein Society. New Series

Volume 6

Wittgenstein
and the
Philosophy
of Information

Alois Pichler, Herbert Hrachovec (Eds.)
Wittgenstein and the Philosophy of Information
Proceedings of the 30th International Ludwig Wittgenstein-Symposium in
Kirchberg, Volume 1
ISBN 978-3-86838-001-9
356pp., Hardcover, EUR 79,00

This is the first of two volumes of the proceedings from the 30th International Wittgenstein Symposium in Kirchberg, August 2007. In addition to new contributions to Wittgenstein research (by N. Garver, M. Kross, St. Majetschak, K. Neumer, V. Rodych, L. M. Valdés-Villanueva), the book contains articles with a special focus on digital Wittgenstein research and Wittgenstein's role for the understanding of the digital turn (by L. Bazzocchi, A. Biletzki, J. de Mul, P. Keicher, D. Köhler, K. Mayr, D. G. Stern), as also discussions - not necessarily from a Wittgensteinian perspective - of issues in the philosophy of information, incl. computational ontologies (by D. Apollon, G. Chaitin, F. Dretske, L. Floridi, Y. Okamoto, M. Pasin and E. Motta).

Volume 7

Philosophy
of the
Information Society

Herbert Hrachovec, Alois Pichler (Eds.)
Philosophy of the Information Society
Proceedings of the 30th International Ludwig Wittgenstein-Symposium in
Kirchberg, Volume 2
ISBN 978-3-86838-002-6
326pp., Hardcover, EUR 79,00

This is the second of two volumes of the proceedings from the 30th International Wittgenstein Symposium in Kirchberg, August 2007. It contains selected contributions on the Philosophy of media, Philosophy of the Internet, on Ethics and the political economy of information society. Also included are papers presented in a workshop on electronic philosophy resources and open source/open access.

Volume 8

Phenomenology
as Grammar

Jesús Padilla Gálvez (Ed.)
Phenomenology as Grammar
ISBN 978-3-938793-91-6
224pp., Hardcover, EUR 59,00

This volume gathers papers, which were read at the congress held at the University of Castilla-La Mancha in Toledo (Spain), in September 2007, under the general subject of phenomenology. The book is devoted to Wittgenstein's thoughts on phenomenology. One of its aims is to consider and examine the lasting importance of phenomenology for philosophic discussion. For E. Husserl phenomenology was a discipline that endeavoured to describe how the world is constituted and experienced through a series of conscious acts. His fundamental concept was that of intentional consciousness. What did drag Wittgenstein into working on phenomenology? In his "middle period" work, Wittgenstein used the headline "Phenomenology is Grammar". These cornerstones can be signalled by notions like language, grammar, rule, visual space *versus* Euclidean space, *minima visibilia* and colours. L. Wittgenstein's main interest takes the form of a research on language.

ontos
verlag

Frankfurt • Paris • Lancaster • New Brunswick
P.O. Box 1541 • D-63133 Heusenstamm bei Frankfurt
www.ontosverlag.com • info@ontosverlag.com
Tel. ++49-6104-66 57 33 • Fax ++49-6104-66 57 34

ontos
verlag

PublicationsOfTheAustrianLudwigWittgensteinSociety
NewSeries

Vol. 1 Friedrich Stadler and Michael Stöltzner
Time and History
Proceedings of the 28. International
Ludwig Wittgenstein Symposium, 2005
ISBN 978-3-938793-17-6
621 pp., Hardcover € 79,00

Vol. 2 Alois Pichler, Simo Säätelä (Eds.)
**Wittgenstein:
The Philosopher and his Works**
ISBN 978-3-938793-28-2
461pp., Hardcover € 98,00

Vol. 3 Christian Kanzian,
Edmund Runggaldier (Eds.)
**Cultures. Conflict - Analysis -
Dialogue**
Proceedings of the 29th International
Ludwig Wittgenstein-Symposium 2006
ISBN 978-3-938793-66-4
431pp., Hardcover € 59,00

Vol. 4 Georg Gasser (Ed.)
How Successful is Naturalism?
ISBN 978-3-938793-67-1
300pp., Hardcover € 69,00

Vol. 5 Christian Kanzian,
Muhammad Legenhausen (Eds.)
Substance and Attribute
ISBN 978-3-938793-68-8
248pp., Hardcover, 69,00

Vol. 6 Alois Pichler, Herbert Hrachovec
**Wittgenstein and the
Philosophy of Information**
Proceedings of the 30th International
Ludwig Wittgenstein-Symposium, 2007,
Volume 1
ISBN 978-3-86838-001-9
356pp., Hardcover,€ 79,00

Vol. 7 Herbert Hrachovec, Alois Pichler
**Philosophy of the Information
Society**
Proceedings of the 30th International
Ludwig Wittgenstein-Symposium, 2007,
Volume 2
ISBN 978-3-86838-002-6
326pp., Hardcover, EUR 79,00

Vol. 8 Jesús Padilla Gálvez (Ed.)
Phenomenology as Grammar
ISBN 978-3-938793-91-6
224 pp., Hardcover, EUR 59,00

Vol. 9 Wulf Kellerwessel
**Wittgensteins Sprachphilosophie in
den „Philosophischen
Untersuchungen"**
Eine kommentierende Ersteinführung
ISBN 978-3-86838-032-3
330 pp., Paperback EUR 39.90

Vol. 10 John Edelman (Ed.)
Sense and Reality
Essays out of Swansea
ISBN 978-3-86838-041-5
235 pp., Hardcover EUR 89.00

Vol. 11 Alexander Hieke, Hannes Leitgeb
Reduction – Abstraction – Analysis
Proceedings of the 31th International
Ludwig Wittgenstein-Symposium in
Kirchberg, 2008
ISBN 978-3-86838-047-7
414pp., Hardcover, EUR 79,00

Vol. 12 Alexander Hieke, Hannes Leitgeb
Reduction
Between the Mind and the Brain
ISBN 978-3-86838-046-0
216pp., Hardback, EUR 69,00

ontos Frankfurt • Paris • Lancaster • New Brunswick
P.O. Box 1541 • D-63133 Heusenstamm bei Frankfurt
www.ontosverlag.com • info@ontosverlag.com
verlag Tel. ++49-6104-66 57 33 • Fax ++49-6104-66 57 34